Exposition of Psalms 119

By Charles Bridges

Table o

PREFACE

A considerable portion of the Sacred Volume (as the Book of Psalms and Canticles in the Old Testament, and a large part of the several Epistles in the New Testament) is occupied with the interesting subject of Christian Experience; and exhibits its character, under different dispensations of religion, and diversified with an endless variety of circumstances, as ever essentially the same. As the same features of countenance and elevation of stature have always marked the human species in the midst of the creation of God; so an identity of feature and "measure of the stature of the fullness of Christ" has, in all ages, and under every shade of outward difference, distinguished the family of God, "as the people that should dwell alone, and should not be reckoned among the nations." This indeed was to have been expected.

Human nature has undergone no change since the fall. In its unrenewed state it is still captivated in the same chains of sin; and, when renewed, it is under the influence of the same Spirit of grace. "That which is born of the flesh is flesh; and that which is born of the Spirit is spirit." The modern believer, therefore, when employed in tracing the records of Patriarchal or Mosaic experience, will mark in the infirmities of the ancient people of God a picture of his own heart, "answering, as in water face answers to face;" and in comparing their gracious exercises with his own, he will be ready to acknowledge—"All these works that one and the selfsame Spirit, dividing to every man severally as He will."

In this view, it is the object of this work to exhibit an Old Testament believer in a New Testament garb, as one "walking in the same spirit, and in the same steps" with ourselves; and, in bringing his features of character to the Evangelical standard, it is presumed, that the correspondence will be found to be complete. "Faith which works by love"—the fundamental distinction of the Gospel—pervades the whole man; with at least an implied reference to the One way of access to God (verses 41, 88, 132, 135), and a distinct regard alike to the promises (verses 25, 32, 49, 74, 169, 170), and to the precepts (verses 66, 166), of Divine revelation. Nor are the workings of this principle delineated with less accuracy. In all the variety of Christian feelings and holy conduct, we observe its operations leading the soul into communion with God, and molding every part into a progressive conformity to His image.

4

When we view the "man after God's own heart," taking God for his portion, associating with His people, and feeding upon His word; when we mark his zeal for his Master's glory; his devotedness and self-denial in his Master's work; when we see him ever ready to confess His name, to bear His reproach, and caring only to answer it by a more steady adherence to His service — do we not in those lineaments of character, recognize the picture of one, who in after times could turn to the churches of Christ, and say — "therefore, I beseech you, be followers of me?"

Or can we recollect the Psalmist's insight into the extent and spirituality of the law of God, and his continual conflict with indwelling sin, awakening in him the spirit of wrestling prayer, and confidence in the God of his salvation; and not be again forcibly reminded of him, who has left upon record the corresponding history of his own experience — "I was alive without the law once; but when the commandment came, sin revived, and I died. We know that the law is spiritual; but I am carnal, sold under sin. O wretched man that I am! who shall deliver me from the body of this death? I thank God, through Jesus Christ our Lord!"

In short, let his instancy in prayer and praise be remembered; his determined and persevering cultivation of heart-religion and practical holiness, his hungering and thirsting after righteousness; his jealous fear and watchful tenderness against sin, and regard for the honor of his God; his yearning compassion over his fellow-sinners; his spiritual taste; his accurate discernment; the "simplicity" of his dependence, and the "godly sincerity" of his obedience; his peace of mind and stability of profession; his sanctified improvement of the cross; his victory over the world; his acknowledgment of the Lord's mercy; his trials of faith and patience; his heavenly liberty in the ways of God; his habitual living in his presence, and under the quickening—restraining—directing, and supporting influence of His word—let these holy exercises be considered, either separately, or as forming one admirable concentration of Christian excellence; and what do we desire more to complete the portrait of a finished servant of God upon the Divine model? Is not this a visible demonstration of the power of the word, "perfecting the man of God, and furnishing him thoroughly unto all good works?"

Having explained the Evangelical character of this Psalm, we may notice its peculiar adaptation to Christian experience. It may be considered as the journal of one, who was deeply taught in the things of God, long practiced in the life and walk of faith. It contains the anatomy of experimental religion, the interior lineaments of the family of God. It is given for the use of believers in all ages, as an excellent touchstone of vital godliness, a touchstone which appears especially needful in this day of profession; not as warranting our confidence in the Savior, or as constituting in any measure our ground of acceptance with God: but as exciting us to "give diligence to make our calling and election sure," and quicken our sluggish steps in the path of self-denying obedience. The Writer is free to confess, that his main design in the study of this Psalm was to furnish a correct standard of Evangelical sincerity for the habitual scrutiny of his own heart; and if in the course of this Exposition, any suggestion should be thrown out, to call the attention of his fellow-Christians to this most important, but, alas! too much neglected duty, he will have reason to "rejoice in the day of Christ, that he has not run in vain, neither labored in vain."

Never let it be supposed, that a diligent, prayerful, probing examination of the "chambers of imagery," "genders to bondage." Invariably will it be found to establish the enjoyment of Scriptural assurance. "Hereby we know that we are of the truth, and shall assure our hearts before him." As therefore the preceptive part of the Gospel thus becomes our guide in the happy path of filial obedience, our beloved rule of duty, and the standard of our daily progress; we shall learn in the use of it to depend more entirely upon the Savior, fresh energy will be thrown into our prayers; and the promises of pardon and grace will be doubly precious to our souls.

These views of the Divine life cannot be found unfriendly to the best happiness of mankind. The Psalm opens with a most inviting picture of blessedness, and describes throughout the feelings of one, encompassed indeed with trials superadded to the common lot of men, but yet evidently in possession of a satisfying portion — of a "joy, with which a stranger does not intermedle." Of those, therefore, who would affix the stigma of melancholy to evangelical religion, we are constrained to remark, that they "understand neither what they say, nor whereof they affirm." The children of Edom have never tasted the "clusters of Canaan," and cannot therefore form any just estimate of that goodly land. Those who have spied the land bring a good report of it, and tell—"Surely it flows with milk and honey, and this is the fruit of it." "The work of righteousness is peace; and the effect of righteousness, quietness and assurance forever."

The structure of this Psalm is peculiar. It is divided into twenty-two parts, according to the number of the letters of the Hebrew Alphabet; each part, and its several verses, beginning with the corresponding letter of the Alphabet. The whole Psalm is in the form of an ejaculatory address, with the exception of the first three verses, which may almost be considered as a preface to the whole, and one other verse in the course of it, where the man of God rebukes the ungodly from his presence, as if intruding into his "hiding-place," and interrupting his communion with God. It is not always easy to trace the connection between the several verses; at least not beyond the several divisions of the Psalm. Probably nothing more was intended, than the record of the exercises of his own heart at different periods, and under different circumstances. If, however, they are not links on the same chain, in continuous and unbroken dependence; they may at least be considered as pearls upon one string, of equal, though independent, value.

The prominent characteristic of the Psalm is a love for the word of God, which is brought before us under no less than ten different names, referring to some latent and distinguishing properties of the Divine word, whose manifold excellencies and perfections are thus illustrated with much elegant variety of diction. In many instances, however the several terms appear to have been varied, to adapt themselves to the metre; while, perhaps, at other times they may be promiscuously used for the whole revelation of God, that the view of its inexhaustible fullness might thus conciliate a more attentive regard to its authority; and might add fresh strength to the obligation to read, believe, love, and live in it.

If the Writer may be permitted to suggest the method, in which this Exposition may be best studied to advantage, he would beg to refer to the advice of the excellent Philip Henry to his children—that they should 'take a verse of Psalm 119 every morning to meditate upon, and so go over the Psalm twice in a year:' and 'that'—said he—'will bring you to be in love with all the rest of the Scripture.' The Writer does not presume to suppose, that this superficial sketch will supply food for meditation year after year. Yet he ventures to hope that it may have its use, in directing the attention from time to time to a most precious portion of Holy Writ; which however unfruitful it may have proved to the undiscerning mind, will be found by the serious and intelligent reader to be "profitable for doctrine, for reproof, for correction, for instruction in righteousness."

The composition of this work has been diversified with as much variety as the nature of the subject would allow. The descriptive character of the book will be found to be interspersed with matter of discussion, personal address, hints for self-inquiry, and occasional supplication, with the earnest endeavor to cast the mind into that meditative, self-scrutinizing, devotional frame, in which the new creature is strengthened, and increases, and goes on to perfection. Such, however, as the work is, the Writer would commend it to the gracious consideration of the great Head of the Church; imploring pardon for what in it may be his own, and a blessing on what may be traced to a purer source: and in giving both the pardon and the blessing, may His holy name be abundantly glorified!

Old Newton Vicarage,
July 20th, 1827.

PREFACE TO THE SIXTEENTH EDITION.

The Writer gratefully acknowledges the kind indulgence, with which his work has been received by the Church of Christ. Oh! may his God and Savior have all the glory, while he is humbled in thankfulness for the high privilege of leading his fellow-sinners into the "ways of pleasantness and peace," and ministering to the spiritual blessing of the family of God!

He has carefully revised the work, and trusts that he has been enabled to give increased perspicuity to the style, and a deeper molding of evangelical statement to the matter. He desired, that every page should be lighted up with the beam of the "Sun of Righteousness," who is the glory of the Revelation of God—the Christian's "All in all." He has endeavored to illustrate true religion, as the work of the Divine Spirit, grounded on the knowledge of Christ, advancing in communion with Him, and completed in the enjoyment of Him, and of the Father by Him. He has also aimed to elevate the standard of Christian privilege, as flowing immediately from Him: by giving such a Scriptural statement of the doctrine of assurance, as may quicken the slothful to greater diligence in their holy profession, and at the same time encourage the weak and fearful to a clearer apprehension of their present salvation.

The work has been recently translated into German under the kind patronage of her Majesty the Queen Dowager. The Writer requests the prayers of his Readers, that this new channel of usefulness may be abundantly blessed for the grand object of extending the influence of vital religion throughout the churches.

Old Newton Vicarage,
October 12, 1842

PREFACE TO THE TWENTY-SECOND EDITION.

This work — once more revised — is now stereotyped, in order to reduce the price, and to open for it a wider circulation. The Writer again commends it to the blessing of God, desiring only that fruit may abound for His glory, and for the edifying of His Church.

Hinton Martell Rectory,
June 4th, 1857

Verses 1 - 25

1. Blessed are the undefiled in the way, who walk in the law of the Lord.

This most interesting and instructive Psalm, like the Psalter itself, "opens with a Beatitude for our comfort and encouragement, directing us immediately to that happiness, which all mankind in different ways are seeking and inquiring after. All would secure themselves from the incursions of misery; but all do not consider that misery is the offspring of sin, from which therefore it is necessary to be delivered and preserved, in order to become happy or blessed." (Bishop Horne)

The undefiled character described in this verse marks, in an evangelical sense, "an Israelite indeed, in whom is no deceit", not one who is without sin, but one who in the sincerity of his heart can say, "I do not understand what I do. For what I want to do I do not do, but what I hate I do."

As his way is, so is his "walk", "in the law of the Lord." He is "strengthened in the Lord, and he walks up and down in His name;" his "ears hearing a word behind him, saying, This is the way—walk in it"— when he is "turning to the right hand or to the left." And if the pardon of sin, imputation of righteousness, the communion of saints, and a sense of acceptance with God; if protection in providence and grace; and—finally and forever, the beatific vision, are the sealed privileges of His upright people, then there can be no doubt, that "blessed are the undefiled in the way." And if temporal prosperity, spiritual renovation and fruitfulness, increasing illumination, fellowship with the Savior, peace within, and— throughout eternity—a right to the tree of life, are privileges of incalculable value; then surely "the walk in the law of the Lord" is "the path of pleasantness and peace." "Truly"—indeed may we say, "God is good to Israel, even to such as are of a clean heart."

But let each of us ask—What is the "way" of my heart with God? Is it always an "undefiled way?" Is "iniquity" never "regarded in the heart?" Is all that God hates habitually lamented, abhorred, forsaken? "Search me, O God, and know my heart: try me, and know my thoughts; and see if there be any wicked way in me, and lead me in the way everlasting."

Again—What is my "walk?" Is it from the living principle of union with Christ? This is the direct—the only source of spiritual life. We are first quickened in Him. Then we walk in Him and after Him. Oh! that this my walk may be steady, consistent, advancing! Oh! that I may be ever listening to my Father's voice, "I am the Almighty God; walk before me, and be perfect!"

Is there not enough of defilement in the most "undefiled way," and enough of inconsistency in the most consistent "walk" to endear to us the gracious declaration of the gospel, "If any man sins, we have an advocate with the Father, Jesus Christ the Righteous?"

2. Blessed are those who keep His testimonies, and who seek Him with the whole heart.

The "testimony," in the singular number, usually denotes the whole canon of the inspired writings—the revelation of the will of God to mankind—the standard of their faith. "Testimonies" appear, chiefly, to mark the preceptive part of Scripture; that part, in which this man of God always found his spiritual delight and perfect freedom. Mark his language: "I have rejoiced in the way of Your testimonies, as much us in all riches. Your testimonies have I taken as a heritage forever; for they are the rejoicing of my heart." Not, however, that this blessedness belongs to the mere outward act of obedience; but rather to that practical habit of mind, which seeks to know the will of God in order to "keep" it. This habit is under the influence of the promise of God, "I will put my Spirit within you, and cause you to walk in my statutes, and you shall keep my judgments, and do them." And in thus "keeping the testimonies of God," the believer maintains the character of one, that "seeks Him with the whole heart."

Oh! how many seek, and seek in vain, for no other reason, than because they do not "seek Him with the whole heart!" The worldling's "heart is divided; now shall he be found faulty." The professor "with his mouth shows much love; but his heart goes after his covetousness." The backslider "has not turned unto Me with his whole heart, but feignedly, says the Lord." The faithful, upright believer alone brings his heart, his whole heart, to the Lord: "When You said, Seek my face, my heart said unto You, Your face, Lord, will I seek." For he alone has found an object, that attracts and fills his whole heart, and, if he had a thousand hearts, would attract and fill them all. He has found his way to God by faith in Jesus. In that way he continues to seek. His whole heart is engaged to know and love more and more. Here alone the blessing is enjoyed, and the promise made good: "You shall seek Me, and find Me, when you shall search for Me with all your heart."

But let me not shrink from the question, Do I "keep His testimonies" from constraint, or from love? Surely when I consider my own natural aversion and enmity to the law of God, and the danger of self-deception in the external service of the Lord, I have much need to pray, "Incline my heart to Your testimonies. Give me understanding—save me, and I shall keep Your testimonies." And if they are blessed, who seek the Lord with their whole heart, how am I seeking Him? Alas! with how much distraction! with how little heart-work! Oh! let me "seek His strength" in order to "seek His face."

Lord! search—teach—incline—uphold me. Help me to plead Your gracious promise, "I will give them a heart to know Me, that I am the Lord; and they shall be my people, and I will be their God; for they shall return unto Me with their whole heart."

3. They also do no iniquity; they walk in His ways.

This was not their character from their birth. Once they were doing nothing but iniquity. It was iniquity without mixture, without cessation—from the fountain-head. Now it is written of them, "they do no iniquity." Once they walked, even as others, in the way of their own hearts, "enemies to God by wicked works." Now "they walk in His ways." They are "new creatures in Christ; old things are passed away; behold! all things are become new." This is their highly-privileged state, "Sin shall have no dominion over them: for they are not under the law, but under grace." They are "born of God, and they cannot practice sin: for his seed remains in them, and they cannot sin, because they are born of God." Their hatred and resistance to sin are therefore now as instinctive, as was their former enmity and opposition to God. Not, indeed, that the people of God are as "the saints made perfect," who "do no iniquity." This is a dream of perfection—unscriptural and self-deluding. The unceasing advocacy of their Heavenly Friend evidently supposes the indwelling power of sin, to the termination of our earthly pilgrimage. The supplication, also, in the prayer of our Lord teaches them to ask for daily pardon and deliverance from "temptation," as for "daily bread." Yes—to our shame be it spoken—we are sinners still; yet—praised be God!—not "walking after the course," not "fulfilling the desires," of sin. The acting of sin is now like the motion of a stone upward, violent and unnatural. If

13

sin is not cast out, it is dethroned. We are not, as before, "its willing people," but its reluctant, struggling captives. It is not "the day of its power."

And here lies the holy liberty of the Gospel—not, as some have imagined—a liberty to "continue in sin, that grace may abound"; but a deliverance from the guilt and condemnation of abhorred, resisted, yet still indwelling, sin. When our better will has cast it off—when we can say in the sight of a heart-searching God, "What we hate, that do we"— the responsibility is not ours: "It is not we who do it, but sin which dwells in us."

Still let us inquire, is the promise of deliverance from sin sweet to us? And does our successful resistance in the spiritual conflict realize the pledge of its complete fulfillment? Blessed Jesus! what do, we owe to Your cross for the present redemption from its guilt and curse, and much more for the blissful prospect of the glorified state, when this hated sin shall be an inhabitant no more forever! Oh, let us take the very print of Your death into our souls in the daily crucifixion of sin. Let us know the "power of Your resurrection," in a habitual "walk in newness of life."

4. You have commanded us to keep Your precepts diligently.

We have seen the character of the Man of God. Let us mark the authority of God, commanding him to a diligent obedience. The very sight of the command is enough for him. He obeys for the command's sake, however contrary it may be to his own will. But has he any reason to complain of the yoke? Even under the dispensation, which "genders unto bondage" most encouraging were the obligations to obedience, "that it may be well with them, and with their children forever." Much more, then, we, under a dispensation of love, can never lack a motive for obedience! Let the daily mercies of Providence stir up the question, "What shall I render to the Lord?" Let the far richer mercies of grace produce "a living sacrifice" to be "presented to the Lord." Let "the love of Christ constrain us." Let the recollection of the "price with which we were bought," remind us of the Lord's ownership in us, and of our obligations to "glorify Him in our body, and in our spirit, which are His." Let us only "behold the Lamb of God;" let us hear His wrestling supplications, His deserted cry, His expiring agonies—the price of our redemption; and then let us ask ourselves—Can we lack a motive?

14

But what is the scriptural character of evangelical obedience? It is the work of the Spirit, enabling us to "obey the truth." It is the end of the purpose of God, who "has chosen us in Christ before the foundation of the world, that we should be holy and without blame before Him in love." It is the only satisfactory test of our profession.

Then let me begin my morning with the inquiry, "Lord, what will You have me to do?" "Teach me Your way, O Lord; I will walk in Your truth; unite my heart to fear Your name." Let me trade with all my talents for You: ever watchful, that I may be employed in Your work; setting a guard upon my thoughts, my lips, my tempers, my pursuits, that nothing may hinder, but rather everything may help me, in keeping Your precepts diligently.

But why do I ever find the precepts to be "grievous" to me? Is it not that some indolence is indulged; or some "iniquity regarded in my heart;" or some principle of unfaithfulness divides my services with two masters, when I ought to be "following the Lord fully?" Oh! for the spirit of "simplicity and godly sincerity" in the precepts of God. Oh! for that warm and constant love, which is the main-spring of devoted diligence in the service of God. Oh! for a larger supply of that "wisdom which is from above," and which is "without partiality and without hypocrisy!"

5. Oh that my ways were directed to keep Your statutes!

The Lord has indeed "commanded us to keep His precepts." But, alas! where is our power? Satan would make the sense of our weakness an excuse for indolence. The Spirit of God convinces us of it, as an incitement to prayer, and an exercise of faith. If, Reader, your heart is right with God, you "consent to the law that it is good;" you "delight in it after the inner man;" you would not have one jot or tittle altered, mitigated, or repealed, that it might be more conformed to your own will, or allow you more liberty or self-indulgence in the ways of sin. But do you not sigh to think, that, when you aim at the perfect standard of holiness, you should, at your best moments, and in your highest attainments, fall so far below it; seeing indeed the way before you, but feeling yourself without ability to walk in it? Then let a sense of your helplessness for the work of the Lord lead you to the throne of grace, to pray, and watch, and wait, for the strengthening and refreshing influences of the Spirit of grace. Here let your faith realize at one and the same view your utter insufficiency, and your complete All-sufficiency.

15

Here behold Him, who is ever presenting Himself before God as our glorious Head, receiving in Himself, according to the good pleasure of the Father, the full supply for this and every successive moment of inexpressible need. Our work is not therefore left upon our own hands, or wrought out at our "own charges." So long as he has the "Spirit of grace" he will be found "sufficient"—Divine "strength will be made perfect in weakness." "Without Him we can do nothing;" "through Him, all things." Even the "worm Jacob shall thresh the mountains," when the Lord says, "Fear not, I will help you."

In connecting this verse with the preceding, how accurately is the middle path preserved, equally distant from the idea of self-sufficiency to "keep the Lord's statutes," and self justification in neglecting them! The first attempt to render spiritual obedience will quickly convince us of our utter helplessness. We might as soon create a world, as create in our hearts one pulse of spiritual life. And yet our inability does not cancel our obligation. Shall God lose His right, because sin has palsied our ability? Is not a drunken servant still under his master's law? and is not the sin which prevents him from performing his duty, not his excuse, but his aggravation? Thus our weakness is that of a heart, which "cannot be subject to the law of God," only because it is carnal, "enmity against God." The obligation therefore remains in full force. Our inability is our sin, our guilt, and condemnation.

What then remains for us, but to return the mandate to heaven, accompanied with an earnest prayer, that the Lord would write upon our hearts those statutes, to which He requires obedience in His word?, "You have commanded us to keep Your statutes diligently." We acknowledge, Lord, our obligation; but we feel our impotency. Lord, help us: we look unto You. "Oh that our ways were directed to keep Your statutes!" "Give what You command—and then command what You will." (Augustine.)

Now, as if to exhibit the fullness and suitableness of the promises of the gospel, the commands and prayers are returned back again from heaven with promises of quickening and directing grace. Thus does the Lord fully answer His end with us. He did not issue the commands, expecting that we could turn our own hearts to them; but that the conviction of our entire helplessness might cast us upon Him, who loves to be sought, and never will be thus sought in vain. And indeed this is a part of the "mystery of godliness," that in proportion as we depend upon Him who is alike, "the Lord our righteousness," and our strength; our desire after holiness will increase, and our prayers become more fervent.

He who commands our duty, perfectly knows our weakness; and he who feels his own weakness is fully encouraged to depend upon the power of his Savior.

Faith is then the principle of evangelical obedience, and the promises of His grace enable us for duty, at the very time that we are commanded to it. In this view are brought together the supreme authority of the Lawgiver, the total insufficiency of the creature, the full provisions of the Savior, and the all-sufficiency of "the God of grace." We pray for what we lack; we are thankful for what we have; we trust for what is promised. Thus "all is of God." Christ "is the Alpha and the Omega, the beginning and the end, the first and the last." Thus "grace reigns" triumphant. The foundation is laid in grace, and the headstone will be brought forth with shoutings, crying, "Grace, grace unto it!" The Savior's work is finished, and Jesus is crowned Lord of all forever.

6. Then shall I not be ashamed, when I have respect unto all Your commandments.

The Lord expects our obedience to be not only "diligent," but universal. Willingly to dispense with the least of the commandments, proves that we have yet to learn the spirit of acceptable obedience. Grace is given and suited for all, no less than for one of them, "that we might walk worthy of the Lord unto all pleasing." One lust "regarded in the heart" is sufficient to keep possession for the tyrant, however others may be restrained. Even Herod could "do many things;" and yet his adulterous wife cherished in his bosom, too plainly proved the sovereignty of sin to be undisturbed. Saul slew all the Amalekites but one; and that single exception to universal obedience marked his unsoundness, cost him the loss of his throne, and brought him under the awful displeasure of his God. And thus the one corrupt unmortified member brings the whole body to hell. Reserves are the canker upon godly sincerity. A secret indulgence, "the rolling of the sweet morsel under the tongue," "the part of the price kept back"—stamps our service as a robbery, not as an offering. We may be free, sincere, and earnest in many parts of our prescribed duty; but this "root of bitterness" renders the whole an abomination.

Sincerity therefore must be the stamp of my Christian profession. Though utterly unable to render perfect obedience to the least of the commandments, yet my desire and purpose will have respect unto them

17

all. I shall no more venture to break the least, than the greatest of them; much less shall I ever think of attempting to atone for the breach of one by the performance of the rest. They are indeed many commandments; yet—like links in a chain—they form but one law; and I know who has said, "Whoever shall keep the whole law, and yet offend in one point, he is guilty of all."

However the professor may confine his regard to the second table (as if the first were ceremonial, or obsolete, or the regulation of the outward man was the utmost extent of the requirement,) I would fix my eye with equal regard to both; yet specially marking any command in either of them; that may appear most directly opposed to my besetting corruptions. Thus "walking in the fear of the Lord," I may hope to walk "in the comfort of the Holy Spirit" and "hereby shall I know that I am of the truth, and shall assure my heart before God."

But where, in my strictest walk, is my hope of acceptance, but in Him, whose obedience has "fulfilled all righteousness" in my stead, and whose death "has redeemed me from the curse" of my unrighteousness, when repentance, prayers, and tears, would have been of no avail? Yet it is only in the path of holiness that we can realize our acceptance. The heart occupied with this world's pleasure knows nothing of this heavenly joy. Its brightness is dimmed—its freshness fades—its life withers—in the very breath of an unholy world. A godly assurance of the present favor of God must be weakened by self-indulgence, unwatchfulness, allowance of secret sins, or neglect of secret duties. "If you return to the Almighty"—said a wise man, "you shall be built up, you shall put away iniquity far from yourself. Then shall you have your delight in the Almighty, and shall lift up your face unto God."

Let us then carefully examine the character of our assurance. Does it rest simply and exclusively upon the testimony of the Gospel? Will it abide the test of the word of God? Is it productive of tenderness of conscience, watchfulness, and circumspection of conduct? Does it exercise our diligence in adding grace to grace, that we may "make our calling and election sure," and that "an entrance may be ministered to us abundantly into the everlasting kingdom of our Lord and Savior Jesus Christ?" How boldly can we plead our Christian confidence in the path of godliness, "I have stuck to Your testimonies; O Lord, put me not to shame. Let my heart be sound in Your statutes, that I be not ashamed."

7. I will praise You with uprightness of heart, when I shall have learned Your righteous judgments.

The righteous judgments of God include the whole revelation of His word—so called—as the rule by which He judges our present state, and will pronounce our final sentence. David's attainments here seemed to be as nothing. So much remained unlearned and unknown, that he could only anticipate the time, when he shall have learned them. "Your commandment"—he exclaims, "is exceedingly broad." When the Apostle, after twenty years' acquaintance with the gospel, expressed it as the one desire of his heart, "That I may know Christ;" evidently he entertained the same humbling views of his high attainments, and the same exalted apprehensions of the value of treasures yet unexplored, and progressively opening before him. Thus the wisest saints are only students in the Divine School. Yet whatever their learning be, it casts them into the mold and spirit of their doctrine. Conceit of one's knowledge, is the greatest enemy to knowledge, and the strongest proof of ignorance; so that, "if any man thinks that he knows anything, he knows nothing yet as he ought to know." "He deceives himself."

But what is the motive, that enlivens the believer in this holy learning? Is it that he may live upon the airy breath of human applause? No, rather that he may "praise his God with uprightness of heart." When our mind is dark, our lips are sealed. But when "He opens our understandings" to "learn His judgments," He will next "open our lips, and our mouth shall show forth His praise." And this indeed is the end for which "His people are formed;" for which they "are called out of darkness into marvelous light." This is the daily frame, in which our God will be glorified. Yet must we live as well as sing His praise. "The praise of the upright heart will be shown in the holy walk and conversation."

But let us watch, that our praise really flows "out of the abundance" of what our hearts have "learned" of His "righteous judgments." For do we not sometimes speak of our Savior with a secret lurking after self-exaltation? May we not really be seeking and serving ourselves in the very act of seeming to serve and honor Him? Surely the very thought of the selfishness that defiles our holiest earthly praise, may well quicken our longings after that world of praise, where the flame burns active, bright, incessant; where we shall offer our sacrifices without defilement, without intermission, without weariness, without end!

8. I will keep Your statutes: O forsake me not utterly.

The resolution to "keep the Lord's statutes" is the natural result of having "learned His righteous judgments." But how happily does David combine "simplicity" of dependence with "godly sincerity" of obedience! Firm in his purpose, but distrustful of his strength, instantly upon forming his resolution, he recollects that the performance is beyond his power; and therefore the next moment, and almost the same moment, he follows it up with prayer, "I will keep Your statutes: O forsake me not utterly." Oh! beware of self-confidence in the Christian course. We stumble or advance, as we lean upon an arm of flesh, or upon an Almighty Savior.

Temporary desertion may be the seasonable chastisement of spiritual wantonness. When grace has been given in answer to prayer, it was not duly prized, or diligently improved. The "Beloved"—in answer to solicitation, "has come into His garden," He knocks at the door, but the spouse is "asleep." The answer to prayer was not expected, not waited for, and therefore not enjoyed; and the sleeper awakes too late, and finds herself forsaken by the object of her desire. Again—when we have given place to temptation; when love for our Savior "waxes cold," and our earnestness in seeking Him is fainting; we must not be surprised, if we are left for a time to the trial of a deserted state.

Yet we sometimes speak of the hidings of God's countenance, as if it were a sovereign act, calling for implicit submission; when the cause should at least be sought for, and will generally be found, in some "secret thing" of indulgence, unwatchfulness, or self-dependence. It was while David "kept silence" from the language of contrition, that he felt the pressure of the heavy hand of his frowning God. And may not the darkness, which has sometimes clouded our path, be the voice of our God, "Your own wickedness shall correct you, and your backslidings shall reprove you; know therefore and see, that it is an evil thing and bitter, that you have forsaken the Lord your God."

But in the engagement of the Lord's everlasting covenant, how clear is the warrant of faith!—how ample the encouragement for prayer, "Forsake me not utterly!" David knew and wrote of the Lord's unchangeable faithfulness to His people; and while he dreaded even a temporary separation from his God more than any worldly affliction, he could plead that gracious declaration, "Nevertheless, my loving-kindness will I not utterly take from him, nor permit my faithfulness to fail."

We would not indeed make the promises of grace an encouragement to carelessness: yet it is indispensable to our spiritual establishment that we receive them in their full, free, and sovereign declaration. How many fainting souls have been refreshed by the assurances, "For a small moment have I forsaken you; but with great mercies will I gather you: with everlasting kindness will I have mercy on you, says the Lord your Redeemer!" "My sheep shall never perish; neither shall any pluck them out of My hand." In a lowly, self-abased, and dependent spirit, we shall best, however, learn to "make our boast in the Lord;" "confident of this very thing, that he who has begun a good work in us, will perform it until the day of Jesus Christ." And even if awhile destitute of sensible consolation, still our language will be, "I will wait upon the Lord, who hides His face from the house of Jacob; and I will look for Him."

Great, indeed, is the danger and evil to the soul, if we apprehend the Lord to have forsaken us, because we are in darkness; or that we are out of the way, because we are in perplexity. These are the very hand-posts, that show us that we are in the way of His own promised leading—painful exercise—faithful keeping—eternal salvation: "I will bring the blind by a way that they knew not; I will lead them in paths that they have not known; I will make darkness light before them, and crooked things straight. These things will I do unto them, and not forsake them." Oh! the rest—the satisfaction of placing an implicit confidence in a covenant-keeping God!

Forsaken we may be—but not utterly. David was forsaken, not like Saul. Peter was forsaken, not like Judas, utterly and forever. What foreboding have you of such desertion? Is your heart willing to forsake Him? Have you no mournings and thirstings for His return? "If, indeed, you forsake Him, He will forsake you." But can you forsake Him? 'Let Him do as seems good to Him (is the language of your heart); I will wait for Him, follow after Him, cleave to His word, cling to His cross.' Mark His dealings with you. Inquire into their reason. Submit to His dispensation. If He forsakes, beg His return: but trust your forsaking God. "Though He slays me, yet will I trust in Him." Though my comfort is clouded, my hope remains unchanging, unchangeable—such as I would not resign for the glory of an earthly kingdom. What are these earnest breathings—this abiding confidence, but His own work in us? And can the Lord "forsake the work of His own hands?" Sooner should heaven and earth pass, than the faithful engagements of the gospel be thus broken.

21

9. How shall a young man cleanse his way? by taking heed thereto according to Your word.

Why is the young man so especially called to cleanse his way? Because God justly claims the first and the best. And is it not a most affecting proof of the alienation of the heart from God, that the youth of man—the bloom and freshness of his mind, "his first love"—should naturally be devoted to the service of sin? Ever since fallen man "begat a son in his own likeness," "the imagination of man's heart has been evil from his youth." For "who can bring a clean thing out of an unclean?" And never does the heart utter the cry, "My Father! You are the guide of my youth," until the misery of wandering without a guide has been painfully felt. And even when Divine grace has awakened the desire to return homewards, the habit of wandering from God, and the long-cherished pollutions of sin, seem to form an almost invincible barrier to progress.

The fearful power of "youthful lusts," and the madness with which the heart is hurried into forbidden indulgences, give solemn weight to the inquiry, "How shall a young man cleanse his way?" And the answer is ready. Let him "take heed thereto according to Your word." Thus did Joseph, and Daniel with his young companions, "cleanse their way" in the defilement of an heathen atmosphere. It was probably the recollection of this purifying efficacy of the word, that induced the venerable Beza to mention in his will, among his chief matters of thankfulness to God—the mercy of having been called to the knowledge of the truth at the age of sixteen; thus, during a course of more than seventy years' walk with God, "escaping the pollutions of the world through lust." But the "way can only be cleansed" by the cleansing of the heart; for how can a corrupt fountain "send forth" other than "bitter waters?" "Out of the heart are the issues of life." Hence the urgent need to cry, "Create in me a clean heart, O God, and renew a right spirit within me."

How precious, therefore, is the word of God, as the means of this cleansing operation! When our Savior had been setting forth Himself as "the way, the truth, and the life," and exhibiting the high privilege of union with Himself, "Now," He adds, "you are clean, through the word which I have spoken unto you." This is "the truth," which He pleaded with His Father as the means of our sanctification. This sets out our purifying hope. Here are the promises, by which we "cleanse ourselves

22

from all filthiness of flesh and spirit, perfecting holiness in the fear of God." Thus is restored to man that golden "crown"—the stamp of his Maker's holiness—which "fell from his head when he sinned."

But oh! how does the recollection force itself upon us, that our way needs daily cleansing! so defiled are our actions, our thoughts, our motives—no more, our prayers and services. Let us then "take heed according to the word of God"—specially thankful for its heavenly light, which guides us to the "Fountain, that is opened for sin and for uncleanness." Let us also, under the same Divine light, seek for the daily sanctifying influence of the Spirit of God. "Who can understand his errors? Cleanse me from secret faults." "Cleanse the thoughts of my heart by the inspiration of Your Holy Spirit." (Prayer-Book.)

10. With my whole heart have I sought You; O let me not wander from Your commandments.

Attention to the word, however important, can never be practically effective without earnest prayer. Indeed this is the character of the Lord's people, "a generation of seekers;" and yet how much do we lose of the comfort of our religion, and obscure the glory of our profession, by neglecting to bring "our whole heart" to this work! When sin is vigorous, and our spiritual affections are dull, and various hindrances combine in prayer—at this crisis strong faith is needed to overcome and to persevere. But here the soul too commonly yields to the difficulty, and contents itself either with heartless complainings, or with just sufficient exertion to quiet the voice of conscience, and produce a delusive peace within. But the Lord will not be found thus. His promise is not to such seekers as these; and if we are satisfied with this state, we must look for a very scanty measure of spiritual success, accompanied with the total absence of spiritual enjoyment.

In a far different spirit David could appeal, "With my whole heart have I sought You." And this assurance, instead of producing self-confidence, will, so far as it is genuine, invariably show itself in a prayerful acknowledgment of our weakness, "O let me not wander from Your commandments." Yet the feeblest desire and attempt to seek the Lord is the Spirit's rising beam in the heart, a "day of small things" not to be "despised." It is distinguished from every other principle by the simplicity of its object, "This one thing I do. One thing have I desired of the Lord; that will I seek after." My God! my Savior! with my whole heart have I sought You. "The desire of my soul is to Your name, and to the remembrance of You. With my soul have I desired You in the night; yes, with my spirit within me will I seek You early."

When the soul is thus conscious of "following the Lord fully," there is a peculiar dread of wandering. In a careless or half-hearted state, wanderings are not watched, so long as they do not lead to any open declension. Secret prayer will be hurried over, worldly thoughts unresisted, waste of time in frivolous pursuits indulged, without much concern. Not so, when the heart is fully in pursuit of its object. There is a carefulness, lest wandering thoughts should become habitual. There is a resistance of the first step, that might lead into a devious path. The soul remembers the "wormwood and the gall," "the roaring lion," and the devouring wolf; and in the recollection of the misery of its former wandering, dreads any departure from the Shepherd's fold.

This blessed state of mind the flock of Christ should cherish with godly jealousy. Yet let it be remembered, that daily progress in the heavenly walk is not maintained by yesterday's grace. Humble and dependent prayer must fetch in a fresh supply continually, "O let me not wander from Your commandments." 'Lord, I feel my heart so prone to wander. My affections are often scattered to the ends of the earth. "Unite my heart to fear Your name." Concentrate every thought, every desire, in Yourself, as the one object of attraction.'

11. Your word have I hid in my heart, that I might not sin against You.

What an aggregate of guilt and misery is comprehended in this short word "sin"! Sin is the greatest curse that ever entered the universe of God, and the parent of every other curse! Its guilt is aggravated beyond the conception of thought. Injury to a Superior—a Father—a Sovereign! Its power is misery wherever it extends—in the family—in the world. In eternity its power is unrestrained. Sometimes the death-bed scene casts a fearful gleam of light upon "the worm that never dies, and the fire that never shall be quenched." But experience alone, can develop its full-grown horrors.

How supremely important therefore is the object of our preservation from sin! and how wisely adapted are the means to the end! That word—which the man of God had just before mentioned as the guide to the cleansing of the way—he hides within his heart—not for concealment, but for security, that it may be ready for constant use. It is not therefore a mere acquaintance with the word, that will avail us. There must be a cordial assent—a sound digestion—a constant respect. It must be to us the rule that we would not transgress—the treasure that we are afraid to lose.

Often indeed Satan shuts out its entrance. He "catches away that which was sown." Too often, again, it is "withered or choked" in the soil. But "the honest and good heart" "hides it, keeps it, and brings forth fruit with perseverance, unto perfection."Here it "dwells richly in all wisdom," the storehouse, as occasion requires; a principle of holiness; a covering from sin. In this view it is recommended by one who had well acquainted himself with its valuable uses: "My son, let them (the Divine precepts) not depart from your eyes; keep sound wisdom and discretion. So shall they be life to your soul, and grace to your neck. Then shall you walk in your way safely, and your foot shall not stumble." David also gives us the same experience: "By the word of Your lips I have kept myself from the paths of the destroyer." And it was probably this recollection, combined with a sense of continual danger, that suggested the prayer, "Order my steps in Your word; and let not any iniquity have dominion over me."

The value of the word is inestimable, as our means of walking with God in the hurry, business, and temptation of the day. The Psalms furnish precious materials for spontaneous prayer; the promises, food for comfort; the rules, such light in perplexity; the instruction, such solid matter for godly conference—all operating for one end—a preservation from sin. Being from the word—a manifestation of the Savior's love— what a keeping of the heart! what a quickening motive! How seasonable in worldly temptation is the warning of the word hidden in the heart, "No man, having put his hand to the plough, and looking back, is fit for the kingdom of God!" So in the spiritual conflict, let this word, "Him who comes to Me, I will never cast out," be hidden in the heart—what a preservation is it against unbelief!

Take the word to the wavering believer, alarmed by ridicule or persecution, "If the world hates you, you know that it hated Me before it hated you." Fearing that he shall never hold out to the end; "I will never leave you nor forsake you." Trembling lest his sins should rise up to his condemnation, "The blood of Jesus Christ the Son of God cleanses from all sin." And then as to duties: Let his Savior's word rebuke his indolence and unwatchfulness, "What! could you not watch with Me one hour? Watch and pray, that you enter not into temptation." Hide in the heart the sorrowful story of His agony in the garden, and His death on the cross, that "sin may appear yet more exceedingly sinful."

But how is the word to gain entrance into hearts like ours? How shall it be "hid" in so unkindly a soil? No power of man surely can plant it there. The Holy Spirit's Almighty agency must be diligently sought; for in proportion as we are filled with His gracious influence shall we be armed, as was our Master, for the effectual resistance of our spiritual temptations.

Lastly, connected with this subject, mark the Christian's character, "In whose heart is my law." His security, "None of his steps shall slide." His happiness, "O how I love Your law." His victory, "The word of God abides in him, and he has overcome the wicked one." All infallibly provided by the covenant promise, "I will put My law in their inward parts, and write it in their hearts." Oh! let us not then shrink from a close contact with the word, though the cost may be the cutting off a right hand for the saving of the life. There is no better test of our security, than our willingness to come to the searching light of the word.

12. Blessed are You, O Lord: teach me Your statutes.

"Praise is lovely for the upright." It is at once their duty and their privilege. But what does highest exercise amount to, when placed on the ground of its own merit? We clothe our ideas with magnificence of language, and deck them out with all the richness of imagery; and perhaps we are pleased with our forms of praise. But what are they in His sight beyond the offering of a contemptible worm, spreading before its Maker its own mean and low notions of Divine Majesty? If a worm were to raise its head, and cry—'O sun! You are the source of light and heat to a widely-extended universe'—it would, in fact, render a higher praise to the sun, than we can ever give to our Maker. Between it and us there is some proportion—between us and God none. Yet, unworthy as the offering confessedly is, He will not despise it. No, more, instead of spurning it from His presence, He has revealed Himself as "inhabiting the praises of Israel;" thus intimating to us, that the service of praise is "set forth in His sight as incense;" and at the same time, that it should be the daily and unceasing exercise of one at his own home.

The true character of praise, however, depends entirely upon the state of the heart. In the contemplative philosopher it is only cheerless, barren admiration: in the believer it becomes a principle of comfort and encouragement. For, can he forget the revelation, which his God has given of Himself in the gospel of His dear Son; how it divests every attribute of its terrors, and shines before us in all the glory of His faithfulness and love? The ascription of praise, "Blessed are You, O Lord," frames itself therefore into the prophet's song, "Who is a God like You, who pardons iniquity, and passes by the transgression of the remnant of His heritage? He retains not His anger forever, because He delights in mercy."

Truly then He is "blessed" in Himself, and delights to communicate His blessedness to His people. Hence we are emboldened to ask for continual "teaching in His statutes," in the truths which He has revealed, and the precepts which He has enjoined; that we may "be followers of Him, as dear children," and "walk with Him in love."

The practical influence, however, of Divine light, constitutes its peculiar privilege. Man's teaching puffs up—God's teaching humbles. Man's teaching may lead us into error as well as into truth—God's teaching is "the unction from the Holy One, by which we know all things." Man's teaching may make us more learned—God's teaching makes us more holy. It persuades, while it enlightens. It draws the heart, inclines the will, and carries out the soul to Christ. The tried character of God encourages us to look for His teaching, "Good and upright is the Lord; therefore will He teach sinners in the way." Our warrant is especially confirmed in approaching Him as our covenant God, "Lead me in Your truth, and teach me; for You are the God of my salvation. Teach me to do Your will: for You are my God."

Reader! do you desire to praise your God? Then learn to frequent the new and living way, "by which alone you can offer your sacrifice acceptably."And while engaged in this holy service, inquire, surrounded as you are with the means of instruction, what progress you are making in His statutes. Seek to have a deeper acquaintance with the character of God. Seek to be the vessels of honor and glory, into which He is pouring more and more continually, "until they be filled with all the fullness of God." Value the unspeakable blessing of Divine teaching, by which you learn to live the life, and begin the blessedness of God.

13. With my lips have I declared all the judgments of Your mouth.

We have seen the word hid in the heart: now we see it poured forth from the lips. The Lord has taught us His statutes; now we declare these judgments of His mouth. But who can declare them with unction and power, except those who are taught of God? Now we are introduced to the high and honorable privilege of becoming a witness for our Savior! Our opportunities of service are our talents, and we trade with a large increase; for "to everyone who has shall be given, and he shall have abundance." But, "our lips are our own"—is the proud language of the world. Blessed be God; "we know that we are not our own." Most gladly do we acknowledge, that He, who fashioned our lips, has the best claim to their service. And when He has added to the claim of creation the right of purchase, what further constraining can we need, to induce the consecration of all that we are, and all that we have, to His glory!

This is a family obligation—to declare the judgments of God's mouth. Thus did Abraham obtain a blessing for his children. Heavenly blessings are the gracious reward of thus honoring our God. This also is the material of our general conversation, fruitful in spiritual results. Thus did Andrew bring Peter, and the woman of Samaria her neighbors, to Jesus. What might we not do for our fellow-sinners, if our conversation with them was the overflowing of a heart full of love; guided by a single desire to glorify our Savior, and to edify His Church! Fearful, indeed, is the guilt of sinful silence; and those, who thus prove their unfaithfulness to God, may well tremble at His awful denunciations. And yet it is possible to be bold in speech for God, when in the closet, the family, or the world, our consciences justly convict us of insincerity: "You who teach another, do you not teach yourself?" Let us seek, therefore, to have our hearts "filled with the Spirit"; otherwise ours will be "the talk of the lips, which tends only to poverty."

This subject illustrates the character of the Lord's people, "The mouth of the righteous speaks wisdom, and his tongue talks of judgment;" their resolution, "My mouth shall show forth Your righteousness and Your salvation all the day; for I know not the numbers thereof;" their prayer, "O Lord, open my lips, and my mouth shall show forth Your praise;" their blessing, "The lips of the righteous feed many. A wholesome tongue is a tree of life." The example of the Savior, here as everywhere, is our perfect and encouraging pattern: "I have preached righteousness in the great congregation; Lo! I have not refrained My lips, O Lord, You know." In this spirit of their Master, the Apostles awed their persecutors into forbearance: "We cannot but speak the things which we have seen and heard."

How sinful is it to employ our lips for any but the Lord! Yet not less sinful is our reluctance to employ them for Him! Surely the day, when perhaps we have been fluent in worldly conversation, and yet have neglected our opportunities of speaking a word for Him, must be considered a lost day! Is there not much cause for watchfulness, prayer, and self-denial; lest our silence should deny Him, whom by every obligation we are bound to confess? If our inability to bear a testimony for our Lord is not painful to us, must we not suspect, if not the sincerity, at least the strength, of our attachment to His precious name? and we can do no better than retire into our closets with the prayer of contrition, "Enter not into judgment with Your servant, O Lord."

14. I have rejoiced in the way of Your testimonies, as much as in all riches.

How natural is it to be speaking of that which is our delight! The man of God was always declaring the Lord's judgments, because they were his rejoicing. There is indeed a real joy in despising earthly joys. "How sweet"—said Augustine, referring to the period of his conversion, "was it in a moment to be free from those delightful vanities, to lose which had been my dread; to part with which was now my joy!" More satisfying is the believer's rejoicing in the way of God, than that of the miser in his untold riches. Here he may safely say to his soul, "Soul, you have much goods laid up for many years; take your ease." And these are the only riches within the reach of all. If we are poor in this world, it is the Lord's providence. If we are poor in grace, it is our own fault. It is because we have despised our Lord's "counsel to buy from Him gold tried in the fire, that we may be rich." And what is this enriching portion?, "Things present or things to come;" something enjoyed, and much more expected: the mercies of eternity added to the blessings of time; the riches of both worlds—all assured to him by the covenant of grace "in the way of the Lord's testimonies."

Is it not then most strange, that, with such treasure in possession and in prospect, the child of God should be so careless in increasing his store, and in confirming his own interest in it? But the riches of God's testimonies have this peculiar property, that they cease to rejoice the heart, when they are not uppermost there. Have there not been times, when we have actually rejoiced in the accession of some worldly good, or the accomplishment of some worldly desire, more than in this heavenly treasure? What then do we count our riches? To thrive in grace, or in the world? To be rich towards God, or for our own indulgence?

But though we would rejoice in the testimonies, and would not, for all this world can afford, lose a verse or a letter of our Bibles, yet we cannot be satisfied with a general interest. Many texts—doctrinal, practical, or experimental—have been specially sealed by the Divine Spirit upon our hearts. This or that promise—yes, all the land of promise, as much as I can set my foot upon—is mine. From these precious testimonies, shall we not increase our little stock, until we have apprehended the full enjoyment of the whole; if indeed the fullness of that which is called "unsearchable" can ever be, in this life at least, completely enjoyed?

But it is not so much in the Lord's testimonies, as "in the way of them," that David rejoiced—the way to God, of which they testify; "the way of holiness," in which they lead—the narrow way of the cross—so contrary to our natural desires and inclinations, that none but the true sheep of Christ can ever enter, or continue in it. Who that walks in these ways will fail to find them, in duties no less than in privileges, "paths of pleasantness and peace?" Our happiness is not withered, but flourishing. "Thus says the Lord, Stand in the ways, and see, and ask for the old paths, where is the good way, and walk therein, and you shall find rest for your souls."

15. I will meditate in Your precepts, and have respect to Your ways.

Our rejoicing in the testimonies of God will naturally flow in a habitual meditation in them. The thoughts follow the affections. The carnal man can never be brought to this resolution. Having no spiritual taste, he has no ability for spiritual meditation. Indeed many sincere Christians, through remaining weakness and depravity, are too often reluctant to it. They are content with indolent reading: and, with scarcely a struggle or a trial, yield themselves up to the persuasion, that they are unable sufficiently to abstract their minds for this blessed employment. But let the trial prove the work. Perseverance will accomplish the victory over mental instability, and the spiritual difficulty will give way to prayer, "Lord! help me."

The fruitfulness of meditation will soon be manifest. Does it not "stir up the gift of God that is in us," and keep the energies of the heart in a wakeful posture of conflict and resistance? Besides this, meditation is the digestive faculty of the soul, which converts the word into real and proper nourishment: so that this revolving of a single verse in our minds is often better than the mere reading of whole chapters. "Your words were found, and I ate them; and Your word was to me the joy and the rejoicing of my heart." Thus the mind becomes the instrument of faith and love—of joy and strength.

But this meditation not only includes the stated times of thought, but the train of holy thoughts, that pass through the mind during the busy hours of the day. This maintains a habitual flow of spiritual desires, and excites the flame of love within, until at length the Psalmist's resolution becomes the inwrought habit of our minds, "I will meditate in Your precepts."

Can we lack a subject for meditation, if indeed the salvation of Jesus has been made known to our souls? While musing upon the glorious theme, does not "the fire burn" within, as if our hearts were touched with a live coal from the altar of God? Chide then, believer, your dull and sluggish spirit, that permits the precious manna to lie ungathered upon the ground, that is slow to entertain these heavenly thoughts, or rather that heavenly guest, whose peculiar office it is to "help our infirmities," and especially to "take of Christ's, and show it to us."

The exercise, however, of this, as of every other duty, may prove a barren form, that imparts neither pleasure nor profit. Let each of us then ask—'What distinct experimental benefit have I received from the word? Do I endeavor to read it with prayerful meditation, until I find my heart filled with it?'

But this communing with the word is not for contemplation, but for practice. By meditating on God's precepts, we learn to have respect unto His ways—carefully "pondering the path of our feet," that we "turn not aside." "Your loving-kindness is before my eyes; and I have walked in Your truth." "My foot," says Job, "has held His steps; His ways have I kept, and not declined. Neither have I gone back from the commandment of His lips; I have esteemed the words of His mouth more than my necessary food."

16. I will delight myself in Your statutes: I will not forget Your word.

As delight quickens to meditation, so does the practical habit of meditation strengthen the principle of delight. In the enjoyment of this delight, the Christian (however small his attainments may be) would rather live and die, than in the pursuit, and even in the possession, of the most satisfying pleasures of a vain and empty world. But if it be a real "delight in the Lord's statutes," it will be universal—when they probe the secret lurking-places within, and draw out to the full light the hidden indulgences of a heart that is yet carnal; when they call for the entire crucifixion of every corrupt inclination, and the unreserved surrender of all to the self-denying service of our God. This spirit is very different from the delight of the hypocrite, which is rather to "know," than to do, the "ways of his God;" and, therefore, who is satisfied with outward conformity, with little or no desire to "understand the errors" of his heart, that he might be "cleansed from secret faults." The spring of our obedience will therefore prove its sincerity; and the reality of our love will be manifested by its fruitfulness and active cheerfulness in our appointed sphere of duty.

We may also observe here an evidence of adoption. Obedience is not a burden, but a delight. The servant may perform the statutes of God; but it is only the son who "delights in them." But what—we may ask—is the spring of adoption? It is "the Spirit of the Son sent into our hearts, whereby we cry, Abba, Father." It is because we are at peace with God through Jesus Christ; because the statutes are the message of reconciliation through Him, that they become delightful to those, who are partakers of this great salvation. "The spirit of adoption," therefore, as the principle of delight, is the spring of acceptable obedience in the Lord's service.

And surely those who are serving Him in this happy filial walk, are not likely to "forget His word." As the eye is continually turned to the object of its affection, so the eye of the soul, that has been fixed with delight on the ways of God, will be habitually resting upon them. As one of the wise heathens observed—'I never yet heard of a covetous old man, who had forgotten where he had buried his treasure.' The reason is abundantly evident. His heart is in it. And this explains the forgetfulness of the ungodly or the formalist. They have no delight in the statutes. And who is not glad to forget what is distasteful? But if we "have tasted that the Lord is gracious"—if we have found a treasure "in the way of His testimonies"—we cannot forget the sweetness of the experience, or where to go to refresh ourselves with the repetition of it.

Forgetfulness of the word is, however, to the Christian, a source of continual complaint, and sometimes also of most distressing temptation. Not that there is always a real charge of guilt upon the conscience. For, as Thomas Boston somewhat quaintly observes—'Grace makes a good heart-memory, even where there is no good head-memory.' But means must be used, and helps may be suggested. Watchfulness against the influence of the world is of the first importance. How much of the good seed is choked by the springing thorns! If our hearts are ever refreshed with spiritual delight, we should be as cautious of an uncalled-for advance into the world, as of exposing an invalid's susceptible frame to a damp or an unhealthy atmosphere. Whatever warmth has been kindled in spiritual duties, may be chilled by one moment's unwary rush into an unkindly climate.

We would also recommend increasing attention to the word, as the means of its preservation—the exercise of "faith," without which it will "not profit"—the active habit of love, bringing with it a more habitual interest in the statutes—all accompanied with unceasing prayer for the gift of the Holy Spirit, made the express subject of promise for this purpose. Under His heavenly teaching and recollection, what delight will be found in the statutes! what blessed remembrance of His word! And what a happy spirit is this delight and remembrance of the word—the affections glowing—the memory pondering—the presence and manifestation of truth keeping the heart in close communion with God! "O Lord God, keep this forever in the imagination of the thoughts of the heart of Your people, and prepare their hearts unto You."

17. Deal bountifully with Your servant, that I may live, and keep Your word.

This prayer appears to have been much upon David's heart, and in its substance and object it is again repeated. Nor does he fail to acknowledge the answer to it. The believer, like David, is a man of large expectations. As regards himself—his own daily provocations and backslidings—he cannot stand upon his own ground. But when he brings with him the name, the blood, the intercession of Jesus; as soon could God deny His own beloved Son, as resist the supplication of those who present this all-prevailing plea. Not only so, but—is He not His own gift to His children, as the pledge of every other gift? And what other pledge can they need, to encourage them to draw near with the largest desire, and the most heavenly expectation? We may, indeed, be too bold in our manner of approach to God; but we cannot be too bold in our expectations from Him. Standing as we do upon such high and sure ground, it is equally dishonorable to Him, and impoverishing to ourselves, to ask only a little of Him. Rather let us, according to His own command, "open our mouths wide; and He will fill them." Rather let us expect that He will deal—not only favorably—but bountifully with His servants—that, as "our God, He will supply all our need according to His riches in glory by Christ Jesus."

And, indeed, the most experienced believer cannot forget, that he is in himself still the same poor, weak, empty, helpless creature as at first. Nothing, therefore, short of a bountiful supply can answer his continual neediness. And such a supply is always at hand. The act of prayer increases the power to pray. The throne of grace is a well, which no power or malice of the Philistines can stop up. We need not say, "We have nothing to draw with, and the well is deep." Faith will enable us "with joy to draw out of this well of salvation." Let us bring our empty vessels, until "there is not a vessel more." Yes—believer—there is indeed a bountiful supply of grace—of every kind—suited to every need—grace to pardon—grace to quicken—grace to bless. Oh! see, then, that you come not empty away. Remember—who it is that pleads before the throne. Remember—that the grace you need is in His hand. From eternity He foreknew your case. He laid your portion by. He has kept it for the time of need; and now He only waits for an empty vessel, into which to pour His supply. He is ready to show you, how infinitely His grace exceeds all thoughts—all prayers—all desires—all praises.

And say—what has been the fruit of your pleading, waiting expectancy at "the throne of grace?" Have you not returned thence with a fresh spring of devotedness in His service, with every selfish thought forgotten in the desire, that you "may live, and keep His word?" Nothing touched or moved your reluctant heart, but the apprehension of bountiful redeeming love. This makes obedience easy—delightful—natural—in a manner unavoidable. It "constrains" to it. The man now lives—not the animal life of appetite—not the sensual life of vanity and pleasure—but the only life that deserves the name. He lives singly, supremely "to Him who died for him, and rose again." He "lives, and keeps His word." His motto and character now is, "To me to live is Christ." He values life only by his opportunities of serving his God. The first archangel knows not a higher object of existence. And how encouraging the reflection, that in this glorious object the lowest servant in the household of God is an equal participant with the most blessed inhabitant of heaven!

18. Open my eyes, that I may behold wondrous things out of Your law.

In order to keep God's word, must we not pray to understand it? What then is the prayer? Not—give me a plainer Bible—but open my eyes to know my Bible. Not—show me some new revelations beside the law—but make me behold the wonders of the law. David had acquired in the Divine school "more understanding than all his teachers;" yet he ever comes to his God under a deep sense of his blindness. Indeed those who have been best and longest taught, are always the most ready to "sit at the feet of Jesus," as if they had everything to learn. It is an unspeakable mercy to know a little, and at the same time to feel that it is only a little. We shall then be longing to know more, and yet anxious to know nothing, except as we are taught of God.

There are indeed in God's law things so wondrous, that "the angels desire to look into them." The exhibition of the scheme of redemption is in itself a world of wonders. The display of justice exercised in the way of mercy, and of mercy glorified in the exercise of justice, is a wonder, that must fill the intelligent universe of God with everlasting astonishment. And yet these "wondrous things" are hidden from multitudes, who should be most deeply interested in the knowledge of them. They are "hidden," not only from the ignorant and unconcerned, but "from the wise and prudent; and revealed" only "to babes"—to those who practically acknowledge that important truth, that a man "can receive nothing, except it be given him from heaven." External knowledge is like the child spelling the letters without any apprehension of the meaning. It is like reading a large and clear print with a thick veil before our eyes. Oh! how needful then is the prayer—'Unveil;', "Open my eyes:" let the veil be taken away from the law, that I may understand it; and from my heart, that I may receive it!

But do not even Christians often find the word of God to be as a sealed book? They go through their accustomed portion, without gaining any increasing acquaintance with its light, life, and power, and without any distinct application of its contents to their hearts. And thus it must be, whenever reading has been unaccompanied with prayer for Divine influence. For we not only need to have our "eyes opened to behold" fresh wonders, but also to give a more spiritual and transforming perception of those wonders, which we have already beheld.

But are we conscious of our blindness? Then let us hear the counsel of our Lord, that we "anoint our eyes with eye-salve, that we may see."

35

The recollection of the promises of Divine teaching is fraught with encouragement. The Spirit is freely and abundantly promised in this very character, as "the Spirit of wisdom and revelation in the knowledge of God." If, therefore, we desire a clearer insight into these "wondrous things" of revelation—if we would behold the glorious beauty of our Immanuel—if we would comprehend something more of the immeasurable extent of that love, with which "God so loved the world, as to give His only-begotten Son," and of that equally incomprehensible love, which moved that Son so cheerfully to undertake our cause—we must make daily, hourly use of this important petition, "Open my eyes!"

19. I am a stranger in the earth: hide not Your commandments from me.

Such is the condition of the child of God—a stranger in the earth! This confession, however, from a solitary wanderer would have had little comparative meaning. But in the mouth of one, who was probably surrounded with every sort of worldly enjoyment, it shows at once the vanity of "earth's best joys," and the heavenly tendency of the religion of the Bible. This has been ever the character, confession, and glory of the Lord's people. We "would not live always;" and gladly do we hear the warning voice, that reminds us to "arise and depart, for this is not our rest." And was not this especially the character, not of David only, but of David's Lord? Born at an inn— "having nowhere to lay His head"— suffering hunger—subsisting upon alms—neglected by His own—He "looked for some to take pity, but there was none, and for His comforters, but He found none"—might He not justly take up the confession, "I am a stranger in the earth?"

This verse exhibits the Christian in many most interesting points of view; distant from his proper home—without a fixed residence—with no particular interest in the world—and submitting to all the inconveniences of a stranger on his journey homewards. Such is his state!

And the word of God includes all that he needs—a guide, a guard, a companion—to direct, secure, and cheer his way. "When you go, it shall lead you; when you sleep, it shall keep you; and when you awake, it shall talk with you." Most suitable then is the stranger's prayer, "hide not Your commandments from me." Acquaintance with the word of God supplies the place of friends and counselors. It furnishes light, joy, strength, food, armor, and whatever else he may need on his way homewards.

The pilgrim-spirit is the pulse of the soul. All of us are traveling to eternity. The worldling is at home in the earth—a pilgrim only by restraint. His heart would say, "It is good for me to be here. Let God dispose of heaven at His pleasure. I am content to have my "portion in this life." The child of God is a stranger in the earth. Heaven is the country of his birth. His kindred—his inheritance—his Savior—his hope—his home—all is there. He is "a citizen of no insignificant city," of "the heavenly Jerusalem." He is therefore a pilgrim in affection, no less than in character. How cheering is the thought, that "here we have no continuing city," if in heart and soul we are "seeking one to come!"

We know, indeed, that we cannot—we would not—call this world our home, and that it is far better to be without it, than to have our portion in it. But do we never feel at home in the earth, thus forgetting our proper character, and our eternal prospects? Do we always live, speak, and act as "strangers in the earth;" in the midst of earthly enjoyments, sitting loose to them, as if our treasure was in heaven? Does our conversation in the society of the world savor of the home, where we profess to be going? Is the world gaining ascendancy in our affection? Let the cross of Calvary be the object of our daily contemplation—the ground of our constant "glorying;" and the world will then be to us as a "crucified" object.

And lastly, let us not forget, that we are looking forward, and making a progress towards a world, where none are strangers—where all are children of one family, dwelling in one eternal home. "In our Father's house," said our gracious Head, "are many mansions: I go to prepare a place for you."

20. My soul breaks for the longing that it has unto Your judgments at all times.

This intense desire and affection is the Christian's answer to his prayers—Open my eyes—Hide not Your commandments from me. For who that is conversant with this blessed revelation but longs to be filled with it? In contrasting this glow with the church of Laodicea, under a brighter dispensation, "neither cold nor hot" which state, we may ask, most nearly resembles our own? Observe also, not only the fervor, but the steady uniformity, of this religion. It was not a rapture, but a habit; constant and uniform; "at all times." With us such enjoyments are too often favored seasons, happy moments; alas! only moments—why not days, and months, and years? The object of our desires is an inexhaustible spring. The longing of the soul can never over-reach its object. The cherished desire, therefore, will become the established habit—the element in which the child of God lives and thrives.

This uniformity is the most satisfactory test of our profession. Often are the judgments prized in affliction, when all other resources fail: or under a pang of conscience when the terror of the Lord is frowning upon the sinner. But the excitement wears off, and the heart returns to its hardness. Often also the impulse of novelty gives a strong but temporary impression. This is very different from the Christian, whose study is stretching out its desires at all times; finding the judgments a cordial or a discipline, a support or a preservation, as his need may require.

Not less important is this habit, as the test of the soul's prosperity. We are not satisfied with occasional fellowship with a beloved friend. His society is the life of our life. We seek him in his own ways, where he is accustomed to resort. We feel the blank of his absence. We look out for his return with joyous anticipation.

Now, is this the picture of our soul's longing for communion with Jesus? We may feel His loss, should the stated seasons of prayer fail in bringing Him near to us. But do we long for Him at all times? Do we "wait for Him in the way of His judgments," where He is usually found? And when spiritual exercises are necessarily exchanged for the occupations of the world, do we seize the leisure moment to catch a word—a glimpse—a look? Is not the heart silent with shame in the recollection of the cold habit of external or occasional duty?

But why this low ebbing of spiritual desire? Do we live near to the throne of grace? Have we not neglected prayer for the influence of the Spirit? Have we not indulged a light, vain, and worldly spirit, than which nothing more tends to wither the growth of vital religion? Or have not the workings of unbelief been too faintly resisted? This of itself will account for much of our dullness; since the rule of the kingdom of grace is, "According to your faith be it unto you." Grace is, indeed, an insatiable principle. Enjoyment, instead of satisfying, only serves to sharpen the appetite. Yet if we are content to live at a low rate, there will be no sensible interest in the consolation of the Gospel. We know, desire, and are satisfied with little; and, therefore, we enjoy but little. We live as borderers on the land, instead of bearing our testimony: "Surely it flows with milk and honey; and this is the fruit of it." This is not the thriving, the cheerfulness, the adorning of the Gospel. It is rather the obscuring of the glory of our Christian profession, and of the happiness of its attendant privileges.

Let not the fervor of desire here expressed be conceived to be out of reach; nor let it be expected in the way of some sudden manifestation or excitement. Rather let us look for it in a patient, humble, and persevering waiting upon the Lord. We may have still to complain of coldness and wanderings. Yet strength to wait will be imperceptibly given: faith will be sustained for the conflict; and thus "our souls will make their boast in the Lord," even though an excited flow of enjoyment should be withheld. One desire will, however, tread upon another, increasing in fullness, as the grand object is nearer our grasp.

At all events, let us beware of resting satisfied with the confession of our lukewarmness to our fellow-creatures, without "pouring out our heart before the Lord." There is a fullness of grace in our glorious Head to "strengthen the things which remain, which are ready to die," as well as at the beginning to "quicken" us when "dead in trespasses and sins." Abundant, also—are the promises and encouragements to poor, dry, barren souls, "I will heal their backslidings; I will be as the dew unto Israel: he shall grow as the lily, and cast forth his roots as Lebanon." For what purpose are promises such as these given, but that they may be "arguments," with which to "fill our mouth," when in the contrition of faith we again venture to "order our cause before God?" And "will He plead against us with His great power?" No! but "He will put His strength in us;" and we shall yet again "run the way of His commandments" with an enlarged heart.

21. You have rebuked the proud that are cursed, which err from Your commandments.

Let the histories of Cain, Pharaoh, Haman, Nebuchadnezzar, and Herod, exhibit the proud under the rebuke and curse of God. He abhors their persons, and their offerings; He "knows them afar off," "He resists them;" "He scatters them in the imaginations of their hearts." Especially hateful are they in His sight, when cloaking themselves under a spiritual garb; "They say, Stand by yourself, come not near me; for I am holier than you. These are a smoke in my nose, a fire that burns all the day." Most of all, is this sin an abomination in His own beloved people. David and Hezekiah are instructive beacons in the church, that they, least of all, must expect to escape His rebuke, "You were a God who forgave them; though You took vengeance on their inventions."

Now the people of the world call the proud happy. But will they be counted so, when they shall be manifestly under the curse of God; when "the day of the Lord shall be upon them to bring them low," yes, to "burn them in the oven" of "His wrath?"

Pride probably influences all, who "err from the Lord's commandments;" yet doubtless "the Righteous Judge" will make an infinite difference between errors of infirmity and obstinate wilfulness. The confession of the man of God, "I have gone astray like a lost sheep "—is widely different in character from the subjects of this awful rebuke and curse. "You have trodden down all those who err from Your statutes; for their deceit is falsehood."

We wonder not at this expression of the mind of God concerning pride. There is no sin more abhorrent to His character. It is as if we were taking the crown from His head, and placing it upon our own. It is man making a God of himself—acting from himself, and for himself. Nor is this principle less destructive to our own happiness. And yet it is not only rooted, but it often rears its head and blossoms, and bears fruit, even in hearts which "hate and abhor" its influence. It is most like its father, the Devil, in serpentine deceitfulness. It is always active—always ready imperceptibly to mix itself up with everything. When it is mortified in one shape, it rises in another. When we have thought that it was gone, in some unexpected moment we find it here still. It can convert everything into nourishment, even God's choicest gifts—yes, the graces of His Spirit. Let no saint, therefore, however near he may be living to God, however favored with the shinings of His countenance—consider himself beyond the reach of this temptation. Paul was most in danger, when he seemed to be most out of it; and nothing but an instant miracle of grace and power saved him from the "snare of the Devil."

Indeed, the whole plan of salvation is intended to humble the pride of man, by exhibiting his restoration to the Divine favor, as a free gift through the atoning blood of the cross. How hateful, therefore, is proud man's resistance to this humbling doctrine of the cross, and the humbling requisitions of the life of faith flowing from it! This makes the sure "foundation" of the believer's hope, "a stone of stumbling" to the unbeliever's ruin. As regards also the means of salvation—how can pride lift up his head in the view of the Son of God, "taking upon Him the form of a servant," that He might bear the curse of man? "Behold, the soul that is lifted up, is not upright in him."

But can a sinner—can a saint—be proud?—one who owes everything to free and sovereign grace—one who has wasted so much time—abused so much mercy—so grieved the Spirit of God—who has a heart so full of atheism—unbelief—selfishness? No, the very pride itself should be the matter of the deepest daily humiliation. Thus the remembrance of it may, under Divine grace, prove an effectual means of subduing it in our hearts. We shall overcome corruption by its own working, and meet our adversary with his own weapons. And if this cursed principle be not wholly destroyed, yet the very sight of its corruption, deepening our contrition, will be overruled for our spiritual advancement.

O blessed end intended by the Lord's dealings with us! to "humble and to prove us" "to know," and to make us know "what was in our heart, that He might do us good at the latter end!" Let us not frustrate His gracious intentions, or build again the things which He would have destroyed. May we love to lie low—lower than ever—infinitely low before Him! Lord! teach us to remember, that "that which is highly esteemed among men, is abomination in Your sight." Teach us to bless You, for even Your sharp and painful discipline which tends to subjugate this hateful pride of our hearts before our Savior's cross!

22. Remove from me reproach and contempt; for I have kept Your testimonies.

The proud under the rebuke of God are usually distinguished by their enmity to His people. They delight to pour upon them "reproach and contempt," with no other provocation given, than that their keeping the testimonies of God condemns their own neglect. This must, however, be counted as the cost of a decided, separate, and consistent profession. Yet it is such a portion as Moses valued above all the treasures of the world; yet it is that reproach, which our Master Himself "despised," as "reckoning it not worthy to be compared with "the joy that was set before Him." For did He bear His cross only on the way to Calvary? It was laid for every step in His path; it met Him in every form of suffering, of "reproach and contempt." Look then at Him, as taking up His daily cross in breathing the atmosphere of a world of sin, and "enduring the contradiction of sinners against Himself." Mark Him consummating His course of "reproach and contempt," by suffering "outside the gate;" and

41

can we hesitate to "go forth unto Him outside the camp, bearing His reproach?"

The trial, however—especially if cast upon us by those whom we have loved and valued, or by those whom we wish to love and value us—proves most severe; and the spreading our case, after David's example, before the Lord, is the only preservation from faintness, "Remove from me reproach and contempt."

Perhaps "contempt" is more hard to bear than "reproach." Even our enemies think of us so much better than we deserve, that it strikes with peculiar poignancy. Yet when the submissive prayer of deprecation is sent us; doubtless some answer—and that the right answer—will be given; and whether the "reproach" be removed, or "grace" given "sufficient" to endure it, the outcome will prove alike for the glory of God, and the prosperity of our own souls.

But let us beware of that "way of escape" in returning to the world, which the insincere are ever ready to pursue. They dare not act according to the full conviction of their consciences: they dare not confront their friends with the avowal of their full determination to form their conduct by the principles of the word of God. This is hard—this is impossible. They know not the "victory which overcomes the world", and, therefore, cannot bear the mark upon their foreheads, "These are those who follow the Lamb wherever He goes." Far better, however, will be the heaviest weight of "reproach and contempt," than any such endeavor to remove it from ourselves.

The desire to escape the cross convicts the heart of unfaithfulness, and makes way for tenfold difficulties in our path. Every worldly compliance against the voice of God is a step into the by-path, which deviates wider and wider from the strait and narrow way, brings discredit upon our professions, proves a stumbling-block in the way of the weak, and will cause us, if not actually to come short, at least to "seem to come short, of the promised rest."

But is the weight of the cross really "above what we are able to bear?" He who bore it for us will surely enable us to endure it for Him, and, upheld by Him, we cannot sink. It is a sweet exchange, by which the burden of sin is removed, and bound to His cross; and what remains to us is the lighter cross of "reproach and contempt,"—the badge of our discipleship. If, then, we have the testimony of our consciences, that in the midst of the persecuting world we "have kept His testimonies," here is our evidence of adoption, of our Father's special love, of the indwelling, comforting, supporting Spirit. Here, then, is our warrant of hope, that the overwhelming weight will be removed from us; and that we shall be able to testify to our Master's praise in the Churches of God, that "His yoke is easy, and His burden is light."

23. Princes also did sit and speak against me; but Your servant did meditate in Your statutes.

David might well give his testimony to "the words of the Lord," that they were "tried words," for perhaps no one had ever tried them more than himself, and certainly no one had more experience of their faithfulness, sweetness, and support. Saul and his "princes might indeed sit and speak against him;" but he had a resource, of which they could never deprive him, "Not as the world gives, give I unto you." As our blessed Master was employed in communion with His Father, and delighting in His work at the time when the "princes did sit and speak against him;" so, under similar circumstances of trial, this faithful servant of God, by meditation in the Lord's statutes, extracted spiritual food for his support; and in this strength of his God he was enabled to "suffer according to His will, and to commit the keeping of his soul to Him in well-doing, as unto a faithful Creator."

The children of Israel in Egypt, Daniel in Babylon, and the disciples of Christ in the early ages of the Church, have each found "this same affliction to be accomplished in themselves." that God is pleased to permit it, to show "that his kingdom is not of this world," to wean His people from earthly dependencies, and to bring out before the world a more full testimony of His name.

One other reason is suggested by this verse—to make His word more precious by the experience of its sustaining consolation in the conflict with the power of the world. Often, indeed, from a lack of a present application of the word—young Christians especially are in danger of being put to rebuke by the scorner's sneer. The habit of scriptural meditation will realize to them a present God, speaking "words of spirit and life" to their souls. The importance, therefore, of an accurate and well-digested acquaintance with this precious book cannot be too highly estimated. In the Christian's conflict it is "the sword of the Spirit," which, if it be kept bright by constant use, will never be wielded without the victory of faith. Such powerful support does it give against fainting under persecution, that the good soldier may ever be ready to thank God, and to take courage. Christ has left it, indeed, as the portion of His people, "In the world you shall have tribulation;" counterbalanced, however, most abundantly, by the portion which they enjoy in Him, "In Me you shall have peace." If, therefore, the one-half of this portion may seem hard, the whole legacy is such as no servant of Christ can refuse to accept, or indeed will receive without thankfulness.

24. Your testimonies also are my delight, and my counselors.

What could we want more in a time of difficulty than comfort and direction? David had both these blessings. As the fruit of his "meditation in the Lord's statutes," in his distress they were his "delight;" in his perplexity they were his "counselors." He would not have exchanged his delight for the best joys of earth. And so wisely did his counselors direct his course, that, though "princes sat and spoke against him," they "could find no occasion nor fault." The testimonies of God were truly his "counselors." He guided his own conduct by the rules laid before him in the book of God, as if he were having recourse to the most experienced counselors, or rather as if the prophets of his God were giving the word from His mouth. Thus the subject as well as the sovereign, had his counsel. On one side was Saul and his counselors—on the other side, David and the testimonies of his God. Which was better furnished with that "wisdom which is profitable to direct?" Subsequently as a king, David was constrained to make "the testimonies of his God his counselors"; and, probably, to his constant regard to their voice he owed much of his earthly prosperity.

In such a dark world as this, beset with temptation at every turn, we preeminently need sound and wise counsel. But all of us carry an evil counselor within us, and it is our folly to listen to his voice. God has given us His word as a sure counselor, and "he who hearkens to its counsel is wise."

Now, do we value the privilege of this heavenly counsel? Every improvement must increase our delight in it; a heartless interest shuts out this blessing. But those who make the word their delight will always find it their counselor. Yet a mere cursory reading will never realize to us its holy delight or counsel. It must be brought home to our own experience, and consulted on those trivial occasions of every day, when, unconscious of our need of Divine direction, we are too often inclined to lean to our own counsel. The Christian is a man of faith, every step of his way. And this habitual use and daily familiarity with the testimonies of God will show him the pillar and the cloud, in all the dark turns of his heavenly road. The word will be to him as the "Urim and Thummin"—an infallible counselor.

Sometimes, however, perplexity arises from the conflict, not between conscience and sinful indulgence (in which case Christian sincerity would always determine the path), but between duty and duty. When, however, acknowledged obligations seem to interfere with each other, the counsel of the word will mark their relative importance, connection, and dependence: the present path in providence: the guidance which has been given to the Lord's people in similar emergencies; and the light which the daily life of our Great Exemplar exhibits before us.

The great concern, however, is to cultivate the habit of mind, which falls in most naturally with the counsel of the word. "Walking in the fear of the Lord," in a simple spirit of dependence, and torn away from the idolatry of taking counsel from our own hearts, we cannot materially err; because there is here a suitableness between the disposition and the promise—a watchfulness against the impetuous bias of the flesh; a paramount regard to the glory of God, and a meek submission to His gracious appointment. If the counsel, however, should prove fallible, the fault is not in the word, but in the indistinctness of our own perception. We need not a clearer rule, or a surer guide, but a more single eye. And if, after all, it may not mark every precise act of duty (for to do this, even all the world "could not contain the books that should be written"), yet it determines the standard to which the most minute acting of the mind should be brought; and the disposition, which will reflect the light of the will of God upon our path.

But let it be remembered, that any lack of sincerity in the heart—any allowance of self-dependence, will always close the avenues of this Divine light and counsel. We are often unconsciously "walking in the light of our own fire, and in the sparks that we have kindled." Perhaps we sought, as we conceived, the guidance of the Lord's counsel, and supposed that we were walking in it. But, in the act of seeking, and as the preparation for seeking, did we subject our motives and inclinations to a strict, cautious, self-suspecting scrutiny? Was the heart schooled to the discipline of the cross? Was "every thought brought into captivity to the obedience of Christ?" Or was not our heart possessed with the object, before counsel was sought at the mouth of God? Oh! how careful should we be to walk warily in those uncertain marks of heavenly counsel, that fall in with the bias of our own inclination! How many false steps in the record of past experience may be traced to the counsel of our own hearts, sought and followed to the neglect and counsel of God; while no circumstance of perplexity can befall us in the spirit of humility, simplicity, and sanctity, when the counsel of the Lord will fail!

An undue dependence upon human counsel, whether of the living or the dead, greatly hinders the full influence of the counsel of the word. However valuable such counsel may be, and however closely it may agree with the word, we must not forget, that it is not the word—that it is fallible, and therefore must never be resorted to in the first place, or followed with that full reliance, which we are warranted to place on the revelation of God.

On the other hand, what is it to have God's word as our "Counselor?" Is it not to have Himself, "the only wise God?" When our Bibles, in seasons of difficulty, are searched in a humble, prayerful, teachable spirit, we are as much depending upon the Lord Himself for counsel, as if we were listening to an immediate revelation from heaven. We need not a new revelation, or a sensible voice from above, for every fresh emergency. It is enough, that our Father has given us this blessed "word as a light to our feet, and a lamp to our path."

Let me then inquire—What is the counsel of God, that speaks directly to myself? If I am an unawakened sinner, it warns me to turn from sin; it invites me to the Savior; it directs me to wait upon God. If I am a professor, slumbering in the form of godliness, it shows me my real condition; it instructs me in the all-sufficiency of Christ, and cautions me of the danger of hypocrisy. If through grace I am made a child of God, still do I need my Father's counsel to recover me from perpetual backsliding, to excite me to increased watchfulness, and to strengthen my confidence in the fullness of His grace, and the faithfulness of His love. Ever shall I have reason for the grateful acknowledgment, "I will bless the Lord, who has given me counsel." And every step of my way would I advance, glorifying my God and Father by confiding in His counsel unto the end: "You shall guide me with Your counsel, and afterwards receive me to glory."

25. My soul cleaves to the dust; quicken me according to Your word.

Sin is no trifle to a child of God. It is his heaviest sorrow. Thus David—thus the Great Apostle found it. And where is the believer who has not full sympathy with their complaints? To have a soul cleaving to the dust, and not to feel the trouble, is the black mark of a sinner, dead in sins—dead to God. To "know the plague of our own heart," to feel our misery, to believe and to apply the remedy, is the satisfactory evidence of a child of God. Dust is the portion of the world, and they wish for no better. But that the soul of the man of God should continually cleave to the dust, is most strange and humbling. And yet such is the influence of his evil nature—such the power of self-will and self-indulgence—such the regard to human praise, and cherishing of self-admiration, that were it not that he "abhors himself" for the very dust that cleaves to him, he would question the existence of a renewing change. He knows what he ought to be. He has tasted the blessedness of "mounting upward on eagles' wings." But every attempt to rise is hindered by the clogging weight that keeps him down.

It is, however, the cleaving of his soul that is so painful—not occasional, but constant—not like the bird of the morning that descends for a moment, and then soars his upward flight; but it seems as if, like the "serpent—dust was to be his food;" as if the spiritual, heaven-born soul was to sink and grovel below. And then, as the dust of the summer-road blinds the eye, and obscures the view—how does this earthliness of soul darken the view of the Savior, dim the eye of faith, and hide the glorious prospects which, when beheld in the clear horizon, enliven the weary pilgrim on his way!

But this complaint is the language of conflict and humiliation—not of despondency. Observe the believer carrying it to the Lord—'Here I lie in the dust, without life or power. Oh! Savior, who "came that I might have life, and that I might have it more abundantly"—Quicken me: Breathe into me Your own life, that I may rise from the dust, and cleave to You.' This cry for quickening grace is the exercise of faith. We have a covenant to plead. Faith is the hand that takes hold of the promise, "according to Your word." Can this word fail? "Sooner shall heaven and earth pass away, than one jot or one tittle pass" from the engagements of a covenant-keeping God. "He is faithful who promised." The man who takes hold of this plea, is "a Prince who has power with God, and prevails."

But how different is the character of the mere professor! ready probably to make the same confession, yet without humiliation, without prayer, without faith. Nothing is more common than to hear the complaint—"My soul cleaves to the dust." The world has such power over us—we are so cold—so dead to spiritual things:' while, perhaps, the complaint is never once brought with wrestling supplication, but rather urged in indolent self-delight, as an evidence of the good state of the heart before God.

Yet it is not the complaint of sickness, but an application to the physician, which advances the recovery of the patient. We do not usually expect to better our condition, by mourning over its badness, or merely wishing for its improvement. Nor is it the confession of sin, but the application to the Great Physician, that marks genuine contrition before God. That confession which evaporates in heartless complaints, belongs not to the tenderness of a renewed heart. But the utterance of genuine prayer is the voice of God's own "Spirit making intercession for us;" and then, indeed, how cheering the encouragement, that He "who searches the hearts, knows what is the mind of the Spirit, because He makes intercession for the saints according to the will of God!"

Some are ready to give up or delay their duty, when they have been unable to bring their heart to it. Thus does "Satan get advantage of us" by our "ignorance of his devices." Quickening grace is not the ground or warrant for duty. Indisposition to duty is not our weakness, but our sin—not therefore to be indulged, but resisted. We must mourn over the dullness which hinders us, and diligently wait for the 'help we every moment need.' God keeps the grace in His own hands, and gives it at His pleasure, to exercise our daily dependence upon Him. The acting of grace strengthens the habit. Praying helps to pray. If the door is closed, "Knock, and it shall be opened." Assuredly it will not long be shut to him, who has faith and patience to wait until it be opened.

Now let me sift the character of my profession. Is it a habitual, persevering, overcoming conflict with sin? Do I not sometimes indulge in fruitless bemoanings of my state, when I had far better be exercising myself in vigorous actings of grace? If I find "my soul cleaving to the dust," am I not sometimes "lying on my face," when I ought to be "taking heaven by violence," by importunate petitions for quickening grace? Are my prayers invigorated by confidence in the word of God? Oh! let me remember that "those who wait upon the Lord" shall shake off the dust to which they have cleaved so long, and "shall mount with wings like eagles," to take possession of their heavenly home.

O Lord, make me more deeply ashamed, that "my soul should cleave to the dust." Breathe upon me fresh influence from Your quickening Spirit. Help me to plead Your word of promise; and oh! may every fresh view of my sinfulness, while it prostrates me in self-abasement before You, be overruled to make the Savior daily and hourly more precious to my soul. For defiled as I am in myself, in every service of my heart, what but the unceasing application of His blood, and the uninterrupted prevalence of His intercession, give me a moment's confidence before You, or prevent the very sins that mingle with my prayers from sealing my condemnation? Blessed Savior! it is nothing but Your everlasting merit, covering my person, and honoring my sacrifice, which satisfies the justice of an offended God, and restrains it from breaking forth as a devouring fire—to consume me upon my very knees.

Verses 26-50

26. I have declared my ways, and You heard me; teach me Your statutes.

A beautiful description of the "simplicity and godly sincerity" of the believer's "walk with God!" He spreads his whole case before his God, "declaring his ways" of sinfulness, of difficulty, and of conduct. And, indeed, it is our privilege to acquaint our Father with all our care and need, that we may be pitied by His love, and guided by His counsel, and confirmed by His strength. Who would not find relief by unbosoming himself to his Father? This showing of ourselves to God—declaring our ways of sin before Him without deceit—is the short and sure way of rest.

"You heard me." "When I kept silence, my bones waxed old through my roaring all the day long." While the voice of ingenuous confession was suppressed, cries and lamentations were disregarded. It was not the voice of the penitent child; and, therefore, "where was the sounding of his father's affections, and of his mercies towards him?" But now, on the first utterance of confession from his lips, or rather on the first purpose of contrition formed in his heart; "while he is yet speaking," the full and free pardon, which had been signed in heaven, comes down with royal parental love to his soul, "I said, I will confess my transgression to the Lord; and You forgave the iniquity of my sin."

Oh! what cannot he testify of the more than parental tenderness, with which "his transgression is forgiven, and his sin covered!" And yet, how necessary to the free declaration of our ways is an acquaintance with the way of forgiveness! Had not our great "High Priest passed into the heavens," how awful would have been the thought, that all things were "naked and opened unto the eyes of Him with whom we have to do!" We could only then have "covered our transgressions as Adam, by hiding our iniquity in our bosom." But now, even though "our ways" are so defiled, so crooked that we cannot but "abhor ourselves," on account of them, we are yet encouraged "boldly" to "declare" them all before God, with the assurance of finding present acceptance, and seasonable grace.

And now, having found the happy fruit of this sincere and child-like spirit, then follows the obligation of walking worthy of this mercy. Hence our need of the prayer for continual teaching. The same heavenly guidance, that brought us into the way of return, we need for every successive step to the end, "Teach me Your way, O Lord: I will walk in Your truth." "I have declared my" ignorance, my sinfulness, and my whole experience before You, looking for Your pardoning mercy, Your teaching Spirit, and assisting grace, "And You have heard me." O continue to me what You have been, and teach me more of Yourself!

The hypocrite may pray after this manner. But he never thus opens his heart, and "declares his ways" beneath his God. And are we sincere in our dealings with Him? How often do we treat our Almighty Friend as if we were weary of dealing with Him! And even when we do "declare our ways" before Him, are we not often content to leave the result as a matter of uncertainty? We do not watch for the answer to our prayer. It will come in the diligent exercise of faith, but not perhaps in our way. We may have asked for temporal blessings, and we receive spiritual. We may have "besought" deliverance from trial, and we receive "grace sufficient" to bear it. But this is the Lord's wise and gracious answer—You heard me. And how sweet are those mercies, which come to us manifestly marked with this inscription, "Received by prayer!" They are such encouragement to pray again. It is not our inevitable weakness, nor our lamented dullness, nor our abhorred wanderings, nor our opposed distractions, nor our mistaken unbelief; it is not any—no, nor all these— that can shut out prayer. If "iniquity" is not "regarded in our heart," we may always hear our Savior's voice, "Verily, verily, I say unto you, Whatever you shall ask the Father in My name, He will give it you. Hitherto have you asked nothing in My name. Ask, and you shall receive, that your joy may be full."

27. Make me to understand the way of Your precepts; so shall I talk of Your wondrous works.

Notice the reiterated cries of the man of God for heavenly light, Teach me Your statutes—make me to understand the way of Your precepts. The need and the encouragement for these cries is equally manifest. Who has ever been known to understand the way of himself? And to whom—walking in a well-ordered conversation—has the Lord ever failed to show it? A man, untaught by the Spirit of God, may be able to criticize, and even clearly to expound, much of the word of God. But such a prayer as this has never ascended from the heart; the necessity of it has never been felt. And, doubtless, from this neglect of prayer have

51

arisen those floating fancies and false and unscriptural doctrines, which crude, unexercised minds have too hastily embraced. Instead of humbly and simply asking, "Make me to understand"—men too often "lean to their own understanding," and are "vainly puffed up" by their fleshly mind, "not holding the Head." Such men may obtain loose fragments of spiritual knowledge; but they will not be in the faith, "grounded and settled." They never know when they are upon safe ground; and being "unlearned and unstable, they wrest the Scriptures"—except the sovereign grace of God interpose, "unto their own destruction."

Never must we forget, that teaching from above is indispensable to a right knowledge of the most simple truths. Ignorance and prejudice pervert the understanding. "Spiritual things can only be spiritually discerned." Divine doctrines can only be apprehended by Divine light. But under heavenly teaching, the deeper and more mysterious truths (so far as they are needful to be understood) are manifested with the same clearness, as the more elementary doctrines: "Eye has not seen nor ear heard, nor have entered into the heart of man, the things which God has prepared for them that love Him. But God has revealed them to us by His Spirit. Now we have received—not the spirit of the world, but the Spirit which is of God, that we might know the things that are freely given to us of God."

Wondrous, indeed, is the spiritual revelation in the knowledge of Himself; including "the hope of His calling;—the riches of the glory of His inheritance in His saints;—the exceeding greatness of His power" manifested to, and wrought in, His people;—no other or less than that "which He wrought in Christ, when He raised Him from the dead." In the understanding of the way, we would be progressing until the new man "grows up into the measure of the stature of the fullness of Christ." The smallest attainment in this knowledge is (as the great day will fully declare) of infinitely greater value than the highest intelligence in the field of earthly science.

But how important is it to grow in this knowledge! Theoretical attainment is at a stand. Spiritual and practical knowledge is always advancing. Little, indeed, comparatively, is necessary for salvation. But much for comfort and steadfastness—much also for the clear discernment of that narrow way of the precepts so difficult to trace, and when traced so difficult to maintain. Not less important is it to keep the object in constant view. Why do I desire to understand that way? That I may commend it to others—that I may talk of Your wondrous works.

Abhorred be the thought of indulging in a self-complacent view of my attainments! But oh! let my God be more admired by me, and glorified in me. And may I advance both myself and others in His obedience and praise!

Often do we complain of restraint in religious conversation. But the prayer—Make me to understand while I talk—will bring "a live coal to our lips" from the altar of God, "Our mouths will then speak out of the abundance of the heart," and "minister grace to the hearers." Humility, teachableness, simplicity, will bring light into the understanding, influence the heart, "open the lips," and unite every member that we have in the service and praise of God.

28. My soul melts for heaviness; strengthen me according to Your word.

Is this David, "whose heart is as the heart of a lion, here utterly melting?" But the sorrows, as the joys of the spiritual man—dealing immediately with the Infinite and Eternal God—are beyond conception. Ordinary courage may support under the trials of this life; but when "the arrows of the Almighty are within us, the poison thereof drinks up our spirit." How, then, can the Christian's lot be so enviable, when their souls thus melt for heaviness? But this, be it remembered, is only "for a season." There is a "needs-be" for it, while it remains: and in the end it "will be found unto praise, and honor, and glory." Never, perhaps, are their graces more lively, or the ground of their assurance more clear, than in these seasons of sorrow. They complain, indeed, of the diversified power of indwelling sin. But their very complaints are the evidence of the mighty working of indwelling grace. For what is it but the principle of faith, that makes unbelief their burden? What but hope, that struggles with their tears? What but love, that makes their coldness a grief? What but humility, that causes them to loathe their pride? What but the secret spring of thankfulness, that shows them their unthankfulness, and shames them for it? And, therefore, the very depth of "that heaviness which melts their souls" away, is the exhibition of the strength of God's work within, upholding them in perseverance of conflict to the end. Would not the believer then, when eyeing in his heaviest moments the most prosperous condition of the ungodly, say, "Let me not eat of their dainties?" Far better, and, we may add, far happier, is godly sorrow than worldly joy. In the midst of his misery, the Christian would not exchange his hope in the gospel—though often obscured by unbelief, and clouded

53

by fear—for all "the kingdoms of the world, and the glory of them." "If the heart knows his own bitterness, a stranger does not intermeddle with his joy." Yet the bitterness is keenly felt. Sin displeases a tender and gracious Father. It has "pierced" the heart that loves him; and shed the blood that saves him. It grieves the indwelling Comforter of his soul. God expects to see him a mourner; and he feels he has reason enough to mourn, "My soul melts for heaviness."

But this cry of distress is sometimes that of the child under his Father's needful chastisement. The world is dethroned, but not extirpated, in the heart. Much dross is yet to be removed. The sources of the too attractive earthly joy must be embittered: and now it is that the discipline of the cross forces the cry, "My soul melts for heaviness." Yet in the midst of heaviness, the child of God cannot forget that he is loved—that he is saved; and the recollection of this sovereign mercy makes his tears of godly sorrow, tears of joy.

But this melting heaviness has not wrought its work, until it has bowed us before the throne of grace with the pleading cry of faith—Strengthen me! For do we stand by the strength of our own resolutions or habits of grace? Unless the Lord renew His supply from moment to moment, all is frail and withering. But what burden or difficulty is too great for Almighty strength? "Fear not, you worm Jacob; you shall thresh the mountains, and beat them small." And especially is our success assured, when the plea is drawn, as it is repeatedly in this Psalm—according to Your word. For what does that word assure us?, "As Your days, so shall Your strength be." "Will He plead against me"—said Job, "with His great power? No! but He will put strength in me." Thus David found it in his own case: "In the day when I cried, You answered me, and strengthened me with strength in my soul." Thus also to the Apostle was the promise given and fulfilled: "My grace is sufficient for you; for My strength is made perfect in weakness." And is not "the God of Israel" still "he who gives strength and power to His people?" still the same "faithful God, who will not suffer them to be tempted above that they are able, but will with the temptation also make a way to escape, that they may be able to bear it?"

When we are most sensible of our utter helplessness, and most simple in our reliance upon Divine strength, then it is, that the "soul melting for heaviness," is most especially upheld and established. "Heaviness in the heart of man makes it stoop; but a good word makes it glad." And how reviving is that "good word" of the Gospel, which proclaims the Savior anointed to "give the garment of praise for the spirit of heaviness," and gifted with "the tongue of the learned, that he might know how to speak a word in season unto him that is weary!" And no less encouraging is it to view Him "melting for heaviness" "sore amazed, and very heavy" under the accumulated weight of imputed guilt; learning by this bitter discipline, "in that He Himself suffered being tempted, to support them that are tempted." Yet was He, like His faithful servant, strengthened according to His Father's word, in the moment of his bitterest agony, by the agency of His own creation. And this faithful support, given to the Head, is the seal and pledge of what every member in every trouble will most assuredly enjoy. "As the sufferings of Christ abound in His people, so their consolation also abounds by Christ." The blessed word will supply all their need—life for their quickening, light for their direction, comfort for their enjoyment, strength for their support, "Strengthen me according to Your word."

Lord, may I ever be kept from despondency—regarding it as sinful in itself, dishonorable to Your name, and weakening to my soul; and though I must "needs be sometime in heaviness through manifold temptations," yet let the power of faith be in constant exercise, that I may be able to expostulate with my soul, "Why are you cast down, O my soul? and why are you disturbed within me? hope in God: for I shall yet praise Him, who is the health of my countenance, and my God."

29. Remove from me the way of lying; and grant me Your law graciously.

Every deviation in principle and conduct from the strait and narrow path, is a way of lying. Every traveler in the way "feeds on the ashes" of his own delusion. Does it seem a marvel, that the man of God should deprecate so earnestly the influence of gross sin? "The brand plucked out of the fire" retains a susceptibility of the fire. The oldest Christian in the family of God might at any moment of unwatchfulness be captivated by the chain of his former sins. Might not the recollection of past compliances with this shameful sin naturally have suggested the prayer—Remove from me the way of lying? But even in the profession of the Gospel, should we "be removed from Him that called us into the grace of Christ unto another gospel;" should erroneous doctrines find a place in our system; and—as the natural consequence of doctrinal errors—should any inconsistency be marked in our practice; should there be any allowed principles of sinful indulgence, self-righteousness, conformity to the world, or shrinking from the daily cross—then, indeed, will the prayer naturally flow from our hearts—Remove from me the way of lying.

Most justly are ways such as these called "ways of lying." They promise what it is impossible, in the nature of things, that they can ever perform: and prove to their deluded followers, that "those who observe lying vanities, forsake their own mercy." We can be at no loss to trace these "ways," to their proper source;—to him, who, "when he speaks a lie, speaks of his own for he is a liar, and the father of it." A lie was his first—alas! too successful—instrument of temptation, by which he "beguiled Eve through his subtlety," and still does he pursue the same deadly work throughout the world lying under his sway, beguiling the blinded "children of disobedience," into the awful deception of mistaking their God, and into the blind choice of preferring "broken cisterns" to "the fountain of living waters."

The gracious knowledge of the law is the only means of the removal of this evil way. David, as a king, had it written by him. He wished it written on him—not the book only before his eyes, but stamped on the heart. The external knowledge is the common benefit of all. The gracious knowledge is the covenant-blessing of the Lord's people—the only effective principle of holiness. The law is still what it was—an enemy to the ungodly—forcing a hateful light upon their conscience; but a delight to the servant of God—framing his will, and directing his conduct. Thus truth extirpates lying. Christ reigns instead of Belial.

Thus also we are enabled to "keep our hearts"—those leading wanderers, that mislead the rest. For wherever we see wandering eyes, wandering feet, and a wandering tongue, all flow from a heart, that has taken its own liberty in wandering from God. But with the law as our rule, and the Spirit as our guide, we shall be directed and kept in a safe and happy path.

Grant me Your law graciously. Grant me a clearer perception of its holy character—a more sensitive shrinking from transgressing it—a more cordial approval of its spirit—a more entire conformity to its directions.

30. I have chosen the way of truth: Your judgments have I laid before me.

Only two ways lie before us for our choice, "the way of lying," and "the way of truth." God by the light of His word guides us into one— Satan by his temptations allures us into the other. The way of lying is the natural choice of man. The choice of the way of truth is the Lord's work in the hearts of His people—the seal of His special eternal love. His teaching shows us the way; and His grace enables us to "choose" it . And who in his subsequent course has ever found reason to alter his first determination? Does Mary regret her "choice of the good part?" One whose solid and reflecting judgment was not likely to make a rash or hasty choice, tells us, of the outset of his course, "What things were gain to me, those I counted loss for Christ." The experience of twenty years— instead of bringing matter for repentance—only confirmed him in his choice: and he repeats his determination with increasing energy of expression; "Yes, doubtless, and I count all things but loss for the excellency of the knowledge of Christ Jesus my Lord." In the same spirit one of the ancient fathers expresses himself: "If I have any possessions, health, credit, learning—this is all the contentment I have of them—that I may have something to despise for Christ, who comprises in His own person all and everything that is most desirable."

The connection of this verse with the preceding well illustrates the bias of the believer's heart. His experience of the deceitfulness of sin, Satan, and his own heart, stirs up the prayer, "Remove from me the way of lying." But his choice is expressed in this verse, "I have chosen the way of truth." The sincere desire to have "the way of lying removed from us," is a clear evidence, that we have already "chosen the way of truth:" that "the spirit of truth has guided us to Him," who is indeed "the way of truth"—the true and only "way to God!" And of all ways that could be set before the Christian, this is the way he would "choose"—as bringing most glory to his God, exalting the Savior, honoring the Spirit of God, and securing the salvation of his own soul. Whatever becomes of me— the Christian would feel—'I would have no other way than this. Yes, though I should perish, I would abide in it. So transcendent is the discovery of the glory of God—scarcely less clear than the glory of heaven itself!'

The practical pathway, however, is often rugged—always narrow. We may have to encounter not only the reviling of an ungodly world, but even the suspicions of our brethren, who may not always understand our motives. Yet if our heart is upright with God, "none of these things will move us. Our choice is made, and we are prepared to abide the cost."

But that our choice may be daily established, let us not forget the treasury of our life, light, and grace. Let us lay the "judgments of God before us." For we have always some new lesson to learn—some new duty to perform—some new snare to avoid. We must therefore walk by rule—as under the eye of a jealous God, who enlightens and cheers our path—under the eye of the ungodly, who "watch for our halting"—under the eye of weak Christians, who might be stumbled by our unsteady walk—under the eye of established Christians, who will be yet further established by the testimony of our consistent profession. The Gospel affords all the material for this strict and accurate walk. All is given that is needed. The obedience that is enjoined is secured. "God working in us," enables us to work for Him; and while we are humbly looking for further supplies, and diligently improving what has been already bestowed, He is pledged by promise to assist, as we are bound by duty to obey.

What then—let me inquire—is the choice which I have made? I would remember that it is for eternity. And if, through the grace that has first chosen me, "I have chosen the way of truth,"—is the effect of this choice daily visible in a life and conversation well ordered according to the word of God? If it is good to "hide that word in my heart," as a safeguard against sin; it is good also "to lay it before" my eyes, as the chart to guide my course—the model to direct my work—the support to uphold my weakness.

31. I have stuck to Your testimonies; O Lord, put me not to shame.

We have just seen the choice of the man of God, and the rule by which he acted upon it. Now we see his perseverance—first choosing the way—then sticking to it. While he complained of "his soul cleaving to the dust," he would yet say—I have stuck to Your testimonies. Thus did he illustrate the apostle's delineation of the Christian's two hearts (as a converted African expressed it), "I delight in the law of God after the inward man; but I see another law in my members, warring against the law of my mind, and bringing me into captivity to the law of sin, which is in my members. So then with the mind I myself serve the law of God; but with the flesh the law of sin." In the midst, however, of the most painful conflicts, the child of God holds fast his confidence. He feels that he hates the sin that he commits, and loves the Savior, whom, in spite of himself, he dishonors; so that, with all his sins and unworthiness, he fears not to put in his claim among the family of God.

But, reader, seriously ask yourself—How did you become a Christian? Was it by birth and education, or by choice? If indeed by grace you have been enabled to "choose the way of truth," then be sure you firmly stick to it; or better, far better, that you had not made choice of it at all. "No man having put his hand to the plough, and looking back, is fit for the kingdom of God.—If you continue in My word, then are you My disciples indeed. It had been better for you not to have known the way of righteousness, than, after you had known it, to turn from the holy commandment delivered to you." Yet, praised be God for the security of perseverance! He who enabled you to "put your hand to the plough" will keep it there in the habit of faith, firm and steadfast. "The Lord will perfect that which concerns you."

Yet this "cleaving to the Lord," can only be maintained by unceasing conflict. The length and weariness of the way, and the slowness of your progress, are sources of constant and harassing trial. Revert, then, to the ground of your original choice. Was it made under the Lord's light and direction? This reason may well bind you to "stick to" it. For are not the ways of God as pleasant—is not Christ as lovely—is not heaven as desirable—as at the beginning? No—have you not even more reason to adhere to your choice, than you had to make it? It was formed before at least you could fully know for yourself. Now "you have tasted"—you have the seal of experience. Is not the crown more joyous in the nearer prospect?

Backslider! "has God been to you a wilderness, and a land of darkness," that you virtually give your testimony after trial—'Satan is the better master, and I will return to him?' The world is the happiest path; and I will walk in it. This is, indeed, choosing a murderer in the stead of a Father, "forsaking the fountain" for the "broken cistern." Oh! must there not be repentance in this path? May that repentance come before it be too late! Ponder who it was, that befriended you in the moment of a dreadful extremity, and snatched you as "a brand from the burning." Ponder the endearing proofs of His love—condescending to become a man, "a man of sorrows," and to die in the agony of the cross, bearing for you the eternal curse of God. And does not gratitude remind you, what returns of faithful service are due from a creature so infinitely indebted to

Him? Surely the steadfast perseverance with which His heart cleaved to His costly work, may serve to put to shame your unsteadiness in "sticking to His testimonies."

Believer! you are determined to abide by your choice—but not in your own strength. Remember him, who one hour declared, that he would sooner die with Christ than deny Him; and the next hour denied Him with oaths and curses. Learn, then, to follow up your resolution with instant prayer, "O Lord, put me not to shame." Leave me not to myself, lest I become a shame to myself, and an offence to Your Church. "I will keep Your statutes. O forsake me not utterly." Dependence upon the Lord, in a deep sense of our weakness, is the principle of perseverance. Never will he shut out the prayer of His faithful servant. He has promised, "My people shall never be ashamed;" and therefore, taking firm hold of His promise, you may "go on your way rejoicing."

32. I will run the way of Your commandments, when You shall enlarge my heart.

A glowing picture of the Christian's delight in the ways of God! If we "have chosen the way of God's commandments," and have been able to "stick to" this way, surely we shall wish to "run in it" with constancy and cheerfulness. We shall want to mend our pace. If we walk, we shall long to "run." There is always the same reason for progress, that there was for setting out. Necessity, advantage, enjoyment, spur us on to the end. Whatever progress we have made, we shall desire to make more; we shall go on praying and walking, and praying that we may walk with a swifter motion; we shall be dissatisfied, yet not discouraged, "faint, yet pursuing." Now this is as it should be. This is after the pattern of the holy Apostle:, "Brethren, I count not myself to have apprehended: but this one thing I do; forgetting those things which are behind, and reaching forth unto those which are before, I press toward the mark for the prize of the high calling of God in Christ Jesus." But the secret as well as the pattern of Christian progress is—looking beyond the Apostle, and the "so great cloud of witnesses, with which we are encompassed"—and "looking unto Jesus." Faith is the principle of life, and supplies the daily motion of life;—directing our eye to Him as "the Author," until He "becomes the Finisher," of our faith. This is at once our duty, our privilege, our happiness, and our strength. This is the point, at which we begin to run; and we "so run, that we may obtain."

But let us more distinctly mark the medium through which this spiritual energy flows—an enlarged heart. Without this influence how could we run this way of God's commandments? Such is the extent and latitude of the course, that a straitened heart is utterly inadequate to carry us through. There must be large treasures of knowledge, in order that from a rich "treasure-house the good things" may pour out abundantly. For indeed spiritual "knowledge" is the principle of "multiplied grace." Scriptural truths, divinely fixed in the understanding, powerfully influence the heart. Christian privilege also greatly advances this important end. In seasons of depression we are "so troubled, that we cannot speak." We cannot pour out our hearts, as at other times, with a large measure of spirit and life. But when "we joy in God, having received the atonement," the spirit is invigorated, as with oil on the wheels, or as "with wings to mount" on high in the service of praise.

Very different, however, is this enlargement of heart from enlargement of gifts. Fluency of utterance is too often fearfully separated from the spiritual life, and utterly unconnected with delight in the way of God's commandments. It is expression, not feeling—counterfeit grace—public, not secret or personal, religion. The yoke of sin is not broken, and the self-deceiver will be found at last among the deluded throng of gifted hypocrites, "punished with everlasting destruction from the presence of the Lord."

Indeed the spiritual principle is far too little realized. At the commencement of the course, conscious guilt straitens the approach to the throne of grace. Unbelief imprisons the soul. And even when the deliverer is known, who "sets at liberty them that are bruised," still the body of death with all its clogging burden and confinement presses down the soul. Unbelief also continues to work, to narrow the conceptions of the gospel, and by the painful recollections of the past, to bring in distrust, distance, and bondage. And most painful is this restraint. For the soul, which is but beginning to see how desirable is the favor of God, feels also an earnest desire to honor Him. And to him who—having fully "tasted that the Lord is gracious"—asks, "What shall I render unto the Lord?" this remaining influence of "the spirit of bondage" is more afflicting, than perhaps was a greater measure of it in a less enlightened stage of his way. Still, however, this legal spirit pursues him. His comforts, ebbing and flowing, according as he is dissatisfied or satisfied with his Christian progress, clearly evince a secret "confidence in the flesh," greatly hindering that "rejoicing in Christ Jesus," which so enlarges the heart.

Thus by the shackles of sin, unbelief, and self-righteousness, we are indeed 'sore let and hindered in running the race set before us.' (Collect for Advent.) The light is obscured. Faith loses sight of its object. What otherwise would be a delight becomes a weariness. Obedience is irksome; self-denial intolerable; the cross heavy. The heart is, as it were, "shut up, and it cannot get forth." Faith is so low: desires are so faint; hopes so narrow, that it seems impossible to make progress. Frequent defeats induce despondency. The world is resorted to. Sin ensnares and captivates. Thus "we did run well; but we have been hindered."

This sad evil naturally leads us to inquire for the remedy. The case is backsliding, not apostasy. The remedy therefore is in that engagement, which embraces a wider expanse of light, and a more full confidence of love. We find that we have not been "straitened" in God, but "in our own affections." If then the rich fool thought of enlarging his barns, when his stores had increased upon him, much more should we "enlarge the place of our tent," that we may make more room for God, encourage larger expectations, if we would have more full manifestations of Him. Let not the vessels fail, before the oil stays. Continually let the petition be sent up, "Oh that You would bless me indeed, and enlarge my coast!" Whatever cause we have to cry out, "My leanness, my leanness!"—still let us, in the exercise of faith and prayer, be waiting for a more cheerful ability to love, serve, and praise. Let us be restless, until the prison-doors are again opened, and the command is issued to the prisoners, "Go forth: and to them that are in darkness—Show yourselves. They shall feed in the ways, and their pastures shall be in all high places." Who knows but the Lord will once more shine upon us; once more unloose our fetters, and renew our strength?

But again and again must we be reminded that every motion must begin with God. I will run—but how? not in my own strength, but by "the good hand of my God upon me," delivering and enlarging my heart. He does not say—I will make no efforts, unless You work for me; but if You will enlarge—I will run. Weakness is not the plea for indolence, but for quickening grace. "Draw me"—says the Church, "we will run after You." Effectual calling will issue in running." Where the Spirit of the Lord is, there is liberty." The secret of Christian energy and success is a heart enlarged in the love of God.

Let me then begin betimes—make haste—keep straight on—fix my eye on the mark, "endure unto the end." I may yet expect in the joy of blessed surprise to exclaim, "Or ever I was aware, my soul made me like the chariots of Ammi-nadib." Godly sorrow had made me serious. Now let holy joy make me active. "The joy of the Lord is my strength;" and I am ready, under the power of constraining love, to work and to toil—to run without weariness—to "march onward" without fainting; not measuring my pace by my own strength, but looking to Him who "strengthens with all might by His Spirit in the inner man."

Happy fruit of wrestling prayer and diligent waiting on God! Joy in God, and strength to walk with Him, with increasing knowledge of Him, increasing communion with Him, and increasing confidence in Him.

33. Teach me, O Lord, the way of Your statutes; and I shall keep it unto the end.

We need no instruction in the way of sin. That has been our way, ever since Adam "sought out his own invention." The ungodly "desire no knowledge of the way of God's statutes." The heart leads the judgment, and "their heart is enmity to the law of God." But for a child of God, this is a prayer for constant use. The outward revelation is of no avail without the inward teaching. The Divine Instructor must interpret and apply His own rule. However plain the word may be, the darkness must be removed from the understanding. Light will not show an object, except the faculty of sight be given. A blind man cannot see at noonday. We know nothing spiritually, except as we are taught of God. The more we are taught, the more we feel our need of teaching, and the more pressing will be our cries for this invaluable blessing. The blind man must be led in the plainest and most direct, as well as in the more difficult and rugged paths. And thus do we need the shining of light from above—not only in the "deep things of God"—but for the reception of the most elementary truths. And yet we want not this knowledge for its own sake—to feed pride or speculation—but for its practical influence. For of what avail is the discovery even of important truth, if we be not molded into its likeness, and constrained "into the obedience of faith?" The connection of every thought with Christian practice, here directed to its proper end, is a most striking proof of the Divine origin of the statutes. The most clear instructions for the regulation of our conduct flow from single sentences or expressions in these "statutes;" and this clearly proves an infinite wisdom in their distribution, a reference in the eternal mind to every detail of practical duty, and a Divine power and unction, applying the word to the several circumstances of daily conduct. For, indeed, what mind but the mind of God could have comprehended in so small a compass such a vast system of instruction? In this view, therefore, the Lord's teaching becomes the spring of obedience. For how can we "keep" a way, which we do not understand? And who was ever "taught the way of the Lord's statutes," who had not his heart constrained and directed by their spiritual beauty and sweetness? In this path we realize union with the Savior; "the love of God is perfected in us;" and our confidence is established before God.

The object nearest to the believer's heart, and which causes him many an anxious—and too often many an unbelieving thought—is the grace of perseverance. Now the Lord's teaching is the principle of perseverance. It is "the light of life," enlightening the mind, and quickening the heart. Under this influence, therefore, we live—we endure—we cannot fail of keeping the way unto the end. Thus the end crowns the work. For with this blessing of perseverance, is sealed to us the hope of victory over our spiritual enemies, and the participation of our Savior's glory. Confidence, indeed, without prayer and dependence upon our glorious Head, is most daring presumption. But that "well-ordered and sure covenant," which "is all our salvation, and all our desire," engages for our continuance in "the way of the Lord's statutes." "I will put My fear in their hearts, that they shall not depart from Me. I will put My law in their inward parts, and write it in their hearts: and I will be their God, and they shall be My people."

34. Give me understanding, and I shall keep Your law; yes, I shall observe it with my whole heart.

'He who is his own teacher'—says Bernard—and one greater than Bernard, 'has a fool for his master.' Man cannot teach what he does not know; and of God, and of His law, he knows nothing. Therefore the beginning of wisdom is a consciousness of ignorance, a distrust of our own understanding, and the heartfelt prayer, "Give me understanding." The spiritual understanding is the gift of Jesus Christ. He directs us to Himself, as its fountain, "I am the light of the world; he who follows Me shall not walk in darkness, but shall have the light of life." This understanding differs from mere intellectual discernment or speculative knowledge. It is the spring of spiritual activity in our walk with God; so that our obedience is not outward and reluctant, but filial delight and wholeness of heart:—we desire not only to keep the law of God to the end, but every day to the end, "with our whole heart."—Such are our obligations towards Him, that we ought to study very accurately the character of our walk with Him; always remembering that service without the heart—the whole heart—is hateful in His sight; and that what is now wilfully withheld, will gradually draw away the rest in apostasy from Him. Now are we seeking more "engagedness of heart" for Him? Then will this prayer be a suitable expression of our need, and the utterance of a humble, resolute petitioner. It is not, however, enough, that we have once received, unless we are constantly receiving. We must ask, that we may receive; but after we have received, we must ask again. Yet is this prayer never offered up, until the soul has in part received what it is here seeking for. The natural man is "wise in his own conceit," and has therefore no idea of his need of Divine teaching.

But we must not be satisfied with even a clear apprehension of the doctrines of the Bible, and of the "truth as it is in Jesus." "Give me understanding"—'not only that I may believe these doctrines, but that I may keep and observe them.' In every path of duty, this cry is repeated, with an importunity that is never wearisome to the ears of our gracious Father. And in how many unnoticed instances has the answer been given, when some clear and heavenly ray has darted unexpectedly into the mind, or some providential concurrence of unforeseen circumstances has disentangled a path before intricate and involved, and marked it before us with the light of a sunbeam! How many whispers of conscience! how many seasonable suggestions in moments of darkness and perplexity, may the observant child of God record, as the answer to this needful prayer! "Whoever is wise, and will observe these things, even they shall understand the loving-kindness of the Lord." Nor will our growth in spiritual understanding fail to evidence itself in the steady consistency of a well-ordered conversation! "Who is a wise man, and endued with knowledge among you? Let him show out of a good conversation his works with meekness of wisdom." If then knowledge is valuable according to its usefulness, one ray of this practical knowledge—the result of prayer for heavenly teaching—is more to be prized than the highest attainments of speculative religion—flowing from mere human instruction.

35. Make me to go in the path of Your commandments; for therein do I
delight.

We are equally ignorant of the path of God's commandments, and
impotent to go in it. We need therefore double assistance. Our mind must
be enlightened; our hearts constrained; else our knowledge of this
humbling path would make us shrink from it. But under the complete
influence of Divine grace, when understanding has been given to discern
the beauty of it, the soul's warmest desire is fixed upon it. Conscious
helplessness looks upward—Make me to go: and He who said to the
paralytic, "Arise, take up your bed, and go to your house," speaks the
same word of quickening life and power to the soul "giving heed,"
"expecting to receive something of Him." It is delightful to acknowledge
of this work, that "all is of God"—that "it is He who works in us both to
will and to do of His good pleasure." To him only can it belong. For
since the natural inclination "is not subject to the law of God, neither
indeed can be," Almighty power must introduce a new and active bias,
"Turn me, and I shall be turned." "Make me to go in the path of Your
commandments."

But even when brought into this path, still we need accelerated
motion to run with increasing alacrity. We need to take "the Lord God
for our strength; and He shall make our feet like hinds' feet, and He shall
make us to walk upon the high places." The path, indeed, is uninviting to
the eye of sense. This distorted vision brings all its difficulties into full
view; hiding all its counter-balancing enjoyments. Let us, however,
exercise that "faith," which is "the substance of things hoped for, the
evidence of things not seen." Let us exhibit our proper character,
"walking by faith, and not by sight," and our discernment of unseen
things will be more clear, and our enjoyment of them more permanent.
The prayer will then be with increasing earnestness, "Make me to go in
the path of Your commandments."

But we must not be content with walking in this way; we must seek to
"delight in it." Delight is the marrow of religion. "God loves a cheerful
giver," and accepts obedience, only when it is given, not when it is
forced. He loves the service of that man, who considers it his highest
privilege to render it, and whose heart rejoices in the way, "as a giant to
run his race." Fervent prayer and cheerful obedience mark the experience
of the thriving Christian. As a true "child of Zion, he is joyful in his

king;" he loves His service, and counts it "perfect freedom"—the rule of love, mercy, and grace.

But is the self-condemned penitent distressed by this description of a child of God? He cannot find the same marks in himself; and he too hastily concludes, that he does not belong to the heavenly family; not considering, that his very grief is caused by his love to, and "delight in" that way in which he is so hindered, and in which he daily prays, "Make me to go." It was, probably, the same sense of weakness and inability, "to go in the path of God's commandments," which urged David's prayer; and if it urges yours, poor trembling penitent—if it sends you to a throne of grace, you will, before long, receive an answer of peace, and "go on your way rejoicing."

This delight in the path is not only following the "man after God's own heart;" but it is the image of David's Lord, and our forerunner in this path. He could testify to His Father, "I delight to do Your will, O My God;" and to His disciples, "I have meat to eat that you know not of. My meat is to do the will of Him that sent Me, and to finish His work." And as a proof of the intenseness of His delight he could, to their great amazement, "go before them" to Jerusalem, unappalled by the "baptism" of blood which awaited Him; yes, even "straitened" with the unquenchable ardor of His love, "until it was accomplished."

36. Incline my heart to Your testimonies, and not to covetousness.

But what "makes us to go in the path of God's commandments?" The force of His Almighty love effectually inclines the will, as with a Divine touch. The day of His power, in which He makes us willing, is a time of love. "I drew them"—says he, "with cords of a man, and with bands of love." Every man, who is conscious of the counteracting bias within, will deeply feel the need of this prayer, "Incline my heart." The native principle of man draws him to his own self—to his own indulgence—pleasure—covetousness—assuming a thousand forms of gratifying self, at the expense of love to God. Few but are ready to condemn this principle in others, while perhaps it may be their own "easily-besetting sin." When the mind is grasping after the world, as if it were our portion, we have the greatest reason to "take heed" to our Lord's admonition, and beware of "covetousness." When we invest earthly gratifications with any inherent excellency—virtually putting them in the place of God—

then will be a season for special supplication—Incline my heart to Your testimonies, and not to covetousness.

There is probably no principle so opposed to the Lord's testimonies. It casts out the principle of obedience, since the love of God cannot co-exist with the love of the world; and the very desire to serve Mammon is a proof of unfaithfulness to God. We mark the deadly influence in direct breaches of the law of God. Balaam, in the indulgence of this propensity, set his will in mad contradiction to God; Ahab was tempted to murder; David, to murder and adultery; Achan, to steal; Judas, both to steal from his fellows, and to betray his Master; Gehazi and Ananias to lying. And besides—what is the matter of common but painful observation—how much of the good seed of the kingdom, that was springing up with the promise of a plentiful harvest, has this weed of rank luxuriance "choked, that it has become unfruitful!" Our Lord's parables, therefore—His providence—His promises—His terms of discipleship—His counsels—His own example of poverty and renunciation of this world's comfort—all are directed against this destructive principle. The power of the love of Christ delivered Matthew and Zaccheus from its influence, and "inclined their hearts to the testimonies of God." And has not faith still the same power to turn the heart from the world, from sin, from self, to Christ? Learn, then, to rest upon the promise of His love, and to delight in His testimonies. Earthly cares will be cast upon him, and earthly prospects will lose their splendor. This life of faith—living in union with a heavenly Savior, involves the only effective principle of resistance. Those who are risen with Christ will be temperate in earthly things, "setting their affections on things above." Such—such alone—will "mortify the members that are upon the earth—evil concupiscence, and covetousness, which is idolatry."

We desire to sit loose to our earthly comforts. Are we enabled to check our natural discontent with the Lord's dealings with us, and to restrain our eagerness to "seek great things for ourselves," by the recollection of His word, "Seek them not?"

Let us not forget, that the inclination—even if it is not brought into active and perceptible motion, is fatally destructive of the life of religion. "Those who will be rich fall into temptation and a snare, and into many foolish and hurtful lusts, which drown men in destruction and perdition." Awful warning to professors!, "The love of money is the root of all evil; which while some have coveted after, they have erred from the faith, and pierced themselves through with many sorrows." A most important exhortation to the people of God!" But you, O man of God, flee these things, and follow after righteousness." If the Lord loves you, He will not indeed lose you; but unless you "take heed, and beware of covetousness," He will not spare you. In the midst, therefore, of temptation without, and a world of sin within, go onwards, with the pilgrim's prayer indelibly fixed on your heart, "Incline my heart to Your testimonies, and not to covetousness."

37. Turn away my eyes from beholding vanity; and quicken me in Your way.

So strongly does the man of God deprecate temptation to self-indulgence, that he prays to be kept at the greatest possible distance from it. That his heart may not be inclined to it: he desires that his eyes may be turned away from beholding it. Keeping the eye is a grand means of "keeping the heart." Satan has so infused his poison into all the objects around us, that all furnish fuel for temptation: and the heart—naturally inclined to evil, and hankering after vanity—is stolen away in a moment. Vanity includes "all that is in the world—the lust of the flesh, the lust of the eye, and the pride of life." All is sin, "because it is not of the Father, but is of the world." Of all that belongs to earth, "the preacher, the son of David"—standing on the vantage-ground, and having taken within his view the widest horizon of this world's excellency, has pronounced his judgment, "Vanity of vanities, says the preacher, vanity of vanities! all is vanity." We have just mentioned "the lusts of other things choking" many a promising profession. Our Lord's solemn caution to His own disciples implies their injury to a sincere profession, "Take heed to yourselves, lest at any time your hearts be overcharged with surfeiting and drunkenness, and cares of this life; and so that day come upon you unawares." Some, indeed, seem to walk, as if they were proof against temptation. They venture to the very edge of the precipice, under a vain assurance that no danger is to be apprehended. But such a confidence is upon the brink of a grievous fall. The tender-hearted child of God, trusting in the promise, that "Sin shall not have dominion over him," knows that he can only enjoy the security of it, while he is shrinking from every occasion of sin. He "hates even the garment spotted by the flesh;" and, remembering how often his outward senses have ministered to the workings of his weak and treacherous heart, he continues in prayer, "Turn away my eyes from beholding vanity!"

69

Probably the recollection of the circumstance of his own sin, would to the end of his life remind David of his special need of this prayer. Yet who that is conscious of his own weakness and corruption, will find the prayer unsuitable to his circumstances of daily temptation? But we must watch as well as pray. For as watchfulness without prayer is presumption, so prayer without watchfulness is self-delusion. To pray that "our eyes" may be "turned from vanity," without "making a covenant with our eyes," that they should not behold it, is like "taking fire in our bosoms," and expecting "not to be burnt," because we have prayed that we might not be burnt. If we pray not to be "led into temptation," we must "watch that we enter not into it." The sincerity of our prayer will be proved by the watchfully avoiding the circumstances and occasions of temptation. The fear of sin will manifest itself by a fear of temptation to sin. "The knife will be put to the throat, if we be given to appetite." We shall be afraid of the wine sparkling in the glass.

But where is the harm of beholding vanity, if we do not follow it? When Eve beheld the forbidden fruit, perhaps she did not think of taking it: and when she took it, she did not think of eating it: but the beginning of sin "is as the letting out of water," whose progress once opened, beats down all before it. And who, after our "beguiled mother," has not found the eye an inlet to sin? When Bunyan's pilgrims were obliged to pass through Vanity Fair, beset on every side with temptations and allurements, they stopped their eyes and ears, and quickening their pace, cried, "Turn away my eyes from beholding vanity!" A striking reproof to us, who too often loiter and gaze, until we begin to covet those vanities, to which, as Christians, we "are dead!"

Is it asked—What will most effectually "turn my eyes from vanity?" Not the seclusion of contemplative retirement—not the relinquishment of our lawful connection with the world; but the transcendent beauty of Jesus unveiled to our eyes, and fixing our hearts. This will "turn our eyes from vanity" in its most glittering forms. The sight of the "pearl of great price" dims the luster of the "goodliest pearls" of earth; at once deadens us to the enticements of the world, and urges us forward in the pursuit of the prize. And is not this our object? It is not enough, that through special mercy I am preserved from temptations. I want to be quickened to more life, energy, delight, and devotedness in the way of my God. The secret of Christian progress is simplicity and diligence. "This one thing I do— forgetting the things that are behind, and reaching forth to those things that are before; I press towards the mark, for the prize of the high calling of God in Christ Jesus." The Spirit leaves no wish in the heart for beholding vanity. The world with all its flowery paths, is a dreary wilderness; and Christ and heaven are the only objects of desire, "He who shuts his eyes from seeing evil, he shall dwell on high; his place of defense shall be the munitions of rocks; bread shall be given him, his water shall be sure. Your eyes shall see the King in His beauty: they shall behold the land that is very far off." Precious promises to those, that flee from temptation, and desire to walk in the ways of God!

38. Establish Your word to Your servant, who is devoted to Your fear.

Often—instead of being quickened in the way—I am fainting under the pressure of unbelief. What then is my resource? Only the word of promise. Lord! seal—establish Your word to Your servant—devoted as I am—as I would be—to Your fear. If "the fear of the Lord is the beginning of wisdom"—a "treasure"—a "strong confidence" "a fountain of life"—how wise—how rich—how safe—how happy—is he who "is devoted to" it! "Blessed" indeed is he—with the favor of his God, the secret of His love, the teaching of His grace, and the mercy of His covenant. The promises of the Old Testament are generally connected with the fear of God, as in the New Testament they are linked with faith. But in truth, so identified are these two principles in their operation, that the faith, by which we apprehend the forgiveness of God, and the privileges of His kingdom, issues in a godly, reverential, filial fear. To be devoted to this fear, completes the character of a servant of God—the highest honor in the universe—the substantial joy of heaven itself. It is an obedience of choice, of reverence, and of love. "Joining himself to the Lord, to serve Him, and to love the name of the Lord—to be His servant." 'Yes, gracious Lord, I had rather be bound than loosed.' I only wish to be loosed from the bonds of sin, that I might be bound to You forever. My heart is treacherous; lay Your own bonds upon me. "O Lord, truly I am Your servant: You have loosed my bonds;" I am "devoted to Your fear." Is this my desire, my mind, my determination, my character? Then let me plead my title to an interest in the promises of the word— rich and free, "exceeding great and precious,"—all mine, "yes and amen in Christ Jesus;" let me plead, that every word may be "established" in my victory over sin, advancing knowledge of Christ, experience of His love, conformity to His image, and, finally, in my preservation in Him unto eternal life.

But how far has the fear of God operated with me as a safeguard from sin, and an habitual rule of conduct? David's confidence in the promises of God, far from lessening his jealousy over himself, only made him more "devoted to the fear" of God. And if my assurance be well grounded, it will ever be accompanied with holy fear; the influence will be known by "standing more in awe of God's word;" having a more steady abhorrence of sin, and a dread of "grieving the Holy Spirit of God." Thus this filial fear produces a holy confidence; while confidence serves to strengthen fear: and their mutual influence quickens devotedness to the work of the Lord.

It is interesting to remark, that the Christian privilege of assurance is not confined to the New Testament dispensation. David's pleading to have the "word of his God established unto him," was grounded upon the tried foundations of faith. And this direct act of faith, as it regards God in Christ, His engagements and His promises, cannot be too confident. The promises are made to the whole Church, that we might each look for our part and interest in them. God loves to have His own seal and hand-writing brought before Him. "Put Me in remembrance"—He says: "let us plead together." "He cannot deny Himself."

Very cheering is it to mark, how the Lord establishes His word in our own experience. Every day He is fulfilling some promise, and a word made good at one time encourages our confidence for another. The word performed in part is an earnest of the whole, assuring us of the time, when we shall acknowledge His faithfulness, "who performs all things for us." Thus, as the word is eternally established on the foundation of the Divine engagements, its certainty is sealed to our own conviction. Our confidence is established, that if He has spoken a word, He may be trusted for that word.

This, then, is the exercise and the power of faith. I bring wants. I bring Your word of promise. Establish Your word to Your servant. You have bought me with a precious price; You have made me Yours: You have subdued my heart to Yourself, so that it is now "devoted to Your fear." Whatever, therefore, Your covenant has provided for my sanctification, my humiliation, my chastisement, my present and everlasting consolation, "Establish this word:" let it be fulfilled in me; for I am "Your servant, devoted to Your fear."

39. Turn away my reproach which I fear: for Your judgments are good.

There is a reproach, which we have no cause to fear, but rather to glory in. It is one of the chief privileges of the Gospel—the honorable badge of our profession. But it was the "reproach" of bringing dishonor upon the name of his God, that David feared, and deprecated with most anxious, importunate prayer. The fear of this reproach is a practical principle of tender watchfulness and circumspection, and of habitual dependence upon an Almighty upholding power. "Hold me up, and I shall be safe,"—will be the constant supplication of one, that fears the Lord, and fears himself. We do not, perhaps, sufficiently consider the active malice of the enemies of the gospel, "watching for our halting;" else should we be more careful to remove all occasions of "reproach" on account of inconsistency of temper or conversation. None, therefore, that feel their own weakness, the continual apprehension of danger, the tendency of their heart to backslide from God, and to disgrace "that worthy name by which they are called," will think this prayer unseasonable or unnecessary, "Turn away my reproach which I fear."

Perhaps also the conflicting Christian may find this a suitable prayer. Sometimes Satan has succeeded in beguiling him into some worldly compliance, or weakened his confidence, by tempting him to look to himself for some warrant of acceptance (in all which suggestions he is aided and abetted by his treacherous heart): and then will this "accuser of the brethren" turn back upon him, and change himself "into an angel of light," presenting before him a black catalogue of those very falls, into which he had successfully led him. Bunyan does not fail to enumerate these "reproaches," as among the most harassing assaults of Apollyon. In his desperate conflict with Christian, he taunts him with his fall in the Slough of Despond, and every successive deviation from his path, as blotting out his warrant of present favor with the King, and blasting all hopes of reaching the celestial city. Christian does not attempt to conceal or palliate the charge. He knows it is all true, and much more besides! but he knows that this is true also, "Where sin abounded, grace has much more abounded." "The blood of Jesus Christ the Son of God cleanses from all sin." Believers! In the heat of your conflict remember the only effective covering. "Above all, taking the shield of faith, with which you shall be able to quench all the fiery darts of the wicked." Do you not hate the sins, with which you have been overtaken? Are you not earnestly longing for deliverance from their power? Then, even while the

73

recollections of their guilt and defilement humble you before the Lord, take fresh hold of the gospel, and you shall "overcome by the blood of the Lamb." Victory must come from the cross. And the soul that is directing its eye there for pardon, strength, and consolation, may sigh out the prayer with acceptance, "Turn away my reproach which I fear."

But how deeply is the guilt of apostasy or backsliding aggravated by the acknowledgment, which all are constrained to make, "Your judgments are good!" How affecting is the Lord's admonition with us!, "What iniquity have your fathers found in Me, that they are gone far from Me, and have walked after vanity, and are become vain? O My people! what have I done to you, and how have I wearied you? testify against Me. I have not caused you to serve with an offering, nor wearied you with incense." No, surely we have nothing to complain of our Master, of His work, or of His wages: but much, very much, to complain of ourselves, of our unwatchfulness, neglect, backsliding; and to humble ourselves on account of the consequent reproach upon our profession.

Never, however, let us cease to cry, that all the reproach which we fear on account of our allowed inconsistencies of profession, may, for the Church's sake, be "turned away from us." Meanwhile, "let us accept it as the punishment of our iniquity;" and, in the recollection of the goodness of the Lord's judgments, still venture to hope and look for the best things to come out of it from our gracious Lord.

40. Behold, I have longed after Your precepts; quicken me in Your righteousness.

Behold! An appeal to the heart-searching God, "You know that I love" Your precepts! The heartfelt acknowledgment of their goodness naturally leads us to long after them. The professor longs after the promises, and too often builds a delusive—because an unsanctifying—hope upon them. The believer feels it to be his privilege and safety to have an equal regard to both—to obey the precepts of God in dependence on His promises, and to expect the accomplishment of the promises, in the way of obedience to the precepts. The utmost extent of the professor's service is the heavy yoke of outward conformity. He knows nothing of an "inward delight and longing after them." Of many of them his heart complains, "This is a hard saying: who can hear it?" The Christian can give a good reason for his delight even in the most difficult and painful precepts. The moments of deepest repentance are his times of sweetest "refreshing from the presence of the Lord." Whatever be the pleasure of indulgence in sin, far greater is the ultimate enjoyment arising out of the mortification of it. Most fruitful is our Savior's precept, which inculcates on His followers self-denial and the daily cross. For by this wholesome discipline we lose our own perverse will; the power of sin is restrained, the pride of the heart humbled; and our real happiness fixed upon a solid and permanent basis. So that, whatever dispensation some might desire for breaking the precept without forfeiting the promise, the Christian blesses God for the strictness, that binds him to a steady obedience to it. To him it is grievous, not to keep it, but to break it. A longing therefore after the precepts, marks the character of the child of God: and may be considered as the pulse of the soul. It forms our fitness and ripeness for heaven.

There are indeed times, when the violence of temptation, or the paralyzing effect of indolence, hides the movements of the "hidden man of the heart." And yet even in these gloomy hours, when the mouth is shut, and the heart dumb, before God, "so troubled, that it cannot speak"—even then, acceptable incense is ascending before the throne of God. We have a powerful intercessor "helping our infirmities"—interpreting our desires, and crying from within, "with groanings that cannot be uttered;" yet such as, being indited by our Advocate within, and presented by our Advocate above, are cheering pledges of their fulfillment. "He will fulfill the desire of them that fear Him: He also will hear their cry, and will save them."

These longings might seem to betoken a vigorous exercise of grace. But shall I be satisfied, while the most fervent desires are so disproportioned to their grand object—so overborne by the corruption of the flesh—and while a heartless state is so hateful to my Savior? Idle confessions and complaints are unseemly and unfruitful. Let me rather besiege the mercy-seat with incessant importunity—'Quicken me in Your righteousness.' 'I plead Your righteousness—Your righteous promise for the reviving of my spiritual life. I long for more lively apprehensions of Your spotless righteousness. Oh! let it invigorate my delight, my obedience, my secret communion, my Christian walk and conversation.' Such longings, poured out before the Lord for a fresh supply of quickening grace, are far different from "the desire of the slothful, which kills him," and will not be forgotten before God. "Delight yourself in the Lord; and He shall give you the desires of your heart." O for a more enlarged expectation, and a more abundant vouchsafement of blessing;

75

that we may burst forth and break out, as from a living fountain within, in more ardent longings for the Lord's precepts!

But it may be asked—What weariness in, and reluctance to duties, may consist with the principle and exercise of grace? Where it is only in the members, not in the mind—where it is only partial, not prevalent—where it is only occasional, not habitual—where it is lamented and resisted, and not allowed—and where, in spite of its influence, the Christian still holds on in the way of duty, "grace reigns" in the midst of conflict, and will ultimately and gloriously triumph over all hindrance and opposition. But in the midst of the humbling views of sin that present themselves on every side, let me diligently inquire—Have I an habitual "hungering and thirsting after righteousness?" And since, at the best, I do but get my longings increased, and not satisfied; let the full satisfaction of heaven be much in my heart. "As for me, I will behold Your face in righteousness; I shall be satisfied, when I awake, with Your likeness."

And what an expectation is this to pretend lo! To think what the infinitely and eternally blessed God is—and what "man is at his best estate," then to conceive of man—the worm of the dust—the child of sin and wrath—transformed into the likeness of God—how weighty is the sound of this hope! What then must its substantiation be? If the initial privilege be glorious, what will the fullness be! Glory revealed to us! transfused through us! becoming our very being! To have the soul filled—not with evanescent shadows—but with massive, weighty, eternal glory! Worlds are mere empty bubbles, compared with this, our sure, satisfying, unfading inheritance.

41. Let Your mercies come also to me, O Lord; even Your salvation, according to Your word.

A prayer of deep anxiety—large desire—simple faith! It is a sinner—feeling his need of mercy—yes, mercies—abundant mercy—mercies for every moment—looking for them only in the Lord's salvation—to be dispensed according to His word. Out of Christ we know only a God, of justice and holiness. In Christ we behold "a just God, and yet a Savior;" and in "His salvation mercy and truth are met together; righteousness and peace have kissed each other." Therefore general notions of mercy without a distinct apprehension of salvation have their origin in presumption, not in warranted faith. For can there be any communication of mercy from an unknown God? Can there be any communion with an angry God? "Acquaint now yourself with Him, and be at peace; thereby good shall come to you" "The Lord's mercies, even His salvation."

Can we conceive the moment, when this prayer is not suited to us? How can we be at any moment safe or happy without the spirit of it? To walk as a saved sinner, "accepted in the Beloved," conformed to His image, devoted to His service, sealed for His kingdom—this is, or should be, the sunshine of every day. Let this prayer live in the heart. Carry continually to the Lord the cry for all His mercies—specially for that, which is the seal and crown of them all—His salvation.

This prayer, however, is peculiarly suitable to the believer, longing to realize that which sometimes is clouded to his view—his personal interest in the Lord's salvation! It must come to me; or I shall never come to it. I want not a general apprehension—I am not satisfied with the description of it. Let it come to me—Let Your mercies be applied, so that I can claim them, and rejoice in them! I see Your salvation come to others. Who needs it more than I? Let it come also to me. "Look upon me, and be merciful to me, as You do to those that love Your name. Remember me, O Lord, with the favor that You bear to Your people; O visit me with Your salvation; that I may see the felicity of Your chosen, that I may rejoice in the gladness of Your nation, that I may glory with Your inheritance."

Now, are we seeking the assurance of this salvation? Are we waiting to realize its present power, saving us from sin—Satan—the world—ourselves—and "blessing us with all spiritual blessings in Christ Jesus?" Should a trial of faith and patience be ordained for us, yet in the end we shall find an enriching store of experience from His wise dispensations. That He has kept us from turning our backs upon His ways, when we had no comfort in them; that He has upheld us with His secret supplies of strength—is not this the work of His own Spirit within, and the pledge of the completion of the work? That He has enabled us, against all discouragements, to "continue instant in prayer," is surely an answer to that prayer, which in our apprehensions of it, had been cast out. That in waiting upon Him, we have found no rest in worldly consolation, is an assurance, that the Lord Himself will be our soul-satisfying and eternal portion. And who is there now in the sensible enjoyment of His love, who does not bless that Divine wisdom, which took the same course with them that has been taken with us, to bring them to these joys? When did a weeping seed-time fail of bringing a joyful harvest?

But let not the ground of faith be forgotten—According to Your word—that it shall come fully—freely—eternally—to him who waits for it. "You meet him that rejoices and works righteousness; those that remember You in Your ways." Many, indeed, are satisfied with far too low a standard of spiritual enjoyments. It is comfortless to live at a distance from our Father's house, when we might be dwelling in the secret of His presence, and rejoicing in the smiles of His love. But let us not charge this dishonorable state upon the sovereignty of the Divine dispensations. Let us rather trace it to its true source—lack of desire—lack of faith—lack of prayer—lack of diligence. What infinite need have we of heavenly influence! What gracious encouragement to seek it! The way was blocked up—mercy has cleared the path, opened our access, "The golden scepter is always held out." Earnest prayer will bring a sure answer. The blessing is unspeakable. Let Your mercies—Your salvation, come to me, O Lord.

42. So shall I have with which to answer him who reproaches me; for I trust in Your word.

What is the salvation which he had just been speaking of? The whole gift of the mercy of God—redemption from sin, death, and hell—pardon, peace, and acceptance with a reconciled God—constant communication of spiritual blessings—all that God can give, or we can want; all that we are able to receive here, or heaven can perfect hereafter. Now if this comes to us—comes to our hearts—surely it will furnish us at all times with an answer to him who reproaches us. The world casts upon us the reproach of the cross. "What profit is there that we have walked mournfully before the Lord of Hosts?" What is there to counterbalance the relinquishment of pleasure, esteem, and worldly comfort? The mere professor can give no answer. He has heard of it, but it has never come to Him. The believer is ready with his answer, 'I have found in the Lord's salvation pardon and peace, "not as the world gives"—and such as the world cannot take away. Here, therefore, do I abide, finding it my happiness not to live without the cross, and testifying in the midst of abounding tribulation, that there are no comforts like Christ's comforts.' This was David's answer, when family trials were probably an occasion of reproach. "Although my house be not so with God, yet He has made with me an everlasting covenant, ordered in all things and sure: for this is all my salvation and all my desire."

But there is a far heavier reproach than that of the world—when the grand accuser injects hard thoughts of God—when he throws our guilt and unworthiness—our helplessness and difficulties, in our face. And how severe is this exercise in a season of spiritual desertion! Except the believer can stay his soul upon "a God who hides Himself, as still the God of Israel, the Savior," he is unprepared with an answer to him who reproaches him. Such appears to have been Job's condition, and Heman's, not to speak of many of the Lord's most favored people, at different stages of their Christian life. Most important, therefore, is it for us to pray for a realizing sense of the Lord's mercies—even of His salvation— not only as necessary for our peace and comfort—but to garrison us against every assault, and to enable us to throw down the challenge, "Rejoice not against me, O my enemy; when I fall, I shall arise; when I sit in darkness, the Lord shall be a light to me." Free grace has saved me—an unspotted righteousness covers me—an Almighty arm sustains me—eternal glory awaits me. Who shall condemn? "Who shall separate us from the love of God which is in Christ Jesus our Lord?"

Now, for this bold front to our enemies, nothing is wanted beyond the reach of the weakest child of God. No extraordinary holiness—no Christian establishment in experience—nothing but simple, humble faith—For I trust in Your word. Faith makes this salvation ours, in all its fullness and almighty power: and, therefore, our confidence in the word will make us "ready always to give an answer to everyone who asks us a reason of the hope that is in us, with meekness and fear." "No weapon that is formed against you shall prosper; and every tongue that rises against you in judgment, you shall condemn. This is the heritage of the servants of the Lord; and their righteousness is of Me, says the Lord."

But how often is our Christian boldness paralyzed by our feeble apprehensions of the salvation of God! Clear and full evangelical views are indispensable for the effective exercise of our weighty obligations. Any indistinctness here, from its necessary mixture of self-righteousness and unbelief, obscures the warrant of our personal interest, and therefore hinders the firm grasp of Almighty strength. Coldness and formality also deaden the power of Christian boldness. Much need, therefore, have we to pray for a realized perception of the freeness, fullness, holiness, and privileges of the Gospel. Much need have we to use our speedy diligence, without delay; our painful diligence, without indulgence: our continual diligence, without weariness; that we be not satisfied with remaining on the skirts of the kingdom; that it be not a matter of doubt, whether we belong to it or not; but that, grace being added to grace, "so an entrance may be ministered to us abundantly, into" all its rich consolations and everlasting joys.

43. And take not the word of truth utterly out of my mouth; for I have hoped in Your judgments.

For the sake of the church and of the world, no less than for our own sakes, let us "give diligence" to clear up our interest in the Gospel. The want of personal assurance is not only a loss in our own souls, but a hindrance to our Christian usefulness. Hence our efforts are often powerless in parrying off the attack of him that reproaches us, as well as to "strengthen the weak hands, and confirm the feeble knees" of our brethren. The charge of hypocrisy, or the want of the "constraining" principle of "the love of Christ," stops the utterance of the word of truth, and obscures our character as a "saint of God," and "a witness" for His name. Justly, indeed, might He punish our unfaithfulness, by forbidding us any more to speak in His name. And therefore the dread of this grievous judgment, and the mourning over precious lost opportunities, stirs up the prayer—'Take not the word of truth utterly out of my mouth—Not only take it not out of my heart; but let it be ready in my mouth for the confession of my Master.'

This valuable prayer may preserve us from denying Christ. Too apt are we to allow worldly communion, habits, and conversation without a word of restraint. Let the whole weight of Christian responsibility be deeply felt—faith in the heart, and confession with the mouth—the active principle, and the practical exercise. Should we be content with the dormant principle, where would be the Church—the witness for God in the world? Shall we shrink from the bold confession of Him, who "despised the shame of the cross" for us? Would not this imply distrust of our own testimony—the word of truth?

It does indeed need wisdom to know when, as well as what, to speak. There is "a time to keep silence," and "the prudent shall keep silence in that time." But is it our cross to be "dumb with silence?" And when we "hold our peace, even from good," is our "sorrow stirred—our hearts hot within us—the fire burning"? No—is not the plea of bashfulness or judicious caution often a self-deluding cover for the real cause of restraint—the lack of the personal apprehension of the Lord's mercy? "I believed, and therefore have I spoken." Oh! let not the word of truth be taken utterly out of our mouth. A stammering confession is better than silence. If we cannot say all we want of, or for our Savior, let us say what we can. 'God's servants are very sensible of the infinite value of the least atom of what belongs to Him.' And a word spoken in weakness may be a word of Almighty power, and a present help to some fainting spirit. In our connection with the world, many occasions will unexpectedly occur, if the heart be but wakeful and active to improve them. The common topics of earthly conversation often furnish a channel for heavenly communion, so that our communications with the world may be like Jacob's ladder, whose bottom rested upon the earth, but the top reached unto the heavens. And oh! what a relief is it to the burdened conscience, to stammer out, if it be but a few words for God, even though there be no sensible refreshings of His presence! Yet if we would speak for Him with power and acceptance, it must be out of the "good treasure and abundance of the heart." For it is only when "the heart is inditing a good matter, speaking of the things touching the King, that the tongue is as the pen of a ready writer."

But let us take up this petition as the expression of the Christian's exercises with his God. 'That word utterly'—observes an eminently-tried believer—'though it seems to be beneath the notice of the mind, when one has got very low, is in reality one of the most blessed words in this most blessed book. How often, when I have formerly been upon the brink of giving up all for lost, and of saying, "Evil, be my good"—the thought has perhaps struck me, that, while I am struggling between despondency and rebellion, and too hard, too cold, too discouraged to look up to Him, the blessed Redeemer is pitying the struggle of my soul; and it has kept me where I was, led me to put off despair at least until tomorrow; and then before tomorrow I have seen something of the grace and glory of the Gospel.'

What then is the advice, which this man of God gives from his own experience? 'When you are most deeply deploring your sins, never fail to thank the Lord, or at least to think how you would thank Him, if you dared lift up a face overwhelmed with shame and defeat, that He has not taken away His truth UTTERLY; that He has left you clinging to some twig of hope, instead of leaving you to end—what thousands who look outwardly very calm—have found—the depth of the precipice of despair.' (Nottidge)

The Psalmist's prayer here is the same confidence of faith, that was expressed in the preceding verse—For I have hoped in Your judgments, an acceptable spirit of approach to God, and an earnest of the revival of life and comfort in the Lord's best time and way.

44. So shall I keep Your law continually forever and ever.

The heaping up of so many words in this short verse, appears to be the struggle of the soul to express the vehemency of its longings to glorify its Savior. And, indeed, the Lord's return to us, unsealing the lips of the dumb, and putting His word again into their mouth, brings with it a fresh sense of constraining obligation. This fresh occupation in His praise and service is not only our present privilege, but an foretaste of our heavenly employment, when the word will never more be taken out of our mouth, but we shall "talk of His wondrous works" "forever and ever." The defects in the constancy and extent of our obedience (as far as our hearts are alive to the honor of God) must ever be our grief and burden; and the prospect of its completeness in a better world, is that, which renders the anticipation of heaven so delightful. There we shall be blessed with suitable feelings, and therefore be enabled to render suitable obedience—even one unbroken consecration of all our powers to His work. Then "shall we keep His law continually forever and ever." Once admitted to the "throne of God," we "shall serve Him day and night in His temple"—without sin—without inconstancy—without weariness—without end! We speak of heaven; but oh! to be there! To be engaged throughout eternity in the service of love to a God of love! In one day's continuance in the path of obedience even here, in the midst of the defilement which stains our holiest services, how sweetly do the moments roll away! But to be ever employed for Him, in that place, where "there shall in no wise enter anything that defiles"—this gives an emphasis and a dignity to the heavenly joy, which may well stamp it as "unspeakable and full of glory." May we not then encourage the hope, that the Lord is making us meet for heaven, by the strength and constancy of our desires to keep the laws of God? And is it not evident, that heaven itself can afford no real delight to one, who feels the service of God on earth to be irksome? He stands self-excluded by the constitution of his nature, by the necessity of the case. He has no heart for heaven, no taste for heaven, no capacity for enjoyment of heaven, "He that is unjust, let him be unjust still; and he who is filthy, let him be filthy still; and he who is righteous, let him be righteous still; and he who is holy, let him be holy still."

Heavenly, gracious Father! who and what are we, that our hearts should be made the unworthy recipients of Your grace? that our will should be subdued into "the obedience of faith?" and that we should be permitted to anticipate that blessed period, when we shall "keep Your law continually, forever and ever?" May this prospect realize the happiness of our present obedience! May He, who has "bought us with a price" for His glory, reign in our hearts, and live upon our lips; that each of us may have His mark upon our foreheads—the seal of His property in us, and of our obligation to Him, "Whose I am, and whom I serve!"

45. And I will walk at liberty: for I seek Your precepts.

Not only perseverance but liberty, is the fruit of the Lord's mercy to our souls—not the liberty of sin—to do what we please—but of holiness—to do what we ought; the one, the iron bondage of our own will; the other, the easy yoke of a God of love. It was a fine expression of a heathen, "To serve God is to reign." Certainly in this service David found the liberty of a king. The precepts of God were not forced upon him; for he sought them. "More to be desired than gold, yes, than much fine gold; sweeter also than honey, and the honey-comb." The way of the Lord, which to the ungodly is beset with thorns and briers, is the king's highway of liberty. The child of God walks here in the gladness of his heart and the rejoicing of his conscience. Even in "seeking these precepts," there is "liberty" and enlargement of heart; a natural motion, like that of the sun in its course, "going forth as a bridegroom, and rejoicing as a strong man to run a race." What must it be then, to walk in the full enjoyment of the precepts! "Where the Spirit of the Lord is, there is liberty." "They shall sing in the ways of the Lord,"—for "how great is His goodness; how great is His beauty!"

Are we then obeying the precepts as our duty, or "seeking" them as our privilege? Do we complain of the strictness of the law, or of the corruption of the flesh? Are the precepts of our own hearts our burden? Is sin or holiness our bondage? The only way to make religion easy, is to be always in it. The glow of spiritual activity, and the healthfulness of Christian liberty, are only to be found in the persevering and self-denying pursuit of every track of the ways of God, "If you continue in My word, then are you My disciples indeed: and you shall know the truth, and the truth shall make you free. If the Son, therefore, shall make you free, you shall be free indeed." To have the whole stream of all our thoughts, actions, motives, desires, affections, carried in one undivided current towards God, is the complete and unrestrained influence of His love upon our hearts.

Let but our eyes be opened, our judgments clearly exercised, our consciences suffered to speak; and this point is clear—Sin is slavery—Holiness is liberty. The sinner may live in bonds with as much delight as if he was in his element. He may seem even to himself to be at large, while in fact he is "shut up, and cannot come forth." For such is the tyranny under which he is bound, that he cannot help himself; and (to use the confession of a heathen) while 'he sees and approves better things, he follows the worse.' Every sin is a fresh chain of bondage, under the check of a cruel master. On the other hand—the Lord's commands—as He Himself declares, and all His servants testify—are "for our good always." His 'service is perfect freedom.' (Liturgy.) The life of liberty is to be under the bonds of holy love and duty. Let the trial be made of two Masters; conviction must follow.

True it is, that the corrupt and rebellious inclinations will "lust" to the end. But as long as indulgence is denied, conflict excited, and the constant endeavor maintained to "bring every thought into captivity to the obedience of Christ," our liberty is established, even where it is not always enjoyed. Every fresh chain, by which we bind ourselves to the Lord, makes us more free. While, then, those who "promise us liberty are themselves the servants of corruption," let us live as the children of God—the heirs of the kingdom—grateful—free—blood-bought souls—remembering the infinite cost at which our liberty was purchased, and the moment of extreme peril when we were saved. When the flesh was weak, and the "law weak through the flesh," and no resolution of ours could break us from the yoke of sin—then it was that "Christ both died, and rose, and revived, that He might be the Lord both of the dead and living," "delivering us from the hand of our enemies, that we might serve Him without fear." And then indeed do we "walk at liberty," when we "break the bands" of all other lords "asunder," and consecrate ourselves entirely to His precepts. "O Lord our God, other lords beside You have had dominion over us; but by You only will we make mention of Your name."

46. I will speak of Your testimonies also before kings, and will not be ashamed.

"Liberty in walking" in the Lord's ways will naturally produce boldness in speaking of them. Compare the conduct of the three unshaken witnesses for the truth before the Babylonish monarch. Mark the difference of the spirit displayed by the Apostles, and especially by Peter, before and after the day of Pentecost. Look at Stephen before the council, and Paul before Felix, Festus, and Agrippa. "God had not given to them the spirit of fear; but of power, and of love, and of a sound mind." Hear the great Apostle testifying of himself, "I am ready to preach the gospel to you that are at Rome also"—at the metropolis of the world, in the face of all opposition and contempt, and at the imminent hazard of my life, "For"—says he, "I am not ashamed of the gospel of Christ." In the same determination of soul, he exhorts his dear son in the faith, "Be not ashamed of the testimony of our Lord, nor of me His prisoner." To how many does "the fear of man bring a snare?" Many a good soldier has faced the cannon's mouth with undaunted front, and yet shrunk away with a coward's heart from the reproach of the cross, and been put to blush even by the mention of the Savior's name. Far better— the Son of Man "strengthening you"—to brave the fiery furnace, or the den of lions in His service, than like Jonah, by flinching from the cross, to incur the sting of conscience and the frown of God.

Professing Christians! Are we ready to bear our testimony for Jesus, against the sneer and ridicule of the ungodly? We are not likely to "be brought before kings and rulers for the Son of Man's sake." Yet no less do we need Divine help and strong faith in withstanding the enmity of a prejudiced relative or scornful neighbor. Young people! you are perhaps in especial danger of being ashamed of your Bible, your religion, your Savior. You may be brought under the snare of the "fear of man," and be tempted to compromise your religion, and to sacrifice your everlasting all from a dread of "the reproach of Christ." But remember Him, who for your sake "before Pontius Pilate witnessed a good confession;" and shall the dread of a name restrain you from sharing His reproach, and banish the obligations of love and gratitude from your hearts? Have you forgotten, that you once owned the service of Satan? and will you not be as bold for Christ, as you were for him? Were you once "glorying in your shame;" and will you now be ashamed of your glory? Oh! remember who has said, "Whoever shall be ashamed of Me and of My words, in this adulterous and sinful generation, of him also shall the Son of Man be ashamed, when He comes in the glory of His Father with the holy angels." Think much and often of this word. Think on this day. Think on the station of "the fearful and unbelieving" on the left hand on that day. Think on their eternal doom. What is a prison, compared to hell? What need to pray and tremble! If you are sincere in your determination, and simple in your dependence, then will the "love of Christ constrain you," not to a cold, calculating, reluctant service; but to a confession of your Savior, bold, unfettered, and "faithful even unto death." Every deviation from the straight path bears the character of being ashamed of Christ. How much have you to speak in behalf of His testimonies, His ways, His love! When in danger of the influence of "the fear of man," look to Him for strength. He will give to you, as He gave to Stephen, "a mouth and wisdom, which all your adversaries shall not be able to gainsay or resist." Thus will you, like them, be strengthened "to profess a good profession before many witnesses."

47. And I will delight myself in Your commandments, which I have loved.

It is but poor comfort to the believer to be able to talk well to others upon the ways of God, and even to "bear the reproach" of His people, when his own heart is cold, insensible, and dull. But why does he not rouse himself to the active exercise of faith, "I will delight myself in Your commandments?" That which is the burden of the carnal heart is the delight of the renewed soul. The former "is enmity against God: and therefore is not, and cannot be, subject to His law." The latter can delight in nothing else. If the gospel separates the heart from sinful delights, it is only to make room for delights of a more elevated, satisfying, and enduring nature. Satan, indeed, generally baits his temptations with that seductive witchery, which the world calls pleasure. But has he engrossed all pleasure into his service? Are there no pleasures besides "the pleasures of sin?" Do the ways of the Lord promise nothing but difficulty and trial? What means then the experience of him, who could "rejoice in them, as much as in all riches," and who "loved them above gold, yes, above fine gold?" The "fatted calf" of our Father's house is surely a most gainful exchange for "the husks" of the "far country." The delights of holiness go deeper than sensual pleasures. The joy of the saint is not that false, polluted, deadly joy, which is all that the worldling knows, and all that he has to look for: but it flows spontaneously from the fountain of living waters, through the pure channel of "the word of God, which lives and abides forever." No, so independent is it of any earthly spring, that it never flourishes more than in the desolate wilderness, or the sick-bed solitude; so that, "although the fig-tree shall not blossom, neither shall fruit be in the vines, yet we will rejoice in the Lord, we will joy in the God of our salvation." Men of the world see what religion takes away, but they see little of what it gives; else would they reproach—not our folly—but their own blindness. "Thus says the Lord God, Behold, My servants shall eat, but you shall be hungry; behold, My servants shall drink, but you shall be thirsty; behold, My servants shall rejoice, but you shall be ashamed; behold, My servants shall sing for joy of heart, but you shall cry for sorrow of heart, and shall howl for vexation of spirit." The love and delight of the soul first fixes on the commandments. Then how natural is the flow of delight in them! even at the very time that we are "abhorring ourselves in dust and ashes" for our neglect of them; and God never has our hearts, until something of this delight is felt and enjoyed. But do we complain of the dullness of our hearts, that restrains this pleasure? Let us seek for a deeper impression of redeeming love. This will be the spring of grateful obedience and holy delight. Let us turn our complaints into prayers, and the Lord will quickly turn them into praises. Let us watch against everything, that would intercept our communion with Jesus. Distance from Him must be accompanied with poverty of spiritual enjoyment., "They shall be abundantly satisfied with the fatness of Your house: and You shall make them drink of the river of Your pleasures. For with You is the fountain of life: and in Your light shall we see light."

48. My hands also will I lift up unto Your commandments, which I have loved: and I will meditate in Your statutes.

David seems at a loss for expressions adequately to set forth the fervency of his love and delight in the ways and word of God. Here we find him lifting up his hands with the gesture of one, who is longing to embrace the object of his desire with both hands and his whole heart. Perhaps also in lifting up his hands unto the commandments, he might mean to express his looking upward for assistance to keep them, and to live in them. But how humbling this comparison with ourselves! Alas! how often from the neglect of this influence of the Spirit of God, do our "hands hang down," instead of being lifted up, in these holy ways! We are too often content with a scanty measure of love: without any sensible "hungering and thirsting after righteousness;" neither able to pray with life and power, nor to hear with comfort and profit, nor to "do good and communicate" with cheerfulness, nor to meditate with spiritual delight, nor to live for God with zeal and interest, nor to anticipate the endurance of the cross with unflinching resolution—the soul being equally disabled for heavenly communion and active devotedness. Shall we look for ease under the power of this deadening malady? Let us rather struggle and cry for deliverance from it. Let us subscribe ourselves before God as wretched, helpless, and guilty. He can look upon us, and revive us. Let us then "take hold upon His covenant," and plead that He will look upon us. Let us "put Him in remembrance" of the glory of His name, which is much more concerned in delivering us out of this frame, by His quickening grace, than in leaving us, stupid, corrupt, and carnal in it. Professor! awake: or beg of the Lord to awaken you! For if your cold sleeping heart is contented with the prospect of a heaven hereafter, without seeking for a present foretaste of its joy, it may be a very questionable matter whether heaven will ever be yours.

Delight, however, will exercise itself in an habitual meditation in the statutes. The breathing of the heart will be, "Oh, how love I Your law! it is my meditation all the day." It is in holy meditation on the word of God, that all the graces of the Spirit are manifested. What is the principle of faith, but the reliance of the soul upon the promises of the word? What is the sensation of godly fear, but the soul trembling before the threatenings of God? What is the object of hope, but the apprehended glory of God? What is the excitement of desire or love, but longing, endearing contemplations of the Savior, and of His unspeakable blessings? Hence we can scarcely conceive of the influence of grace separated from spiritual meditation on the word. It is this which, under Divine teaching, draws out its hidden contents, and exhibits them to the soul, as the objects upon which the principles and affections of the Divine life are habitually exercised. Not that any benefit can be expected from meditation, even upon the word of God, as an abstract duty. If not deeply imbued with prayer, it will degenerate into dry speculative study. Without some distinct practical application, it will be unedifying in itself, and unsatisfactory for its important ends—the discerning of the mind of God, and feeding upon the rich provision of the Gospel.

Why then is the Bible read only—not meditated on? Because it is not loved. We do not go to it, as the hungry man to his food, as the miser to his treasure. The loss is incalculable. Our superficial knowledge has no practical influence. It is only as we "search," that we "know it for our good."

Let it then be a matter of daily inquiry. Does my reading of the word of God furnish food for my soul, matter for prayer, direction for conduct? Scriptural study, when entered upon in a prayerful spirit, will never, like many other studies, be unproductive. The mind that is engaged in it, is fitly set for bearing fruit; it will "bring forth fruit in due season." Meditation kindles love, as it is the effect of love, "While I was musing, the fire burned." "Whoever looks into the perfect law of liberty, and continues in it, this man is blessed in his deed." But let us take heed, that the root of religion in the soul is not cankered by the indulgence of secret sin. The largest supply of Christian ordinances will fail to refresh us, except the heart be kept right with God in simplicity of faith, love, and diligence in the service of Christ.

Come then, Christian, let us set our hearts to a vigorous, delighting devotedness to the statutes of our God. "It is not a vain thing for us; because it is our life." But to regard some of the words only would be to obey our own will, not God's. Let us lift up our hands to them all. How shadowy is the joy of speculative contemplation, if it does not draw the heart to practical exercise! Let faith return our obligations in the full apprehension of the Lord's mercy. And then will love constrain us to nothing less than "a living sacrifice" to His service. If the professor sleeps in notional godliness, let us employ our active meditation in searching for the mine that lies not on the surface, but which never fails to enrich diligent, patient, persevering labor.

49. Remember the word unto Your servant, upon which You have caused me to hope.

What is faith? It is hope upon God's word. The warrant of faith is therefore the word. The object of faith is He who causes us to hope. He has not forgotten—He cannot forget, His word. But He permits—no, commands His servants to remind Him of it in order to exercise their faith, diligence, and patience. Often, indeed, "hope deferred makes the heart sick." But it is not needless delay—not ignorance of the fittest time—not forgetfulness—not changeableness—not weakness.

Meanwhile, however, constantly plead the promise—Remember the word unto Your servant. This is the proper use of the promises, as "arguments with which to fill our mouths, when we order our cause before God." When thus pleaded with the earnestness and humility of faith, they will be found to be the blessed realities of unchanging love.

Now—have not circumstances of Providence, or the distinct application of the Spirit, made some words of God especially precious to your soul? Such words are thus made your own, to be laid up against some future time of trial, when you may "put your God in remembrance" of them. Apply this exercise of faith to such a word as this, "Him who comes to Me, I will in no wise cast out." Then plead your interest in it as a coming sinner, "Lord, I hope in this Your word." "You have caused me to hope" in it. "Remember this word unto Your servant." Thus is prayer grounded upon the promise, which it forms into a prevailing argument, and sends back to heaven; nothing doubting, but that it will be verified in God's best time and way.

Take another case; God has engaged Himself to be the God of the seed of believers. His sacramental ordinance is the seal of this promise. The believer brings his child to this ordinance, as the exercise of his faith upon the faithfulness of God. Let him daily put his finger upon this promise, Remember the word unto Your servant, upon which You have caused me to hope. This is, as Augustine said of his mother, 'bringing before God His own handwriting.' Will He not remember His word? Faith may be tried, perhaps long tried. "But He abides faithful. He cannot deny Himself." Faith trusts—not what the eye sees, but what the word promises.

Again—Have we ever found God's word hoped on, a covering and strength against besetting sin? This will surely be an encouragement to cry under the same temptation—Remember Your word. "He who has delivered, does deliver, and will even to the end deliver." He "has done great things for us." And is not this an earnest of continued mercy? "Because You have been my help, therefore under the shadow of Your wings will I rejoice." Thus may we confidently receive a promise as the distinct message to our soul, when we are conscious of a readiness to receive the whole word as the rule of our life. And does it not set an edge upon prayer, to eye a promising God, and to consider His promises—not as hanging in the air, without any definite direction or meaning, but as individually spoken and belonging to myself as a child and servant of God? This is the experience and comfort of the life of faith. This unfolds the true secret of living to God; ending at last with the honorable death-bed testimony, "Behold, this day I am going the way of all the earth: and you know in all your hearts and in all your souls, that not one thing has failed of all the good things, which the Lord your God spoke concerning you; all have come to pass to you; and not one thing has failed thereof."

50. This is my comfort in my affliction; for Your word has quickened me.

David was encouraged to plead the word of promise in prayer, from the recollection of its comfort in his affliction. For the man of God is not exempted from affliction, but he is comforted in it with God's comforts, flowing from the fountain-head. And truly no comforts are like God's comforts, and there are none beside His. They are indeed strong consolations, both in their foundation and their influence; supporting—not only in the prospect, but under the actual pressure of trouble, and fully proportioned to the need of the most sinking calamity. Never therefore are we left unsupported in such a time, or called to drink a cup of unmingled tribulation. In the moments of our bitterest sorrow, how are we compelled to stand amazed at the tenderness, which is daily and hourly exercised towards us! We have always some word exactly suited to our affliction, and which we could not have understood without it; and "a word" thus "spoken in due season, how good is it!" One word of God, sealed to the heart, infuses more sensible relief, than ten thousand words of man. When therefore the word assures of the presence of God in affliction; of His continued pity and sympathy in His most severe dispensations; and of their certain issue to our everlasting good; must not we say of it, This is our comfort in our affliction? How does the Savior's love stream forth from this channel on every side; imparting life, refreshment, strength to those, who but for this comfort would have "fainted," and "perished in their affliction!" This indeed was the end, for which the Scriptures were written; and such power of consolation have they sometimes administered to the afflicted saint, that tribulation has almost ceased to be a trial, and the retrospect has been the source of thankful recollection.

But first the word becomes life—then comfort. And those only, who have felt the quickening power of the word, can realize its consolations. Be thankful, then, Reader, if, when dead in sins, it "quickened you;" and, when sunk in trouble, once and again it has revived you. Yet do not think, that it is any innate power of its own, that works so graciously for you. No. The exhibition of the Savior is the spring of life and consolation. It is because it "testifies of Him," "the consolation of Israel" "afflicted in all our afflictions"—and never failing to uphold with "grace sufficient for us." It is not, however, the word without the Spirit, nor the Spirit generally without the word; but the Spirit by the word—first putting life into the word, and then by the word quickening the soul. The word then is only the instrument. The Spirit is the Almighty agent. Thus the work is the Lord's; and nothing is left for us, but self-renunciation and praise.

Verses 51-75

51. The proud have had me greatly in derision; yet have I not declined from Your law.

The scorn of an ungodly world is one of the afflictions, which realize to us the comfort of the word. And this is a trial, from which no exemption is to be expected, "All that will live godly in Christ Jesus shall suffer persecution." Not even David—though a king—a man of wisdom and prudence, and therefore not likely to give unnecessary offence; and whose character and rank might be expected to command respect—not even was he shielded from the derision of the proud on account of the profession and service of his God. Thus it ever was and ever will be. Faith in the doctrine of Christ, and conformity to the strict commandments of the gospel, must expose us to the taunts of the unbeliever and the worldling. Yet, where the heart is right with God, the derision of the proud, instead of forcing us to decline from the law of God, will strengthen our adherence to it. David answered the bitter derision of Michal with a stronger resolution to abide by his God, "I will yet be more vile than thus." He counted it his glory, his duty, his joy. None, however, but a believer knows what it is to bear this cross: and none but a real believer can bear it. It is one of the touchstones of sincerity, the application of which has often been the means of "separating the precious from the vile," and has unmasked the self-confident professor to his own confusion. Oh! how many make a fair profession, and appear "good soldiers of Jesus Christ," until the hour of danger proves them deserters, and they reap only the fruits of their self-confidence in their own confusion!

It is, therefore, of great importance to those who are just setting out in the warfare, to be well armed with the word of God. It kept David steadfast amid the derision of the proud; and it will keep young Christians from being frightened or overcome by the sneer of an ungodly world. But that it may "dwell in us richly in all wisdom," and be suited to our own case, it will be well, under circumstances of reproach, to acquaint ourselves with the supporting promises and encouragements to suffer for righteousness' sake. Above all, the contemplation of the great sufferer Himself—meeting this poignant trial in meekness, compassion, and prayer—will exhibit "a refuge from the storm, and a shadow from the heat, when the blast of the terrible ones is as the storm against the wall." The mere professor knows not this refuge; he possesses not this armor; so that when "affliction or persecution arises for the word's sake, immediately he is offended."

Christian! be satisfied with the approbation of your God. Has He not adopted you into His family, stamped you with His image, assured you by His Spirit, sealed you for His kingdom? And is not this "honor that comes from God only" enough—far more than enough—to counterbalance the derision of the proud? Think of the day, when "the rebuke of the people shall be taken away from off all the earth," when "he will confess their name before His Father, and before His angels," when "the saints shall judge the world," when "the upright shall have dominion over them in the morning." Can we be Christians, if this sure prospect does not infinitely more than compensate for all "the hard speeches, which ungodly sinners have spoken against us?"

Thus—blessed be God—the weapons of our warfare are drawn from the Divine armory; and therefore depending on the grace, and following the example, of Jesus, we suffer, as the way to victory—the road to an everlasting crown.

52. I remembered Your judgments of old, O Lord; and have comforted myself.

The Lord's dealings with His people were a frequent subject of meditation to the Psalmist, and now were they his present support under "the scourge of the tongue." Evidently they are put upon record for the encouragement of future generations. We are ready to imagine something peculiar in our own case, and to "think it strange concerning the fiery trial which is to try us, as though some strange thing happened unto us." But when we remember the Lord's judgments of old, with His people, we comfort ourselves in the assurance, that "the same afflictions are accomplished in our brethren, that have been in the world;" and that "as the sufferings of Christ have abounded in them, so their consolation also abounded by Christ." They also encountered the same derision of the proud, and always experienced the same support from the faithfulness of their God. We do not sufficiently consider the mercy and gracious wisdom of God, in occupying so much of His written word with the records of His judgments of old. One class will pay a prominent attention to the preceptive, another to the doctrinal, parts of revelation—each forgetting that the historical records comprise a full and striking illustration of both, and have always proved most supporting grounds of consolation to the Lord's people. The important design in casting so large a portion of the small volume of Revelation into an historical form, is every way worthy of its author. "Whatever things were written before, were written for our learning; that we through patience and comfort of the Scriptures might have hope;" and how admirably adapted the means are to the end, the diligent student in the Scripture field will bear ample witness. Willfully, therefore, to neglect the historical portion of the sacred volume, from the idea of confining our attention to what we deem the more spiritual parts of scripture—would show a sad deficiency of spiritual apprehension, and deprive ourselves of the most valuable instruction, and most abundant comfort. This neglect would exclude us from one eminent means of increasing "patience," in the example of those "who through faith and patience inherit the promises;" of receiving "comfort," in the experience of the faithfulness of God manifested in every age to His people: and of enlivening our "hope," in marking the happy issue of the "patience of the saints," and the heavenly support administered unto them. So far, therefore, are we from being little interested in the Scriptural records of past ages, that it is evident that the sacred historians, as well as the prophets, "ministered not unto themselves, but unto us the things which are now reported."

Let us select one or two instances as illustrative of this subject. Why were the records of the deluge, and of the overthrow of the cities of the plain, preserved, but as exhibitions to the church, that "the Lord"—the Savior of Noah, the eighth person, and the deliverer of just Lot, "knows how to deliver the godly out of temptations, and to reserve the unjust unto the day of judgment to be punished?" What a source of comfort then to the tempted people of God is the remembrance of these judgments of old! Take again the wonderful history of the overthrow of the Egyptians, and the consequent deliverance of God's ancient people. How often does the church recollect this interposition as a ground of assurance, that under similar circumstances of trial, the same illustrious displays of Divine faithfulness and love may be confidently expected! She looks back upon what the "arm of the Lord has done in ancient days, and in the generation of old," as the pattern of what He ever would be, and ever would do, for His purchased people. Thus also God Himself recalls to our mind this overthrow and deliverance as a ground of present encouragement and support, "According to the days of your coming out of the land of Egypt will I show unto him marvelous things"—and the Church echoes back this remembrance in the expression of her faith, gratitude, and expectation for spiritual blessings: "He will subdue our iniquities, and You will cast all their sins into the depths of the sea." Such is the interesting use that may be made of the historical parts of Scripture! Such is the comfort to be derived from the remembrance of the Lord's judgments of old! And is not the recollection of His judgments of old with ourselves, productive of the same support? Does not the retrospect of His dealings with our own souls serve to convince us, that "all His paths are mercy and truth?" The assurance is therefore warranted alike by experience and by Scripture, "We know that all things work together for good to them that love God, to them who are the called according to His purpose."

53. Horror has taken hold upon me, because of the wicked that forsake Your law.

The remembrance of the Lord's judgments of old, while it brings comfort to His people as regards themselves, stirs up a poignancy of compassionate feeling for the ungodly. And indeed to a feeling and reflecting mind, the condition of the world must excite commiseration and concern! A "whole world lying in wickedness!" lying therefore in ruins! the image of God effaced! the presence of God departed! Horror has taken hold of me! to see the law of Him, who gave being to the world, so utterly forsaken! so much light and love shining from heaven in vain! The earthly heart cannot endure that any restraint should be imposed; much less that any constraint, even of love, should be employed to change its bias, and turn it back to its God. Are you then a believer? then you will be most tender of the honor of the law of God. Every stroke at His law you will feel as a stroke at your own heart. Are you a believer? then will you consider every man as your brother; and weep to see so many of them around you, crowding the broad road to destruction, and perishing as the miserable victims of their own deceivings. The prospect on every side is, as if God were cast down from His throne, and the creatures of His hand were murdering their own souls.

But how invariably does a languor respecting our own eternal interest affect the tenderness of our regard for the honor of our God; so that we can look at the wicked that forsake God's law, with comparative indifference! Awful indeed is the thought, that it ever can be with us a small matter, that multitudes are sinking! going down into perdition! with the name of Christ—under the seal of baptism—partakers of the means of gospel grace—yet perishing! Not, indeed, that we are to yield to such a feeling of horror, as would paralyze all exertion on their behalf. For do we owe them no duty—no prayer—no labor? Shall we look upon souls hurrying on with such dreadful haste to unutterable, everlasting torments; and permit them to rush on blinded, unawakened, unalarmed! If there is a horror to see a brand apparently fitting for the fire, will there not be a wrestling endeavor to pluck that brand out of the fire? Have we quite forgotten in our own case the fearful terrors of an unconverted state—the Almighty power of wrath and justice armed against us—the thunder of that voice, "Vengeance belongs to Me, I will recompense, says the Lord?" Oh! if the love of the Savior and the love of souls were reigning with more mighty influence in our hearts, how much more devoted should we be in our little spheres of labor! how much more enlarged in our supplications, until all the kingdom of Satan were subject to the obedience of the Son of God, and conquered by the force of His omnipotent love!

But if the spirit of David, renewed but in part, was thus filled with horror in the contemplation of the wicked, what must have been the affliction—what the intensity of His sufferings, "who was holy, harmless, undefiled, separate from sinners"—yes, "of purer eyes than to behold iniquity"—during thirty-three years of continued contact with a world of sin! What shall we say of the condescension of His love, in wearing "the likeness of sinful flesh"—dwelling among sinners—yes, "receiving sinners, and eating with them!"

Blessed Spirit! impart to us more of "the mind that was in Christ Jesus," that the law of God may be increasingly precious in our eyes, and that we may be "exceedingly jealous for the Lord God of Hosts!" Help us by Your gracious influence to plead with sinners for God, and to plead for sinners with God!

54. Your statutes have been my songs in the house of my pilgrimage.

Come, Christian pilgrim, and beguile your wearisome journey heavenward by "singing the Lord's song in this strange land." With the statutes of God in your hand and in your heart, you are furnished with a song for every step of your way, "The Lord is my shepherd; I shall not want. He makes me to lie down in green pastures: He leads me beside the still waters. He restores my soul: He leads me in the paths of righteousness for His name's sake. Yes, though I walk through the valley of the shadow of death I will fear no evil; for You are with me; Your rod and Your staff, they comfort me. You prepare a table before me in the presence of my enemies: You anoint my head with oil; my cup runs over. Surely goodness and mercy shall follow me all the days of my life; and I will dwell in the house of the Lord forever." How delightfully does this song bring before you Him, who having laid down His life for you, engages Himself as your Provider, your Keeper, your Guide, your faithful and unchangeable Friend! Such a song, therefore, will smooth your path, and reconcile you to the many inconveniences of the way; while the recollection that this is only the house of your pilgrimage and not your home; and that "there remains a rest for the people of God," will support the exercise of faith and patience to the end. How striking the contrast between the wicked that forsake the law, and the Christian pilgrim, who makes it the subject of his daily song, and the source of his daily comfort! Yes, these same statutes, which are the yoke and burden of the ungodly, lead the true servant of the Lord from pleasure to pleasure; and, cherished by their vigorous influence, his way is made easy and prosperous. Evidently, therefore, our knowledge and delight in the Lord's statutes will furnish a decisive test of our real state before Him.

But it is important to remember that our cheerful song is connected with a pilgrim-spirit. Never forget that we are not at home; only happy strangers on our passage homewards. Here we have no settled habitation—no rest. We are looking for a better country: and as we look, we are seeking for it. Our "hearts are in the ways of it." Every day advances us nearer to it. In this spirit the statutes of the Lord will be our song. Here are the deeds of conveyance—our title made sure to an estate—not small, of little account, or of uncertain interest—but "an inheritance" of incalculable value, made over to us. Here we have sure direction—such as cannot mislead us—for the attainment of it. Here we are stimulated by the examples of our fellow-pilgrims, who have reached their home; and as we follow their track, many are the cordials by the way, and home brightens in the nearer prospect.

What reason have we then every moment to guard against the debasing, stupifying influence of the world, which makes us forget the proper character of a pilgrim! And what an habitual conflict must be maintained with the sloth and aversion of a reluctant heart to maintain our progress in the journey towards Zion! Reader! have you entered upon a pilgrim's life? Then what is your solace and refreshment on the road? It is dull, heavy, wearisome, to be a pilgrim without a song. And yet it is only the blessed experience of the Lord's statutes, that will tune our song. "If therefore you have tasted that the Lord is gracious;" if He has thus "put a new song into your mouth," oh! do not permit any carelessness or neglect to rob you of this heavenly anticipation. And that your lips be not found mute, seek to maintain a lively contemplation of the place where you are going—of Him who as your "forerunner is for you entered" there—and of the prospect, that, having "prepared a place for you, He will come again, and take you to Himself; that where He is, there you may be also." In this spirit, and with these hopes before you, you may take up your song, "O God, my heart is fixed: I will sing and give praise. I will bless the Lord at all times—His praise shall continually be in my mouth." Thus may you go on your pilgrimage "singing in the ways of the Lord," and commencing a song below, which in the world of praise above, shall never, never cease.

55. I have remembered Your name, O Lord, in the night, and have kept Your law.

How did this man of God live in the statutes of God! In the day they were his pilgrim song—in the night his happy meditation. And, truly, if we can ever spend the waking moments of the night with God, "the darkness is no darkness with us, but the night shines as the day." Many a tried believer has found this cordial for the restlessness of a wakeful night more restorative to the quiet and health of his earthly frame, than the most sovereign specifics of the medical world. "So He gives His beloved sleep." And if in any night of affliction we feel the hand of the Lord grievous to us, do we not find in the remembrance of the Lord a never-failing support? What does our darkness arise from, but from our forgetfulness of God, blotting out for a while the lively impressions of His tender care, His unchanging faithfulness, and His mysterious methods of working His gracious will? And to bring up as it were from the grave, the remembrance of God's name, as manifested in His promises, and in the dispensation of His love; this is indeed the "light that is sown for the righteous," and which "springs up out of darkness." It is to eye the character of the Lord as All-wise to appoint, Almighty to secure, All-compassionate to sympathize and support. It is to recollect Him as a "father pitying his children;" as a "friend who loves at all times," and who "sticks closer than a brother." And even in those seasons of depression, when unwatchfulness or indulgence of sin have brought the darkness of night upon the soul, though the remembrance of the name of the Lord may be grievous, yet it opens the way to consolation. It tells us, that there is a way made for our return; that "the Lord waits, that He may be gracious;" and that in the first step of our return to our Father, we shall find Him full of mercy to his backsliding children. Thus, though "weeping may endure for a night, joy comes in the morning."

Study the Lord's revelation of His own name; and what more full perception can we conceive of its support in the darkest midnight of tribulations? "And the Lord descended in the cloud, and stood with him (Moses), and proclaimed the name of the Lord. And the Lord passed by before him, and proclaimed—The Lord, the Lord God, merciful and gracious, long-suffering, and abundant in goodness and truth, keeping mercy for thousands, forgiving iniquity, transgression, and sin, and that will by no means clear the guilty." Can we wonder that such a name as this should be exhibited as a ground of trust? "The name of the Lord is a strong tower: the righteous runs into it and is safe." "Those who know Your name will put their trust in You." Even our suffering Lord appears to have derived support from the remembrance of the name of the Lord in the night of desertion, "O my God, I cry in the daytime, and You do not hear; and in the night-season, and am not silent. But You are holy, O You who inhabits the praises of Israel!" And from the experience of this source of consolation, we find the tempted Savior directing His tempted people to the same support, "Who is among you who fears the Lord, who obeys the voice of His servant, who walks in darkness, and has no light? let him trust in the name of the Lord, and stay upon his God."

The main principles of the Gospel are involved in this remembrance of the Lord's name. Memory is the storehouse, in which the substance of our knowledge is treasured up. Recollections without faith are shadowy notions. But we have confidence that our God in Himself—and as engaged to us—is all that the Bible declares Him to be. How vast then are our obligations to His dear Son—the only medium, by which His name could be known or remembered, "who has" so "declared Him!" And here is the spring of practical religion. We shall keep His law when we remember His name. A sense of our obligations will impel us forward in diligence, heavenly-mindedness, and self-devotedness in our appointed sphere. Obedience will partake far more of the character of privilege than of duty, when an enlightened knowledge of God is the principle of action.

56. This I had, because I kept Your precepts.

How is it, believer, that you are enabled to sing of the Lord's statutes—and to remember His name? This you have, because you keep His precepts. Thus you are able to tell the world, that in keeping His "commandments there is great reward"—that the "work of righteousness is peace; and the effect of righteousness, quietness, and assurance forever." Christian! let your testimony be clear and decided—that ten thousand worlds cannot bestow the happiness of one day's devotedness to the service of your Lord. For is it not in this path that you realize fullness of joy in "fellowship with the Father, and with His Son Jesus Christ?" "He that has My commandments, and keeps them, he it is that loves me; and he who loves Me shall be loved of My Father; and I will love him, and will manifest Myself to him—My Father will love him; and we will come unto him, and make our abode with him." If you were walking more closely with God in "the obedience of faith," the world would never dare to accuse religion as the source of melancholy and despondency. No man has any right to the hope of happiness in a world of tribulation, but he who seeks it in the favor of his God. Nor can any enjoy this favor, except as connected, in the exercise of faith, with conformity to the will, and delight in the law, of his God. Thus not only are the "statutes of the Lord right," but they "rejoice the heart." There is a sweetness and satisfaction in the work, as well as a good flowing out of it—a current as well as a consequent privilege—cheering the soul in the act of exercise, just as the senses are regaled at the very instant with the object of their gratification.

But let us remark how continually David was enriching his treasury of spiritual experience with some fresh view of the dealings of God with his soul: some answer to prayer, or some increase of consolation, which he records for his own encouragement, and for the use of the Church of God. Let us seek to imitate him in this respect; and we shall often be enabled to say as he does—This I had—this comfort I enjoyed—this support in trouble—this remarkable manifestation of His love—this confidence I was enabled to maintain—it was made my own, because I kept Your precepts.

This I had—not, this I hoped for. He speaks of "the promise of the life that now is"—that by which God clears away the charge, "It is vain to serve Him; and what profit is it, that we have kept His ordinances?" Nor is it any boasting of merit, but only an acknowledgment of the gracious dispensation of his God. Such a reward for such poor service, can only be undeserved "mercy," having respect, not to the worthiness of the work, but to the faithfulness of the promise. Perfect keeping, according to the legal requirements, there cannot be. Evangelical perfection, in aiming at the mark, and constantly pressing onward towards it, there may be.

How important therefore is it—in the absence of this Christian confidence—to examine, "Is there not a cause?" and what is the cause? Have not "strangers devoured my strength; and I knew it not?" Is the Lord "with me as in months past?"—with me in my closet?—with me in my family?—with me at my table?—with me in my daily employments and conversation with the world? When I hear the faithful people of God telling of His love, and saying—This I had; must I not, if unable to join their cheerful acknowledgment, trace it to my unfaithful walk, and say— This I had not, because I have failed in obedience to Your precepts; because I have been careless and self-indulgent; because I have slighted Your love; because I have "grieved Your Holy Spirit," and forgotten to ask for the "old paths, that I might walk therein, and find rest to my soul?" O let this scrutiny and recollection of our ways realize the constant need of the finished work of Jesus, as our ground of acceptance, and source of strength. This will bring healing, restoration, increasing devotedness, tenderness of conscience, circumspection of walk, and a determination not to rest, until we can make this grateful acknowledgment our own. At the same time, instead of boasting that our own arm, our own diligence, or holiness, "have gotten us" into this favor, we shall cast all our attainments at the feet of Jesus, and crown Him Lord of all forever.

57. You are my portion, O Lord; I have said that I would keep Your words.

Man, as a dependent being, must be possessed of some portion. He cannot live upon himself. It must, however, be not only good, but his own good—something that he may lay claim to as his own. It must also be a large portion, because the powers and capacities to be filled are large. If he has not a satisfying portion, he is a wretched empty creature. But where and how shall he find this portion? "There be many that say, Who will show us any good? Lord! lift up the light of Your countenance upon us." And then the goodness of the Lord, in having offered Himself as the portion of an unworthy sinner! So that we can now lay claim to Him, as having wholly and fully made Himself over to us, and having engaged to employ His perfections for our happiness! "I will be your God." Surely every good is centered in the chief good—the fountain of all blessings, temporal, spiritual, eternal. What, then, is the folly, madness, and guilt, of the sinner, in choosing his "portion in this life:" as if there were no God on the earth, no way of access to Him, or no happiness to be found in Him? That such madness should be found in the heart of man, is a most affecting illustration of his departure from God. But that God's own "people should commit these two evils—forsaking the fountain of living waters, and hewing out for themselves broken cisterns"—this is the fearful astonishment of heaven itself.

But we cannot know and enjoy God as our portion, except as He has manifested Himself in His dear Son. And in the knowledge and enjoyment of Him, can we envy those who "in their lifetime receive their good things," and therefore have nothing more to expect? Never, indeed, does the poverty of the worldling's portion appear more striking, than when contrasted with the enjoyment of the child of God, "Soul"—said the rich fool, "you have much goods laid up for many years." But God said, "This night your soul shall be required of you." Augustine's prayer was, "Lord, give me Yourself!" And thus the believer exults, "Whom have I in heaven but You? and there is none upon earth that I desire but You. Return unto your rest, O my soul. The Lord Himself is the portion of my inheritance and of my cup. You maintain my lot. The lines have fallen to me in pleasant places; yes, I have a goodly heritage. I will bless the Lord, who has given me counsel."

Elsewhere the believer makes this confession to himself, "The Lord is my portion—says my soul." Here, as if to prove his sincerity, he "lifts up his face unto God." "You are my portion, O Lord." And surely the whole world cannot weigh against the comfort of this Christian confidence. For it is as impossible, that His own people should ever be impoverished, as that His own perfections should molder away. But a portion implies, not a source of ordinary pleasure, but of rest and satisfaction, such as leaves nothing else to be desired. Thus the Lord can never be enjoyed, even by His own children—except as a portion—not only above all, but in the place of all. Other objects indeed may be subordinately loved: but of none but Himself must we say, "He is altogether lovely.""In all things He must have the preeminence"—one with the Father in our affections, as in His own subsistence. The moment that any rival is allowed to usurp the throne of the heart, we open the door to disappointment and unsatisfied desires.

But if we take the Lord as our portion, we must take Him as our king. I have said—this is my deliberate resolution—that I would keep Your words. Here is the Christian complete—taking the Lord as his portion, and His word as his rule. And what energy for holy devotedness flows from the enjoyment of this our heavenly portion! Thus delighting ourselves in the Lord, He gives us our heart's desire; and every desire identifies itself with His service. All that we are and all that we have, are His; cheerfully surrendered as His right, and willingly employed in his work. Thus do we evidence our interest in His salvation; for "Christ became the author of eternal salvation unto all those who obey Him."

Reader! inquire—was my choice of this Divine portion considerate, free, unreserved? Am I resolved that it shall be steadfast and abiding? that death itself shall not separate me from the enjoyment of it? Am I ready to receive a Sovereign as well as a Savior? Oh! let me have a whole Christ for my portion! Oh! let Him have a whole heart for His possession. Oh! let me call nothing mine but Him.

'The heart touched with the loadstone of Divine love: trembling with godly fear, yet still looking towards God by fixed believing—points at the love of election. He who loves may be sure he was loved first. He who chooses God in Christ for his delight and portion, may conclude confidently, that God has chosen him to enjoy Him, and be happy in Him forever.' (Leighton)

58. I entreated Your favor with my whole heart; be merciful unto me according to Your word.

Delight in the Lord as our portion, naturally leads us to entreat His favor as "life," and "better than life," to our souls. And if we have said that we would keep His words, we shall still entreat His favor—to strengthen and encourage us in His way. We shall entreat it with our whole hearts, as though we felt our infinite need of it, and were determined to wrestle for it in Jacob's spirit, "I will not let You go, except You bless me." If we have known what unspeakable happiness it is to be brought into the favor of God "by the blood of Christ;" and if by "Him also we have access unto that grace wherein we stand," how shall we prize the sense of Divine favor, the light of our Father's countenance! We shall never be weary of this source of daily enjoyment. It is to us as the light of the sun, which shines every day with renewed and unabated pleasure. We "joy in God, through our Lord Jesus Christ, by whom we have now received the atonement." Mercy, however, is the source of that favor which we entreat; and the word is the warrant of our expectation— Be merciful to us according to Your word. As sinners, we need this favor. As believers, we entreat it in the assurance that praying breath, as the breath of faith, will not be spent in vain. Any indulged indolence, or neglect, or unfaithfulness—relaxing our diligence, and keeping back the whole heart from God—will, indeed, never fail to remove the sunshine from the soul. But the blood of Christ still opens the way of return to the backslider, even though he may have wandered, as it were, to the ends of the earth. For "if from thence you shall seek the Lord your God, you shall find Him, if you seek Him with all your heart and all your soul.""A whole heart" in seeking the Lord, is the seal of the Lord's heart in returning to us, "I will rejoice over them"—says He, "to do them good; and I will plant them in this land assuredly, with my whole heart, and with my whole soul."

Reader! if you are a child of God, the favor of God will be to you the "one thing needful." In other things, you will not venture to choose for yourself; "for who knows what is good for man in this life?" But in this choice you will be decided. This grand, incomparable desire will fill your heart. This will be to you as the portion of ten thousand worlds. Nothing will satisfy besides.

You may, indeed, be a child of God without the enjoyment of the blessing; but not so, if you be content to be without it. If the wise sovereignty of our God is pleased to withhold it, still the child in submission will entreat it. Much more, when it is withdrawn in righteous chastening of carelessness or folly, will the cry be reiterated upon the ground of the covenant—Be merciful to me according to Your word.

59. I thought on my ways, and turned my feet to Your testimonies.

The Psalmist's determination, lately mentioned, to keep God's word, was not a hasty impulse, but a considerate resolve, the result of much thinking on his former ways of sin and folly. How many, on the other hand, seem to pass through the world into eternity without a serious thought on their ways! Multitudes live for the world—forget God and die! This is their history. What their state is, is written as with a sunbeam in the word of truth, "The wicked shall be turned into hell, and all the nations that forget God." When "no man repents him of his wickedness, saying, What have I done?"—this banishing of reflection is the character and ruin of an unthinking world. Perhaps one serious thought might be the new birth of the soul to God—the first step of the way to heaven. For when a man is arrested by the power of grace, he is as one awaking out of sleep, lost in solemn and serious thoughts—'What am I? where am I? what have I been? what have I been doing? I have a soul, which is my everlasting all—yet a soul without a Savior—lost—undone. What is my prospect for its happiness? Behind me is a world of vanity, an empty void. Before me a fearful unknown eternity. Within me an awakened conscience, to remind me of an angry God, and a devouring hell. If I stay here, I perish; if I go forward, I perish; if I return home to my offended Father, I can but perish.' The resolution is formed; "'I will arise," and fight my way through all difficulties and discouragements to my Father's house.' Thus does every prodigal child of God "come to himself;" and this his first step of return to his God involves the whole work of repentance. The wanderer thinks on his ways, and turns his feet to the testimonies of his God; witnessing, to his joyful surprise, every hindrance removed, the way marked with the blood of his Savior, and his Father's smiles in this way welcoming his return homeward. This turn is the practical exercise of a genuine faith; and "because he considers, and turns away from all his transgressions that he has committed, he shall surely live—he shall not die."

But this considerate exercise is needed, not only upon the first entrance into the ways of God, but in every successive step of our path. It will form the habit of daily "communion with our own heart;" without which, disorder and confusion will bewilder our steps. Probably David did not know how far his feet had backslidden from the ways of his God, until this serious consideration of his state brought conviction to his soul—so imperceptible is the declining of the heart from God! Nor is it a few transient thoughts or resolutions, that will effect this turn of the heart to God. A man may maintain a fruitless struggle to return to God for many years in sincerity and earnestness; while the simple act of faith in the power and love of Jesus will at once bring him back. Thus, while "thinking on his ways," let him walk in Christ as the way of return—and he will walk in the way of God's testimonies with acceptance and delight. In this spirit of simplicity, he will listen to the first whisper of the convincing voice of the Spirit, which marks the early steps of return from secret declension from God. He will also thankfully accept the chastening rod, as the Lord's appointed instrument of restoring His wandering children to Himself. For so prone are they to turn their feet away from the Lord—so continually are they "turning aside like a deceitful bow."—and so deaf are they, from the constitution of their sinful nature, to the ordinary calls of God; that, in love and tender faithfulness to their souls, He is often constrained, by the stroke of His heavy hand, to arrest them in their career of thoughtlessness, and turn them back to Himself. Most suitable then for such a state is the prayer of Basil—'Give me any cross, that may bring me into subjection to Your cross; and save me in spite of myself!'

60. I made haste, and delayed not, to keep Your commandments.

A superficial conviction brings with it a sense of duty, without constraining to it. Men stand reasoning and doubting, instead of making haste. But a sound conviction sweeps away all excuses and delays. No time will be lost between making and performing resolutions. Indeed, in a matter of life and death—of eternal life and eternal death—the call is too clear for debate, and there is no room for delay. Many a precious soul has been lost by waiting for "a more convenient season"—a period, which probably never arrives, and which the willful neglect of present opportunity provokes God to put far away. Today is God's time. Tomorrow ruins thousands. Tomorrow is another world. "Today—while it is called today; if you will hear His voice" "make haste, and delay not." Resolutions, however sincere, and convictions, however serious, "will pass away, as the morning cloud and as the early dew," unless they are carefully cherished, and instantly improved. The bonds of iniquity will soon prove too strong for the bonds of your own resolutions; and in the first hour of temptation, conviction left to chance to grow, will prove as powerless as the "seven green withs" to bind the giant Samson. If ever delays are dangerous, much more are they in this concern of eternity. If therefore convictions begin to work, instantly yield to their influence. If any worldly or sinful desire is touched, let this be the moment for its crucifixion. If any affection is kindled towards the Savior, give immediate expression to its voice. If any grace is reviving, let it be called forth into instant duty. This is the best—the only—expedient to fix and detain the motion of the Spirit now striving in the heart: and who knows but the improvement of the present advantage may be the moment of victory over difficulties hitherto found insuperable, and may open the path to heaven with less interruption, and more steady progress?

It is from the neglect of this haste that convictions often alternately ebb and flow so long, before they settle in a sound conversion. Indeed the instant movement—making haste, and delaying not—marks the principle of the spiritual life. This was the prodigal's resolution, no sooner formed than in action. He said, "I will arise, and go to my father—and he arose, and came to his father." When Matthew heard the voice, "Follow Me—he left all, rose up and followed Him." When Zaccheus was called from the top of the sycamore-tree, "Make haste, and come down, for today I must abide at your house—he made haste, and came down, and received Him joyfully."

Ah! as you prize a hope for eternity; as you wish to "flee from the wrath to come," and to "flee for refuge to the hope set before you"—beware of smothering early convictions. They may prove the first dawn of eternal day upon the soul—the first visit of the quickening Spirit to the heart. Guard them with unceasing watchfulness. Nourish them with believing prayer. "Exercise" them unto practical "godliness." "Quench not the Spirit." Let not the spark be extinguished by opposition of the world. Let it not expire for lack of the fuel of grace. Let it not lie dormant or inactive. "Stir up the gift of God which is in you." Every exercise, every motion, adds grace to grace, and increases its vigor, health, and fruitfulness. The more we do, the more we find we can do. The withered hand, whenever stretched forth in obedience to the Savior's word, and in dependence on His grace, will never lack a supply of spiritual strength. Every successive act strengthens the disposition, until a continual succession has formed the ready and active habit of godliness. Thus the Lord works in setting us to work. Therefore think—determine—turn—make haste, and delay not; and we wish you God speed; "we bless you in the name of the Lord."

Professor! did you realize eternity, would you hover as you do between heaven and hell? If you were truly alive and awake, no motion would be swift enough for your desire to "flee from the wrath to come"—to flee for refuge to lay hold on the hope set before you." If ever God should touch your heart to feel the heavenly sweetness of communion with Him, will there be no regret, that the privilege was not sooner sought and enjoyed? Had I betaken myself earlier to a hearty interest in the ways of God, how much more knowledge, experience, and comfort should I have attained! how much more honor should I have brought to God! how much more profit to my fellow-sinners! Remember, every day of carnal pleasure or lukewarm formality is a day lost to God—to your own happiness—to eternity.

A word to the believer—Have you any doubts to clear up, any peace to regain in the ways of the Lord? Make haste to set your heart to the work. Make haste to the blood of atonement. Be on the watch to "hear the Shepherd's voice," even if it be the voice of reproof. Promptness is a most important exercise of the habit of faith. Delay brings guilt to the conscience. The blessing of conviction—the comfortable sense of acceptance—the freedom of the Lord's service—is sacrificed to sloth and procrastination. The work that is hard today will be harder still tomorrow, by the resistance of this day's convictions. A greater cost of self-denial, a heavier burden of sorrow, and increasing unfitness for the service of God, will be the issue of delay. Be continually therefore looking for some beam of light to descend, and some influence of grace to flow in upon you from your exalted Head. A simple and vigorous faith will quickly enliven you with that love, delight, rejoicing in the Lord, readiness to work, and cheerfulness to suffer, which will once again make the ways of God "pleasantness and peace" to your soul.

61. The bands of the wicked have robbed me; but I have not forgotten Your law.

Are we not too apt to cull out the easy work of the Gospel, and to call this love to God? Whereas true love is supreme, and ready to be at some loss, and to part with near and dear objects, knowing that He "is able to give us much more than" we lose for Him. Our resolution to keep His commandments will soon be put to the test. Some trial to the flesh will prove whether we flinch from the cross, or study to prepare ourselves for it. Few of us, perhaps, have literally known this trial of David. But the lesson to be learned from his frame of mind under it, is of great importance to all who profess to have their "treasure in heaven." It teaches us, that only exercised faith will sustain us in the time of trouble. This faith will enable us instantly to recollect our heavenly portion, and to assure our interest in it, in a remembrance of the law of our God. Had David forgotten God's law, no other resource of comfort opened before him. But it was ready—substantiating to his mind "the things that were not seen and eternal." Look again at the Apostle's deliberate estimate of this very trial—not only bearing his loss, but absolutely forgetting it in the enjoyment of his better portion, "Yes, doubtless, and I count all things but loss for the excellency of the knowledge of Christ Jesus my Lord, for whom I have suffered the loss of all things; and do count them but dung, that I may win Christ."

The temper of mind under such trials as this, serves indeed most clearly to discover the real bent of the heart. If we are in possession of a spiritual and heavenly portion, we shall bear to be robbed by the bands of the wicked, and yet, "hold fast our profession." David, under this calamity, "encouraged himself in the Lord his God." Job, under the same visitation, "fell upon the ground, and worshiped." The blessings, indeed, we lose, are but as a feather compared with the blessings which we retain. The Providence of God is an abundant support for His children. Their prospects (not to speak of their present privileges) effectually secure them from ultimate loss, even in the spoiling of their worldly all. Thus the early Christians permitted the bands of the wicked to rob them—no, "they took joyfully the spoiling of their goods; knowing in themselves, that they had in heaven a better and an enduring substance." We have, indeed, little reason to be frightened from religion by the anticipation of its trials. The exchange of the world for God, and of the service of sin for the ways of heaven, leaves no room for regret in life, in death, or in eternity. The Christian's darkest hour is ten thousand times brighter than the brightest day of the ungodly. The hope of the crown will enable us to bear the cross, and to realize its sanctifying support as a matter for unbounded praise.

But how desolate are the poor votaries of the world in the hour of trouble! Ignorant of the all-sufficiency of the refuge of the gospel; instead of being driven to it by the gracious visitations of God, they would rather retreat into any hiding-place of their own, than direct their steps backward to Him. Their circumstances of distress are most intensely aggravated by the sullen rebellion of the heart, which refuses to listen to those breathings of the Savior's love, that would guide them to Himself, as their sure, peaceful, and eternal rest! Would that we could persuade them to cast their souls in penitence and faith before His blessed cross! The burden of sin, as Bunyan's pilgrim found, would then drop from their backs. And this burden once removed—other burdens, before intolerable, would be found comparatively light; no—all burdens would be removed in the enjoyment of the Christian privilege of casting all—sin—care—and trouble, upon Jesus. Contrast the state of destitution without Him, with the abundant resources of the people of God. We have a double heaven—a heaven on earth, and a heaven above—one in present sunshine—the other in "the city, which has no need of the sun"— where our joys will be immediate—unclouded—eternal. Thus our portion embraces both worlds. Our present "joy no man takes from us;" and we have "laid up treasures in heaven," where the bands of the wicked can "never break through, nor steal."

Christian! does not your faith realize a subsistence of things not seen? The only realities in the apprehension of the world are "the things that are seen, and are temporal." Your realities are "the things that are not seen, and are eternal." Then, remember—if you be robbed of your earthly all, your treasure is beyond the reach of harm. You can still say, "I have all, and abound." You can live splendidly upon your God, though all is beggary around you. You confess the remembrance of the law of your God to be your unfailing stay, "Unless Your law had been my delights, I should then have perished in my affliction."

62. At midnight I will rise to give thanks unto You: because of Your righteous judgments.

Another exercise of sacred pleasure is the ways of the Lord! His portion was always satisfying to this holy man, and he was daily feeding upon it with fresh delight. There was no occasion for the painful restrictions and mortifications of a monastery to oblige him to self-denying observances. Much less was there any desire, by these extraordinary services, to work out a righteousness of his own, to recommend him to the favor of God. His diligence in this heavenly work was the spontaneous effusion of a heart "filled with the Spirit." Presenting the morning and the evening service "seven times a day," was not enough for him; but he must rise at midnight to continue his song of praise. These hours sometimes had been spent in overwhelming sorrow. Now they were given to the privileged employment of praise. Indeed it seems to have been his frequent custom to stir up his gratitude by a midnight review of the Lord's daily manifestations of mercy. A most exciting example—especially for the child of sorrow, when "wearisome nights are appointed to him," and he "is full of tossings to and fro unto the dawning of the day!" Thus "let the saints be joyful in glory; let them sing aloud upon their beds." We observe this Christian enjoyment under circumstances of outward trial. When "at midnight—their feet made fast in the stocks—Paul and Silas prayed, and sang praises to God:" they gave thanks, because of His righteous judgments.

We often complain of our lack of spirituality in the Divine life—how much our body hinders the ascent of the soul heavenwards—how often drowsiness overcomes our evening communion with our God; the "weakness of the flesh" overpowering the "willingness of the Spirit." But, after making all due allowances for constitutional infirmity, how far are we "instant in season and out of season" in the mortification of the flesh? Do we earnestly seek for a heart delighting in heavenly things? The more the flesh is denied for the service of God, the more we shall be elevated for the enjoyment, and realize the privilege of the work; and instead of having so often to mourn that our "souls cleave to the dust," we shall "mount upwards with eagles' wings," and even now by anticipation, take our place before "the throne of God and the Lamb." Such is the active influence of self-denial in exercising our graces, and promoting our comfort! Oh! how much more fervent would be our prayers— how much more fruitful in blessings—were they enlivened with more abundant delight in the 'angelic work of praise!' (Baxter.) The theme is always before us. The subject of the heavenly song should constantly engage our songs on earth—Jesus and His love—the "worthiness of the Lamb that was slain"—His "power, and riches, and wisdom, and strength, and honor, and glory, and blessing." Midnight wakefulness would be far sweeter than slumber; yes, night itself would be turned into day, did the judgments of God, as manifested in the glory of the Savior, thus occupy our hearts. Lord! tune my heart to Your praise, and then no time will be unseasonable for this blessed employment. Time thus redeemed from sleep will be an foretaste of the unwearied service of heaven.

63. I am a companion of all who fear you, and of those who keep your precepts.

Those that love the Lord's service naturally associate with kindred spirits—with those that fear Him, and keep His precepts. These two features identify the same character: as cheerful obedience is always the fruit of filial fear. These then are the Lord's people; and union with Him is in fact union with them. Sometimes the society of the refined and intelligent of this world may be more congenial to our natural taste. But ought there not to be a restraint here? Ought not the Christian to say, "Surely the fear of God is not in this place?" and "should I love them that hate the Lord?" Let those of us, who live in close, and to a certain degree necessary, contact with the world, subject their hearts to an evening scrutiny on this subject. 'Has the society of this day refreshed my soul, or raised my heart to spiritual things? Has it promoted a watchful temper? Or has it not rather "quenched the spirit" of prayer, and restrained my communion with God? To meet the Christian in ordinary courtesy, not in unity of heart, is a sign of an unspiritual walk with God. Fellowship with God is "walking in the light." "Fellowship one with another" is the natural flow. "The communion of saints" is the fruit and effect of communion with God.

The calls of duty, or the leadings of Providence, may indeed unavoidably connect us with those, who "have no fear of God before their eyes." Nor should we repel them, by religiously affecting a sullen or uncourteous habit. But such men, whatever be their attractions, will not be the companions of our choice. Fellowship with them is to "remove the ancient landmark;" to forget the broad line of separation between us and them; and to venture into the most hazardous atmosphere. If indeed our hearts were ascending, like a flame of fire, with a natural motion heavenwards, and carrying with them all in their way, the choice of the companions of our pilgrimage would be a matter of little importance. But so deadening to our spirit is the conversation of the men of this world (however commanding their talents, or interesting their topics), that even if we have been just before enlivened by the high privilege of communion with God, the free and self-indulgent interchange of their society will benumb our spiritual powers, and quickly freeze them again. To underrate therefore the privileged association with them that fear God, is to incur—not only a most awful responsibility in the sight of God; but also a most serious hazard to our own souls.

If then we are not ashamed to confess ourselves Christians, let us not shrink from walking in fellowship with Christians. Even if they should exhibit some repulsive features of character, they bear the image of Him, whom we profess to love inexpressibly and incomparably above all. They will be our companions in our eternal home; they ought therefore to be our brothers now. How sweet, and holy, and heavenly, is this near relation with them in our common Lord! Shall we not readily consent to his judgment, who pronounced "the righteous to be more excellent than his neighbor?" "Iron sharpens iron." If then "the iron be blunt," this will be one of the best means of "whetting the edge." The most established servants of God gladly acknowledge the sensible refreshment of this union of heart. It is marked in the word of God, as the channel of the communication of heavenly wisdom—as a feature in the character of the citizens of Zion—and as that disposition, which is distinguished with manifest tokens of the Savior's presence; and which the great day will crown with the special seal of His remembrance. "They that feared the Lord spoke often one to another; and the Lord hearkened, and heard" it; "and a book of remembrance was written before Him for them that feared the Lord, and that thought upon His name. And they shall be Mine, says the Lord of Hosts, in that day when I make up My jewels."

64. The earth, O Lord, is full of Your mercy: teach me Your statutes.

What full provision is made for man's happiness! The first creation was full of mercy. God knew that He had created a being full of want. Every faculty wanted some suitable object, as the source of enjoyment in the gratification—of suffering in the denial; and now has He charged

Himself with making provision for them all—so perfect, that no want is left unprovided for.

But what a picture does the earth now present on every side—a world of rebels! yet a world full of the mercy of the Lord! "O Lord, how manifold are Your works! in wisdom have You made them all. The earth is full of Your riches. The eyes of all wait upon You, and You give them their meat in due season. You open Your hand, and satisfy the desire of every living thing." And how does the contemplation of the Lord's mercy in providence encourage our faith, in the expectancy of spiritual privileges! "O Lord! You preserve man and beast. How excellent is Your loving-kindness, O God! therefore the children of men put their trust under the shadow of Your wings. They shall be abundantly satisfied with the fatness of Your house; and You shall make them drink of the river of Your pleasures." 'As You largely bestow Your blessings upon all creatures according to their nature and condition, so I desire the spiritual blessings of the lively light of Your law and word, which are fitting and convenient for the being and happiness of my soul.' As an ignorant sinner, "what I see not, teach me." Teach me Your statutes; that which You have appointed, as the way of duty, and the path to glory—that path which I am utterly unable to discover, or when discovered, to walk in, without the help of Your grace. And indeed the hearts of His people are the vessels, into which the Lord is continually pouring more and more of Himself, until they shall "be filled with all the fullness of God." Every good, according to its character and degree, is diffusive. And thus the goodness or mercy of God pervades His whole universe—natural—plentiful—free—communicative.

Yet none but a believer will understand how to use the plea which is here employed. The mercy that he sees on every side, is to him a pledge and earnest of that mercy, which his soul needs within. The world indeed in its present fallen state, when seen through the medium of pride and discontent, exhibits a picture of misery, not of mercy; and only ministers occasion for complaint against the Creator. But the believer—feeling the infinite and eternal desert of sin—cannot but know, that the lowest exercise of goodness in God is an act of free undeserved mercy. No wonder then that he sees mercy in everything—in every part of the universe of God—a world full of mercy. The very food we eat, our clothing, our habitations, the contrivances for our comfort, are not mere displays of goodness, but manifestations of mercy. Having forfeited all claim upon the smallest consideration of God, there could have been no just ground of complaint, had all these blessings been made occasions of suffering, instead of comfort and indulgence.

Indeed is it not a marvel, that when man—full of mercy—is lifting up his hand against his God—employing against him all the faculties, which His mercy gave and has preserved—that God should be so seldom provoked to strike by their aggravated provocations? What multitude— what weight—what variety of mercy does He still shower upon us! Even our hair, though seemingly so unimportant, the seat of loathsome, defiling, and even mortal disease—is the object of His special care. All the limbs of the body, all the faculties of the mind, all the affections of the heart, all the powers of the will: keeping us in health, and capable of acting for our own happiness—how does He restrain them from those exercises or movements which might be fatal to our happiness!

And then the question naturally recurs—and to a spiritual mind will never weary by its recurrence—Whence flows all this mercy? Oh! it is delightful indeed to answer such an inquiry—delightful to contemplate Him, "in whom" we are not only "blessed with all spiritual blessings;" but who is also the medium, through which our temporal comforts are conveyed to us. How sweet to eye these mercies, as bought with the most precious blood that ever was known in the world, and to mark the print of the nails of our crucified Friend stamped upon the least of them! We allow it to add a relish to our enjoyments, that we can consider them as provided by some beloved friend; and should not our mercies be doubly sweet in remembrance of that munificent Friend, who purchased them for us so dearly; who bestows them upon us so richly; yes, who gives Himself with them all?

Have we heard of this mercy of God? And do we feel the need of it for ourselves—for every moment? Then let us apply to the throne of grace in the free and open way of acceptance and access. Let us go to the King (as Benhadad's servants to the king of Israel,) in the spirit of self-condemnation and faith. Our acceptance does not depend (as in the case referred to) upon a "perhaps;" but it rests upon the sure word of promise, "Him who comes to Me, I will in no wise cast out."

65. You have dealt well with Your servant, O Lord, according to Your word.

There is a time for all things in the believer's experience—for confession, prayer, and praise. This Psalm mostly expresses the confessions and prayers of the man of God—yet mingled with thankful acknowledgments of mercy. He had prayed, "Deal bountifully with Your servant." Perhaps here is the acknowledgment of the answer to his prayer—You have dealt well with Your servant, O Lord, according to Your word. And who among us has not daily reason to make the same acknowledgment? Even in those trials, when we have indulged hard thoughts of God, a clearer view of His judgments, and a more simple dependence upon His faithfulness and love, will rebuke our impatience and unbelief, and encourage our trust. Subsequent experience altered Jacob's hasty view of the Lord's dealings with him. In a moment of peevishness, the recollection of the supposed death of a beloved son, and the threatened bereavement of another, tempted him to say, "All these things are against me." At a brighter period of his day, when clouds were beginning to disperse, we hear that "the spirit of Jacob revived: And Jacob said, It is enough; Joseph my son is yet alive, I will go and see him before I die." And when his evening sun was going down almost without a cloud, in the believing act of "blessing the sons of" his beloved "Joseph," how clearly does he retract the language of his former sinful impatience!, "God, before whom my fathers, Abraham and Isaac, did walk—the God which fed me all my life long to this day—the Angel which redeemed me from all evil, bless the lads!" This surely was in the true spirit of the acknowledgment—You have dealt well with Your servant, O Lord, according to Your word.

And how is it that any of us have ever harbored a suspicion of unbelief? Has God in any one instance falsified His promise? Has "the vision" failed to come at the end? Has it ever "lied?" Has He not "confirmed His promise by an oath," "that we might have two immutable things" as the ground of "strong consolation?" Any degree less than the full credit that He deserves, is admitting the false principle, that God is a man, that He should lie, and the son of man, that He should repent. It weakens the whole spiritual frame, shakes our grasp of the promise, destroys our present comfort, and brings foreboding apprehensions of the future. Whereas, if we have faith and patience to wait, "in the mount the Lord shall be seen." "All things" may seem to be "against us," while at the very moment, under the wonder-working hand of God, they are "working together for our good." When therefore we "are in heaviness through manifold temptations," and we discover a "needs-be" for it all; and "the trial of faith is found unto praise and honor and glory"—when we are thus reaping the fruitful discipline of our Father's school, must we not put a fresh seal to our testimony—You have dealt well with Your servant, O Lord? But why should we delay our acknowledgment until we come out of our trial? Ought we not to give it even in the midst of our "heaviness?" Faith has enabled many, and would enable us, to "glorify God in the fires;" to "trust" Him, even when "walking in darkness, and having no light;" and, even while smarting under His chastening rod, to acknowledge, that He has dealt well with us.

But if I doubt the reasonableness of this acknowledgment, then let me, while suffering under trials, endeavor to take up different language. 'Lord, You have dealt ill with Your servant; You have not kept Your word.' If in a moment of unbelief my impatient heart, like Jacob's, could harbor such a dishonorable suspicion, my conscience would soon smite me with conviction—'What! shall I, who am "called out of darkness into marvelous light"—shall I, who am rescued from slavery and death, and brought to a glorious state of liberty and life, complain? Shall I, who have been redeemed at so great a price, and who have a right to "all the promises of God in Christ Jesus," and who am now an "heir of God, and joint heir with Christ," murmur at my Father's will? Alas, that my heart should prove so foolish, so weak, so ungrateful! Lord! I would acknowledge with thankfulness, and yet with humiliation, You have dealt well with Your servant, according to Your word.' But how sinfully do we neglect these honorable and cheering acknowledgments! Were we habitually to mark them for future remembrance, we should be surprised to see how their numbers would multiply. "If we should count them, they are more in number than the sand." And truly such recollections—enhancing every common, as well as every special mercy—would come up as a sweet savor to God "by Christ Jesus.""Bless the Lord, O my soul, and all that is within me, bless His holy name; and do not forget all His benefits."

66. Teach me good judgment and knowledge; for I have believed Your commandments.

If the perception of the Lord's merciful dealings with my soul is obscure—Teach me good judgment and knowledge. Give me a clear and enlarged apprehension, that I may be ready with my acknowledgment, "All the paths of the Lord are mercy and truth." Or even with an enlightened assurance of His wise and faithful dispensations, still would I urge this petition before Him, as needful for every step of my path.

Indeed this prayer illustrates the simplicity and intelligence of Christian faith—always desiring, asking, and expecting the most suitable blessings. For what blessings can be more suitable to an ignorant sinner, than good judgment and knowledge: knowledge of ourselves, of our Savior, of the way of obedience—and good judgment, to apply this knowledge to some valuable end? These two parts of our intellectual furniture have a most important connection and dependence upon each other. Knowledge is the speculative perception of general truth. Judgment is the practical application of it to the heart and conduct. No school, but the school of Christ—no teaching, but the teaching of the Spirit—can ever give this good judgment and knowledge. Solomon asks it for himself—Paul for his people. Both direct us to God as the sole fountain and author.

We cannot fail to observe a very common defect in Christians;— warm affections connected with a blind or loose judgment. Hence, too often, a lightness in religion, equally unsteady in profession and in practice—easily satisfied with a narrow compass in the vast field of Scripture, instead of grasping a full survey of those truths, which are so intimately connected with our Christian establishment and privilege. Much perplexing doubt, discouragement, and fear; much mistaken apprehension of important truth, much coldness and backsliding of heart and conduct, arises from the want of an accurate and full apprehension of the scriptural system.

This prayer has a special application to the tender and sensitive child of God. The disease of his constitution is too often a scrupulous conscience—one of the most active and successful enemies to his settled peace and quietness. The faculty of conscience partakes, with every other power of man, of the injury of the fall; and therefore, with all its intelligence, honesty, and power, it is liable to misconception. Like a defect of vision, it often displaces objects: and, in apparently conflicting duties, that which touches the feeling, or accords with the temper, is preferred to one, which, though more remotely viewed, really possessed a higher claim. Thus it pronounces its verdict from the predominance of feeling, rather than from the exercise of judgment—more from an indistinct perception of the subject presented to the mind, than from a simple immediate reference "to the law and testimony." Again—matters of trivial moment are often insisted upon, to the neglect of important principles. External points of offence are more considered, than the habitual mortification of the inward principle. Conformity to the world in dress and appearance is more strongly censured than the general spirit of worldliness in the temper and conduct of outward non-conformists; while the spirit of separation from the world, is totally disregarded. Thus are non-essentials confounded with fundamentals—things indifferent with things unlawful, from a narrow misconception of what is directly forbidden and allowed. Conscience, therefore, must not be trusted without the light of the word of God; and most important is the prayer— Teach me good judgment and knowledge.

The exercises of this state of feeling are both endless and causeless. In the well-intended endeavor to guard against a devious track, the mind is constantly harassed with an over-anxious inquiry, whether the right path is accurately discovered; and thus at once the pleasure and the progress of the journey are materially hindered. The influence therefore of this morbid sensibility is strenuously to be resisted. It renders the strait way more strait. It retards the work of grace in the soul. It is usually connected with self-righteousness. It savors of, and tends to produce, hard thoughts of God. It damps our cheerfulness in His service, and unfits us for the duty of the present moment. What however is more than all to be deprecated, is, that it multiplies sin; or, to speak more clearly, it superinduces another species of sin, besides the actual transgression of the law of God. For opposition to the dictates of conscience in any particular is sin, even though the act itself may be allowed by the law of God. We may therefore sin in the act of doing good, or in obedience to the liberty and enjoyment of the gospel, as well as in the allowed transgression of the law. Indeed, under the bondage of a scrupulous conscience, we seem to be entangled in the sad necessity of sinning. The dictates of conscience, even when grounded upon misconception, are authoritative. Listening to its suggestions may be sinning against "the liberty, with which Christ has made us free," and in which we are commanded to "stand fast." No human authority can free from its bonds. Resistance to its voice is disobedience to God's viceregent, and therefore, in a qualified sense at least, disobedience to God Himself. And thus it is sin, even when that which conscience condemns may be innocent.

The evil of a scrupulous conscience may often be traced to a diseased temperament of body, to a naturally weak or perverted understanding, to the unfavorable influence of early prejudice—to a lack of simple exercise of faith, or perception of the matters of faith. In these cases faith may be sincere, though weak; and the sin, such as it is, is a sin of infirmity, calling for our pity, forbearance, prayer, and help. In many instances however, willful ignorance, false shame that will not inquire, or a pertinacious adherence to deep-rooted opinion, is the source of the disease. Now such persons must be roused, even at the hazard of wounding the conscience of the more tenderly scrupulous. But as the one class decidedly sin, and the other too frequently indulge their infirmity, the excitement will probably be ultimately useful to both. Both need to have the conscience enlightened; and to obtain "a right judgment in all things"—by a more diligent "search in the Scriptures"—by "seeking the law at the mouth of the priest"—and, above all, by earnest prayer with the Psalmist—Teach me good judgment and knowledge. Thus they will discern between what is imperative, and what is indifferent; between what is lawful, and what is expedient. If "whatever is not of faith is sin," then the only prospect of the removal of the doubt will be increase of faith—that is, a more full persuasion of the Divine warrant and instruction. "Howbeit there is not in everyone this knowledge:" yet the exhortation speaks alike to all, "Grow in grace, and in the knowledge of our Lord and Savior Jesus Christ." Indeed the most favorable symptoms of scrupulosity (except where the disease originates in external causes) partake of the guilt of willful ignorance; because none can be said sincerely to ask for good judgment and knowledge, who do not diligently improve all means of obtaining it. If therefore, the scrupulous shrink from honestly seeking the resolution of their difficulties in private conferences (where they are to be had) with Ministers or experienced Christians, so far they must be considered as wilfully ignorant. We would indeed "receive them," "bear with their infirmities," and encourage them to expect relief from their hard bondage in the way of increasing diligence, humility, and prayer. While their minds are in doubt concerning the path of duty, their actions must be imperfect and unsatisfactory. Let them therefore wait, inquire, and pray, until their way be made plain. This done, let them act according to their conscience, allowing nothing that it condemns, neglecting nothing which it requires. The responsibility of error (should error be eventually detected) will not be—the too implicit following of the guidance of conscience—but the want of due care and diligence for its more clear illumination. Generally, however, the rule will apply, "If your eye be single, your whole body shall be full of light."

But, besides the scrupulous conscience, the imperfectly enlightened conscience presents a case equally to be deprecated. Often does it charge to a sinful source those incessant variations of feelings, which originate in bodily indisposition, or accidental influence of temptation. Sins of infirmity are confounded with sins of indulgence: occasional with habitual transgressions of duty. Only a part of the character is brought under cognisance: and while short-comings or surprisals are justly condemned: yet the exercise of contrition, faith, love, and watchfulness, is passed by unnoticed. Thus the gospel becomes the very reverse of the appointment of its gracious Author. It brings ashes for beauty, mourning for the oil of joy, and the spirit of heaviness for the garment of praise. If this evil is "not a sin unto death," it is "a sore evil under the sun," which may often give occasion for the prayer—Teach me good judgment and knowledge; that, in the simplicity of faith, I may be blessed with a tender conscience, and be delivered from the bondage of a scrupulous, and from the perplexity of an unenlightened, conscience. Let my heart never condemn me where it ought not. Let it never fail to condemn me where it ought.

But, alas! the perception of our need of this good judgment and knowledge, is far too indistinct and uninfluential. We need to cry for these valuable blessings with deeper earnestness, and more diligent and patient waiting upon God. Divine wisdom is a treasury, that does not spend by giving; and we may ask to be enriched to the utmost extent of our wants, "in full assurance of faith." But this faith embraces the whole revelation of God—the commandments as well as the promises. And thus it becomes the principle of Christian obedience. For can we believe these commandments to be as they are represented, "holy, just, and good," and not delight in them? "In those is continuance"—said the prophet, "and we shall be saved." Convinced of their perfection, acknowledging their obligations, loving them, and living in them, we shall "come to full age" in the knowledge of the Gospel, and, "by reason of use have our senses exercised to discern both good and evil."

67. Before I was afflicted I went astray; but now have I kept Your word.

The teaching of good judgment and knowledge will lead us to deprecate, instead of desiring, a prosperous state. But should the Christian, by the appointment of God, be thrown into the seductive atmosphere, he will feel the prayer that is so often put into his lips, most peculiarly expressive of his need, "In all time of our wealth—Good Lord, deliver us!" (Litany.) A time of wealth is indeed a time of special need. It is hard to restrain the flesh, when so many are the baits for its indulgence. Such mighty power is here given to the enemy, while our perception of his power is fearfully weakened! Many and affecting instances are recorded of the hardening of the heart even of the Lord's people, in the deadening influence of a proud and worldly spirit. But the fate of the ungodly is written as with a sunbeam for our warning, "When Jeshurun waxed fat, he kicked—I spoke to you in your prosperity; but you said, I will not hear." But how awful will be the period, when the question shall speak to the conscience with all the poignancy of self-conviction, "What fruit had you then in those things whereof you are now ashamed?" What is the end of this flowery path? "Death!" "Surely You set them in slippery places: You cast them down into destruction. How are they brought into desolation as in a moment! They are utterly consumed with terrors" "the prosperity of fools shall destroy them."

Our Savior's allotment for His people, "In the world you shall have tribulation"—marks not less His wisdom than His love. This is the gracious rod, by which He scourges back His prodigal children to Himself. This is the wise discipline, by which He preserves them from the poisoned sweetness of carnal allurements, and keeps their hearts in a simple direction towards Himself, as the well-spring of their everlasting joy. With all of them this one method has been pursued. All have been taught in one school. All have known the power of affliction in some of its varied forms of inward conflict or outward trouble. All have found a time of affliction a time of love. All have given proof, that the pains bestowed upon them have not been in vain. Thus did Manasseh in affliction beseech "the Lord, and humble himself greatly before the Lord God of his fathers." Thus also in afflictions the Lord "heard Ephraim bemoaning himself;" and beheld Israel "seeking Him early," and the forlorn wandering child casting a wishful, penitent look towards his Father's house, as if the pleasures that had enticed his heart from home, were now embittered to the soul.

And thus the Christian can give some account of the means, by which his Father is leading and preparing him for heaven. Perhaps he did not at first see the reason. It was matter of faith, not of consciousness. But in looking back, how clear the path, how valuable the benefit, Before I was afflicted, I went astray: but now have I kept Your word. 'I never prized it before. I could indeed scarcely be said to know it. I never understood its comfort, until affliction expounded it to me. I never until now saw its suitableness to my case.' But what an heightened aggravation of guilt, when these especial mercies fail of their gracious end—when

123

vanity, worldliness, and sin still reign with uncontrolled sway! Ah! when sinners are unhumbled "under the mighty hand of God"—when they are afflicted, and not purged by affliction—when it is said of them, "They received not correction"—it seems the forerunner of that tremendous judgment, "Why should you be stricken any more?"

Heavenly Father! keep Your poor, weak, erring child from this fearful doom. Let not that measure of prosperity, which You may be pleased to give, prove my curse. But especially let every cross, every affliction which You are pleased to mingle in my cup, conform me more to my Savior's image, restrain my heart from its daily wanderings, endear Your holy ways and word to my soul, and give me sweeter anticipations of that blessed home, where I shall never wander more, but find my eternal happiness in keeping Your word.

68. You are good, and do good: teach me Your statutes.

The blessed effects of chastisement, as a special instance of the Lord's goodness, might naturally lead to a general acknowledgment of the goodness of His character and dispensation. Judging in unbelieving haste, of His providential and gracious dealings, feeble sense imagines a frown, when the eye of faith discerns a smile, upon His face; and therefore in proportion as faith is exercised in the review of the past, and the experience of the present, we shall be prepared with the ascription of praise—You are good. This is indeed the expression—the confidence—the pleading—of faith. It is the sweet taste of experience—restraining the legality of the conscience, the many hard and dishonorable thoughts of God, and invigorating a lively enjoyment of Him. Indeed 'this is the true and genuine character of God. He is good—He is goodness. Good in Himself—good in His essence—good in the highest degree. All the names of God are comprehended in this one of Good. All the acts of God are nothing else but the effluxes of His goodness distinguished by several names according to the object it is exercised about. When He confers happiness without merit, it is grace. When He bestows happiness against merit, it is mercy. When He bears with provoking rebels, it is patience. When He performs His promise, it is truth. When He commiserates a distressed person, it is pity. When He supplies an indigent person, it is bounty. When He supports an innocent person, it is righteousness. And when He pardons a penitent person, it is mercy. All summed up in this one name—Goodness. None so communicatively good as God. As the notion of God includes goodness, so the notion of goodness includes diffusiveness. Without goodness He would cease to be a Deity; and without diffusiveness He would cease to be good. The being good is necessary to the being God. For goodness is nothing else in the notion of it but a strong inclination to do good, either to find or to make an object, wherein to exercise itself, according to the propensity of its own nature; and it is an inclination of communicating itself, not for its own interest, but for the good of the object it pitches upon. Thus God is good by nature; and His nature is not without activity. He acts consistently with His own nature—You are good, and do good.' (Charnock)

How easily is such an acknowledgment excited towards an earthly friend! Yet who has not daily cause to complain of the coldness of his affections towards his God? It would be a sweet morning's reflection to recollect some of the innumerable instances, in which the goodness of God has been most distinctly marked, to trace them in their peculiar application to our own need; and above all to mark, not only the source from which they come, but the channel through which they flow. A view of covenant love does indeed make the goodness of God to shine with inexpressible brightness "in the face of Jesus Christ;" and often when the heart is conscious of backsliding, does the contemplation of this goodness under the influence of the Spirit, prove the Divinely appointed means of "leading us to repentance." Let us therefore wait on, even when we see nothing. Soon we shall see, where we did not look for it. Soon we shall find goodness unmingled—joy unclouded, unspeakable, eternal.

Meanwhile, though the diversified manifestations—the materials of our happiness, in all around us, be countless as the particles of sand, and the drops of dew; yet without heavenly teaching they only become occasions of our deeper misery and condemnation. It is not enough that the Lord gives—He must teach us His statutes. Divine truths can only be apprehended by Divine teaching. The scholar, who has been longest taught, realizes most his need of this teaching, and is most earnest in seeking it. Indeed, "the earth is full of the goodness of the Lord," yet we may be utterly ignorant of it. The instances of goodness in the shape of a cross, we consider to be the reflection on it. Nothing is goodness in our eyes, that crosses our own inclination. We can hardly bear to hear of the cross, much less to take it up. We talk of goodness, but yield to discontent. We do not profess to dislike trial—only the trial now pressing upon us—any other cross than this; that is, my will and wisdom rather than God's. Is there not, therefore, great need of this prayer for Divine

125

teaching, that we may discern the Lord's mercies so closely crowded together, and make the due improvement of each? Twice before had the Psalmist sent up this prayer and plea. Yet he seems to make the supplication ever new by the freshness and vehemency of his desires. And let me ever make it new by the remembrance of that one display of goodness, which casts every other manifestation into the shade, "God so loved the world, that He gave His only-begotten Son."

This constitutes of itself a complete mirror of infinite and everlasting goodness—the only intelligent display of His goodness—the only manifestation, that prevents from abusing it. What can I say to this—but You are good, and do good? What may I not then expect from You! "'Teach me Your statutes." Teach me the Revelation of Yourself—Teach me the knowledge of Your Son. For "this is life eternal, that I might know You, the only true God, and Jesus Christ whom You have sent.'"

69. The proud have forged a lie against me; but I will keep Your precepts with my whole heart.

If the Lord does us good, we must expect Satan to do us evil. Acting in his own character, as a "liar and the father of it," he readily puts it into the hearts of his children to forge lies against the children of God! But all is overruled by the ever-watchful care and providence of God, for the eventual good of His church. The cross frightens the insincere, and removes them out of the way; while the steadfastness of His own people marvelously displays to the world the power and triumph of faith. A most delightful source of encouragement in this fiery trial is, to take off the eye from the objects of sense, and to fix it upon Jesus as our pattern, no less than our life. For every trial, in which we are conformed to His suffering image, supplies to us equal direction and support. Do "the proud forge lies against us?" So did they against Him. "The disciple is not above his master, nor the servant above his Lord. It is enough for the disciple, that he be as his master, and the servant as his Lord. If they have called the Master of the house Beelzebub, how much more shall they call them of his household?" "Consider Him, therefore, that endured such contradiction of sinners against Himself, lest you be wearied and faint in your minds."

But is it always lies that are forged against us? Is there no worldliness, or pride, or inconsistency in temper and walk, that opens the mouths of the enemies of the gospel, and causes "the way of truth to be evil spoken of?" Do they not sometimes "say all manner of evil" against some of us, for Christ's sake; yet alas! not altogether "falsely?" "Woe unto the world, because of offences! for it must needs be that offences come; but woe to that man, by whom the offence comes!" If, however, the reproach of the world be "the reproach of Christ," "let us hold fast the profession of our faith without wavering; for He is faithful that promised." Insincerity of heart can never support us to a consistent and persevering endurance of the cross. A heart divided between God and the world will ever be found faulty and backsliding. Wholeness of heart in the precepts of God adorns the Christian profession, awes the ungodly world, realizes the full extent of the Divine promises, and pours into the soul such a spring-tide of enjoyment, as more than counterbalances all the reproach, contempt, and falsehood, which the forge of the great enemy is employing against us with unceasing activity, and relentless hatred. Yet do not forget, believer, that these proofs of the malicious enmity of the proud must often be received as the gentle stroke of your Father's chastisement. Let the fruits of it, then, be daily visible in the work of mortification—in the exercise of the suffering graces of the gospel—in your growing conformity to His image—and in a progressive fitness for the world of eternal uninterrupted love.

70. Their heart is as fat as grease; but I delight in Your law.

A dreadful description of the hardened state of the proud forgers of lies! Yet not of their state only, but of every sinner, who stands out in willful rebellion against God. The tremendous blow of almighty justice has benumbed his heart, so that the pressure of mountains of sin and guilt is unfelt! The heart is left of God, "seared with a hot iron," and therefore without tenderness; "past feeling;" unsoftened by the power of the word: unhumbled by the rod of providential dispensations, given up to the heaviest of all spiritual judgments! But it is of little avail to stifle the voice of conscience, unless the same power or device could annihilate hell. It will only "awake out of sleep, like a giant refreshed with wine," and rage with ten-fold interminable fury in the eternal world, from the temporary restraint, which for a short moment had benumbed its energy. Willful resistance to the light of the gospel, and the strivings of the Spirit, constrained even from a God of love the message of judicial abandonment, "Make the heart of this people fat, and make their ears heavy, and shut their eyes; lest they see with their eyes, and hear with their ears, and understand with their heart, and convert, and be healed." Who then among us will not cry—From hardness of heart, and contempt of Your word and commandment, Good Lord! deliver us! (Litany.) Tenderness is the first mark of the touch of grace, when the heart becomes sensible of its own insensibility, and contrite on account of its own hardness. 'Nothing'—said Jerome, in a letter to a friend—'makes my heart sadder, than that nothing makes it sad.' But when "the plague of our own heart" begins to be "known," and becomes a matter of confession, humiliation, prayer; the promise of "a new heart" is as life from the dead. The subject of this promise delights in God's law; and this amid the sometimes overwhelming power of natural corruption, gives a satisfactory witness of a change "from death unto life."

Christian! can you daily witness the wretched condition of the ungodly, without the constraining recollection of humiliation and love? What sovereign grace, that the Lord of glory should have set His love upon one so vile! What mighty power, to have raised my insensible heart to that delight in His law, which conforms me to the image of His dear Son! Deeply would I "abhor myself:" and gladly would I acknowledge, that the service of ten thousand hearts would be a poor return for such unmerited love. What, oh, "what shall I render to the Lord!"—Prayer for them who are still lying in death—praise for myself quickened from death. But what can give the vital breath, pulse, feeling, and motion? "Come, from the four winds, O breath; and breathe upon the slain, that they may live."

Let us apply, for the purpose of daily self-examination, this description of the heart, either as given up to its natural insensibility, or as cast into the new mold of delight in the law of God. Such an examination will prove to us, how much even renewed souls need the transforming, softening influences of grace. "The deceitfulness of sin hardens the heart" to its original character, as fat as grease, unfeeling, incapable of impression, without a Divine touch. O Lord, let not my heart be unvisited for one day, one hour, by that melting energy of love, which first made me feel, and constrained me to love.

71. It is good for me that I have been afflicted; that I might learn Your statutes.

If I mark in myself any difference from the ungodly—if I can feel that my natural insensibility is yielding to the influence of grace—if I am enabled to "delight in God's law," which before I had neglected as a "strange thing," if this softening transformation has been wrought in the school of affliction; let me thankfully acknowledge—It is good for me that I have been afflicted. None indeed but the Lord's scholars can know the benefit of this school and this teaching. The first lessons are usually learned under the power of the word pricking and piercing the heart; yet issuing in joyous good. All special lessons afterward will probably be learned here. 'I never'—said Luther—'knew the meaning of God's word, until I came into affliction. I have always found it one of my best schoolmasters.' This teaching distinguishes the sanctified from the unsanctified cross, explaining many a hard text, and sealing many a precious promise—the rod expounding the word, and the Divine Teacher effectually applying both.

Indeed, but for this discipline we should miss much of the meaning and spiritual blessing of the word. For how can we have any experimental acquaintance with the promises of God, except under those circumstances for which the promises are made? When, for example, but in the day of trouble, could we understand the full mercy of such a gracious word, as, "Call upon Me in the day of trouble: I will deliver you, and you shall glorify Me?" And how much more profitable is this experimental learning than mere human instruction! When, therefore, we pray for a clearer apprehension and interest in the blessed book, and for a deeper experience of its power upon our hearts; we are, in fact, often unconsciously supplicating for the chastening rod of our Father's love. For it is the man "whom the Lord chastens," that He "teaches out of His law." Peter, indeed, when on the mount of transfiguration, said, "It is good for us to be here. Let us build here three tabernacles." Here let us abide, in a state of comfort, indulgence, and sunshine. But well was it added by the sacred historian, "Not knowing what he said." The judgment of David was far more correct, when he pronounced, that it was good for him that he had been afflicted. For so often are we convicted of inattention to the voice of the Lord—so often do we find ourselves looking back upon forsaken Sodom, or lingering in the plain, instead of pressing onward to Zoar, that the indulgence of our own liberty would shortly hurry us along the pathway of destruction. Alas! often do we feel the spirit of prayer to be quenched for a season by "a heart overcharged with the cares of this life"—or by the overprizing of some lawful comfort—or by a temper inconsistent with our Christian profession—or by an undue confidence in the flesh. And at such seasons of backsliding, we must count among our choicest mercies the gracious discipline, by which the Lord schools us with the cross, that we may learn His statutes.

After all, however, this must be a paradox to the unenlightened man. He can only "count it" all grief—not "all joy—when he falls into diverse temptations." His testimony is—It is evil—not it is good—for me that I have been afflicted. And even God's children, as we have before remarked, do not always take up this word while smarting under the rod. The common picture of happiness is freedom from trouble, not, as Scripture describes it, the portion of trouble. Yet how true is God's judgment, when it is the very end of affliction to remove the source of all trouble, and consequently to secure—not to destroy—solid happiness! We must however determine the standard of real good by its opposition—not its accordance—to our own fancy or indulgence. The promise of "every good thing" may be fulfilled by a plentiful cup of affliction. Present evil may be "working together for" ultimate "good." Let God take His own way with us. Let us interpret His providences by His covenant—His means by His end—and instead of fainting under the sharpness of His rod, we shall earnestly desire the improvement of it.

Are you, then, tried believer, disposed to regret the lessons you have already learned in this school? Or have you purchased them at too dear a cost? Do you grieve over the bleedings of a contrite heart, that have brought you under the care of the healing physician? Or could you by any other way have obtained so rich a knowledge of His love, or have been trained to such implicit obedience to His will? As Jesus, "though He were a Son, yet learned He obedience by the things which He suffered;" so may we "rejoice, inasmuch as we are partakers of His sufferings," and be thankful to learn the same obedience, as the evidence and fruit of our conformity to Him.

The Lord save us from the greatest of all afflictions, an affliction lost! "Be instructed, O Jerusalem, lest My soul depart from you; lest I make you desolate, a land not inhabited." "He who being often reproved, hardens his neck, shall suddenly be destroyed, and that without remedy." A call to tremble and repent, to watch and pray, and "turn to Him that smites us!"

Oh! is there one of that countless throng surrounding the everlasting throne, who has not sung, "It is good for me that I have been afflicted?" "And one of the elders answered, saying unto me, What are these which are arrayed in white robes? and whence came they? And I said unto him,

Sir, you know. And he said unto me, These are they which came out of great tribulation, and have washed their robes, and made them white in the blood of the Lamb."

72. The law of Your mouth is better unto me than thousands of gold and silver.

Well might David acknowledge the benefit of affliction, since he had thus learned in God's statutes something that was better to him than thousands of gold and silver. This was indeed an enlightened judgment for one to form, who had so small a part of the law of God's mouth, and so large a portion of this world's treasure. And yet, if we study only his book of Psalms to know the important uses and privileges of this law, and his son's book of Ecclesiastes, to discover the real value of paltry gold and silver, we shall, under Divine teaching, be led to make the same estimate for ourselves. Yes, believer, with the same, or rather with far higher delight than the miser calculates his thousands of gold and silver, do you tell out the precious contents of the law of your God. After having endeavored in vain to count the thousands in your treasure, one single name sums up their value, "the unsearchable riches of Christ." Would not the smallest spot of ground be estimated at thousands of gold and silver, were it known to conceal under its surface a mine of inexhaustible treasure? This it is that makes the word so inestimable. It is the field of the "hidden treasure." "The pearl of great price" is known to be concealed here. You would not, therefore, part with one leaf of your Bible for all the thousands of gold and silver. You know yourself to be in possession of the substance—you have found all besides to be a shadow. "I lead"—says the Savior, "in the way of righteousness, in the midst of the paths of judgment; that I may cause them that love me to inherit substance; and I will fill their treasures." The grand motive, therefore, in "searching the Scriptures," is because "they testify of Christ." A sinner has but one want—a Savior. A believer has but one desire—to "know and win Christ." With a "single eye," therefore, intent upon one point, he studies this blessed book. "With unveiled face he beholds in this glass the glory of the Lord:" and no arithmetic can compute the price of that, which is now unspeakably better to him than the treasures of the earth.

Christian! bear your testimony to your supreme delight in the book of God. You have here opened the surface of much intellectual interest and solid instruction. But it is the joy that you have found in the revelation of the Savior, in His commands, in His promises, in His ways, that leads you to exclaim, "More to be desired are they than gold, yes, than much fine gold!" Yes, indeed—every promise— every declaration—centering in Him, is a pearl; and the word of God is full of these precious pearls. If then they be the richest who have the best and the largest treasure, those who have most of the word in their hearts, not those who have most of the world in their possession—are justly entitled to this preeminence. "Let then the word of Christ dwell in us richly in all wisdom." For those who are rich in this heavenly treasure are men of substance indeed.

True—this is a correct estimate of the worth of God's law—better than this world's treasure. But is it better to me? Is this my decided choice? How many will inconsiderately acknowledge its supreme value, while they yet hesitate to relinquish even a scanty morsel of earth for an interest in it! Do I then habitually prefer this law of God's mouth to every worldly advantage? Am I ready to forego every selfish consideration, if it may only be the means of uniting my heart more closely to the Book of God? If this be not my practical conviction, I fear I have not yet opened the mine. But if I can assent to this declaration of the man of God, I have made a far more glorious discovery than Archimedes; and therefore may take up his expression of joyful surprise—'I have found it! I have found it!' What? That which the world could never have given me—that of which the world can never deprive me.

And—Lord—help me to prize the law as coming from Your mouth. Let it be forever written upon my heart. Let me be daily exploring my hidden treasures. Let me be enriching myself and all around me with the present possession and interest in these heavenly blessings.

Yet how affecting is it to see men poor in the midst of great riches! Often in the world we see the possessor of a large treasure—without a heart to enjoy it—virtually therefore a pauper. Oftener still in the Church do we see professors (may it not be so with some of us?) with their Bibles in their hands—yet poor even with the external interest in its "unsearchable riches." Often also do we observe a want of value for the whole law or revelation of God's mouth. Some parts are highly honored to the depreciation of the rest. But let it be remembered that the whole of Scripture "is given by inspiration of God and is therefore profitable" for its appointed end. Oh! beware of resting satisfied with a scanty treasure. Prayer and diligence will bring out not only "things new," but the "old" also with a new and brighter glow. Scraping the surface is a barren exercise. Digging into the affections is a most enriching employ. No vein in this mine is yet exhausted. And rich indeed shall we be, if we gather only one atom of the gold each day in prayerful meditation. But as you value your progress and peace in the ways of God—as you have an eye to your Christian perfection—put away that ruinous thought—true as an encouragement to the weak, but false as an excuse to the slothful—that a little knowledge is sufficient to carry us to heaven.

73. Your hands have made me and fashioned me: give me understanding, that I may learn Your commandments.

In the vast universe of wonder, man is the greatest wonder—the noblest work of God. A council of the Sacred Trinity was held respecting his creation, "God said, Let us make man in our image, after our likeness." Every part of creation bears the impress of God. Man—man alone—bears His image, His likeness. Everywhere we see His track—His footsteps. Here we behold His face. What an amazing thought, that the three Eternal subsistents in the glorious Godhead, should have united in gracious design and operation towards the dust of the earth! But thus man was formed—thus was he raised out of his parent dust, from this low original, to be the living temple, and habitation of Divine glory—a Being full of God. The first moment that he opened his eyes to behold the light and beauty of the new-made world, the Lord separated him for His own service, to receive the continual supply of His own life. His body was fitted as a tabernacle for his soul, "curiously wrought" by the hand of God; and all its parts and "members written in this book, which in continuance were fashioned, when as yet there was none of them." Most naturally therefore does the contemplation of this "perfection of beauty" raise the adoring mind upward, "I will praise You; for I am fearfully and wonderfully made; marvelous are Your works; and that my soul knows right well." Your hands have made me and fashioned me.

Could we suppose that man was formed to eat, to sleep, and to die—that, after taking a few turns upon the grand walk of life, he was to descend into the world of eternal silence, we might well ask the question of God, "Why have You made all men in vain?" But the first awakening of man from his death-like sleep enlightens him in the right knowledge of the end of his creation. If I am conscious of being the workmanship of God, I shall feel my relationship to Him, and the responsibility of acting according to it. I would plead then this relation before Him in asking for light, life, and love. I cannot serve You as a creature, except I be made a new creature. Give me a spiritual being, without which my natural being cannot glorify You. You have indeed "curiously wrought" my frame; but sin has marred all. Make me Your spiritual "workmanship, created in Christ Jesus." Give me understanding—spiritual knowledge, that I may learn Your commandments, "Renew a right spirit within me."

But the natural man feels no need of this prayer. No, he is puffed up in his own wisdom. He cannot receive the Divine testimony, which levels him, while he "understands not," with "the beasts that perish," and tells him, that he must "become a fool, that he may be wise." But should he ever know his new state of existence, he will offer up this prayer eagerly and frequently; and every step of his way heavenward he will feel increasing need of Divine "wisdom and spiritual understanding."

How does the song of heaven remind us of this end of our creation!, "You are worthy, O Lord, to receive glory, and honor, and power! for You have created all things; and for Your pleasure they are, and were created." In harmony with this song we must acknowledge, that the "Lord has made all things for Himself"—that He "created all things for His glory." And the recollection that He "created us by Jesus Christ," brings before us the grand work of redemption, and the work of the new creation consequent upon it. He who created us in His own image, when that image was lost, that He might not lose His property in us, put a fresh seal upon His natural right, and "purchased us with His own blood." Oh! let us not be insensible to this constraining motive to learn His commandments. "You are not your own, for you are bought with a price; therefore glorify God in your body and in your spirit, which are God's."

74. Those who do fear You, will be glad when they see me: because I have hoped in Your word.

How cheering is the sight of a man of God! How refreshing his converse! How satisfactory and enlivening is the exhibition of his faith! The goodness of God to one becomes thus the joy and comfort of all. What an excitement is this to close communion with our God, that the light which we thus receive will shine on those around us! What a comfort will it be even in our own hour of temptation, that the hope, which we may then be enabled to maintain in the word of God, shall prove the stay, not only of our own souls, but of the Lord's people! Many a desponding Christian, oppressed with such fears as this, "I shall one day perish by the hand of Saul"—when he hears of one and another exercised in the same trials, and who have hoped in God's word, and have not been disappointed, will be glad when he sees them. Thus David recorded his conflicts, that we may not despair of our own; and his triumphs, that "in the name of our God we might set up our banners." "I had fainted, unless I had believed to see the goodness of the Lord in the land of the living. Wait on the Lord, be of good courage, and He shall strengthen your heart: wait, I say, on the Lord." Thus also, under affliction, he was comforted with the thought of comforting others with the history of his own experience, "My soul shall make her boast in the Lord: the humble shall hear thereof, and be glad. O praise the Lord with me, and let us magnify His name together. He has put a new song in my mouth, even praise to our God. Many shall see it, and fear, and shall trust in the Lord. Bring my soul out of prison, that I may praise Your name; the righteous shall compass me about, for You shall deal bountifully with me."

In this view, the believer, who has been "sifted in the sieve" of temptation, without the least "grain" of faith or hope "falling upon the earth," stands forth as a monument of the Lord's faithfulness, to "strengthen the weak hands, and confirm the feeble knees, and to say to them that are of fearful heart, Be strong, fear not." Those that are "fearful, and of little faith," are glad when they see him. They "thank God" for him, and "take courage" for themselves. What a motive is this to keep us from despondency; that, instead of destroying by our unbelief, those who are already "cast down," we may enjoy the privilege of upholding their confidence, and ministering to their comfort! And how should the weak and distressed seek for and prize the society of those, who have been instructed by the discipline of the Lord's school!

Believer! what have you to tell to your discouraged brethren of the faithfulness of your God? Cannot you put courage into their hearts, by declaring that you have never been "ashamed of your hope?" Cannot you tell them from your own experience, that Jesus "is for a foundation-stone, a tried stone, a sure foundation?" Cannot you show them, that, because He has borne the burden of their sins, He is able to "bear their griefs, and to carry their sorrows?" that you have tried Him, and that you have found Him so? Oh! be animated to know more of Christ yourself; let your hope in Him be strengthened, that you may cause gladness in the hearts of those that, see you; so that, "whether you be afflicted, or whether you be comforted, it may be for their consolation and salvation."

135

But, O my God! how much cause have I for shame, that I impart so little of Your glorious light to those around me! Perhaps some poor trembling sinner has been glad when he saw me, hoping to hear something of the Savior from my lips, and has found me straitened, and cold, and dumb. Oh! that I may be so "filled with the Spirit," so experienced in Your heavenly ways, that I may invite "all that do not fear to come to me," that I may "declare what You have done for my soul;" so that, "when men are cast down, they may say, There is lifting up."

75. I know, O Lord, that Your judgments are right, and that You in faithfulness have afflicted me.

This is the Christian's acknowledgment—fully satisfied with the dispensation of God. This is his confidence—so invigorating to his own soul—so cheering to the church. The Lord's dealings are called His judgments—not as having judicial curses, but as the acts of His justice in the chastening of sin. Perhaps also—as the administration of His wise judgments in their measure and application. But here is not only the confession of the Lord's general judgment, but of His especial faithfulness to Himself. And this he knew—not from the dictates of the flesh (which would have given a contrary verdict), but from the testimony of the word, and the witness of his own experience. It could not be doubted—much less denied—'I know, O Lord, that Your rules of proceeding are agreeable to Your perfect justice and wisdom; and I am equally satisfied, that the afflictions that You have laid upon me from time to time, are only to fulfill Your gracious and faithful promise of making me eternally happy in Yourself.' Blessed fruit of affliction! when we can thus "see the end of the Lord, that the Lord is very pitiful, and of tender mercy"—that His "thoughts towards us are thoughts of peace, and not of evil!" "The patience and faith of the saints" teach this difficult but most consoling lesson, in deciphering the mysterious lines in God's providence.

The child of God under the severest chastisement must acknowledge justice. Our gracious reward is always more—our "punishment always less, than our iniquities deserve." "Why should a living man complain?" In trouble he is indeed—but not in hell. If he complain, let it be of none but himself, and his own wayward choice. I know, O Lord, that Your judgments are right—and who can doubt the wisdom? Who would charge the operator with cruelty, in cutting out the proud flesh, that was bringing death upon the man? Who would not acknowledge the right judgment of his piercing work? Thus, when the Lord's painful work separates us from our sin, weans us from the world, and brings us nearer to Himself, what remains for us, but thankfully to acknowledge His righteousness and truth? Unbelief is put to rebuke; and we, if we have indulged suspicion "that God has forgotten to be gracious," must confess, "This is our infirmity."

This assurance of the Lord's perfect justice, wisdom, and intimate knowledge of our respective cases, leads us to yield to His appointments in dutiful silence. Thus Aaron, under his most afflictive domestic calamity, "held his peace." Job under a similar dispensation was enabled to say, "The Lord gave, and the Lord has taken away: blessed be the name of the Lord!" Eli's language in the same trial was, "It is the Lord; let Him do what seems Him good." David hushed his impatient spirit, "I was dumb; I opened not my mouth, because You did it." And when Shimei cursed him, he said, "Let him alone; let him curse; for the Lord has bidden him." The Shunammite, in the meek resignation of faith, acknowledged, "It is well." Hezekiah kissed the rod, while it was smiting him to the dust, "Good is the word of the Lord which You have spoken." Thus uniform is the language of the Lord's people under chastisement—I know, O Lord, that Your judgments are right.

But the confession of justice may be mere natural conviction. Faith goes further, and speaks of faithfulness. David not only acknowledges God's right to deal with him as He saw fit, and even His wisdom in dealing with him as He actually had done, but His faithfulness in afflicting—not His faithfulness though He afflicted—but in afflicting him; not as if it were consistent with His love, but as the very fruit of His love. It is not enough to justify God. What abundant cause is there to praise Him! It is not enough to forbear to murmur. How exciting is the display of His faithfulness and love! Yes—the trials appointed for us are none else than the faithful performance of His everlasting engagements. And to this cause we may always trace (and it is our privilege to believe it, where we cannot visibly trace it) the reason of much that is painful to the flesh. Let us only mark its gracious effects in our restoration—instruction—healing of our backslidings, and the continual purging of sins—and then say—'Is not the faithfulness of God gloriously displayed?' The Philistines could not understand Samson's riddle—how "Meat could come out of the eater, and sweetness out of the strong." As little can the world comprehend the fruitfulness of the Christian's trials; how his gracious Lord sweetens to him the bitter waters of Marah, and makes the cross not so much the punishment as the remedy of sin. He finds therefore no inclination, and he feels that he has no interest in having any change made in the Lord's appointments, revolting as they may be to the flesh. He readily acknowledges that His merciful designs could not have been accomplished in any other way; while under trials many sweet tokens of love are given, which, under circumstances of outward prosperity, could not have been received with the same gratitude and delight.

You that are living at ease in the indulgence of what this poor world can afford, how little does the Christian envy your portion! How surely in some future day will you be taught by experience to envy his! The world's riches are daily becoming poorer, and its pleasures more tasteless; and what will they be, and how will they appear, when eternity is at hand! Whereas affliction is the special token of our Father's love, conformity to the image of Jesus, and preparation for His service and kingdom. It is the only blessing that the Lord gives, without requiring us to ask for it. We receive it, therefore, as promised, not as threatened; and when the "peaceable fruits of righteousness," which it works in God's time and way, spring up in our hearts, humbly and gratefully will we acknowledge the righteousness of His judgments, and the faithfulness of His corrections.

Verses 76-100

76. Let, I pray You, Your merciful kindness be for my comfort: according to Your word unto Your servant.

What! does the Psalmist then seek his comfort from the very hand that strikes him? This is genuine faith, "Though He slay me, yet will I trust in Him." The very arm that seems to be uplifted for my destruction, shall be to me the arm of salvation.

Several of the preceding verses have spoken of affliction. The Psalmist now prays for alleviation under it. But of what kind? He does not "beseech the Lord, that it might depart from him." No. His repeated acknowledgments of the supports given under it, and the benefits he had derived from it, had reconciled him to commit its measure and continuance to the Lord. All that he needs, and all that he asks for, is, a sense of His merciful kindness upon his soul. Thus he submits to His justice in accumulated trials, and expects consolation under them, solely upon the ground of His free favor. Indeed, it is hard to hold on under protracted affliction without this precious support. Patience may restrain murmuring but a sense of love alone keeps from fainting. Holiness is our service—affliction is our exercise—comfort is our gracious reward. All the candles in the world, in the absence of the sun, can never make the day. The whole earth, in its brightest visions of fancy, destitute of the Lord's love, can never cheer nor revive the soul. Indeed, it matters little where we are, or what we have. In the fullness of refreshing ordinances, unless the Lord meets us, and blesses us with His merciful kindness for our comfort, it is "a thirsty land, where no water is." Absalom might as well have been at Geshur as at Jerusalem, so long as he "saw not the king's face." Nothing that the Lord "gives us richly to enjoy" will satisfy, if this source of refreshment be withheld. The worldling's inquiry is, "Who will show us any good?" The Christian forms his answer into a prayer, "Lord! lift up the light of Your countenance upon me." Let Your merciful kindness be for my comfort. This gives the enjoyment of every real good, and supplies the place of every fancied good. It is a blessing that never cloys, and will never end: and every fresh taste quenches the thirst for earthly pleasures. "Whoever drinks of this water"—says our Divine Savior, "shall thirst again. But whoever drinks of the water that I shall give him shall never thirst!" "Delight yourself in the Lord; and He shall give you the desires of your heart."

But, Reader, do you wish to realize this comfort? Then seek to approach your God by the only way of access. Learn to contemplate Him in the only glass in which a God of love is seen, "in the face of Jesus Christ." Guard against looking for comfort from any other source. Beware especially of that satisfaction in creature-cisterns which draws you away from "the fountain of living waters." Learn also to prize this comfort supremely, and not to be content without some enjoyment, or even with a scanty measure of enjoyment; but rather let every day's refreshment be made a step for desiring and attaining renewed and sweeter refreshment for tomorrow. Some, however, appear to look at David's experience, as if at present they could hardly expect to reach its happiness: and so they go on in a low, depressed, and almost sullen state, refusing the privileges, which are as freely offered to them as to others. But such a state of mind is highly dishonorable to God. Let them earnestly plead their interest in the word of promise—According to Your word to Your servant. Let them lay their fingers upon one or all of the promises of their God. Let them spread before the Lord His own handwriting and seals; and their Savior has said, "According to your faith be it unto you." "The king is held in the galleries;" and, if He should "make as though He would go farther," He is willing that we should "constrain Him, saying, Abide with us." No veil now but the veil of unbelief need hinder us from seeing an unclouded everlasting smile of merciful kindness upon our heavenly Father's reconciled face. Only let us see to it, that He is the first, the habitual object of our contemplation, the satisfying well-spring of our delight—that He is the one desire, to which every other is subordinate, and in which every other is absorbed.

Lord Jesus! I would seek for a renewed enjoyment in Your merciful kindness. I would not forget, that it was this that brought You down from heaven—that led You to endure the death of the cross—that has washed me in Your precious blood—that visits me with many endearing tokens of Your love. Oh, let all my days be spent in the sense of this merciful kindness for my comfort, and in rendering to You the unworthy returns of grateful, filial service.

77. Let Your tender mercies come to me, that I may live; for Your law is my delight.

Sin is no light trouble to the man of God. Mercy, therefore, is to him no common blessing. Never can he have—never can he ask, enough. Hence his repeated cries. Mercy brought him out of sin and misery. Mercy keeps—holds him on—assures him to the end. Every blessing comes in the way of mercy. The most careful walker according to the gospel rule, needs mercy. The elect are "vessels of mercy"—filled up to the brim with mercy. The crown of glory at last is received at the hands of mercy.

The distinguishing character of God is, that His mercies are tender mercies—a father's pitying—yearning mercies. When His returning prodigal expected probably upbraiding looks, if not a frown of banishment, how did these tender mercies bury, not only his sins, but also his very confessions in the depths of the sea, and welcome him without a cloud to his forsaken home! The same tender considerations put away from His children all anxiety respecting "what they shall eat, or what they shall drink, or wherewithal they shall be clothed. As a Father He also "chastens" them, "he suffers their manners"—He "spares them, as a man spares his own son that serves him;" and, finally, He determines respecting each of them by an act of sovereign power, "You shall call Me, My Father, and shall not depart from Me." In a yet more endearing character He speaks, "As one whom his mother comforts, so will I comfort you. They may forget; yet will I not forget You."

Yet have we no just apprehension of these tender mercies, unless they come to us. In the midst of the wide distribution, let me claim my interest. Let them come to me. Praised be God! the way is open to me. The mere report is unfruitful. I cannot speak of them with glow and unction. The application of them is life—not the mere breathing of spiritual existence, but the life of my life—the living principle of devotedness and enjoyment—living to and for God in every form and sphere, in every hour and action of the day; my feebleness becoming strength in the Lord; "walking up and down in His name." This truly is "reigning in life;" rising to more of its honor and dignity, and reaching forth to more of its excellence and happiness.

But let us not lose sight of the abundant overflowing spring, from which our life is maintained. "In Christ was life;" and He "came that we might have life, and that we might have it more abundantly." There can be, therefore, no exercises of life without a vital union to Christ—the source of life. Shall we then give up the hope of believing in Christ, until we feel the influence of this spiritual principle? This would be indeed like refusing to abide in the vine, until we could bring forth fruit; whereas the branch, while separated from the vine, must ever be fruitless and withered. We must receive life from Christ, not bring it to Him. Faith implants us in Him; and "Christ dwelling in the heart by faith" becomes the life of the soul, animating it in the ways of God.

This life, therefore, will manifest itself in delight in God's law. We shall not be satisfied to live upon the mere surface of the gospel (which is barren and unproductive, as any other surface, in spiritual usefulness), but we shall search into its hidden treasures, and draw forth its real life and consolation. This "delight" will furnish a plea for our use at the throne of grace. 'If this is the fruit and acting of the life of Your own implanting, Lord! cherish it. Let me live by the influence of Your tender mercies. I venture to plead my delight in Your law, as an evidence of my adoption into Your family. And, therefore, I would renew my plea and my petition—Let Your tender mercies come to me, that my life may be not only existence, but enjoyment—the beginning, the earnest, of the everlasting life and bliss of heaven.'

78. Let the proud be ashamed: for they dwelt perversely with me without a cause: but I will meditate in Your precepts.

The prophecy with which God Himself condescended to open the history of the church, has ever since been in the course of accomplishment. "Enmity between the seed of the serpent and the seed of the woman," has been the prevailing character and course of the world. "An unjust man is an abomination to the just; and he who is upright in the way is abomination to the wicked." David, however, prayed for the confusion of his enemies—not in a vindictive spirit, as if thirsting for their destruction; but as opening the way for his own more free service of God, and as a chastening, that might eventually turn to their salvation, "Fill their faces with shame, that they may seek Your name, O Lord!" That his prayer was the expression of his tender compassion, rather than of resentful feeling, is sufficiently evident from his affectionate weeping concern for their immortal interests. Prayers of the same deprecating character dropped from the lips of the gentle and compassionate Savior:

while the objects of His awful deprecations were interested in the most yearning sympathies of His heart. A regard also for the honor of God dictated this prayer. David knew that the malice of his enemies against him was only the working of their enmity against God; that it was not so much him that they hated and persecuted, as God in him. And therefore as a servant of God he could appeal, "Do not I hate them, O Lord, that hate You? and am not I grieved at those that rise up against You? I hate them with perfect hatred; I count them my enemies." The followers of a despised Savior must indeed expect to be severely distressed with the perverseness of the proud. But when, like their Master, they can testify that it is without a cause, how cheering are their Master's words! "Blessed are you, when men shall revile you, and persecute you, and shall say all manner of evil against you falsely for My sake. Rejoice, and be exceeding glad; for great is your reward in heaven."

And have you, reader, been exercised with trials from an ungodly world? Has the derision of the proud, or the slight or ill-treatment of the ungodly, never excited revengeful feelings within? Have you always been enabled to set your Savior's example before you, and "in patience possessing your soul," to refer your cause to your Almighty Friend? "O Lord, I am oppressed, undertake for me." Remember, He has engaged to take up your cause, "Shall not God avenge His own elect, which cry day and night unto Him, though He bear long with them?—I tell you that He will avenge them speedily."

But learn in the hour of trial where to go, and what to do. Go to the word of God for direction and support. Meditate in His precepts. There is often a hurry of mind in times of difficulty, which unhinges the soul from the simple exercise of faith. But habit brings practice, and steadiness, and simplicity, enabling us most sweetly to fix our hearts upon the word of God, and to apply its directions and encouragements to the present exigency. Our enemies fight against us with an arm of flesh. We resist them with the armor of the word of God. And how inestimably precious is the armor, refuge, strength, and consolation, here provided for us against every effort to disturb our peace, "or separate our hearts from the love of God, which is in Christ Jesus our Lord!"

143

79. Let those who fear You turn to me, and those that have known Your
testimonies.

As the believer finds trouble from the world, he prays that he may
find help from the Lord's people. The very sight of our Father's family is
cheering. It brings not only fellowship but help. For the wise distribution
of gifts in the body—each having his own gift—was ordained for the
mutual help and sympathy of the several members. It is painful therefore
to see Christians often walking aloof from each other, and suffering
coldness, distance, differences and distrust to divide them from their
brethren. Who then will not pray, that He, who has the hearts of all His
people in His hand, would turn the hearts of those that fear Him and
know His testimonies, unto their brethren? It was the honor of Mordecai,
that he was "accepted of the multitude of his brethren." In the primitive
church, "Demetrius had good report of all men, and of the truth itself;"
and the members of the church generally "did eat their meat with
gladness and singleness of heart; praising God, and having favor with all
the people." 'Then,' as Chrysostom exultingly exclaims, 'the Church was
a little heaven.' Then they could say to each other, "Behold, how good
and pleasant it is for brethren to dwell together in unity!" and even their
Heathen neighbors were awed and constrained into the confession, "See
how these Christians love one another."

Alas! that our Jerusalem should no longer exhibit the picture of a
"city compact together"—that so many "walls of partition" should
separate brother from brother, so that our Zion has very rarely been
exhibited in her "perfection of beauty," when "the multitude of them that
believed were of one heart and of one soul." Prejudice and misconception
divided Job from his friends. Want of forbearance cankered the union of
the members of the church of Rome, and even prevailed to separate chief
friends—Paul and Barnabas. Diversity of sentiment injured the influence
of brotherly love at Corinth. And thus it has been in every successive age
of the church; so that the full answer to the Redeemer's prayer, and the
grand display to the world of the Divine original of the gospel, is yet to
be manifested. But as "the communion of saints" was the peculiar feature
of primitive Christianity, and ever since has formed an article of her
faith; in proportion as we return to the primitive standard, we shall hold
closer fellowship with each other—as "members of one body"
"considering one another, to provoke unto love and to good works"

"bearing one another's burdens;"—and "receiving one another, as Christ also received us, to the glory of God."

Lack of Christian self-denial presents the main hindrance to this "keeping the unity of the spirit in the bond of peace." But—admitting that some of the brethren are "weak in the faith" in comparison with ourselves—are we then to be 'rolling endlessly the returning stone,' obtruding always the same stumbling-offence upon them? We are "not to please ourselves" in compelling them to adopt our views; but rather to "receive them, and bear their infirmities." Accursed be that charity, that is preserved by "the shipwreck of faith!" But though scriptural truth must never be denied, there are times when it may be forborne. The Apostle "knew and was persuaded of the Lord Jesus, that there was nothing unclean of itself;" yet he would rather allow even the misconception of conscience, until clearer light should be given, than endanger the unity of the church. Liberty must give place to love; and for himself, he would rather restrain himself from lawful indulgence, than hazard the safety of a weaker brother, or turn from one that loved his Savior. Wherever, therefore, in the judgment of Christian charity, we discover those "that love our Lord Jesus Christ in sincerity," we must be ready to give them our very hearts, to view them as brethren, as one with ourselves, and to welcome them with brotherly love, as those whom, with all their infirmities, Jesus "is not ashamed to call His brethren." We must be ready to turn to them, as those that fear God, and have known His testimonies.

And does not the believer's anxiety for the company and assistance of the Lord's people rebuke Christian professors, who are far too closely linked to the society of the world? Surely, if the lovely attraction of many of its most avowed votaries can compensate for the absence of their Savior's image, they can have but little relish for that heavenly enjoyment, which unites the children of God together in close and hallowed communion with God. And do we not see a proof of the deteriorating influence of this worldly spirit, in their readiness to feel disgust at the infirmities of the real brethren of the Lord, and to neglect the image of Christ in them, from the unsightliness of the garb, which may sometimes cover it?

But let us mark the completeness of the Christian—combining the fear with the knowledge of God. Knowledge without fear would be self-confidence. Fear without knowledge would be bondage. But the knowledge of His testimonies, connected with an acquaintance with His

145

ways, molds the character of men of God into the spirit of love; and qualifies them, "as fathers" in the gospel, to counsel the weak and inexperienced. Should we, however, be excluded from the privilege of their communion; or should they be prevented from turning to us; may it not be the appointed means of leading us to a more simple dependence on Divine teaching and grace, and to a more blessed anticipation of our Father's house in heaven, where all will be harmony, peace, and love? 'We shall carry truth and the knowledge of God to heaven with us; we shall carry purity there, devotedness of soul to God and our Redeemer, Divine love and joy, if we have these beginnings here, with whatever else of permanent excellence, that has a settled, fixed seat and, place in our souls now: and shall there have them in perfection. But do you think we shall carry strife to heaven? shall we carry anger to heaven? Envyings, heart-burnings, animosities; shall we carry these to heaven with us? Let us labor to divest ourselves, and strike off from our spirits everything that shall not go with us to heaven, or is equally unsuitable to our end and way, that there may be nothing to obstruct and hinder our "abundant entrance" at length into the everlasting kingdom.'

80. Let my heart be sound in Your statutes, that I be not ashamed.

The perverseness of the proud will be sure to put them to shame. As the preservative from this shame, David prays therefore for a sound heart—filled with solid principle—delivered into the mold of the word—like the sacrifices of the law—entire for God. Often had he prayed for Divine teaching—now he begs for soundness in the Lord's statutes. How many "have made shipwreck of faith and of a good conscience," from an unsound heart! Ignorant of the spirituality of God's requirements, and resting in an outward obedience, they falsely conceive themselves to be "alive without the law," and "touching the righteousness that is of the law, blameless." Others go a little beyond the surface; while the want of "simplicity and godly sincerity," of brokenness of heart, love to the Savior, and dependence upon His grace, sooner or later discovers to their eternal confusion, that "the root of the matter is" not "in them." "Their root shall be as rottenness, and their blossom shall go up as dust. Their goodness is as a morning cloud, and as the early dew it goes away." An unsound professor, like beautiful fruit, may attract the careless eye; but a more narrow inspection will show a worm at the core, which has spoiled nearly to the surface. Such religion is only a shriveled mass of inactive formality—a dead image of a living thing.

Alas! how common is it to profess to take Christ for a Savior, while the heart is evidently worshiping Mammon as its God!—constrained— not inclined—to the Lord's statutes! How possible is it to be "carnally-minded" in the daily routine of spiritual exercises! How important is the recollection, that no change of place, of company, or of circumstances, can of itself effect a change of heart! "Saul among the prophets" was Saul still; with "another heart" indeed, but not a new heart. Sin was restrained, but not crucified. He "went out," therefore, as one of his progenitors, "from the presence of the Lord," and perished, a miserable apostate from the statutes of his God. Will profession—knowledge— gifts— feelings—privileges—avail for a sound heart? Need we speak of Judas—a follower—no, even, an apostle of Jesus Christ—living in a familiar communion with his Lord—yet with all his privileges—all his profession, "gone to his own place"—the melancholy victim of his own self-deceitfulness? Need we allude to Balaam, "the man whose eyes were open—which heard the words of God—which saw the vision of the Almighty"—who could in the ken of his eye mark the goodness of the Lord's inheritance, and even in the distant horizon catch a glimpse of "Jacob's star and scepter," and yet "loved the wages of unrighteousness?" Need we bring to the mind's eye Ananias and Sapphira? Alexander—and others of like stamp—all of whom once shone as stars in the skies of the church—need we speak of the end of these men, to give energy to the prayer—Let my heart be sound in Your statutes?

How fearful the thought of being "a branch in the true vine" only by profession! to be "taken away" at length, "cast forth as a branch— withered—gathered—cast into the fire—burned!" It is in the inner man that hypocrisy sets up its throne; whence it commands the outward acts into whatever shape or form may be best suited to effect its purpose. The upright Christian will therefore begin with calling in the help and light of God to ascertain the soundness of his heart. "Search me, O God, and know my heart; try me, and know my thoughts; and see if there be any wicked way in me." Can there be a true and solid work, where there is a professed change of heart, and no manifested change of temper and conduct? Can that heart, which is found upon inquiry to be earthly— unprofitable under the power of the word, "regarding" secret "iniquity"— seeking bye-ends of praise, reputation, or gain—and for the attainment of

147

these ends shrinking from the appointed cross—can that heart be sound in the Lord's statutes? Impossible.

But, on the other hand, do you find that your trust in God is sincere, your desire towards Him supreme, your obedience to Him entire? Prize those evidences of soundness of heart. Thank God for them. They are the workings of His mighty Spirit in your heart—perhaps the answer to the prayer which that same Spirit had indited, Let my heart be sound in Your statutes. Diligently improve all the means of grace for keeping your heart in a vigorous state. Be daily—yes, continually—abiding in the vine, and receiving life and health from its fullness. Be much conversant with the word of God—loving it for itself—its holiness—its practical influences. Be chiefly afraid of inward decays—of a barren, sapless notion of experimental truth; remembering, that except your profession be constantly watered at the root, "the things that remain in you will be ready to die." Specially "commune with your own heart." Watch it jealously, because of its proneness to live upon itself—its own graces or fancied goodness (a sure symptom of unsoundness)—instead of "living by the faith of the Son of God." Examine your settled judgment, your deliberate choice, your outgoing affections, your habitual, allowed practice; applying to every detection of unsoundness the blood of Christ, as the sovereign remedy for the diseases of a "deceitful and desperately wicked heart."

But it may be said—will not these exercises of godly jealousy hinder our Christian assurance? Far from it. They will form an efficient preservative from carnal security. They will induce increasing tenderness, activity, and circumspection, in our daily walk; and thus, instead of retarding the enjoyment of our heavenly privilege, they will settle the foundation of a peaceful temperament. It is a light and careless frame, that is the real hindrance to confidence. An unsound professor knows nothing of the true spirit of adoption—nothing of that holy familiarity, with which a child of God unbosoms himself to his heavenly Father; and if he preserves an empty name in the church, he will be put to shame before the universe of God. But the sound heart is connected with "a hope that makes not ashamed"—the full blessing of scriptural confidence. For the heart is made sound by the "sprinkling of the blood of Christ;" and when thus "sprinkled from an evil conscience," we "have boldness" to "draw near"—yes, even to "enter into the holiest," "in full assurance of faith." Blessed privilege of access and communion with our reconciled God! Every moment endears the Savior to our souls, and enlivens the hope of his glorious coming, as the joyful consummation of all the prospects of faith, "Herein is our love made perfect, that we may have boldness in the day of judgment."

81. My soul faints for Your salvation; but I hope in Your word.

The salvation of the Gospel was the constant object of faith and desire to the Lord's people under the old dispensation. Long had the church triumphed in the glowing anticipation, as if in the full possession of the promised blessing, "It shall be said in that day, Lo, this is our God; we have waited for Him, we will be glad and rejoice in His salvation. I will greatly rejoice in the Lord; my soul shall be joyful in my God; for He has clothed me with the garments of salvation; He has covered me with the robe of righteousness; as a bridegroom decks himself with ornaments, and as a bride adorns herself with her jewels." And as it was the joy of their living moments, so was it the support and consolation of their dying hours. "I have waited for Your salvation, O Lord!" was the expression of the dying patriarch's faith. And how cheering were the last words of this "sweet Psalmist of Israel," whose soul was now fainting for God's salvation, even in his dark and foreboding family prospect! "Although my house be not so with God, yet has He made with me an everlasting covenant, ordered in all things and sure: for this is all my salvation, and all my desire, although He make it not to grow." Good old Simeon, in the break of the gospel-day, was ready to "depart in peace, for his eyes had seen God's salvation." And shall not we, under this heavenly influence, naturally appropriate these feelings of ancient believers to ourselves? What interpreter but experience will be needed to explain them? The uneasiness felt by any interruption of our enjoyment, will show the soul to be fainting for this salvation. Nothing will satisfy but the Savior. The tempting offer of "all the kingdoms of the world, and the glory of them," will fail in attraction. Still the cry will be, "Say unto my soul, I am Your salvation. Let Your mercies come also unto me, O Lord; even Your salvation, according to Your word."

As the lowest expectant of this salvation, am not I richer than the sole possessor of this world's portion? And therefore if the Lord hides His face, I would look to no other quarter; I would stay by Him, and "wait on Him," though days and months and years may pass away, "until He have mercy upon me." My soul faints for His salvation: and—pressing to my lips the fullest cup of earth's best joy—my heart would burst with despair of satisfaction, "but" that "I hope in His word." "By this hope I am saved." In "the patience of hope" I am resolved to wait until the last moment, lying at the footstool of my Savior. I am looking for the "assurance of this hope"—when, in the joyous anticipation of eternity, and with "the earnest of" the heavenly "inheritance" in my soul, I shall echo the voice of my coming Savior, "Even so come, Lord Jesus."

Oh, how precious and important a part of our armor is Hope! As a "helmet," it has "covered our head in the day of battle" from many a "fiery dart of the wicked." In times of darkness—when the restless foe hides the prospect from the eye of faith, and the child of God can scarcely, if at all, mount up and sing—even then hope remains, and lights a candle in moments dark as the chamber of the grave, "Yet the Lord will command His loving-kindness in the daytime; and in the night-season His song shall be with me, and my prayer unto the God of my life." And when the afflicted, tempest-tossed soul is trembling at the prospect of impending danger—at this moment of infinite peril, Hope holds out the "anchor sure and steadfast;" so that in the awful crisis, when "deep calls unto deep, and all the waves and billows are going over us," most unexpectedly "an entrance is ministered unto us abundantly," in the Lord's best time, into our desired haven. And it is this hope alone that sustains us. Were we to conceive of God according to the notions of our own hearts, we should give way to most unbelieving patience. But the Divine character—as it shines forth in the word with such love and wisdom, such tenderness and grace—invigorates our hope. The strength of the strongest of God's people proves but small, when afflictions press heavily, and expected help is delayed. But though the soul faints, it cannot fail. We depend not on what we see or feel, but on what the word promises. If God has engaged, it must be fulfilled, be the difficulties— no, impossibilities—what they may. Fixed, therefore, upon this sure foundation, with our father Abraham, "against hope" from what we see, "we believe in hope" from what God has promised. Thus the word is faith's sure venture for eternity—stamped with such a marvelous, mysterious impression of Divine glory and faithfulness, and communicating such Divine power and refreshment, that the believer cannot but produce his experience of its efficacy for the support of his tempted brethren, "I had fainted, unless I had believed to see the goodness of the Lord in the land of the living. Wait on the Lord: be of good courage, and He shall strengthen your heart: wait, I say, on the Lord."

82. My eyes fail for Your word, saying, When will You comfort me?

Though the believer may be enabled, in the habitual working of faith, to sustain his hope in the word, yet "hope deferred makes the heart sick." Still, Christian, as you value the promise, trust the assurance. Do not be discouraged by present appearances. The sunshine is behind the cloud. "The vision is for an appointed time; though it tarry, wait for it." "The Lord is not slack concerning His promise," but we are hasty in looking for it. The failing of our eyes is the impatience of the will, "limiting God" to our own time, ways, and means. Faith may be exercised in not seeing His reasons—not being able to harmonize His promises with His providences, or His outward dispensations with His Divine perfections. But let us leave this to Him, and be "still, and know that He is God." We shall find in the end, that perseverance in waiting has turned to double advantage; and that even when the present answer to prayer, and also sensible comfort and acceptance have been withheld; yet that important blessings have been accomplished, and the merciful purposes given in bringing the wayward will into more entire subjection to Himself. Yes— the blessing will be so much the sweeter, from being given in the Lord's best time. Waiting time—whatever weariness may attend it—is precious time, and not a moment of it will be lost. The Lord secretly upholds faith and patience, so that every step of feeble perseverance in the way brings with it unspeakable delight. Even while our eyes fail for the fulfillment of the word, peace is found in submission and joyful expectation; and instead of a time of hardness, indolence, or carelessness, the Lord's return is anticipated the more intensely, as His absence had been felt to be the most painful trial. For as well might the stars supply the place of the sun, as outward comforts, or even the external duties of religion, supply to the waiting soul the place of an absent God.

Never, however, let us forget, that the real cause of separation between God and a sinner is removed. The way of access is opened by the blood of Jesus; and in this way we must be found waiting, until He look upon us. Here will our cry, "When will You comfort me?" be abundantly answered; and though the sovereignty of God be exhibited in the time and measure of His consolations, yet the general rule will be, "According to your faith, be it unto you."

But if unbelief clouds our comfort, turn the eye more simply to the "word" as testifying of Jesus. Here alone is the ground of comfort; and the more confidently we expect, the more patiently we will look. Nor shall we ever look in vain. Sin will be rebuked. But restoration and acceptance are assured. We shall obtain—not the spurious comfort of delusion—but those wholesome comforts, founded upon the word of promise, and connected with contrition, peace, love, joy, and triumph. The gospel shows hell deserved, and heaven purchased thus combining conviction and faith. Indeed, conviction without faith, would be legal sorrow; as assurance without conviction would be gospel presumption. Paul's experience happily united both. Never was man at the same moment more exercised with conflict, and yet more established in assurance. Thus may we maintain our assurance as really in wrestling trouble as in exulting joy; honoring the Lord by an humble, patient spirit—in Bernard's resolution—'I will never come away from You without You'—in the true spirit of the wrestling patriarch, "I will not let You go, except You bless me."

But we sometimes seem to go "mourning without the sun," "shut up, and we cannot come forth"—straitened in our desires and expectations—doing little for the Lord—with little enjoyment in our own souls, and little apparent usefulness to the Church. At such seasons it is our clear duty and privilege to "wait upon the Lord, that hides His face from the house of Jacob, and to look for Him." "He waits that He may be gracious. He is a God of Judgment; and blessed are all those who wait for Him." He waits—not because He is reluctant to give, but that we may be fitted to receive.

83. For I am become like a bottle in the smoke, yet do I not forget Your statutes.

What an affecting picture of misery! Not only were his patience and hope—but his very body, "dried up" by long-continued affliction. This is he, who in the prime of youth was "ruddy and of a beautiful countenance, and goodly to look to,"—now shriveled up like a bottle of skin, hung up in the smoke! Such is the mark that the rod of "chastening" leaves on the body of humiliation. The soul is strengthened—the body withers—under the stroke.

What might naturally have been expected to have been the result of this lengthened exercise? Saul, under protracted trial, resorted to the devil for relief. An infidel nation took occasion from thence to throw off the yoke. Even a good man, under a few hours' trial, murmurs against God—no, even defends his murmuring. How did this man of God behave? When his soul was fainting, his hope in the word kept him from sinking. Under the further continuance of the trial, the same recollection gives him support—yet do I not forget Your statutes.

Now—Christian—do not expect a new way to heaven to be made for you. Prepare for the cross. It may be—as with David—a heavy, long-continued burden, and, should it come—look on it as your appointed trial of faith, and your training discipline for more enduring conflicts. And remember that your determined resolution rather to pine away in affliction, than "make a way of escape" by sin—is the proof of the reality of His own grace in you, and of His faithful love towards you. Think how honorably He manifests your relation to Christ, by causing "His sufferings to abound in you," and making you "bear in your body the marks of the Lord Jesus." And do you not thus realize, as you could not otherwise do, the sympathy of our High Priest, who was Himself "a root out of a dry ground, having no form nor loveliness, and no beauty that He should be desired—despised and rejected of men" to the end? Oh, what a supporting cordial to His afflicted people is the sympathy of this suffering, tempted Savior!

But to look at David, under his long-continued trials, preserving his recollection of the Lord's statutes—what a striking evidence of the presence of his God, and the sustaining power of his word! If we then—blessed with much larger Scriptures than he—fail in deriving from them the same support, it can only be, that we do not search them in a dependent, prayerful, and humble spirit—that we do not simply look for the revelation of Christ; to mark His glory, and to increase in the knowledge of Him. In this spirit we should have more to say of the comfort of remembering the Lord's statutes; and of their upholding influence, when all other stays were found as "the trust in the shadow of Egypt—shame and confusion."

Job's history strikingly illustrates both the trial and its sanctified results. When "scraping himself with a potsherd, and sitting down among the ashes,"—the temporary victim of Satanic power—he might well have taken up the complaint, I am become like a bottle in the smoke. But when in this hour of temptation he was enabled to resist the tempter in the person of his own wife, and commit himself with implicit resignation into the hands of his faithful God, "What! shall we receive good at the hand of God, and shall we not receive evil?"—was not this the confidence—Yet do I not forget Your statutes?

153

This confidence is indeed an encouraging seal of the Lord's love to our souls. For we never should have remembered His statutes, had He not written His covenant promises upon our hearts. And how much more honorable to our God is it than the desponding complaint, "The Lord has forsaken me, and my God has forgotten me!" Let us watch then against a proud sullenness under every little trial—such as the coldness of friends, the unkindness of enemies, or our Father's providential dispensations. How sinful to allow hard thoughts of Him, whose name and character, "without variableness or shadow of turning," is "Love!" A steady trust in the long and wearisome seasons of tribulation, is indeed "to glorify God in the fires." Nothing honors Him so much as this enduring, overcoming faith, persevering in despite of opposition, in destitution of all outward prospects of relief. It is when "against hope we believe in hope, not staggering at the promise of God through unbelief," that we are "strong in faith, giving glory to God."

84. How many are the days of Your servant? When will You execute judgment on them that persecute me?—
85. The proud have dug pits for me, which are not after Your law.

Though a steady confidence in severe and protracted exercise may enable us, not to forget the statutes; yet we shall hasten to carry our complaint before Him. How many are the days of Your servant?—my days of affliction under the "fury of the oppressor." To complain of God is dishonorable unbelief. To complain to God is the mark of His "elect, which cry day and night unto Him, though He bears long with them." Christians! study this instructive pattern; and, when exposed to the lawless devices of the proud, do not forget your hiding-place. God in Christ is your stronghold, "whereunto you may continually resort. He has given commandment to save you." Your trial has done its appointed work, when it has brought you to Him; and inclined you, after your blessed Master's example, instead of taking the vengeance into your own hands, to commit yourself and your cause "to Him that judges righteously." 'And this,' as Archbishop Leighton excellently observes, 'is the true method of Christian patience—that which quiets the mind, and keeps it from the boiling tumultuous thoughts of revenge; to turn the whole matter into God's hands; to resign it over to Him, to prosecute when and as He thinks good. Not as the most, who had rather, if they had power, do for themselves, and be their own avengers: and, because they have not power, do offer up such bitter curses and prayers for revenge unto God, as are most hateful to Him, and differ wholly from this calm and holy way of committing matters to His judgments. The common way of referring things to God is indeed impious and dishonorable to Him, being really no other than calling Him to be a servant and executioner of our passion. We ordinarily mistake His justice, and judge of it according to our own precipitate and distempered minds. If wicked men be not crossed in their designs, and their wickedness evidently crushed, just when we would have it, we are ready to give up the matter as desperate; or at least to abate of those confident and reverent thoughts of Divine justice which we owe Him. However things go, this ought to be fixed in our hearts, that He who sits in heaven judges righteously, and executes that His righteous judgment in the fittest season.'

Usually the Psalmist is expressing his love for the law. Here he is complaining against his enemies; yet still implying the same spirit, that the pits, which the proud dug for him, were not after God's law. The martyr's cry under the altar shows the acceptance of this complaint; "seeing it is a righteous thing with God to recompense tribulation to them that trouble" His people, "and to them that are troubled rest." Some of us indeed have known but little of "cruel mockings" and bitter persecutions. Let such be thankful for the merciful exemption from this "hardness:" but let them gird on their armor for the conflict. Let none of us, in the determination to "live godly in Christ Jesus," expect to escape "persecution." Let us "count the cost" of suffering for Christ, whether we shall be able to abide it. For the mere spiritless notions, or for the unenlivened forms of religion, of which we have never felt the power, nor tasted the sweetness, it would be little worth our while to expose ourselves to inconvenience. But if we understand the grand substantials of the gospel—if we are clearly assured of their reality, practically acknowledge their influence, and experimentally realize their enjoyment, we shall dare the persecuting malice of the proud in defense of a treasure dearer to us than life itself. Should we, however, be too rich to part with all for Christ, or too high in the estimation of the world to confess His despised followers, it will be no marvel, or rather a marvel of mercy, if He should sweep away our riches, and suffer the proud to dig pits for us. To make this world "a wilderness or a land of darkness" to us, may be His wisely-ordained means to turn us back to Himself as our portion, to His word as our support, to His people as our choice companions, and to heaven as our eternal rest.

86. All Your commandments are faithful: they persecute me wrongfully; help me.

In the lengthened duration of trials, the eyes fail with looking upward, the voice of prayer grows faint, and in a moment of weakness, the faithfulness of God is almost questioned, as if we should go mourning to the very end of our days. It is at such a season that He who delights to "comfort them that are cast down," realizes to the view of faith the unchangeable faithfulness of His commandments with respect to His people. In this recollection we can "look up and lift up our heads," and "go on our way," if not "rejoicing," yet at least with humble acquiescence; assured, that in the perseverance of faith and hope, we shall ultimately be "more than conquerors through Him that loved us."

Many Old Testament histories beautifully illustrate the reward of this simplicity of faith in temporal emergencies. When Asa's "hands were made strong by the hands of the mighty God of Jacob," "his bow abode in strength." When at a subsequent period he "trusted in man, and made flesh his arm, and his heart departed from the Lord," he became, like Samson, "weak, and as another man." So true is it, that no past communications of Divine strength can stand in the stead of the daily habit of dependence upon the Lord, without which we are utterly helpless, and are overthrown in every conflict. Our best prosperity, therefore, is to leave our cause in His hands, looking upward in the simplicity of wretchedness for His help: 'All Your commandments are faithful; they persecute me wrongfully; help me. Wretched and forlorn I am; but Your truth is my shield.'

Believer! This is your only posture of resistance. Should you enter the field of conflict without this "shield of faith," some crevice will be found in your panoply, through which a "fiery dart" will inflict a poisonous wound." But how can faith be exercised without a distinct acquaintance with the object of faith? We cannot repose trust in, or expect help from, an unknown God—an offended God, whom every day's transgression has made our enemy. There must, then, be reconciliation, before there can be help. Those, therefore, who are unreconciled by the death of Christ, cry for help to a God, who does not hear, accept, or answer, them. But when Christ is known as "the peace," and the way of access to God, what instance can there be of trial or difficulty, when our reliance upon the Lord will fail? Not indeed that we shall always return from the throne of grace with the wished-for relief. For too often we bring our burden before the Lord, and yet through distrust neglect to leave it with Him. Oh! let us remember, when we go to Jesus, that we go to a tried, long-proved, and faithful friend. Dependence upon Him is victory. "The good fight" is the fight "of faith." We are best able to resist our enemy upon our knees; and even such a short prayer as this—Help me—will bring down the strength of Omnipotence on our side. But we might as well expect to crush a giant with a straw, as to enter the spiritual conflict with weapons of carnal warfare. Every trial realizes experimentally the help of a faithful Savior. He does indeed deliver gloriously; and leaves us nothing to do, but to "stand still," wonder, and praise. "Fear not, stand still, and see the salvation of the Lord, which He will show to you today; for the Egyptians, whom you have seen today, you shall see them again no more forever."

87. They had almost consumed me upon earth; but I forsook not Your precepts.

And why did they not quite consume him? Because "the eyes of the Lord run to and fro throughout the whole earth, to show Himself strong in behalf of them, whose heart is perfect toward Him." "Surely the wrath of man shall praise You; the remainder of wrath shall You restrain." And why have not our spiritual enemies consumed us upon earth? "Satan has desired to have us, that he may sift us as wheat." But—says the Savior, "I have prayed for you, that your faith fail not." "My sheep shall never perish; neither shall any pluck them out of My hand." Steadfastness of profession is the evidence of the life of faith: grounded upon this security, the more we are shaken, the more we shall hold fast. Neither long-continued distress, nor determined opposition, will turn us from the ways of God. We would rather forsake all that our heart held dear upon earth, than the precepts of our God. With whatever intensity of affection we love father and mother (and the influence of the Gospel has increased the sensibilities of relative affection), we remember who has said, "He who loves father and mother more than Me, is not worthy of Me." Unlike the deluded professor, we have counted the cost of the "tribulation and persecution" of the Gospel; and the result has only served to confirm our love and adherence to our heavenly Master. Shall not we find in heaven—no, do not we find in the gospel—a far better portion than we lose?

When, therefore, we are tempted to neglect the precepts, or when we fail to live in them, and to delight in them, let us each bring our hearts to this test: 'What would I take in exchange for them? Will the good-will and approbation of the world compensate for the loss of the favor of God? Could I be content to forego my greatest comforts, to "suffer the loss of all things," yes, of life itself, rather than forsake one of the ways of God? When I meet with such precepts as link me to the daily cross, can I throw myself with simple dependence upon that Savior, who has engaged to supply strength for what He has commanded?' How often in times of spiritual temptation, if not of temporal danger, they had almost consumed us upon earth! but "in the mount" of difficulty "the Lord has been seen." Oh! let each of us mark our road to Zion with multiplied Ebenezers, inscribed Jehovah-jireh, Jehovah-nissi. "By this I know You favor me, because my enemy does not triumph over me. And as for me, You uphold me in my integrity, and set me before Your face forever."

What a fine testimony of the upholding grace of God! How could a helpless believer stand against such an appalling array? Yet it is a great, but a true word, suitable for a babe in Christ, as well as for an Apostle, "I can do all things through Christ that strengthens me." Yes, I can "wrestle even against principalities and powers" of darkness, if I be "strong in the Lord, and in the power of His might."

88. Quicken me after Your loving-kindness: so shall I keep the testimony of Your mouth.

We need continual quickening to maintain our steadfastness in the precepts. "God, who is rich in mercy, for His great love with which He loved us, even when we were dead in sins, has quickened us, together with Christ." But without daily quickening after the same loving-kindness, "the things which remain will be ready to die." For every breath of prayer, Divine influence must flow, "Quicken us, and we shall call upon Your name." For the work of praise, without the same influence we are dumb., "Let my soul live, and it shall praise You." For the exercise of every spiritual grace, there must be the commanding voice of our Divine Head, "Awake, O north wind; and come, you south: blow upon my garden, that the spices thereof may flow out." Thus is the creature laid in the dust, and all the glory is given to God. "Not that we are sufficient of ourselves to think anything as of ourselves; but our sufficiency is of God."

Why is it, then, that at one time we spring to duty as the joy of our life; while at other times the soul is so chained down under the power of corruption, that it scarcely can put forth the feeblest exercise of life? The source of our life is the same;, "Hid with Christ in God." But the power of the flesh hinders its every motion. Such a spiritual sloth has benumbed us—such backwardness to prayer, and disrelish for heavenly things! These are sins deeply humbling in themselves, and aggravated by the neglect of the plentiful provision laid up in Christ, not only for the life, but for the peace, joy, and strength of the soul. Nothing but indolence or unbelief straitens our supplies. Oh! stir up the prayer for quickening influence, and we shall be rich and fruitful. Sometimes also self-confidence paralyzes our spiritual energy. We expect our recovery from a lifeless state by more determined resolutions, or increased improvement of the various means of grace. Let these means indeed be used with all diligence, but with the fullest conviction that all means, all instruments, all helps of every kind, without the influence of the Spirit of grace, are dead. "It is the Spirit that quickens; the flesh profits nothing."

These records of David's prayers strikingly mark the intensity of his desire to live to God. Every decay of strength and activity was, as it were, death to him, and awakened his reiterated cries. Do we desire to keep the testimony of His mouth? Do we mourn over our shortcomings in service? Oh! then, for our own sake, for the Lord's sake, and for the church's and the world's sake, let our petitions be incessant each one for himself—'Quicken me—Quicken this slothful heart of mine. Enkindle afresh the sacred spark within, and let me be all alive for You.' Let faith be kept alive and active at the throne of grace, and all will be alive; our obligation will be deeply felt, and practically acknowledged.

The title here given to the directory of our duty—the testimony of God's mouth—adds strength to our obligations. Thus let every word we read or hear be regarded as coming directly from the mouth of God. What reverence, what implicit submission does it demand! May it ever find us in the posture of attention, humility, and faith, each one of us ready to say, "Speak, Lord, for Your servant hears!"

89. Forever, O Lord, Your word is settled in heaven.
90. Your faithfulness is unto all generations; You have established the earth, and it abides.
91. They continue this day according to Your ordinances, for all are Your servants.

The Christian extends his survey far beyond the limits of his individual sphere. His view of the operations of God in creation enlarges his apprehensions of the Divine attributes, and especially that of unchanging faithfulness. Indeed, the very fact of a creation in ruins—a world in rebellion against its Maker, failing of the grand end of existence, and yet still continued in existence—manifests His faithfulness unto all generations. How different is the contemplation of the Christian from that of the philosopher! His is not a mere cold, speculative admiration, but the establishment of his faith upon a clear discovery of the faithfulness of God. Thus he stays his soul upon the assured unchangeableness of the Divine word, "Concerning Your testimonies, I have known of old, that You have founded them forever. Your word is true from the beginning: and everyone of Your righteous judgments endures forever." How striking is the contrast between the transient glory of man's goodness, and the solid foundation of all the promises, hopes, and prospects of the children of God!, "The grass withers, and the flower fades; but the word of our God shall stand forever." "Unbelief" is the character of our "evil hearts." Man chooses his own measure and objects of faith; he believes no more than he pleases. But it is a fearful prospect, that the threatenings of God rest upon the same solid foundation with His promises. "Heaven and earth shall pass away but My word shall not pass away."

Need we any further proof of His faithfulness? Look at the earth established by His word of power. See how "he hangs it upon nothing," as if it might fall at any moment;—and yet it is immovably fixed—it abides—and with all its furniture, continues according to His ordinances. This—though the scoff of the infidel—is the encouragement to Christian faith. It is at once a token of His covenant with nature, that "while the earth remains, seed-time and harvest, and cold and heat, and summer and winter, and day and night, shall not cease;" and an emblem of His covenant with the seed of David, that He "will not cast them off for all that they have done." Thus every view of the heavens—yes—every time we set our foot on the earth—shows the unchangeableness of His everlasting covenant, and the security of the salvation of His own people.

In this vast universe, all are His servants. "The stars in their courses" "fire and hail, snow and vapors, stormy wind—fulfill His word. He sends forth His commandment upon earth: His word runs very swiftly." Man—the child of his Maker, "created in His image"—destined for His glory—is the only rebel and revolter. Most affecting is the appeal, that his own

Father and God is constrained to make concerning him, "Hear, O heavens, and give ear, O earth; for the Lord has spoken. I have nourished and brought up children, and they have rebelled against Me!"

Is not then the universe of nature a parable of grace—setting out on every side—in every view—a cheering display of the faithfulness of God? If His providence fails not, will the promise of His covenant disappoint us? Why should He change? Does He see or know anything now, that He has not foreseen and foreknown from eternity? What more sure ground of salvation than the unchangeableness of God? If I can prove a word to have been spoken by God, I must no more question it than his own Being. It may seem to fail on earth; but it is forever settled in heaven. The decrees of the kings of the earth, "settled" on earth, are exposed to all the variations and weakness of a changing world. They may be revoked by themselves or their successors, or they may die away. The empty sound of the "law of the Medes and Persians that alters not," has long since been swept away into oblivion. But while "the word settled" on earth has "waxed old like a garment," and perished; the word settled in heaven—is raised above all the revolutions of the universe, and remains as the throne of God—unshaken and eternal; exhibiting the foundation of the believer's hope and of the unbeliever's terror to be alike unalterably fixed.

But we also remark the foreknowledge as well as the faithfulness of God. From the eternity that is past, as well for the eternity that is to come, Your word is settled in heaven. Before this fair creation was marred, yes, before it was called into existence, its ruin was foreseen, and a remedy provided. "The Lamb was slain from the foundation of the world," and fore-ordained before that era. Concurrent with this period, a people "were chosen in Him," and forever the word was settled in heaven., "All that the Father gives Me shall come to Me." For the establishment of the Redeemer's kingdom upon earth "the decree is declared;" however earth and hell may combine against it, "Yet have I set My king upon My holy hill of Zion." And what a blessed encouragement in the grand work of bringing back "the lost sheep of the house of Israel," and those "other sheep" with them, "which are not of this fold" is it, that we do not depend upon the earnestness of our prayers, the wisdom of our plans, or the diligence of our endeavors; but upon "the word" forever settled in heaven!, "The Redeemer shall come to Zion, and unto them that turn from transgression in Jacob, says the Lord. As for Me, this is My covenant with them, says the Lord—My Spirit that is upon You, and

My words which I have put in your mouth, shall not depart out of your mouth, nor out of the mouth of your seed, nor out of the mouth of your seed's seed, says the Lord, from henceforth, and forever." "I have sworn by Myself, the word is gone out of My mouth in righteousness, and shall not return—That unto Me every knee shall bow, every tongue shall swear."

92. Unless Your law had been my delights, I should then have perished in my affliction.

The support of the word is as sure as its basis—and that in the time when other supports sink—in affliction. David—like his great prototype—was a man of affliction—sometimes ready to perish—always kept up by the law of his God. How many a false professor has been tried and cast by this hour of affliction! But he who has been sifted by temptation—who has "endured the hardness" of persecution, as a "good soldier of Jesus Christ,"—and who is ready rather to be "consumed upon earth," than to shrink from his profession—this is he whom his Master "will lift up, and not make his foes to rejoice over him." It is the established rule of the kingdom, "Them that honor Me I will honor." "Because you have kept the word of My patience, I also will keep you from the hour of temptation, which shall come upon all the world, to try them that dwell upon the earth."

The law of God opens to us a clear interest in every perfection of His Godhead—every engagement of His covenant. What wonder then, that it brings delights, which the world can never conceive, when bowed down with accumulated affliction? However the believer's real character may be hidden from the world, the hour of trial abundantly proves, both what the law can do for him, and what a lost creature he would have been without it. In affliction, friends mean well; but of themselves they can do nothing. They can only look on, feel, and pray. They cannot "speak to the heart." This is God's prerogative: and His law is His voice.

But for this support, Jonah probably would have perished in his affliction. In the belly of the fish, as "in the belly of hell," he appears to have recollected the experience of David under deep and awful desertion; and in taking his language out of his mouth, as descriptive of his own dark and terrific condition, a ray of light and hope darted upon his dungeon-walls. Indeed it is a mystery, how a sinner, destitute of the support and comfort of the word of God, can ever uphold himself in his trials. We marvel not, that often "his soul should choose strangling, and death, rather than his life."

But in order to derive support from the law, it must be our delights—yes—that it may be our delights it must be the matter of our faith. For what solid delight, can we have in what we do not believe? Must it not also be our joy in prosperity, if we would realize its support in affliction? For this, how ineffectual is the mere formal service! Who ever tasted its tried consolations in the bare performance of the outward duty? It must be read in reality; it will then be taken as a cordial. Let it be simply received, diligently searched, and earnestly prayed over; and it will guide the heavy-laden to Him, who is their present and eternal rest. The tempest-tossed soul will cast anchor upon it., "Remember the word unto Your servant, upon which You have caused me to hope." One promise applied by the Spirit of God is worth ten thousand worlds. And each promise is a staff—if we have but faith to lean upon it—able to bear our whole weight of sin, care, and trial.

Is then affliction our appointed lot? If "man is born"—and the child of God twice born, "to trouble, as the sparks fly upward,"—how important is it to lay in a store of supply from this inexhaustible treasury, against the time when all human support will fail! Supplied hence with heavenly strength, we shall be borne up above the weakness and weariness of the flesh. And as the riches of this storehouse are "the riches of Christ," let those parts be most familiar to us, which mark His person, His character, offices, life, sufferings, and death, resurrection and glory, together with the promises, encouragements, and prospects directly flowing from this blessed subject—and oh! what a treasure-house shall we find, richly furnished with every source of delight, and every ground of support!

93. I will never forget Your precepts; for with them You have quickened me.

An admirable resolution! the blessed fruit of the quickening power of the word in his deep affliction. He had before acknowledged this supernatural efficacy, "Your word has quickened me." Now he more distinctly mentions it, as the instrumental only—not the efficient—cause—With them You have quickened me. Had the power been in the word, the same effect would have immediately and invariably followed. Nor should we have been constrained to lament the limited extent of its influence. How many, Christian, shared with you in the outward

163

privileges; but perhaps unto none was the life-giving blessing given, save unto yourself—the most unlikely—the most unworthy of all! Thus does "God work in us both to will and to do"—not according to any prescribed law, but "of His good pleasure." The grace therefore is not from, but through, the means. Almighty God is the source of the life. The word is the instrument—yet so "quick," so melting, so attractive, that we might ask, out of what rock was that heart hewn, that is proof against its power? Yet while the precepts work nothing without the agents they are the ordinary course, by which the Lord quickens whom He will.

And do not we find them still lively channels of refreshment? Surely, then, we will hold to our purpose of not forgetting the precepts. The leaves of the word of God are the leaves of the tree of life, as well as of the tree of knowledge. They not only enlighten the path, but they supply life for daily work and progress. "The words that I speak unto you"—said Jesus, "they are spirit, and they are life:" so that the times when we have been most diligent in our meditation and obedience to the precepts, have been uniformly the seasons of our most holy consolation.

Men of the world, however, with accurate recollections of all matters, connected with their temporal advantage, are remarkably slow in retaining the truths of God. They plead their short memories, although conscious that this infirmity does not extend to their important secular engagements. But what wonder that they forget the precepts, when they have never been quickened with them—never received any benefit from them? The word of God is not precious to them: they acknowledge no obligation to it: they have no acquaintance with it. It has no place in their affections, and therefore but little abode in their remembrance.

But this resolution is the language of sincerity, not of perfection. The child of God is humbled in the conscious forgetfulness of the Lord's precepts. And this consciousness keeps his eye fixed upon Jesus for pardon and acceptance: while every fresh sense of acceptance strengthens his more habitual remembrance. Then, as for his natural inability to preserve an accurate recollection of Divine things—let him not estimate the benefit of the word by the results in the memory, so much as by the impression upon the heart. The word may have darted through the mind, as a flash of lightning, that strikes and is gone; and yet the heart may have been melted, and the passing flash may have shed a heavenly ray upon a dubious path. If the heart retains the quickening power, the precepts are not forgotten, even though the memory should have failed to preserve them.

But whatever word of conviction, direction, or encouragement, may have come to us, affix this seal to it—I will never forget Your precepts. It may be of signal use in some hour of temptation. The same Spirit that breathed before upon it may breathe again; if not with the same present sensible power, yet with a seasonable and refreshing recollection of past support.

94. I am Yours; save me; for I have sought Your precepts.

What a high and honorable character is stamped upon the lowest believer! He is the Savior's unalienable property, his portion, the "workmanship" of His hand, the purchase of His blood, the triumph of His conquering love. He is given to Him by His Father, "preserved in Him, and called." The evidence of his character is found in seeking the Lord's precepts. "Whom we serve" will prove "whose we are." "His servants you are, to whom you obey." "Know that the Lord has set apart him that is godly for Himself." "The carnal mind is not subject to the law of God, neither indeed can be. So then those who are in the flesh" cannot seek the Lord's precepts. A new and spiritual bias, therefore, is the visible stamp and seal of the Lord's interest in us.

True it is, that our Divine Savior can never be robbed of His property—that His people are saved in Him, beyond the reach of earth and hell to touch them. Yet are they dependent still—always sinners—every day's provocation making them more sinners than before; needing, therefore, from day to day, fresh power, fresh keeping, and, above all, fresh cleansing and acceptance. But what a powerful plea for mercy may we draw from the Lord's interest in us! Will not a man be careful of his children, his treasure, his jewels? 'Such am I. Your sovereign love has bought me—made me Yours—I am Yours; save me. You have saved me; "You have delivered my soul from death; will You not deliver my feet from falling?" Save me from the love of sin, from the daily guilt and power of sin; from the treachery of my own foolish heart from all this, and all besides, which You see ensnaring to my soul. If I am not Yours, whence this desire, this endeavor to seek Your precepts? What mean my privileged moments of communion with You? What mean the yet unsatisfied desires after a conformity to Your image? Lord, I would humbly plead Your own act, Your free and sovereign act, that made me Yours. Save me, because You have brought Your salvation near to me, and sealed me Yours. I need mercy to begin with me; mercy to accompany me; mercy to abide with me forever. I am Yours; save me.'

And what irresistible energy does it give to our pleading, that this was the sole purpose, that brought down the Son of God from Heaven! "I came down"—said he, "from heaven, not to do My own will, but the will of Him that sent Me. And this is the Father's will which has sent Me, that of all which He has given Me I should lose nothing." Of this purpose He was enabled to testify at the conclusion of His work, "Those that You gave Me I have kept, and none of them is lost, but the son of perdition."

But some cry for salvation, who neglect duty, and thus make void their plea. Can we make our interest good, by seeking His precepts? Is it the way in which we love to walk? Then let us not desist from our plea before God, until our heart listens to the voice of love, centering every blessing of creation, redemption, and heavenly calling, in the privilege of adoption, "Thus says the Lord, that created you, O Jacob, and He who formed you, O Israel Fear not, for I have redeemed you: I have called you by your name; you are Mine. You are My servant; O Israel, you shall not be forgotten of Me. I have blotted out, as a thick cloud, your transgressions; and as a cloud your sins." I have regarded this your plea. I have heard this your prayer—I am Yours, save me.

95. The wicked have waited for me to destroy me; but I will consider Your testimonies.

Am I, as a believer, safe as the Lord's property, and in the Lord's keeping? Yet must I expect that the wicked, the ungodly, as the instruments of Satan, will not cease to distress me. The Psalmist had before alluded to this trial, as driving him to his refuge. And, indeed, this is the constant character of the believer's walk—enduring the enmity of the ungodly, and seeking his refuge in the word of God—in that hiding-place of safety to which the word directs him. How striking is the proof of the irreconcilable variance between God and the world—the world encouraging all that is contrary to God, and persecuting His image in His people! Yet the word opens to us a sure defense. If our "soul is among lions," cannot we testify to the astonishment of the world, "My God has sent His angel, and has shut the lions' mouths, that they have not hurt me?" We hear indeed the roaring of the winds and waves; but we hear also the voice hushing the storm to rest, "Peace, be still."

The experience of this trial and support beautifully illustrates the promise, "He who believes shall not make haste." He whose hope is firmly fixed on that "tried corner-stone," which God Himself has "laid in Zion as a sure foundation" "shall not be greatly moved;" no—he "shall not be moved" at all, by the wicked waiting for him to destroy him. In the hour of difficulty, instead of perplexing himself with successive expedients for his safety (sought more from human contrivance, than from asking counsel at the mouth of God) he "possesses his soul in patience," and calmly commits all events to the Lord. Such a man "shall not be afraid of evil tidings! his heart is fixed, trusting in the Lord." 'This trust is grounded on the word of God, revealing His power and all-sufficiency, and withal His goodness, His offer of Himself to be the stay of the soul, commanding us to rest upon Him. People wait on I know not what persuasions and assurances; but I know no other to build faith on but the word of promise. The truth and faithfulness of God opened up His wisdom, and power, and goodness, as the stay of all those that, renouncing all other props, will venture on it, and lay all upon Him. "He who believes, sets to his seal that God is true:" and so he is sealed for God; his portion and interest secured. "If you will not believe, surely you shall not be established."'

But it is the considering of the Lord's testimonies that draws out their staying support. The soul must be fixed upon them, as "tried words, purified seven times in the fire." And in this frame, I will, under all distresses, all circumstances of trial, or even of dismay, consider Your testimonies. I will consider the faithfulness of those blessed declarations, "There shall not an hair of your head perish. Touch not My anointed." "He who touches you, touches the apple of My eye." With this armor of defense, I shall not be afraid, even should I hear the "evil tidings," that the wicked have waited for me, to destroy me. Or even should I be destroyed, I know that Your testimonies cannot fail—that my rock is perfect, "that there is no unrighteousness in Him;" and therefore, "though a host should encamp against me, my heart shall not fear; though war should rise against me, in this will I be confident." Whether, then, I am delivered from the wicked, and live, "I live unto the Lord;" or whether I fall into their snare, and "die—I die unto the Lord;" for I will consider Your testimonies, assured that all Your purposes shall be accomplished concerning me, as You have said, "I will never leave you, nor forsake you." "You will keep him in perfect peace, whose mind is stayed on You, because he trusts in You."

96. I have seen an end of all perfection; but Your commandment is exceeding broad.

A deeper insight into the Lord's testimonies is the sure result of considering them. Weigh them in the balances against this world's excellency; the world and the word—each with all its fullness. Of the one perfection we see an end—of the other—none. This world is a matter of experience and observation. We have seen an end—not of some—but of all its perfection. It wants sufficiency. It stands us in no stead in the great emergencies of affliction—death—judgment—eternity. It wants solidity in its best substance. "In its wisdom is grief!" All its delicacies and indulgences—after having, like the King of Jerusalem, "not withheld the heart from any joy"—all end in the verdict of disappointment, "Behold! all was vanity and vexation of spirit!" Its continuance is but for a moment. The soul is born for eternity. Therefore it must have a portion to last as long as itself. But the world, with its lusts and fashions, passes away. All that it can offer is a bubble—a shadow. In its best riches, honors, and pleasures—in the utmost that its perfection can yield—in its height and prime of enjoyment—what is it in itself—what is it able to do for us? "All is vanity." And yet such is the alienation of the heart from God, that it is first tried to the very uttermost, before any desire to return homeward is felt or expressed. And even then, nothing but the Almighty power of God can bring the sinner back. He would rather perish in his misery, than "return to his rest."

Now contrast with the emptiness of the world the fullness of the commandment of God. Our whole duty to our God, our neighbor, and ourselves, is here laid open before us—commanding without abatement, and forbidding without allowance—making no excuse for ignorance—frailty or forgetfulness—reaching not only to every species of crime, but to everything tending to it. This is perfection, of which we never see an end. Every fresh view opens—not the extent—but the immensity of the field; and compels us at length to shut up our inquiries with the adoring acknowledgment—Your commandment is exceeding broad. Its various parts form one seamless piece; so that no particle can be separated without injury to the whole. As all the curtains of the tabernacle connected by taches and loops, made but one covering for the ark, and the loosening or disjunction of the smallest point disannulled the fitness of the whole; so it belongs to the perfection of the commandment, that "whoever shall keep the whole law, and yet offend in one point, he is guilty of all." The spirituality of its requirements equally illustrates its Divine perfection. An angry look is murder; an unchaste desire is adultery; the "stumbling-block of iniquity" "covetousness"—in the heart is idolatry; the thought as well as the act—the first conception of sin, as well as the after-commission—brings in the verdict—Guilty—Death.

Can we, then, endure the sight of its exceeding breadth? Yes—for the commandment of the gospel is equally broad, and covers all. We know who has stood in our place—who has satisfied Sinai's unalterable requirements, and borne its awful curse. Broad as it may be, the love which has fulfilled it is immeasurable. As a covenant, therefore, it has now lost its terrors. As a rule, we love it for its extent, and for its purity; for the comprehensiveness of its obligations, and for the narrowness of its liberty for indulgence; nor would we wish to be subject to a less severe scrutiny, or a more lenient administration.

Reader! if you have learned the exceeding breadth and spirituality of the law (the first lesson that is taught and learned in the school of Christ), your views of yourself and your state before God will be totally changed. Before, you were "thanking God" in your heart, "that you were not as other men are." Now you will be "smiting upon your bosom, saying— God be merciful to me a sinner!" Before, perhaps, you might have thought yourself, "touching the righteousness which is of the law, blameless." Now you will glory in your new and more enlightened choice, "What things were gain to me, those I counted loss for Christ." Once you considered yourself "alive," when you were really dead. Now that "the commandment is come" in its heart-searching spirituality and conviction to your soul, you "die" that you may live. Blessed change from the law to the gospel, "from death to life!" "I through the law am dead to the law, that I might live unto God."

Such is the effect of the transition from a legal to an evangelical ground. Before, we were reckless of sin, and therefore reckless of the gospel. As the one fell lightly upon our conscience, the other held a light estimation in our judgment. While we had no disturbance from the law, we had no delight in the gospel. But now that we see in the true mirror, we are at once alarmed and enlightened. Praised be God! we now take the true estimate—we degrade to the uttermost righteousness by works— we exalt to the uttermost righteousness by faith. In the one we see pollution—in the other perfection.

169

97. O how love I Your law! it is my meditation all the day.

Mark the man of God giving utterance to his feelings of heavenly delight—expressing most, by intimating that he cannot adequately express what he desires. He seems unable to restrain his acknowledgments of Divine influence springing up in his heart—O how love I Your law! This experience is most distinctive of a spiritual character. The professor may read, and understand, and even externally obey the law; but the believer only loves it; and he lives in it, as if he could not live without it. To the professor it is a task imposed to satisfy conscience; "the veil upon the heart" darkens all his spiritual apprehension, and consequently excludes spiritual delight. To the child of God, it is food and medicine, light and comfort—yes, "life from the dead." The law of precept in the word is a "law of liberty"—a law of love—in his heart. His former obedience was the bondage of fear. But how different is the effect of constraining love! He now delights to view it in every lineament. He dwells upon every feature with intense enjoyment. Before, it was his confinement—his chain. Now, it is his liberty—his ornament. He is not what he was, "Old things are passed away: behold, all things are become new."

Think what good reason there is to love the law. It is the epistle of our most beloved friend—not to be slighted, but to be placed in our bosom, nearest our hearts. It sets out that relief, without which the conscience would have been tortured by the never-dying worm. There is more of glory—more of God—in this, than in any other manifestation of His name. It has ever been the mirror, that has reflected Christ to His church. The spiritual eye discerns Him in every part. Now—Reader—do you search for Him in His law? Do you love His law, because it "testifies of Him?" Do you pray for His Spirit, that His law may guide you to Him? This is the evidence that you have "turned unto the Lord, when the veil is taken away," and you "with unveiled face behold in this glass the glory of the Lord." Then if you do love His law, you will love the whole of it—its obligations as well as its privileges. You will love it at all times, even when it is thwarting your own will and way. The whole law is light and love—wisdom and faithfulness.

But love of the law fastens the soul to the beloved object, It is my meditation all the day. When you cannot have it in your hand, it will be found, if indeed your soul is in a prosperous state, "hid in your heart."

There it is kept as your most precious treasure; while you live upon it with unwearied appetite as your daily bread, and exercise yourself in it as your daily rule. Oh, how worthy is it of all the love of the warmest heart! The deepest students are most humbled for their want of suitable enlargement.

But this heavenly spirit can only be grounded upon a sense of reconciliation. Can an unreconciled sinner be interested in the law, in every page of which he reads his own condemnation? This explains the enmity of the ungodly. But the cultivation of this spirit upon the ground of the gospel is a most important principle of the Christian steadfastness, the want of which has been the source of fearful delusion; and in the exercise of which we shall realize a deeper insight and more spiritual discernment of Scriptural truth. Warm affections will be far more influential than talent, or mere external knowledge.

This habit of love and holy meditation will spread its influence over our whole character. It will fill our hearts with heavenly matter for prayer, diffuse a sweet savor over our earthly employments, sanctify the common bounties of Providence, realize the presence of God throughout the day, command prosperity upon our lawful undertakings, and enlarge our usefulness in the church. Thus the man of God is formed in his completeness, symmetry, and attraction—such as the world is often constrained secretly to admire, even where the heart is unready to follow.

Lord! implant in my heart a supreme love to Your law. Write it upon my heart—even that new law, "the law of the Spirit of life in Christ Jesus." May I love it so, that I may be always meditating upon it, and by continual meditation yet more enlarging my love and delight in it! So let it prove an ever-springing source of heavenly enjoyment and holy conversation!

98. You through Your commandments have made me wiser than my enemies; for they are ever with me. 99. I have more understanding than all my teachers: for Your testimonies are my meditation. 100. I understand more than the ancients, because I keep Your precepts.

What a fruitful harvest did David reap from his glowing love, and "daily meditation on the law of God!" He became wiser than his enemies in "subtlety"—than all his teachers in doctrine—than the ancients in experience. Yet he is not speaking of his extraordinary gifts as a prophet, but of his knowledge gained by ordinary means. Nor is he here boasting of his own attainments: but commending the grace of God in and towards him—You through Your commandments have made me wiser. How much more wisdom does the persecuted believer draw from the word of God, than his persecutors have ever acquired from the learning of this world! Those, however, who have been effectually taught of God, need to be daily taught of Him. While they rest upon their God, and seek counsel in His word, they are wise indeed; yet when they trust to their own wisdom, and turn to their own counsel, they become a bye-word and occasion of offence by their own folly. Was David wiser than his enemies or his teachers, when he dissembled himself before Achish—or when he yielded to the indulgence of lust—or when in the pride of his heart he numbered the people? Alas! how often do even God's children befool themselves in the ways of sin!

But how did David attain this Divine wisdom? Not by habits of extensive reading—not by natural intelligence—but by a diligent meditation in the testimonies. In order to avail ourselves, however, of this means—a simple reception of the Divine testimony is of absolute importance. We can never obtain that assurance of the certainty of our faith, which is indispensable to our peace, or resist the influence of unenlightened teachers, or the long-established worldly maxims of the ancients, except by entire submission to the supreme authority of Scripture. Many sincere Christians—especially at the outset of their course—are much hindered—either by the skepticism of others, or of their own minds; or from their previous habit of studying the Bible in the light of carnal wisdom, or in dependence upon human teaching. Such need special prayer for humility of mind and simplicity of faith. Under this gracious influence they will discern that path to glory, which in infinite condescension is made so plain, that "the wayfaring men, though fools, shall not err therein," and the unlearned believer, who has the word before his eyes, in his heart, and in his life, shall become "perfect, thoroughly furnished unto all good works."

In our Christian progress, David's habit of scriptural meditation will prove of essential service. For while those who "confer with flesh and blood" cannot have their counselors always at hand; we, seeking our wisdom from the word of God, have the best Counselor ever with us, teaching us what to do, and what to expect. Obedience also, as well as meditation, directs our way. David found understanding, because he kept the precepts. And David's Lord has pointed out the same path of light: "If any man will do God's will, he shall know of the doctrine." "You meet him who rejoices, and works righteousness—those that remember You in Your ways." Your ways truly are ways of light, joy, and love!

Now let us turn in, and inquire—What is our daily use of the word of God? Are we satisfied with a slight looking, or do we seek an intimate acquaintance with it! Is its influence ever present—ever practical? Do we prize it as a welcome guest? Is it our delightful companion and guide? Oh! meditate in this blessed book. "Eat the word," when you "have found it; and it will be unto you the joy and rejoicing of your heart." The name of Jesus—its great subject—will be more precious—your love will be inflamed—your perseverance established—and your heart enlivened in the spirit of praise. Thus bringing your mind into close and continual contact with the testimonies of God, and pressing out the sweetness from the precious volume, it will drop as from the honeycomb, daily comfort and refreshment upon your heart.

Verses 101 - 125

101. I have refrained my feet from every evil way, that I might keep Your word.

David's wisdom was of a practical—not of a merely intellectual or speculative—character. It taught him to "keep the Lord's precepts;" and in order to this, to refrain his feet from every evil way. And will not advancing wisdom show itself by increasing tenderness of conscience and carefulness of conduct? The professor is afraid of hell; the child of God—of sin. The one refrains from the outward act—the other seeks to be crucified to the love of sin. Observe not only the practice, but the motive—that he might keep the word. Shall we not "abhor that which is evil," that we might "cleave to that which is good" "abstaining from all appearance of evil" lest unconsciously we should be drawn into the atmosphere of sin, "hating even the garment spotted by the flesh"—fearing the infection of sin worse than death? But how fearful the danger of self-deception! What need to entreat the Lord to "see if there be any wicked way in us?" Oh! for the large supply of grace and unction, to maintain an upright walk before a heart-searching God; to "keep ourselves from our iniquity;" and in dependence upon the promises, and in the strength of the gospel, to "perfect holiness in the fear of God!"

But how awful to hear men talk of keeping the word in a loose and careless profession! For how can it be kept, if the heart has not felt its holiness? For this is its beautiful peculiarity; that, in order to keep it, there must be a separation from sin. The two things are incompatible with each other. The two services are at variance at every point; so that the love of sin must be cast out, where the love of God is engrafted in the heart. Yet so strongly are we disposed to every evil way, that only the Almighty power of grace can enable us to refrain from one or another crooked path. Often is the pilgrim (yes, has it not too often happened to ourselves?) held back by a temporary ascendancy of the flesh—by a little license given to sin—or by a relaxed circumspection of walk. At such seasons, the blessed privilege of keeping the word is lost. We are sensible of a declining delight in those spiritual duties, which before were our "chief joy." And "is there not a cause?" Have we not provoked our gracious God by harboring his enemy in our bosom—no more—by pleading for its indulgence? Has not "the Holy Spirit been grieved" by neglect, or by some worldly compliance: so that His light has been obscured, and His comforting influence quenched? No consolations, consistent with the love and power of sin, can ever come from the Lord. For the holiness of the word of God cannot be either spiritually understood, or experimentally enjoyed, but in a consistent Christian walk. And yet, such is the true blessedness of the word, that the very expectation of keeping it may operate as a principle of restraint from every evil way.

Is there any bondage in this restraint from sin? Oh, no! Sin is slavery; and therefore deliverance from it is "perfect freedom." There is indeed a legal restraint much to be deprecated, when the conscience is goaded by sins of omission or of wilfulness; and the man, ignorant of, or imperfectly acquainted with, the only way of deliverance, hopes to get rid of his burden by a more circumspect walk. But not until he casts it at the foot of the cross, and learns to look wholly to Jesus his deliverer, can he form his resolution upon safe and effectual grounds. Oh, may I therefore seek to abide within a constant view of Calvary! Sin will live everywhere but under the cross of Jesus. Here it withers and dies. Here rises the spring of that holiness, contrition, and love, which refreshes and quickens the soul. Here let me live: here let me die.

Blessed Lord! You know that I desire to keep Your word. Prepare my heart to receive and to retain it. May I so "abide in Christ," that I may receive the sanctifying help of His Spirit for every moment's need! And while I rejoice in Him as my Savior, may I become daily more sensible of every deviation from the straight path! May my eye guide my feet! "Looking to Jesus," may I have light and grace! And may daily grace be given to refrain my feet from every evil way, that I may keep Your word!

102. I have not departed from Your judgments; for You have taught me.

If I have refrained my feet from sin—if I have not departed from God's judgments—to Him be all the glory. Oh, my soul! Are you not a wonder to yourself? So prone to depart—to be carried away by uncertain notions—by the oppositions of Satan—by the example or influence of the world—how is it, that you are able to hold on your way? Because the covenant of the Lord engages Your perseverance, "I will put My fear in their hearts, that they shall not depart from Me." While conscious of my own corrupt bias to depart, let me humbly and thankfully own the work of Divine teaching. Man's teaching is powerless in advancing the soul one step in Christian progress. The teaching from above is "the light of life." It gives not only the light, but the principle to make use of it. It not only points the lesson, and makes it plain: but imparts the disposition to learn, and the grace to obey. So that now I see the beauty, the pleasantness, the peace, and the holiness of the Lord's judgments, and am naturally constrained to walk in them. Oh, how much more frequent would be our acknowledgment of the work of God, did we keep nearer to the Fountain-head of life and light! How may we trace every declension in doctrine and practice—all our continual estrangement from the Lord's judgments—to following our own wisdom, or depending upon human teaching! "Trusting in man," is the departing of the heart from the Lord. I never shall depart from sin by the influence of human persuasion. I never shall depart from the Lord, so long as I have the witness in my heart—You teach me.

Reader! what has been your habit and progress in the judgments of God? Have you been careful to avoid bye-paths? Has your walk been consistent, steady, advancing "in the fear of the Lord, and in the comfort of the Holy Spirit?" If there has been no allowed departure from the ways of God, it has been the blessed fruit of "ceasing from your own wisdom," and the simple dependence upon the promise "written in the prophets—And they shall be all taught of God." And how delightfully does this heavenly teaching draw your heart with a deeper sense of need and comfort to the Savior! For, as He Himself speaks, "Every man therefore that has heard, and has learned of the Father, comes unto Me." Remember—it was no superior virtue or discernment that has restrained your departure from God, but—You have taught me the way to come to God; the way to abide in Him—Christ the way—Christ the end. And His teaching will abide with you. It will win you by light and by love, and by a conquering power allure your heart with that delight in His judgments, and fear of offending against them, that shall prove an effectual safeguard in the hour of temptation. Watch the first step of departure—the neglect of secret prayer—the want of appetite for the sincere word—the relaxing of diligence—the loss of the savor of godliness. Be careful therefore that the teaching of the Lord be not lost upon you. Inquire into your proficiency in His instructive lessons. And do not forget to prize His teaching rod—that loving correction, of which David had felt the blessing, and which He so often uses, to keep His children from departing from His judgments.

Lord! do lead me by the hand, that I may make daily progress in Your judgments. Restrain my feet from "perpetual backsliding." All human instruction will be ineffectual to keep me from departing from Your judgments, except You teach me. Neither grace received, nor experience attained, nor engagements regarded, will secure me for one moment without continual teaching from Yourself.

103. How sweet are Your words to my taste! yes, sweeter than honey to my mouth.

None but a child of God could take up this expression. Because none besides has a spiritual taste. The exercises of David in this sacred word were delightfully varied. Its majesty commanded his reverence. Its richness called forth his love. Its sweetness excited his joy. Its holy light, keeping his heart close with God, naturally endeared it to his soul. How barren is a mere external knowledge of the Gospel! The natural man may talk or even dispute about its precious truths. But he has never tasted them—at least not so as to relish and feed on them. The highest commendation cannot explain the sweetness of honey to one who has never tasted it. Thus nothing but experience can give a spiritual intelligence. But what we have really tasted, we can warmly commend, "Oh! taste and see that the Lord is good." Having once tasted of His Divine goodness, the sweetest joys of earth will be insipid, distasteful, and even bitter.

Do we ask—what is it that gives this unutterable sweetness to the word? Is it not that name, which "is as ointment poured forth?" Is it not "the savor of the knowledge of Christ", that revives the soul in every page with the breath of heaven? For can the awakened sinner hear, that "God so loved the world, that He gave His only-begotten Son, that whoever believes in Him should not perish, but have everlasting life"— and not be ready to say—How sweet are Your words to my taste! yes, sweeter than honey to my mouth? Can the weary soul listen to the invitation to "all that labor and are heavy-laden;" and not feel the sweetness of those breathings of love? Who can tell the sweetness of those precious words to the conflicting, tempted soul—displaying the Divine sovereignty in choosing him, the unchanging faithfulness in keeping him, and the Almighty power of the Divine will in the gift of

177

eternal life? And how can the believer hear his Savior "knock at the door" of his heart, calling him to fresh communion with Himself: and not turn to Him with the ardent excitement of his love, "All Your garments smell of myrrh, and aloes, and cassia, out of the ivory palaces, whereby they have made You glad!"

But are there not times, when we gather no sweetness from the word? It is with the spiritual, as with the natural food—a want of appetite gives disgust, instead of sweetness and refreshment. An indolent reading of the word without faith—without desire—without application—or with a taste vitiated by contact—with the things of sense—deadens the palate, "The full soul loathes an honeycomb: but to the hungry soul every bitter thing is sweet."

But how melancholy is the thought of the multitudes, that hear, read, understand the word, and yet have never tasted its sweetness! Like Barzillai, they have no sense to "discern between good and evil." Full of the world, or of their own conceits—feeding on the delusive enjoyments of creature-comforts—nourishing some baneful corruption in their bosoms—or cankered with a spirit of formality—they have no palate for the things of God; they are "dead in trespasses and sins." But how sweet is the word to the hungering and thirsting taste! We eat, and are not satisfied. We drink, and long to drink again. "If so be we have tasted that the Lord is gracious, as new-born babes" we shall "desire the sincere milk of the word, that we may grow thereby." We shall take heed of any indulgence of the flesh, which may hinder the spiritual enjoyment, and cause us to "loathe" even "angels' food" as "light bread." Instead of resting in our present experience of its sweetness, we shall be daily aspiring after higher relish for the heavenly blessing. And will not this experience be a "witness in ourselves" of the heavenly origin of the word? For what arguments could ever persuade us that honey is bitter, at the moment when we are tasting its sweetness? Or who could convince us that this is the word of man, or the imposture of deceit, when its blessed influence has imparted peace, holiness, joy, support, and rest, infinitely beyond the power of man to bestow? But let this enjoyment—as the spiritual barometer—the pulse of the soul—accurately mark our progress or decline in the Divine life. With our advancement in spiritual health, the word will be increasingly sweet to our taste: while our declension will be marked by a corresponding abatement in our desires, love, and perception of its delights.

104. Through Your precepts I get understanding: therefore I hate every false way.

The Psalmist having spoken of the pleasure, now speaks of the profit—of the word—the teaching connected with its sweetness. Before, he had mentioned the avoiding of sin in order to profit—now, as the fruit of profit. So closely are they linked together. Man's teaching conveys no understanding—God's teaching not only opens the Scriptures, but "opens the understanding to understand them," and the heart to feel their heavenly warmth of life. Thus having learned "the principles of the doctrine of Christ," we shall "go on to perfection" "growing in grace, in the knowledge of Christ." Many inconsistencies belong to the young and half—instructed Christian. But when through the precepts he gets understanding, he learns to walk more uniformly and steadily, abiding in the light. In this spirit and atmosphere springs up a constant and irreconcilable hatred of every false way; as contrary to the God he loves. These ways will include a thousand devious paths—all meeting in one fearful end—often discovered too late. In doctrine can we too much turn away from the thought of putting anything—the Church, ordinances, repentance, prayers—in the place of Jesus—another "foundation" in the stead of that which God Himself "laid in Zion?" Oh, for spiritual understanding to hate this false way with a deadly hatred! What think we of the ways of the sinful world—so long trusted to for happiness—yet so delusive? The sinner thinks that he has found a treasure, but it proves to be glittering trash—burdensome instead of enriching—only leaving him to the pain of disappointed hope. Rightly are such ways called false ways; and of those that tread in them, it is well said, "This their way is their folly." Strewed they may be with the flowery "pleasures of sin." But they are "hard" in their walk, and ruinous in their end. Inquire of those, whose past wanderings justly give weight and authority to their verdict— 'What is your retrospective view of these ways?' Unprofitableness. 'What is your present view of them?' Shame. 'What prospect for eternity would the continuance in them assure to you?' "Death." Let them then be not only avoided and forsaken, but abhorred; and let every deviation into them from the straight path, however pleasing, be "resisted" even "unto blood."

But let me ask myself, Have I detected the false ways of my own heart? Little is done in spiritual religion, until my besetting sins are searched out. And let me not be satisfied with forbearance from the outward act. Sin may be restrained, yet not mortified; nor is it enough that I leave it for the present, but I must renounce it forever. Let me not part with it as with a beloved friend, with the hope and purpose of renewing my familiarity with it at a "more convenient season:" but let me shake it from me, as Paul shook off the viper into the fire, with determination and abhorrence. What! can I wish to hold it? If through the precepts of God I have got understanding, must not I listen to that solemn, pleading voice, "Oh! do not this abominable thing that I hate?" No, Lord: let me "pluck it out" of my heart, "and cast it from me." Oh, for the high blessing of a tender conscience! such as shrinks from the approach, and "abstains from all appearance of evil;" not venturing to tamper with any self-pleasing way; but hating it as false, defiling, destructive! I have noticed the apple of my eye—that tenderest particle of my frame—that it is not only offended by a blow or a wound; but that, if so much as an atom of dust find an entrance, it would smart, until it had wept it out. Now such may my conscience be—sensitive of the slightest touch of sin—not only fearful of resisting, rebelling, or "quenching the Spirit," but grieving for every thought of sin that grieves that blessed Comforter—that tender Friend! To hate every false way, so as to flee from it, is the highest proof of Christian courage. For never am I better prepared to "endure hardness as a good soldier of Jesus Christ," than when my conscience is thus set against sin. Would not I then submit to the greatest suffering, rather than be convicted of unfaithfulness to my God?

Lord! turn my eyes, my heart, my feet, my ways, more and more to Your blessed self. Shed abroad Your love in my heart, that sin may be the daily matter of my watchfulness, grief, resistance, and crucifixion.

105. Your word is a lamp unto my feet, and a light unto my path.

The nightly journeys of Israel were guided by a pillar of fire—directing not only their course, but every step and movement. Thus is our passage in a dark and perilous way irradiated by the lamp and light of the word. But except the lamp be lighted—except the teaching of the Spirit accompany the word, all is darkness—thick darkness. Let us not then be content to read the word without obtaining some light from it in our understanding—in our experience—in our providential path. Did we more habitually wait to receive, and watch to improve the light, we should not so often complain of the perplexity of our path. It would generally determine our steps under infallible guidance: while in the presumptuous neglect of it—like Israel of old—we are sure to come into trouble.

Yet it may sometimes be difficult to trace our light to this heavenly source. A promise may seem to be applied to my mind, as I conceive, suitable to my present need. But how may I determine, whether it is the lamp of the word; or some delusive light from him, who can at any time, for the accomplishment of his own purpose, transform himself "into an angel of light?" Or if a threatening be impressed upon my conscience, how can I accurately distinguish between the voice of "the accuser of the brethren," and the warning of my heavenly guide? Let me mark the state of my own mind. If I am living in the indulgence of any known sin, or in the neglect of any known duty—if my spirit is careless, or my walk unsteady; a consoling promise, being unsuitable to my case, even though it awakened some excitement of joy, would be of doubtful application. The lamp of God under the circumstances supposed, would rather reflect the light of conviction than of consolation. For, though God as a Sovereign may speak comfort when and where He pleases; yet we can only expect Him to deal with us according to the prescribed rules of His own covenant; chastening, not comforting, His backsliding people. In a spirit of contrition, however, I should not hesitate to receive a word of encouragement, as the lamp of God to direct and cheer my progress; being conscious of that state of feeling, in which the Lord has expressly promised to restore and guide His people. Let me also inquire into the terms and character of the promise. When He "that dwells in the high and holy place," engages to dwell "with him also that is of a contrite and humble spirit;" any symptoms of tenderness and humility would naturally lead me to consider this word of promise, as sent by my kind and watchful Father, to be a lamp unto my feet, and a light unto my path.

Again—a distinct and experimental view of the Savior in His promises, endearing Him to me, and encouraging my trust in His faithfulness and love—this is manifestly light from above. Or if the purpose of the promise answers any proper end—to excite or to encourage to any present duty connected with the promise; I cannot doubt, but the lamp of the Lord is directing my path.

For example—when the promise was given to Joshua, "I will not fail you, nor forsake you;" he could not misconstrue "a word" so "fitly spoken" "in a time of need." And when the same promise was subsequently given to the Church, the application was equally clear, as a dissuasive from inordinate attachment to the things of time and sense, and an encouragement to entire dependence upon the Lord.

Further—The practical influence of the word will also enable me clearly to distinguish the light of heaven from any illusion of fancy or presumption. The effect of an unconditional promise of deliverance given to the Apostle in a moment of extremity, was exhibited in a diligent use of all the appointed means of safety. An absolute promise of prolonged life given to Hezekiah when lying at the point of death, produced the same practical result, in a scrupulous attention to the means for his recovery. Upon the warrant of a general promise of Divine protection, Ezra and the Jews "fasted, and besought their God for this." Now in these and other instances, the power of the word, working diligence, simplicity, and prayer, evidently proved its sacred origin. An assurance of safety proceeding from another source, would have produced sloth, carelessness, and presumption; and therefore may I not presume the quickening word in darkness and perplexity, to be the Lord's lamp unto my feet, and light unto my path, "to guide my feet into the way of peace?"

Let me apply the same test to the threatenings of the word. Their influence, meeting me in a watchful and humble walk with God, I should at once consider as the suggestion of the great enemy of the soul, ever ready to whisper distrust and despondency to the child of God. But in a self-confident, self-indulgent state, I should have as little hesitation in marking an alarming word to be the light of the word of God. It would be well for me at such a time to be exercised with fear; not as arguing any insecurity in my state; but as leading me to "great searchings of heart," to increasing watchfulness, humiliation, and prayer. "The commandment is a lamp, and the law is a light: and reproofs of instruction are the ways of life." Oh, that I may be enabled to make use of this lamp to direct every step of my heavenly way!

Whence then—it may be asked—the various tracks even of the sincere servants of God? Though there is clear light in the word, yet there is remaining darkness in the most enlightened heart. There is no eye without a speck, no eye with perfect singleness of vision—consequently without some liability to error. There is light for the teachable—not for the curious;—light to satisfy faith—not caviling. Add to this the office of the ministry—the Lord's gracious ordinance for Christian instruction and establishment; not to enslave, but to direct the judgment in the light of the word. To honor this ordinance is therefore the path of light. To neglect it, is the exposure to all the evils of a wayward will and undisciplined judgment.

Lord! as every action of the day is a step to heaven, or hell—Oh! save me from ever turning my face away from the path, into which Your word would guide me. Enable me to avail myself of its light, in the constant exercise of faith, prudence, and simplicity.

106. I have sworn, and I will perform it, that I will keep Your righteous judgments.

The blessing of the guidance of the Lord's word naturally strengthens our resolution to walk in its path. And as if a simple resolution would prove too weak, the Psalmist strengthens it with an oath. No more, as if an oath was hardly sufficient security, be seconds it again with a firm resolution—I have sworn, and I will perform it. 'There shall be but one will between me and my God; and that will shall be His, not mine.' Some timid Christians, under a morbid sense of their own weakness, would shrink from this solemn engagement. And some, perhaps, may have burdened their consciences with unadvised or self-dependent obligations. Still, however, when it is a free-will offering, it is a delightful service, well-pleasing to God. Such it was in the days of Asa, when "all Judah rejoiced at the oath: for they had sworn with all their heart, and sought Him with their whole desire; and He was found of them." Vows under the law were both binding and acceptable. Nor are they less so—in their spirit at least—under "the perfect law of liberty." A holy promise originating in serious consideration, and established by a more solemn obligation, so far from being repugnant to the liberty of the gospel, appears to have been enjoined by God Himself; no, His people are described as animating each other to it, as to a most joyous privilege; as a renewed act of faith and daily dedication.

Yet we would warn the inconsiderate Christian not to entangle his conscience by multiplied vows (as if they were—like prayer—a component part of our daily religion); nor by perpetual obligation—whether of restraint or of extraordinary exercises; nor by connecting them with trifles—thus weakening the deep solemnity of the purpose.

183

Christian simplicity must be their principle. Our engagements to God must be grounded on His engagements to us. His faithfulness—not ours—must be our confidence. There is no innate power in these obligations; and except they be made in self-renouncing dedication, they will only issue in despondency and deeper captivity in sin.

But the inconsiderateness of the unwary is no legitimate argument against their importance. If Jephthah was entangled in a rash and heedless vow, David manifestly enjoyed the "perfect freedom" of the "service" of his God, when "binding his soul with a bond" equally fixed, but more advised, in its obligation. And have we; with "the vows of God upon us," baptismal vows—perhaps also confirmation or sacramental vows—found our souls brought into bondage by these solemn engagements? Does not a humbling sense of forgetfulness suggest sometimes the need of a more solemn engagement? And may we not thus secure our duty without being ensnared by it? Have not covenanting seasons often restrained our feet from devious paths, and quickened our souls in His service? Daily, indeed, do we need "the blood of sprinkling" to pardon our innumerable failures, and the Spirit of grace to strengthen us for a more devoted obligation. But yet in dependence upon the work and Spirit of Christ, often have these holy transactions realized to us a peace and joy, that leads us to look back upon such times and seasons of favored enjoyment. "If," therefore, "we sin" in a "perpetual backsliding" from these engagements, it is still our privilege without presumption to believe, that "we have an advocate with the Father, Jesus Christ the righteous; and He is the propitiation for our sins." And as for necessary grace, there is One who has said, "My grace is sufficient for you;" and that One has given no less a proof of His interest in us, than by dying for us. May we not therefore trust, that He will "perfect that which concerns us;" that He will "work all our works in us" "to will and to do of His good pleasure?"

Perhaps however "a messenger of Satan "may "buffet us." "You have broken your bond; now will it be worse with you than before." But did not Jesus die for sins of infirmity, and even of presumption? Does every failing annul the marriage covenant? So neither does every infirmity or backsliding dissolve our covenant with God. Was our faithfulness the basis of this covenant? Rather, does not "the blood of this covenant" make constant provision for our foreseen unfaithfulness? And does not our gracious God overrule even our backsliding to establish a more simple reliance upon Himself, and a more circumspect and tender walk before Him?

But let us take a case of conscience. A Christian has been drawn away from a set season of extraordinary devotion by some unforeseen present duty, or some unlooked-for opportunity of actively glorifying God. Has he then broken his obligation? Certainly not. It was, or ought to have been, formed with an implied subserviency to paramount duty. It cannot, therefore, be impaired by any such providential interference. Yet let it not be a light matter to remove a free-will offering from the altar. Let godly care be exercised to discover the subtle indulgence of the flesh in the service of God. Let double diligence redeem the lost privilege of more immediate and solemn self-dedication. In guarding against legal bondage, let us not mistake the liberty of the flesh for the liberty of the Gospel. Let us be simple and ready for self-denying service; and the Lord our God will not fail to give "some token for good."

"Come" then, my fellow-Christian, "and let us join ourselves to the Lord in a perpetual covenant, never to be forgotten" by God: never to be forsaken by us. Let each of us renew our surrender, "O Lord, truly I am Your servant;" I offer myself to You: "You have loosed my bonds;" oh! bind me to Yourself with fresh bonds of love, that may never be loosed. Glad am I that I am anything—though the lowest of all; that I have anything—poor and vile as it is—capable of being employed in Your service. I yield myself to You with my full bent of heart and will, entirely and forever; asking only, that I may be "a vessel for the Master's use."

107. I am afflicted very much: quicken me, O Lord, according to Your word.

It would seem, that this holy saint's covenanting season was a time of deep affliction: while his determined resolution to keep God's word of obedience, gave boldness to his pleading, that God would perform His word of promise—Quicken me, O Lord, according to Your word. And this is our high privilege, that we are permitted to pour our troubles into the ear of One, who is able perfectly to enter into, and to sympathize with us in them; "who knows our frame," who has Himself laid the affliction upon us: yes, more than all, who in "all our affliction is" Himself "afflicted;" and who "suffered being tempted, that He might be able to support them that are tempted." There are none—not even those most dear to us—to whom we can unbosom ourselves, as we do to our heavenly Friend. Our wants, griefs, burdens of every kind—we roll them all upon Him, with special relief in the hour of affliction. An affecting contrast to those who are indeed afflicted very much; whose souls, "drawing near unto death," and knowing no refuge, are ready to burst with their own sorrows, "the sorrow of the world"—unmitigated—unrelieved, "working death!"

There is a "needs-be" for the afflictions of the Lord's people. The stones of the spiritual temple cannot be polished or fitted to their place without the strokes of the hammer. The gold cannot be purified without the furnace. The vine must be pruned for greater fruitfulness. The measure of discipline varies indefinitely. But such is the inveteracy of fleshly lusts, that very much affliction may often be the needful regimen. Yet will it be tempered by one, who knows the precise measure, who can make no mistakes in our constitutions, and whose fatherly pity will chasten "not for His pleasure, but for our profit." And need we speak of the alleviations of our trials, that they are infinitely disproportioned to our deserts—that they are "light, and but for a moment," compared with eternity—that greater comfort is given in the endurance of them, than we even ventured to anticipate from their removal—that the fruit at the end more than balances the trials themselves? Need we say—how richly they ought to be prized, as conforming us to the image of our suffering Lord; how clearly we shall one day read in them our Father's commission, as messengers of love; and how certainly "the end of the Lord" will be "that the Lord is very pitiful and of tender mercy?"

Perhaps affliction—at least very much affliction—may not be our present lot. Yet it is our duty, and wisdom, as the good soldier in the time of truce, to burnish our armor for the fight. "Let not him that girds on his harness boast himself as he who puts it off. Because the wicked have no changes, therefore they fear not God." The continual changes in Christian experience may well remind us of the necessity of "walking humbly with God," that we may not, by an unprepared spirit, lose the blessing of the sanctified cross. How many of the Lord's dear children may bear Ephraim's name, "For God has caused me to be fruitful in the land of my affliction!" Sometimes they are so conscious of the present good, that they dread affliction leaving them, more, probably, than the inexperienced professor dreads its coming.

But great affliction is as hard to bear as great prosperity. Some whose Christian profession had drawn out the esteem of others—perhaps also their own complacency—have shown by "faintness in the day of adversity their strength to be small," and themselves to be almost untaught in this school of discipline—shaken, confused, broken. Special need indeed have we under the smart of the rod, of quickening grace to preserve us from stout-heartedness or dejection. We think we could bear the stroke, did we know it to be paternal, not judicial. Have we, then, "forgotten the exhortation, which speaks unto us as unto children?" Do "we despise the chastening of the Lord?" 'Quicken me, Lord, that I may be preserved in a humble, wakeful, listening posture, to hear and improve the message of Your blessing of the sanctified cross.' Do we "faint, when we are rebuked of Him?" "Quicken me, O Lord," that I sink not under the "blow of Your hand." Thus will this Divine influence save us from the horrible sin of being offended with God in our fretting spirit. We shall receive His chastisement with humility without despondency, and with reverence without distrust; hearkening to the voice that speaks, while we tremble under the rod that strikes: yet so mingling fear with confidence, that we may at the same moment adore the hand which we feel, and rest in mercy that is promised. Our best support in the depths of affliction is, prayer for quickening according to Your word! and which of the exercised children of God has ever found one jot, or one tittle of it to fail? "Patience working experience, and experience hope, and hope making not ashamed," in the sense of "the love of God shed abroad upon the heart by the Holy Spirit which is given unto us"—all this is the abundant answer to our prayer, "You who have shown me great and sore troubles, shall quicken me again, and shall bring me up again from the depths of the earth. You shall increase my greatness, and comfort me on every side." Nothing will bear looking back to with comfort, like those trials, which though painful to the flesh, have tended to break our spirit, mold our will, and strengthen the simplicity of our walk with God.

108. Accept, I beseech You, the free-will offerings of my mouth, O Lord: and teach me Your judgments.

As the first-fruits of his entire self-devotion to the Lord; as the only sacrifice he could render in his affliction; and as an acknowledgment of his answered prayer for quickening grace, behold this faithful servant of God presenting the free-will offerings of his mouth for acceptance. Such he knew to be an acceptable service. For the sacrifices of the Old Testament were not only typical of the One sacrifice for sin, but of the spiritual worship of the people of God. To those who are interested in the atonement of Jesus, there needs "no more sacrifice for sin." That which is now required of us, and in which we would delight, is to "take with us words, and turn to Him, and say unto Him—Take away all iniquity, and receive us graciously; so will we render the calves of our lips."

No offering but a free-will offering is accepted. Such was the service under the law: such must it be under the gospel. Yet neither can this offering be accepted, until the offerer himself has found acceptance with his God. "The Lord had respect," first to the person of "Abel," then "to his offering." But if our persons are covered with the robe of acceptance—if the "offering up of the body of Jesus Christ once for all" has "perfected" us before God: however defiled our services may be, however mixed with infirmity, and in every way most unworthy; even a God of ineffable holiness "beholds no iniquity" in them. No offering is so pure as to obtain acceptance in any other way; no offering so sinful as to fail of acceptance in this way. Most abundant, indeed, and satisfactory is the provision made in heaven for the continual and everlasting acceptance of our polluted and distracted services, "Another angel came, and stood at the altar, having a golden censer; and there was given unto him much incense, that he should offer it, with the prayers of all saints, upon the golden altar which was before the throne. And the smoke of the incense, which came with the prayers of the saints, ascended up before God out of the angel's hand." With such a High Priest and Intercessor, not only is unworthiness dismissed, but boldness and assurance of faith is encouraged.

But, as we remarked, it was a free-will offering that we here presented—the overflowings of a heart filled with love. No constraint was necessary. Prayer was delightful. He was not forced upon his knees. Let me seek fellowship with Him in presenting my free offering before my God. Does not He love it? Does not His free love to me deserve it? Did not my beloved Savior give a free-will offering of delight and of joy? And shall not His free-flowing love be my pattern and my principle? Shall His offering be free for me, and mine, be reluctant for Him? Shall He be ready with His blood for me, and I be backward with my mouth for Him? O my God, work Your own Almighty work—make me not only living, but "willing in the day of Your power." Let the stream flow in the full tide of affectionate devotedness. Blessed Jesus! I would be Yours, and none other's. I would tell the world, that I am captivated by Your love, and consecrated to Your service. Oh, let me "rejoice for that I offered willingly." Great grace is it, that He is willing to accept my service. For what have I to offer, that is not already "his own?" But let me not forget to supplicate for further instruction—'Teach me Your judgments, that I may be directed to present a purer offering; that by more distinct and accurate knowledge of Your ways, my love may be enlarged, and my obedience more entire, until I "stand perfect and complete in all the will of God."'

109. My soul is continually in my hand, yet do I not forget Your law.
110. The wicked have laid a snare for me: yet I erred not from Your precepts.

Precarious health, or familiarity with dangers, may give peculiar emphasis to the phrase—My soul is continually in my hand. David, in his early public life, was in constant apprehension from the open violence and the secret machinations of his bitter enemy. Hunted down "as a partridge in the mountains," and often scarcely escaping the snare which the wicked laid for him; at one time he could not but acknowledge, "there is but a step between me and death;" at another time he was tempted to say, "I shall now perish one day by the hand of Saul." Subsequently the hand of his own son was aimed at his throne and his life. Yet could no peril shake his undaunted adherence to the law and precepts of God.

What was the life of Jesus upon earth? Through the enmity of foes— various, opposite, yet combined—his soul was continually in his hand. Yet how wonderful was his calmness and serenity of mind, when surrounded by them all, like "lions" in power, "dogs" in cruelty, wolves in malice! A measure of this spirit belongs to every faithful disciple—not natural courage, but "the spirit of power," as the gift of God, enabling him in the path of the precepts "to withstand in the evil day, and having done all, to stand."

Let us again mark this confidence, illustrated in the open trials of the servants of God. Mark the Apostle, when "the Holy Spirit witnessed to him in every city, that bonds and imprisonment awaited him. None of these things"—said he, "move me. I am ready not to be bound only, but also to die at Jerusalem for the name of the Lord Jesus." He could look "tribulation, or persecution, or peril, or sword," in the face; and, while he carried his soul continually in his hand, in true Christian heroism, in the most exalted triumph of faith, he could say in the name of himself and his companions in tribulation, "No, in all these things we are more than conquerors." Nothing could make him flinch. Nothing could turn him back. Nothing could wring the love of the service of his God out of his heart. His principle was found invincible in the hour of trial—not, however, as a native energy of his heart, but "through Him that loved him." Did he not speak and live in the spirit of this fearless confidence— Yet do I not forget Your law? Daniel's history again shows the utter impotency of secret devices to produce apostasy in the children of God. When the wicked, after many an ineffectual attempt to "find occasion or fault," were driven to lay a snare for him in "the law of his God," this noble confessor of the faith continued to "kneel upon his knees three times a day, and prayed and gave thanks before his God, as he did aforetime." The den of lions was far less fearful in his eyes than one devious step from the straight and narrow path. Sin was dreaded as worse than a thousand deaths. He surely then could have said—Yet I erred not from Your precepts.

But how striking must it have been to David, in his imminent peril, to have seen the "counsel of Ahithophel"—regarded as oracular, when employed in the cause of God—now, when directed against the church, "turned to foolishness!"—an instance, only "one of a thousand," of the ever-watchful keeping of the Great Head and Guardian of His Church. Thus does He over-rule the devices of the enemy for the establishment of His people's dependence upon Himself. "The wrath of man praises Him," and He "takes the wise in his own craftiness."

But the day of difficulty is a "perilous time" in the church. "Many shall be purified, and made white, and tried." Have we been able to sustain the shock in a steady adherence to the law and precepts of God? This is indeed the time, when genuine faith will be found of inestimable value. In such a time, David experienced the present blessing of having chosen the Lord for his God. When clouds began to gather blackness, and surrounding circumstances to the eye of sense engendered despondency—faith realized All-sufficient support; and "David encouraged himself in the Lord his God." And is not David's God "our God, the health of our countenance," the guide of our path, the God of our salvation? Oh, let us not rest, until his confidence becomes ours, "What time I am afraid, I will trust in You."

But the cross, which proves and establishes the Christian, sifts the unsound professor as chaff. Nothing but this solid principle of faith can resist either the persecution or the snare. Many desire conformity to Christ and His people in everything but in their cross. They would attain their honor without the steps that led them to it. Dread this flinching spirit. Reject it—as did our Lord—with indignation. It "savors not of God." It is the voice of Satan, who would promise a pillow of carnal ease under our heads—a path of roses under our feet—but a path of slumber, of delusion, and of ruin.

The time of special need is at hand with us all, when we shall need substance and reality for our support—the true confidence of a living faith. Those who have never felt the nearness of eternity, can have but a faint idea of what we shall need in the hour when "flesh and heart fail," to fix a sure unshaken foot upon "the Rock of ages." "Watch, therefore," for you know not how soon you may be ready to say, My soul is in my hand, quivering on the eve of departure to the Judge. "Let your loins be girded about, and your lights burning! and you yourselves like men that wait for the Lord, when He will return from the wedding; that when He comes and knocks, they may open unto Him immediately. Blessed are those servants, whom the Lord, when He comes, shall find watching; verily I say unto you, that He shall gird Himself, and make them to sit down to meat, and will come forth and serve them."

111. Your testimonies have I taken as an heritage forever, for they are the rejoicing of my heart.

'Precious Bible: what a treasure!' The testimonies of God—the declaration of his will in doctrine—obligation—and privilege! David had felt their value, as the stay of his soul in shaking and sifting trial. But how did he claim his interest in them? Not by purchase, or by merit, it was his heritage. As a child of Abraham, he was an "heir according to promise." They—all that is contained in them, "the Lord Himself," the sum and substance of all, "was the portion of his inheritance." Man looks at his heritage. 'This land—this estate—or this kingdom is mine.' The child of God looks round on the universe—on both worlds—on God Himself with His infinite perfections—and says, "All things are mine." My title is more sure than to any earthly heritage. Every promise is sprinkled with "the blood of the everlasting covenant," as the seal of its blessings, and the pledge of their performance.

But not only are they my heritage;—by my own intelligent choice I have taken them to be so. A blessing is it to have them. But the blessing of blessings is to have them made good—applied—sealed—made my own; so that, like the minor come to age, I take possession of my heritage, I live on it, I live in it, it is my treasure, my portion. If a man is known by his heritage, let me be known by mine. Let it "be known and read of all men," that I count not the world my happiness, but that I take my Bible, 'Here is my heritage. Here I can live royally—richer upon bare promises than all the treasures of earth could make me. My resources never fail when all besides fail. When all earthly heritage shall have passed away, mine endures forever.'

Let me not then entertain a low estimate of this precious heritage. "Heirs of promise" are entitled to "strong consolation." What belongs to a "joint-heir with Christ," interested in the unchanging love of Jehovah from eternity, but the language of triumphant exultation? The first view, as it passed before my eyes, was the rejoicing of my heart; and never could I be satisfied, until I had taken it as my soul-satisfying and eternal portion.

Need we then entreat you, believer, to show to the world, that the promises of your heritage are not an empty sound—that they impart a Divine reality of support and enjoyment—and that an interest in them habitually realized is a blessed, a heavenly portion? Should your heart, however, at any time be captivated by the transient prospect before your eyes: should you be led to imagine some substantial value in this world's treasures—you will have forgotten the peculiar preeminence of your heritage—its enduring character. But what are the gaudy follies—the glittering emptiness of this passing scene, in comparison with your heavenly prospects, or even of your present sources of enjoyment!

We can readily account for the affecting indifference with which "the men of the world" barter away these treasures, as Esau did his birthright, for very trifles. They have no present interest in them. "They have their portion in this life. They have received their consolation." But, oh! how soon, having spent their all, will they "begin to be in" infinite, eternal "want!" Yet, having no interest in this heavenly heritage, they can have no pleasure in surveying it. If, therefore, conscience imposes upon them the drudgery of casting their careless eye over it, what wonder if they should find nothing to enliven their hopes, or to attract their hearts? What communion can worldly hearts hold with this heavenly treasure? What spiritual light, as the source of heavenly comfort, can penetrate this dark recess? As well might the inhabitant of the subterraneous cavern expect the cheerful light of the sun, as the man, whose eyes and heart are in the center of the earth, enjoy the spiritual perception of an interest in the heritage of the people of God. If, however, the darkness and difficulties of the word are pleaded in excuse for ignorance; let those indolent triflers confess, how small a portion of that persevering devotedness, which has been employed in gathering together the perishing stores of this world, has been given to search into this hidden mine of unsearchable riches!

O my soul, if I can lay claim to this blessed heritage, I envy not the miser his gold! Rather would I adore that grace, which has "made me to differ" from him; and given me a far happier and far richer heritage. But let me be daily enriching myself from this imperishable store; so that, poor as I am in myself, and seeming to "have nothing," I may in reality be "possessing all things." Let the recollection of the rich heritage of light, comfort, peace, and strength, furnished in the word, be my abundant joy: and bind my heart to a closer adherence to its obligations, and to a more habitual apprehension of its privileges.

112. I have inclined my heart to perform Your statutes always, even to the end.

The Psalmist had just been rejoicing in his privileges. He now binds himself to his obligations—and that not for a day—but even to the end. Observe where he begins his work—not with the eye—the ear—the tongue—but with the heart, "for out of the heart are the issues of life." And yet this inclining of the heart to the Lord's statutes is as much the work of God as to create a world; and as soon could "the Ethiopian change his skin, or the leopard his spots," as we could "do good, who are accustomed to do evil." David was very far from meaning, that any act of his own power could turn the channel of his affections out of their natural course. But prayer, such as he had often poured out, sets every principle of the soul in action, and, in dependence upon the Holy Spirit, he inclines his heart. Thus we do what we do; but God enables us, 'preventing us, that we may have a good will, and working with us, when we have that good will' (Are. X.)—not working without or against us, but in us—through us—with us—by us. His preventing grace makes the first impressions, and His assisting grace enables us to follow. Weak indeed are our purposes, and fading our resolutions, unsupported by Divine grace. Yet renewing strength is given to the "waiting" Christian, even to "mount up on eagles' wings, to run without weariness, and to walk without fainting." Conscious as we are, that "without Christ we can do nothing," it is no less true, that we "can do all things through Christ which strengthens us." Let us exercise, then, the grace already given, in dependence upon a continued supply; and turning to Him with freedom and delight, we shall incline our hearts with full purpose to perform His statutes always, even unto the end. This is God's way of quickening the dead soul to life and motion; alluring it by an inexpressible sweetness, and at the same moment, by an invincible power, drawing it to Himself.

Every step indeed to the end will be a conflict with indwelling sin, in the form of remaining enmity, sloth, or unbelief. But how encouraging is it to trace every tender prayer, every contrite groan, every spiritual desire, to the assisting, upholding influence of the "free spirit of God!" The continual drawing of the Spirit will be the principle to perseverance. The same hand that gave the new bias for a heavenward motion will be put forth to quicken that motion even unto the end. 'I can hardly hold on,'—the believer might say—'from one step to another.' How can I then dare to hope, that I shall hold on a constant course—a daily conflict to the end? But was it not Almighty power that supported the first step in your course? And is not the same Divine help pledged to every successive step of difficulty? Doubt not, then, that "He is faithful that has promised:" dare to be "confident of this very thing, that He which has begun a good work in you, will perform it until the day of Jesus Christ." And in this confidence go on to "work out your salvation with fear and trembling; for it is God which works in you both to will and to do of His good pleasure."

113. I hate vain thoughts, but Your law do I love.

The fall of man has misplaced his affections. Love was originally made for God and His law;—hatred, for sin. Now man loves what he ought to hate, and hates what he ought to love. The work of Divine grace is to restore the disordered affections to their proper center, and to bestow them on their right object;—hating vain thoughts, and loving the law of God. Few think of the responsibility of their thoughts; as if they were too trifling to be connected with any solemn account. The enlightened soul, however, learns to make a conscience of his thoughts. Here is the seminal principle of sin. How must a radical remedy be applied?

Vain thoughts are the natural produce of the unrenewed heart, and of the yet unrenewed part of the believer's heart. Who that "knows the plague of his own heart," and the spirituality of the Christian walk with God, does not constantly complain of their baneful influence? The child of God longs that his "every thought may be brought into captivity to the obedience of Christ." But he "sees another law in his members, warring against the law of his mind;" so that "when he would do good, evil is present with him." When he would "attend upon the Lord without distraction;" many times, even in a single exercise, does he forget his sacred employment. Sin seems to enter into every pore of his soul; and a cloud of vain thoughts darkens every avenue to communion with God. He would gladly say, "My heart is fixed, my heart is fixed;" but he finds his affections wandering, as "the eyes of the fool, in the ends of the earth," as if there were no object of Divine attraction to his soul. We do not hear the worldling, or indeed the servant of God in his worldly employments, complaining of this burden. He can bring to deep, important, and anxious concerns of this world, all that intensity and fixedness of attention which the emergency may demand. Indeed, the wily adversary would rather assist than hinder this concentration of mind, as diverting the soul from the far more momentous and interesting subjects of eternity. But never do the "sons of God come to present themselves before the Lord," except "Satan comes also among them."

Vain thoughts are his ceaseless hindrances to our spiritual communion with God. Are we aware of the subtlety, and therefore the peculiar danger, of this temptation? We should instinctively start from an enticement to open transgression. The incursion of defiling or blasphemous thoughts would be such a burden, that we should "have no rest in our spirit," while they remain undisturbed within us. But perhaps neither of these temptations are so formidable as the crowd of thoughts of every kind, incessantly running to and fro in the mind; the indulgence of which, though not actually sinful in itself, yet as effectually restrains the soul from communion with God, as the most hateful injections. These are "the little foxes, that spoil the tender grapes." No—the thoughts may be even spiritual in their nature, and yet vain in their tendency; because unsuitable to the present frame, and calculated, and indeed intended by the great enemy, to divert the mind from some positive duty. Who has not felt a serious thought upon an unseasonable subject, and an unseasonable time, to be in its consequences a vain thought—the secret impulse of the false "angel of light," dividing the attention between two things, so that neither of them may be wholly done, done to any purpose, done at all? If at any time "iniquity has been regarded in the heart;" if the world in any of its thousand forms has regained a temporary ascendancy; or if lusting imaginations are not constantly "held in" as "with bit and bridle;" these vain thoughts, ever ready to force their entrance, will at such seasons "get an advantage of us." Restless in their workings, they keep no sabbaths: and can only be successfully met by a watchful and unceasing warfare.

It may indeed be sometimes difficult, in the midst of this continual trial, to maintain a clear sense of adoption. But this is the distinctive mark of Christian sincerity:—Do we cordially hate them, as exceedingly sinful in the sight of God, hurtful to our own souls and contrary to our new nature? If we cannot altogether prevent their entrance, or eject them from their settlement, are we careful not to invite them, not to entertain them, not to suffer them to "lodge within us?" This active hatred is a satisfactory proof that they are not so much the natural suggestion of the heart, as the injections of the enemy of our peace. They are at least so directly opposed to our better will and dominant bias, that we may say, "If I do that I would not, it is no more I that do it, but sin that dwells in me." Our affliction and conflict with them prove that they dwell with us—not as welcome guests, or as the family of the house—but as "thieves and robbers." Their indulgence constitutes our sin. Their indwelling may be considered only as our temptation. They supply, indeed, continual matter for watchfulness, humiliation, and resistance; yet so far as they are abhorred and resisted, they are rather our infirmities than our iniquities, and leave no stain of actual guilt upon the conscience. An increasing sense of the sinfulness of sin, and of the extent of duty, will indeed show their deeper aggravations and more persevering opposition. Still, however, even while we groan under their defiling, distracting influence, in our best services, we may assure our confidence in Him, who "spares us, as a man spares his own son that serves him," and who will gather up the broken parts of our prayers with merciful acceptance.

But the subjugation of this evil—even though we be secured from its condemnation—is a matter of the deepest concern. Forget not—oh, may the impression be indelible!—that it was for these vain thoughts that the Savior was nailed to the cross. Here lies the ground of self-loathing—the quickening principle of conflict and exertion. Let the heart—the seat of this evil disease—be continually washed in the cleansing blood of Calvary; for until the corrupt fountain be cleansed, it must ever "send forth bitter waters." Let it be diligently "kept," and carefully filled, so that it may be a "good treasure bringing forth good things." Let there be the continued exercise of that "watchfulness" "which is unto prayer," combined with an unflinching adherence to plain and obvious duty. Let the temptation to desist awhile from services so polluted, that they appear rather to mock God than to worship Him, be met on the onset with the most determined opposition. Once admit this suggestion, and our active enemy will pour in successive incursions of vain thoughts into our perplexed and yielding minds, to turn us back step by step in our attempts to approach God. If, therefore, we cannot advance as we could wish, let us advance as we can. If a connected train of thought or expression fails us, let us only change—not surrender—our posture of resistance; substituting sighs, desires, tears, and "groanings"—for words, and casting ourselves upon our God in the simple confidence of faith, "Lord, all my desire is before You, and my groaning is not hid from You. You tell my wanderings: put my tears into Your bottle: are they not in Your book?" It is far better to wander in duty than from it. For if any duty be neglected on account of the defilement that is mingled with it, for the same reason we must neglect every other duty, and, as the final consequence, the worship of God would be abolished from the earth.

Much of our successful warfare, however, depends upon an accurate and well-digested acquaintance with our own hearts—upon a discovery of the bias of the mind in our unoccupied moments, and of the peculiar seasons and circumstances that give most power to temptation. This once known, set a double watch against those doors, by which the enemy has been accustomed to find his most convenient and unobstructed entrance.

But we must not forget the effective means suggested by David's experience—the love of God's law. Here rises the native enmity against God—not as the Creator, but the Law-giver—and therefore against His law as the dictate of His will. Here, then, is the power of grace subduing this enmity. Not only I fear, and therefore through fear I keep, but I love Your law. And 'He who loves a holy law'—remarks an excellent old writer—'cannot but hate a vain thought.' For if the law be the transcript of the image of God, the thoughts affectionately drawn out towards him must naturally fix the image of the beloved friend upon the mind, and by a sweet constraint fasten down the thoughts to Divine contemplation. Are we then ever winged with an elevating love to the Savior? And do we not find our hearts start out from their worldly employments with frequent glances and flights towards the object of our desire? And will not this communion of love gradually mold the soul into a fixed delight, exciting our hatred, and strengthening our resistance of every sinful affection?

Thus, as love to the law stirs up the powers of the renewed man, "spiritual wickedness" will be abhorred, conflicted with, and overcome.

Yet these defilements will remain to die with the last breathings of the old man; which, though crucified indeed and expiring, will struggle with fearful strength and unabated enmity to the end. And let them remain, as humbling mementos of our unclean nature, "shaped in iniquity, and conceived in sin;" and as enlivening our anticipations of that blessed place, where "shall in no wise enter anything that defiles;" where vain thoughts, and whatever beside might "separate between us and our God," will be unknown forever. Meanwhile let them endear to us the free justification of the Gospel; let them lead us daily and hourly to "the fountain opened for sin and for uncleanness;" and enhance in our view that heavenly intercession, which provides for the perfect cleansing and accepting of services even such as ours.

Blessed contemplation! Jesus prays not for us, as we do for ourselves. His intercession is without distraction—without interruption. If we are then so dead, that we cannot, and so guilty, that we dare not, pray, and so wandering in our vain thoughts, that our prayers appear to be scattered to the winds, rather than to ascend to heaven—if on these accounts combined, we "are so troubled, that we cannot speak:" yet always is there One to speak for us, of whom "a voice from heaven" testified for our encouragement, "saying—This is My beloved Son, in whom I am well pleased." With such hopes, motives, and encouragements, let us "continue instant in prayer," until we pray, and that we may pray. Let us supplicate our Lord with restless importunity, that His omnipotent love would take hold of these hearts, which every moment sin and Satan seem ready to seize. At the same time, conscious of our hatred of every interruption to His service, and of the simplicity of our affection to His holy law, let us hold fast that confidence before Him, which will issue in perfect peace and established consolation.

114. You are my hiding place, and my shield; I hope in Your word.

We have seen the unremitting vigilance of the enemy pursuing the man of God in his secret retirement with painful distraction. See how he runs to his hiding-place. Here is our main principle of safety—not our strivings or our watchfulness, but our faith. Flee instantly to Jesus. He is the sinner's hiding-place, "the man,"—that wondrous man, "in whom dwelt all the fullness of the Godhead bodily." Yes, Jesus exposed

Himself to the fury of "the tempest," that He might become a hiding-place, for us. The broken law pursued with its relentless curse—'The sinner ought to die'—But You are my hiding-place, who has "redeemed me from the curse of the law, being made a curse for me." "The fiery darts" pour in on every side: but the recollection of past security awakens my song of acknowledgment, "You have been a strength to the poor, a strength to the needy in his distress, a refuge from the storm, a shadow from the heat, when the blast of 'the terrible ones is as a storm against the wall." Our hiding-place covers us from the power of the world. "In Me"—says our Savior, "you shall have peace. Be of good cheer! I have overcome the world." Helpless to resist the great enemy, our Lord brings us to His wounded side, and hides us there. We "overcome him by the blood of the Lamb." To all accusations from every quarter, our challenge is ready, "Who shall lay anything to the charge of God's elect?" From the fear of death, our hiding-place still covers us. "Jesus through death has destroyed him that had the power of death." Against the sting of this last enemy, a song of thanksgiving is put into our mouth, "O death! where is your sting? O grave! where is your victory? Thanks be to God, which gives us the victory through our Lord Jesus Christ." Thus is "the smoking flax," which the malice of Satan strives to extinguish, not "quenched;" nor is "the bruised reed," which seems beyond the hope of restoration, "broken."

But the completeness of our security is graphically portrayed—You are my hiding-place, to cover from danger—my shield, also to protect me in it. Either I shall be kept from trouble, that it shall not come; or in trouble, that it shall not hurt me. The hiding-place alone would be imperfect security, as being limited to one place. But my shield is moveable, wherever be the point of danger or assault. I can "quench the dart" that is aimed at my soul.

But a hiding-place implies also secrecy. And truly the believer's is "a hidden life," beyond the comprehension of the world. He mixes with them in the common communion of life. But while seen of man, he is dwelling "in the secret of the Lord's tabernacle," safe in the midst of surrounding danger, guarded by invincible strength. Often, indeed, must the world be surprised at his constancy, amid all their varied efforts to shake his steadfastness. They know not "the secret of the Lord, which is with them that fear Him." And never could he have had a just conception of the all-sufficiency of his God, until he finds it above him, around him, underneath him, in all the fullness of everlasting love—his hiding-place, and his shield. Thus in the heart of the enemy's country "he dwells on high, and his place of defense is the munitions of rocks."

But are we acquainted with this hiding-place? How have we discovered it? Are we found in it, and careful to abide in it? Within its walls "that wicked one touches us not." Yet never shall we venture outside the walls unprotected, but his assault will give us some painful remembrance of our unwatchfulness. And then do we prize our shield, and run behind it for constant security. Remember, every other hiding-place "the waters will overflow." Every other shield is a powerless defense. Surely then the word which has discovered this security to us, is a firm warrant for our hope. And, therefore, every sinner, enclosed in the covert of love, will be ready to declare—I hope in Your word.

115. Depart from me, you evil-doers; for I will keep the commandments of my God.

Safe and quiet in his hiding-place, and behind his shield, David deprecates all attempts to disturb his peace—Depart from me, you evil-doers. He had found them to be opposed to his best interests; and he dreaded their influence in shaking his resolution for his God. Indeed such society must always hinder alike the enjoyment and the service of God. "Can two walk together, except they be agreed?" And can we be "agreed," and walk in fellowship with God, except we be at variance with the principles, the standard, and conduct of a world that is "enmity against Him?" Not more needful was the exhortation to the first Christians than to ourselves, "Save yourselves from this untoward generation." True fellowship with God implies therefore a resolute separation from the ungodly. Secure in the hiding-place, and covered with the shield of our covenant God, let us meet their malice, and resist their enticements, with the undaunted front of "a good soldier of Jesus Christ."

Not that we would indulge morose or ascetic seclusion. We are expressly enjoined to courtesy and kindness; to that wise and considerate "walk towards them that are without," which "adorns the doctrine of God our Savior," and indeed in some instances has been more powerful even than the word itself, to "win souls to Christ." But when they would tempt us to a devious or backsliding step—when our connection with them entices us to a single act of conformity to their standard, dishonorable to God, and inconsistent with our profession—then must we take a bold and unflinching stand—Depart from me, you evil-doers for I will keep the commandments of my God.

This resolution gives no countenance to the self-delusive notion of maintaining an intimate connection with professed evil-doers, for the kind purpose of recommending our religion to their acceptance—a scheme, which requires a rare degree of caution and simplicity to attempt without entangling the conscience; and which, for the most part at least, it is to be feared, is only a specious covering for the indulgence of a worldly spirit. If the men of the world are to be met, and their society invited, for the accomplishment of this benevolent intention, it must be upon the principle of the Lord's command to his prophet, "Let them return unto You: but return not You to them." The amiable desire to "please our neighbor" is limited to the single end, that it should be "for his good to edification." And whenever this end and restriction has been overlooked, it is sufficiently evident that self-gratification has been the moving principle: and that the distinctive mark of the Christian character—bearing the cross, and confessing the name of our Divine Master—has been obscured.

Sometimes, however, in the struggle of conscience, an apprehension of danger is not altogether forgotten, and the question is asked, with some trembling of spirit, "How far may I conform to the world, without endangering the loss of my religion?" But, not to speak of the insincerity and self-deception of such a question, it would be better answered by substituting another in its place, "How far may I be separate from the world, and yet be destitute of the vital principle?" Scrutinize, in every advancing step toward the world, the workings of your own heart. Suspect its reasonings. Listen to the first awakened conviction of conscience. Though it be only a whisper, or a hint, it is probably the indication of the Divine will. And never forget, that this experiment of worldly conformity, often as it has been tried, has never answered the desired end. However this compromise may have recommended ourselves, no progress has been made in recommending our Master; since His name—whether from unwatchfulness or cowardice on our part, or from the overpowering flow of the world on the other side—has probably in such society scarcely passed over our lips with any refreshment or attentiveness. Indeed, so far from commending our religion by this accommodation, we have succeeded in ingratiating ourselves in their favor, only so far as we have been content to keep it out of sight; while at the same time, our yielding conformity to their taste, and habits, and conversation, has virtually sanctioned their erroneous standard of conduct; and tended to deceive them with the self-complacent conviction, that it approaches as near to the Scriptural elevation, as is absolutely required. The final result, therefore, of this attempt to recommend the Gospel to those who have no "heart for it," is—that our own consciences have been ensnared, while they retain all their principles unaltered.

It must surely be obvious, that such a course is plainly opposed to the revealed declarations of Scripture, and bears the decisive character of unfaithfulness to our Great Master. We might also ask, whether our love to the Lord can be in fervent exercise, while we "love them that hate Him?"—whether our hatred of sin can be active and powerful, while we can find pleasure in the society of those, whose life "without God in the world," is an habitual, willful course of rebellion against Him?—whether we can have any deep or experimental sense of our own weakness, when thus venturing into temptation?—whether by unnecessary contact with the world, we can expect to "go upon hot coals," and our "feet not be burned?"—or, in fact, whether we are not forgetting the dictates of common prudence in forsaking the path of safety for a slippery, but more congenial path? Is no harm to be anticipated from a willful, self-pleasing association? Is it likely to be less dangerous to us than it was to an Apostle? or, because we conceive ourselves to have more strength, shall we use less watchfulness, and show more presumption?

But, supposing Scripture not to determine the path of duty with infallible certainty; let this line of conduct be subjected to the impartial scrutiny of our own hearts, and of the effects, whether neutral or positively detrimental, which have resulted from it to ourselves, or to the church. Have we not felt this fellowship with evil-doers to be an hindrance in keeping the commandments of our God? If it has not always ended in open conformity to their maxims; or if, contrary to our apprehensions, it does not appear to sanction their principles, yet have we realized no deadening unfavorable influence? Has the spirit of prayer sustained no injury in this atmosphere? Have we never felt the danger of imbibing their taste—the spirit of their conversation and general conduct; which, without fixing any blot upon our external profession, must insensibly estrange our best affections from God! And have we never considered the injury of this worldly association to the Gospel in weakening by an apparent want of decision "on the Lord's side," the sacred cause which we are pledged to support; and obscuring the spiritual character of the people of God as a distinct and separate people? In a providential connection with evil-doers, we go safely in the spirit of humility, watchfulness, and prayer; and this connection, felt to be a cross, is not likely to prove a snare. But does not union of spirit with them, to whom David says, with holy determination—Depart from me— and to whom David's Lord will one day say, "Depart!"—prove a want of fellowship with his spirit, and an essential unfitness for communion with the society of heaven? The children of this world can have no more real communion with the children of light, than darkness has with light. As great is the difference between the Christian and the world, as between heaven and hell—as between the sounds, "Come, you blessed," and, "Depart, you cursed." The difference, which at that solemn day will be made for eternity, must, therefore, be visibly made now. They must depart from us, or we from God. We cannot walk with them both. 'Defilement'—as Mr. Cecil remarks—'is inseparable from the world.' We cannot hold communion with God, in the spirit of the world; and, therefore, separation from the world, or separation from God, is the alternative. Which way—which company—is most congenial to our taste? Fellowship will be a component part of our heavenly happiness. Shall we not then walk on earth with those, with whom we hope to spend our eternity, that our removal hence may be a change of place only, not of company? May we have grace to listen to our Father's voice of love, "Therefore, come out from among them, and be separate, says the Lord; and touch not the unclean thing: and I will receive you, and will be a Father to you, and you shall be My sons and daughters, says the Lord Almighty."

116. Uphold me according unto Your word, that I may live: and let me not be ashamed of my hope.

Lest the Psalmist should seem to have been self-confident in his rejection of the society of the ungodly, and his determination to adhere to his God; here, as on former occasions, mindful of his own weakness, he commits himself to the upholding grace of God. He does not content himself with commanding the evil-doer to depart. He pleads for his God to come to him. He wants not only the hindrances to be removed, but the vouchsafement of present supporting grace. Such is our urgent continual need! Every circumstance has its temptation. Every change of condition is specially trying—and what is he in himself? unstable as water! Indeed the highest Archangel before the throne stands only as he is upheld by the Lord, and may unite with the weakest child in the Lord's family in the acknowledgment, "By the grace of God I am what I am." Much more, therefore, must I, pressed on every side with daily conflict and temptation, and conscious of my own weakness and liability to fall, "come to the throne of grace," for "grace to help in time of need." My plea is the word of promise—according to Your word, "as your days, so shall your strength be." "Fear not"—is the language of my upholding God, "for I am with you; be not dismayed, for I am your God: I will strengthen you: yes, I will help you: yes, I will uphold you with the right hand of My righteousness." Blessed be the goodness that made the promise, and that guides the hand of my faith, as it were, to fasten upon it!

But why do I need the promise? why do I plead it? but that I may live—that I may know that life, which is found and enjoyed "in the favor" of God? Nothing seems worth a serious thought besides; nothing else deserves the name. And therefore new life, "life more abundantly"— let it be the burden of every prayer—the cry of every moment. Thus upheld by the Lord's grace, and living in His presence, I hope to feel the increasing support of my Christian hope. Though I have just before expressed it in God's word—though I have "made my boast in the Lord," as my hiding-place and my shield, yet conscious helplessness leads me earnestly to pray—Let me not be ashamed of my hope.

Yes—Jesus is the sinner's hope, "the hope set before" His people, to which they "flee for the refuge" of their souls. And well may our "hope" in Him be called "an anchor of the soul, sure and steadfast." How does the distressed church plead with the hope of Israel, and put her God in remembrance of this His own name, that she might not be ashamed of her hope! And how does she—with every member of her body— eventually learn by this pleading, to say in the confidence of faith, "I know whom I have believed!" And is there not a solid ground for this confidence? Is not the "stone that is laid in Zion for a foundation," a "tried stone?" Has it not been tried by thousands and millions of sinners—no, more, tried by God Himself, and found to be "a sure foundation?" Yet still, that I may "hold fast the beginning of my confidence," and "the rejoicing of my hope, firm unto the end," I must persevere in prayer—Uphold me according unto Your word.

David, when left to his own weakness, was ashamed of his hope:, "I said in my haste, I am cut off from before Your eyes." At another time, when upheld in a season of accumulated trial, "he encouraged himself in the Lord his God." Thus I see "wherein my great strength lies," and how impotent I am, when left to myself. What a mercy, that my salvation will never for a single moment be in my own keeping! what need have I to pray to be saved from myself! How delightful is the exercise of faith in going to the Strong for strength! The issue of my spiritual conflicts is certain. He who is the author, will ever be the upholder, of the "hidden life" in His people. It is a part of His own life, and therefore can never perish. The Tempter himself will flee, when he marks the poor, feeble, fainting soul, upheld according to the word of his God, and placed in safety beyond the reach of his malice. Not, however, that, as I once supposed, my weakness will ever be made strong; but that I shall daily grow more sensible of it, shall, stay myself more simply upon infinite everlasting strength; and "most gladly shall I glory in my infirmities, that the power of Christ may rest upon me."

117. Hold me up, and I shall be safe; and I will have respect unto Your statutes continually.

Such is my sense of need and peril, that my only refuge lies in "continuing instant in prayer." I must send up one cry after another into my Father's ear for the support of His upholding grace. For not only the consciousness of my weakness, but the danger of the slippery path before me, reminds me, that the safety of every moment depends upon my upholding faithful God. The ways of temptation are so many and imperceptible—the influence of it so appalling—the entrance into it so deceitful, so specious, so insensible—my own weakness and unwatchfulness so unspeakable—that I can do nothing but go on my way, praying at every step—Hold me up, and I shall be safe. Often, indeed, can I remember, when "my feet were almost gone, my steps had well-near slipped:" that I have been enabled to record, "Your mercy, O Lord, held me up."

How beautiful is the picture given of the church of old! "Who is this that comes up from the wilderness, leaning upon her Beloved?" This state of dependence was familiar to the Psalmist, and aptly delineates his affectionate, though conflicting, confidence. "My soul follows hard after You: Your right hand upholds me." The recollection of the care of his

God, from his earliest life, supplied encouragement for his present faith, and matter for unceasing praise, "By You have I been held up from the womb; You are He who took me out of my mother's affections: my praise shall be continually of You." We cannot wonder, then, that this confidence should sustain his soul in the contemplation of the remaining steps of his pilgrimage, and his prospects for eternity. "Nevertheless"—says he, "I am continually with You: You have holden me by Your right hand. You shall guide me with Your counsel, and afterwards receive me to glory." And, indeed, the more lively my spiritual apprehensions are, the more I shall realize the Lord by the operations of His grace as well as of His providence, "compassing my path and my lying down;" lest any hurt me, keeping me night and day."

Is it inquired—how the Lord holds up His people in this slippery path? "Of the fullness of Jesus they all receive, and grace for grace;" so that "the life which they now live in the flesh, they live by the faith of the Son of God." And, therefore, if I am upheld, it is by the indwelling of the Spirit, who supplies from His infinite fountain of life all the strength and support I need throughout my dangerous way. By His Divine influence the dispensations of Providence also become the appointed means of drawing and keeping me near to my God. If, therefore, prosperity is endangering my soul, and strengthening my worldly bonds, may I not trust to the ever-watchful kindness of the Lord, to keep me low, and not to permit me to be at ease in my forgetfulness? If the pleasures of sense, if the esteem of the world, or the good report of the church, are bringing a bewitching snare upon my soul, my God will lead me into the pathway of the cross—in the "valley of humiliation."

Here, then, is the secret of an unsteady walk—the neglect of leaning upon an Almighty arm! How fearfully is the danger of self-confidence unveiled! Standing by my own strength, very soon shall I be made to feel, that I cannot stand at all. No "mountain" seemed to "stand stronger" than Solomon's: yet when he became the very "fool" that he describes, "trusting in his own heart"—how quickly was it removed!

Peter thought in the foolishness of his heart, that he could have walked upon the water unsupported by the arm of his Lord: but a moment's sense of weakness and danger brought him to his right mind: "and, beginning to sink, he cried, saying—Lord! save me!" Well would it have been for him, if his deliverance at that moment of peril had effectually rebuked his presumption. We should not then have heard from the same lips that language of most unwarranted self-confidence:

"Although all shall be offended, yet will not I:—if I should die with You, I will not deny You in any wise." Poor deluded disciple! You are on the brink of a grievous fall! Yet was he held up from utterly sinking. "I have prayed for you"—said the gracious Savior, "that your faith fail not." And thus held up by the same faithful intercession of my powerful friend (whose prayers are not weak as mine, "nor will He fail or be discouraged" by my continual backslidings), "I" too—though in the atmosphere of danger, in the slippery path of temptation, shall be safe—safe from an ensnaring world—safe from a treacherous heart—safe in life—safe in death—safe in eternity. Thus does an interest in the covenant encourage—not presumption—but faith, in all its exercises of humility, watchfulness, diligence, and prayer; in this appointed way does the Lord securely "keep the feet of His saints."

Let me not, then, forget, either my continual liability to fall if left to myself, or the faithful engagements of my covenant God, to "keep me from falling." While I recollect for my comfort, that I "stand by faith," still is the exhortation most needful, "Be not high-minded, but fear." "By faith I stand," as it concerns God; by fear as it regards myself. As light is composed of neither brilliant nor somber rays, but of the combination of both in simultaneous action, so is every Christian grace combined with its opposite, "that it may be perfect and entire, wanting nothing." Hope, therefore, combined with fear, issues in that genuine, evangelical confidence, in which alone I can walk safely and closely with God. Let, then, the self-confident learn to distrust themselves, and the fearful be encouraged to trust their Savior; and in each let the recollection of grace and help given "in time of need," lead to the steadfast resolution—I will have respect unto Your statutes continually. However self-denying they may be in their requirements: however opposed in their tendency to "the desires of the flesh and of the mind," I take my God as the surety of my performance of them; and I desire to love them as the rule of my daily conduct, and the very element of heavenly happiness to my soul.

118. You have trodden down all them that err from Your statutes: for their deceit is falsehood. 119. You put away all the wicked of the earth like dross; therefore I love Your testimonies.

The Psalmist's determination to keep the statutes of God was strengthened by marking His judgments on those that erred from them. And thus the Lord expects us to learn at their cost. The cheerful, grateful respect to His statutes marks also a difference of character indicative of a difference of state. "His saints are in His hand, or sitting down at His feet;" His enemies are trodden down under His feet in full conquest, and disgraceful punishment. His own people He has exalted to be "heirs of God, and joint-heirs with Christ." Even now "he has made them to sit together in heavenly places in Christ Jesus;" and shortly will they "be a crown of glory in the hand of the Lord, and a royal diadem in the hand of their God;" while the ungodly are put away like dross from the precious gold. "Reprobate silver shall men call them, because the Lord has rejected them." The same difference He makes even in chastening— upholding His own children under the scourging rod, lest they faint; but "breaking the wicked with a rod of iron, and dashing them in pieces."

This separation has been from the beginning; in His conduct to the first two children of men; and in His selection of Enoch, Noah, and Abraham, from the world of the ungodly, "as vessels of honor, meet for the Master's use." In after ages, He made Egypt "know, that He put a difference between the Egyptians and Israel." They were His own "people, that should dwell alone," and not "be reckoned among the nations"—a people, whom He had "formed for Himself, that they should show forth His praise." And the same difference He has made ever since, between His people and the world—in their character—their way—their exercises of mind—their services—their privileges—and their prospects. At the day of judgment, the separation will be complete—final— everlasting. "'When the Son of Man shall come in His glory, and all the holy angels with Him, then shall He sit upon the throne of His glory; and before Him shall be gathered all nations; and He shall separate them one from another, as a shepherd divides his sheep from the goats. And He shall set the sheep on His right hand, but the goats on the left; and these shall go away into everlasting punishment; but the righteous into life eternal."

But mark the character—They err from God's statutes—not in their minds, through ignorance; but "in their hearts" through obstinacy. They do not say, 'Lord, we know not,' but, "We desire not the knowledge of Your ways." It is not frailty, but unbelief; not want of knowledge, but love of sin—willful, damnable. Justly, therefore, are they stamped as the wicked of the earth, and marked out as objects of the Lord's eternal frown—expectants of the "vengeance of eternal fire."

And is not this a solemn warning to those "that forget God"—that "they shall be turned into hell;" to "the proud"—that in "the day that shall burn as an oven, they shall be as stubble;"—to the worldly—that in some "night" of forgetfulness, their "souls will be required of them;"—to the "hypocrites in heart"—that they "are heaping up wrath?" Thus does the eye of faith discern through the apparent disorder of a world in ruins, the just, holy, and wise government of God. "Clouds and darkness are round about Him; righteousness and judgment are the habitation of His throne." If the wicked seem to triumph, and the righteous to be trodden down under their feet, it shall not be always so. "The end" and "wages of sin is death." "The ungodly shall not stand in the judgment, nor sinners in the congregation of the righteous."

How awful, then, and almost desperate their condition! Their deceit is falsehood; "deceiving and being deceived"—perhaps given up to believe their own lie—perhaps one or another "blessing themselves in their own heart," saying, 'I shall have peace, though I walk in the imagination of my own heart, to add drunkenness to thirst.' What, then, is our duty? Carnal selfishness says, 'Be quiet—let them alone'—that is, "Destroy them by our" indolence and unfaithfulness, "for whom Christ died." But what does Scripture, conscience, no more—what does common humanity say? "Cry aloud, spare not." Awake the sleepers—sound the alarm, "Now is the accepted time—the day of salvation!" the moment to lift up the prayer, and stretch forth the hand for plucking the brands out of the fire. Tomorrow, the door may be shut, never to be opened more.

How awful the judgment of being put away like dross! Look at Saul, when put away—going out, to harden himself in the sullen pride of despondency. Hear the fearful doom of Israel, "Son of man, the house of Israel is to me become dross; all they are brass, and tin, and iron, and lead, in the midst of the furnace; they are even the dross of silver. Therefore says the Lord God—Because you are all become dross, behold, therefore I will gather you into the midst of Jerusalem, as they gather silver, and brass, and iron, and lead, and tin into the midst of the furnaces to blow the fire upon it, to melt it; so will I gather you in My anger and in My fury; and I will leave you there, and melt you." But how should this justice of the Lord's proceedings endear His statutes to us! It is such a sensible demonstration of His truth, bringing with it such a close conviction of sovereign mercy to ourselves—not less guilty than they! Add to this—If He were less observant of sin—less strict in its punishment as a transgression of His word—we should lose that awful display of the holiness of the word, which commends it supremely to our love, "Your word is very pure; therefore Your servant loves it."

120. My flesh trembles for fear of You; and I am afraid of Your judgments.

The justice of God is a tremendously awful subject of contemplation, even to those who are safely shielded from its terrors. The believer, in the act of witnessing its righteous stroke upon the wicked of the earth, cannot forbear to cry out—My flesh trembles for fear of You. Thus did the holy men of old tremble, even with a frame approaching horror, in the presence of the Divine judgments. David trembled at the stroke of Uzzah, as if it came very near to himself. "Destruction from God"—says holy Job, "was a terror to me: and by reason of His highness I could not endure." Such also was the Prophet's strong sensation, "When I heard, my belly trembled; my lips quivered at Your voice: rottenness entered into my bones." And thus, when God comes to tread down and put away His enemies for the display of the holiness of His character, and to excite the love of His people—those that stand by, secure under the covert of their hiding-place—cannot but "take up their parable and say—Alas! who shall live, when God does this!" The children of God reverence their Father's anger. They cannot see it without an awful fear; and this trembling at His judgments upon the ungodly covers them from the heavy stroke. Those that refuse to tremble shall be made to feel, while those that are afraid of His judgments shall be secure. "Only with Your eyes shall you behold, and see the reward of the wicked." "I trembled in myself," said the prophet, "that I might rest in the day of trouble." Even the manifestations of His coming "for the salvation of His people" are attended with all the marks of the most fearful terror—as if His voice would shake the earth to its very foundation, "You caused judgment to be heard from heaven—the earth feared and was still: when God arose to judgment, to save all the meek of the earth."

To mark this trembling as the character of the child of God, we need only contrast it with the ungodly scoffing, "Where is the God of judgment? Where is the promise of His coming? The Lord will not do good, neither will He do evil." Thus do men dare to "run upon the thick bosses of His bucklers;" instead of trembling for fear of Him! This "stoutness against the Lord," excites the astonishment of the hosts of heaven; so discordant is it to their notes of humble praise, "Who shall not fear You, O Lord, and glorify Your name; for Your judgments are made manifest!" Such is the special acceptance of this trembling spirit, that some shadow of it obtained a respite even for wicked Ahab, and a pardon for the penitent Ninevites; while its genuine "tenderness of heart" screened Josiah from the doom of his people, and will ever be regarded with the tokens of the favor of this terrible God. "To this man," says he, "will I look, even to him that is poor, and of a contrite spirit, and that trembles at My word."

Believers in Christ! rejoice in your deliverance from that "fear which has torment." Yet cherish that holy reverential fear of the character and judgments of God, which will form your most effectual safeguard "from presumptuous sins." The very supposition, that, if God had not engaged Himself to you by an unchangeable covenant, His fearful judgments would have been your eternal portion, is of itself sufficient to mingle the wholesome ingredient of fear with the most established assurance. What! can you look down into the burning bottomless gulf beneath your feet, without the recollection—If I were not immovably fastened to the "Rock of Ages" by the strong chain of everlasting love, this must have been my abode through the countless ages of eternity. If I had not been thus upheld by the grace, as well as by the providence, of God, I might have dropped out of His hand, as one and another not more rebellious than I have fallen, into this intolerable perdition! O God! my flesh trembles for fear of You; and I am afraid of Your judgments.

Thus the dread of the judgments of God is not necessarily of a slavish and tormenting character. "His saints" are called to "fear Him;" and their fear, so far from "gendering unto bondage," is consistent with the strongest assurance; no, even is its fruit and effect. It is at once the principle of present obedience, and of final perseverance. It is the confession of weakness, unworthiness, and sinfulness, laying us low before our God. It is our most valuable discipline. It is the "bit and bridle" that curbs the frowardness of the flesh, and enables us to "serve God acceptably," in the remembrance, that, though in love He is a reconciled Father, yet in holiness He is "a consuming fire."

Now, if we are under the influence of this reverential awe and seriousness of spirit, we shall learn to attach a supreme authority and consideration to the least of His commands. We shall dread the thought of wilfully offending Him. The fear of grieving Him will be far more operative now, than was the fear of hell in our unconverted state. Those who presume upon their gospel liberty, will not, probably, understand this language. But the humble believer well knows how intimately "the fear of the Lord" is connected with "the comfort of the Holy Spirit," and with his own steady progress in holiness, and preparation for heaven.

121. I have done judgment and justice: leave me not to my oppressors.
122. Be surety for Your servant for good: let not the proud oppress me.

There is something very solemn in the reflection, that God has set up a Viceregent in the heart—an internal Judge, who takes cognizance of every thought, every emotion, every act—determining its character, and pronouncing its sentence. This tribunal tries every cause without respect to persons, time, place, or any circumstances, that might seem to separate it from other cases under the same jurisdiction. No criminal can escape detection from defect of evidence. No earthly power can hinder the immediate execution of the sentence. The sentence then, of this awful Judge, whether "accusing or excusing," is of infinite moment. The ignorant expression—'Thank God, I have a clear conscience!' is used alike by the self-righteous and the careless. The awakened sinner, however, pleads guilty to its accusations, and knows not how to answer them. Blessed be God for the revelation of His gospel, which proclaims the blood of Jesus—sprinkling the conscience—silencing its charges—and setting before the sinner the way of peace! And now through Jesus, "the new and living way" of access to God, conscience, sitting on the throne—speaks peace and acceptance; and though sins of infirmity will remain, defiling every thought, desire, and act; yet, like the motes on the face of the sun in the clearest day, they have little or no influence to obstruct the shining of the cheerful light upon the heart.

The clearing of conscience is however connected with Christian integrity. "If our heart condemn us not, then have we confidence toward God." This "testimony of conscience" has often been "the rejoicing" of the Lord's people, when suffering under unremitted reproach or proud oppression. They have been enabled to plead it without offence in the presence of their holy, heart-searching God—no, even when in the near prospect of the great and final account, they might have been supposed to shrink from the strict and unerring scrutiny of their Omniscient Judge.

But observe the influence of this testimony upon our spiritual comfort. David was at this time under persecution—no new trial to a child of God and one that will never cease, so long as Satan has instruments at his command. But see the blessing which conscious uprightness gave to his prayers: I have done judgment and justice: leave me not to my oppressors. Can my heart and conscience respond to this appeal? Then may I plead my cause before God, Leave me not to my oppressors. Let not the proud oppress me. Plead my cause with them. Let my righteousness be made known. Let it be seen, that You "will not leave me in their hand, nor condemn me when I am judged. Let integrity and uprightness preserve me: for I wait on You." But if any deviation from the exact rule of righteousness between man and man has been allowed—if the world charge me as ungodly, because they have proved me unrighteous—then let me not wonder, that "the consolations of God shall be small with me;" nor let me expect a return of the Lord's cheering manifestation, until the Achan has been removed from the camp, and by confession to God, and reparation to man, I have "given glory to the Lord God of Israel."

But let not this appeal be thought to savor of Pharisaical pride. He pleads not merit. He only asserts his innocence—the righteousness of his cause—not of his person. Though upright before man, he ever felt himself a sinner before God. The highest tone of conscious integrity is therefore consistent with the deepest prostration of evangelical humility. The difference is infinite between the proud Pharisee and the upright believer. The Pharisee makes the appeal with undisturbed self-delight and self-righteous pleading. The believer would ever accompany it with the Tax-collector's prayer for mercy. Instantly—in a deep conviction of need—he appends the supplication—Be surety for Your servant for good. The keen eye of the world may possibly not be able to affix any blot upon my outward profession; but, "if you, Lord, should mark iniquities, O Lord, who shall stand?" The debt is continually accumulating, and the prospect of payment as distant as ever. I might well expect to be left to my oppressors, until I should pay all that was due unto my Lord. But behold! "Where is the fury of the oppressor?" The surety is found—the debt is paid—the ransom is accepted—the sinner is free! There was a voice heard in heaven, "Deliver him from going down to the pit: I have found a ransom." Yes, the Son of God Himself became "surety for a stranger," and "smarted for it." At an infinite cost—the cost of His own precious blood—He delivered me from my oppressors—sin—Satan—the world—death—hell. "It was exacted: and he answered." As Judah in the place of Benjamin, he was ready to stand in my stead before his Father, "I will be surety of him: of my hand shall you require him." As Paul in the stead of Onesimus, he was ready to plead, before the same tribunal, "If he has wronged you, or owes you anything, put that on my account; I will repay it."

Let this subject be ever present to my mind. Well indeed was it for me, that Jesus did not "hate suretyship." Had He refused the vast undertaking, how could I have answered before the bar of God? Or had He undertaken only for those who loved Him, again should I have been left without a plea. But when as my surety He has brought me under His yoke, and made me His servant, I can plead with acceptance before His throne, Be surety for Your servant for good—for the good, which You know me to need—my present and eternal deliverance from my proud oppressors. And do not I need such a surety every moment? And need I be told how fully He has performed the Surety's part? So that I may boldly say, "Who is he who condemns? it is Christ that died. It is Christ that lives. There is therefore now no condemnation to them that are in Christ Jesus."

123. My eyes fail for Your salvation, and for the word of Your righteousness.

And do your eyes, tried believer, begin to fail? So did your Redeemer's before you. He, whom you have been recollecting as your Surety, when He stood in your place, burdened with the intolerable load of your sin—bearing the weighty strokes of Infinite justice upon His soul—He too was constrained to cry out, "My eyes fail, while I wait for my God." Listen, then, to your deserted Savior counseling His deserted people; "gifted with the tongue of the learned, that he should know how to speak a word in season to you that are weary" "Who is among you that fears the Lord, that obeys the voice of His servant; that walks in darkness, and has no light? Let him trust in the name of the Lord, and stay upon his God."

That our Surety will plead for our good, doubt not. Yet "the vision is for an appointed time." "But shall not God avenge His own elect, which cry day and night unto Him, though He bear long with them?" Salvation—a gift of such comprehensive and enduring blessing—is it not worth the waiting trial? Wonderful is that arrangement, by which the word of grace is made the word of righteousness! God has bound Himself to us by His promises of grace, which are not, Yes and no, but "Yes and amen"—under His own hand and seal. Who that has tried them, but will "set to his seal that God is true?" Cheering indeed is the thought, that, amid the incessant changes in Christian experience, our hope is unchangeably fixed. We may not indeed always enjoy it; but our salvation does not depend upon our present enjoyment of its consolation. Is not the blessing as certain—yes—is not our assurance of an interest in it as clear, when we are brought to the dust under a sense of sin, as if we were "caught up into the third heaven" in a vision of glory?

In a season of desertion, therefore, while we maintain a godly jealousy over our own hearts, let us beware of a mistrustful jealousy of God. Distrust will not cure our wound, or quicken us to prayer, or recommend us to the favor of God, or prepare us for the mercy of the Gospel. Complaining is not humility. Prayer without waiting is not faith. The path is plain as noon-day. Continue to believe as you can. Wait on the Lord. This is the act of faith, depending on Him—the act of hope, looking for Him—the act of patience, waiting His time—the act of submission, resigned even if He should not come. Like your Savior, in His "agony" of desertion, "pray more earnestly." Condemn yourself for the sins of which you are asking forgiveness. Bless Him for His past mercy, even if you should never taste it again. Can He frown you from His presence? Can He belie His promise to His waiting people? Impossible! No! while He has taken away the sensible apprehensions of His love, and in its room has kindled longing desires for the lost blessing; is not this to show Himself—if He be "verily a God that hides Himself"—yet still "the God of Israel, the Savior?" Though He delays His promise, and holds us as it were in suspense; yet He would have us know, that He has not forgotten the word of His righteousness. But this is His wise and effectual mode of trying His own gift of faith. And it is this "trial of faith"—and not faith untried—that will be "found to praise, and honor, and glory at the appearing of Jesus Christ."

The full consolation of the Gospel is therefore the fruit of patient, humble waiting for the Lord, and of earnest desire, conflicting with impatience and unbelief, and at length issuing in a state of child-like submission and dependence. The man who was here expressing his longing expectation for God's salvation, was evidently, though unconsciously, in possession of the promise. Nor would he at this moment have exchanged his hope, clouded as it was to his own view, for all "the pleasures of sin," or the riches of the world. Although at this moment he appeared to be under the partial hidings of his Father's countenance, yet it is important to observe, that he was not satisfied, as

215

an indolent professor, to "lie upon his face" in this sad condition. His "eyes failed with looking upward"—stretched up with earnest expectation to catch the first rising rays of the beaming Sun of Righteousness. He knew, what all Christians know, who walk closely with God, that his perseverance in waiting upon God, would issue in the eventual fulfillment of every desire of his heart.

But can we assuredly plead the word of His righteousness for the anticipation of the object of our desire? Have we always an express promise answering to our expectations, "putting God in remembrance" of His word? Possibly we may have been asking not "according to His will," and therefore may have "charged God foolishly," as if He had been unfaithful to His word, when no engagement had been pledged: when we had no warrant to build upon from the word of His righteousness. If, however, our petition should be found to be agreeable to His word of promise, and faith and patience hold on in submission to His will, we must not, we cannot, suppose, that one tittle that we have asked will fail. Whether the Lord deliver us or not, prayer and waiting will not be lost. It is a blessed posture for Him to find us in, such as will not fail to ensure His acceptance, even though our request should be denied. An enlivening view of the Savior is in reserve for us; and the word of righteousness will yet speak, "This is the rest, with which you may cause the weary to rest: and this is the refreshing." To every passing doubt and rising fear, oppose this word of His righteousness.

But let me bring my own heart to the test. Am I longing for the manifestation of God? Surely if I am content with what I already know, I know but very little of the unsearchable depths of the love of Christ; and I have abundant need to pray for more enlarged desires, and a more tender enjoyment of His Divine presence. If faith is not dead, yet it may have lost its conquering and quickening vigor. Let me then exercise my soul in diligent, careful, patient waiting upon God, equally removed from sloth and frowardness—and I shall yet find the truth of that consoling word of His righteousness, "Light is sown for the righteous, and gladness for the upright in heart."

124. Deal with Your servant according unto Your mercy, and teach me Your statutes.

125. I am Your servant; give me understanding, that I may know Your testimonies.

A sense of mercy, and the privilege of Divine teaching, were the earnest of the Lord's salvation, for which the eyes of his servant were failing, and for which he was waiting in dependence upon the sure word of His righteousness. And indeed these two wants daily press upon every servant of God as matter for earnest supplication. Both are intimately connected. A deeper sense of mercy will bind us more strongly to His statutes; while a more spiritual teaching in the statutes will humble us in a sense of sin, and consequent need of mercy. As it respects the first—if there is a sinner upon the earth, who needs the special mercy of God, it is His own servant. For as the Lord sees abundantly more excellence in his feeblest desire, than in the professor's most splendid external duties; so He sees far more sinfulness and provocation in the workings of his sin, than in the palpably defective services of professors, or in the open transgression of the wicked of the earth. Let him scrutinize his motives, thoughts, and affections, even in his moments of nearest and happiest approach unto his God; and he will find such defilement cleaving to every offering, with all the aggravations of mercy, light, and knowledge, given, that the confession of his soul, when comparing himself with his fellow-sinners, will be, "Of whom I am chief." And therefore, as a servant of God, I can only come before Him upon the ground of mercy. For my best performances I need an immeasurable world of mercy—pardoning—saving—everlasting mercy; and yet by the blood of Jesus I dare to plead—Deal with Your servant according unto Your mercy.

But then I am ignorant as well as guilty; and yet I dare not pray for teaching—much and hourly as I need it, until I have afresh obtained mercy. These two blessings lead me at once to the foundation of the gospel—in the work of Christ, and the work of the Spirit—mercy flowing from the blood of the Son—teaching from the office of the Spirit. Mercy is the first blessing, not only in point of importance, but in point of order. I must know the Lord as a Savior, before I can go to Him with any confidence to be my teacher. But when once I have found acceptance for my petition—Deal with Your servant according to Your mercy—my way will be opened to enlarge my petition—yes, once and again to repeat it—Teach me Your statutes. Give me understanding, that

I may know Your testimonies—that I may know with intelligent conviction; walk, yes, "run in the way of Your commandments" with "an enlarged heart." For let me never forget, that I am "redeemed from the curse" only—not from the service "of the law"—yes, redeemed from its curse, that I may be bound to its service. And does not my especial relation to my God as His servant, furnish me with a plea for His acceptance? For when this "earth is full of His mercy"—much more may I, as belonging to His house, plead for the special mercy of His teaching—His own covenant promise—so needful for His servant, who desires to know, that he may do, His will.

But if I am the Lord's servant, how did I become so? Time was (let me be ashamed and confounded at the remembrance of it) when I was engaged for another master, and in another service. But His sovereign grace called me from the dominion of sin—from the chains of Satan—from the bondage of the world, and drew me to Himself. "His I am—and Him I serve." His service is my highest privilege: His reward of grace is my glorious hope. "If any man serve Me," says my Master, "let him follow Me: and where I am, there shall also My servant be. If any man serve Me, him will My Father honor." As His servant, therefore, I cast myself with confidence upon His mercy, and expect to be dealt with according to that mercy. No—I shall be denied nothing that I "ask according to His will." For He has condescended to call me—not His servant, but "his friend"—yes more, to call himself "my brother."

Lord! You have showed me this great favor and grace, to make me Your servant. I would be Yours forever. I love Your service too well to wish to change it; yet must I mourn over my dullness, my backwardness in doing Your will, and walking in Your way. Oh! teach me Your statutes more clearly, more experimentally! Give me understanding to discern their heavenly sweetness and their holy liberty, that I may live in a more simple and devoted obedience to them, until I come to see Your face, and to be Your servant in Your heavenly temple, "no more to go out."

Verses 126 - 149

126. It is time for You, Lord, to work; for they have made void Your law.

If I desire a more spiritual understanding of the revelation of God, how can I but mourn to witness its awful neglect and contempt? It seems as if the ungodly not only sin against it, but that they would drive it out of the world. They make it void—denying its power to rule, to annul its power to punish. Oh! let us cherish that distinguishing feature of the Lord's people, "sighing and crying for all the abominations of the land;" so that we cannot hear or see the name of God dishonored, without feeling as for our Father's wounded reputation. Can we suffer the men of the world quietly to go on their course? Must we not throw in our weight of influence, whatever it may be, to stem the flowing torrent: and when (as, alas! is too often the case) all efforts are unavailing, carry the cause to the Lord, "It is time for You, Lord, to work?" This pleading does not contradict the law of love, which requires us to love, pray for, and to bless our enemies; for the Lord's people are not angry for their own cause, but for His. David had no regard to his own honor, but to God's law. He had not injured his enemies. "He had labored to overcome their evil with good." He had often wept for their sins, and prayed for their conversion. But all was in vain. 'Now, Lord, take the rod in Your own hand. "It is time for You, Lord, to work.'" This was true zeal—zeal of the Spirit, not of the flesh. How gracious is our God in permitting His servants thus to plead with Him, and, as it were, to give Him no rest, until "he shall arise, and work," and sit upon the throne of the kingdoms of the earth!

But why does He not break out with some overpowering manifestation of His power? They are "his sword and rod" for the chastening of His people, to discipline their watchfulness into constant exercise. They are the trial of their faith—believing the Lord's justice against apparent inconsistency; and of their patience, "waiting the set time of deliverance." Thus they become a profitable ministry for the church—and this valuable end accomplished, God works His work upon them, and "will avenge His own elect speedily."

Meanwhile—waiting for this "little while," let us "live by faith." Let us be found on the Lord's side—laboring for sinners—pleading with their hardness and rebellion in our Master's name, and for our Master's sake. Let all the weight of personal exertion and influence, consistent example, and wrestling supplication, be concentrated in "coming to the help of the Lord against the mighty." Let us see to it, that if we cannot do what we would, we do what we can. And if at last we be overborne by the torrent of ungodliness, we shall find our refuge and rest in pleading with our Lord for the honor of His name—Remember this, that the enemy has reproached, O Lord, and that the foolish people have blasphemed Your name. "His Spirit shall not always strive with man." Often, when He has seen it time for Him to work, have His judgments made the earth to tremble. "Sodom and Gomorrah" have "known the power of His anger," and are "set forth for an example, suffering the vengeance of eternal fire." And when His time to work is fully come, what is all the resistance of earth and hell, but as "setting the briars and thorns against Him in battle?" "I would"—says he, "go through them. I would burn them together." A word—a frown—a look—is destruction. "He is wise in heart, and mighty in strength. Who has hardened himself against Him, and has prospered?" Or "who has resisted His will?"

But what shall we say of that stupendous work of His hand, by which—when men had made void His law—when no restrictions could bind, no forbearance win them—when He "saw that there was no man, and wondered that there was no intercessor, therefore His arm brought salvation unto him, and His righteousness, it sustained him." Surely, if we could conceive the hosts of heaven to have taken up this expression of ardent concern for the glory of God, It is time for You, Lord, to work—they could little have thought of such a work as this—they could never have conceived to themselves such an unlooked-for, combined display of power, justice, and mercy. To set at nothing then this work—is it not to refuse all hope—all remedy? To persist in making void the law after so magnificent an exhibition of Almighty working—must it not expose the transgressors to reap the fruit of their own obstinacy, and to prepare to meet Him as their Judge, whom they refuse to receive as their Savior? Nor must they wonder, if the Lord's people, with a holy indignation against sin, and a fervent zeal for His glory, should appeal to His faithfulness for the fulfillment of His judgments—It is time for You, Lord, to work: for they have made void Your law.

127. Therefore I love Your commandments above gold; yes, above fine gold.

Therefore I love Your commandments. Yes—shall they not have double valuation in my eyes, for the scorn and reproach which the world cast upon them? They count them dross—I love them above gold—yes, above fine gold. This hope, confidence, and idol of the worldling, the love of which has been the ruin of thousands—is not the commandment of God more to be desired than it? "The merchandise of it is better than the merchandise of silver, and the gain thereof than fine gold. It is more precious than rubies and all the things you can desire are not to be compared unto it." Here has the Lord unlocked to us His golden treasure, and enriched our souls with "the unsearchable riches of Christ."

This image brings the miser before us. His heart and treasure are in his gold. With what delight he counts it! with what watchfulness he keeps it! hiding it in safe custody, lest he should be despoiled of that which is dearer to him than life. Such should Christians be: spiritual misers: counting their treasure, which is above fine gold; and "hiding it in their heart," in safe keeping, where the great despoiler shall not be able to reach it. Oh, Christians! how much more is your portion to you than the miser's treasure! Hide it; watch it; retain it. You need not be afraid of covetousness in spiritual things: rather "covet earnestly" to increase your store; and by living upon it, and living in it, it will grow richer in extent, and more precious in value.

But have I through Divine grace been enabled to withdraw my love from the unworthy objects which once possessed it: and to fix it on that which alone offers satisfaction? Let me attempt to give a reason to myself of the high estimation in which I hold it, as infinitely transcending those things, which the world venture their all—even their temporal happiness—to obtain. Therefore I love the commandments of God above gold: yes, above fine gold—because, while the world and my own heart have only combined to flatter me, they have discovered to me my real state, as a self-deceived, guilty, defiled sinner before God: because they have been as a "schoolmaster to bring me to Christ"—the only remedy for sin, the only rest for my soul. I love them; because they have often supplied wholesome reproofs in my wanderings, and plain directions in my perplexity. I love them; because they restrict me from that which would prove my certain ruin; and because in the way of

221

obedience to them the Lord has "accepted me with my sweet savor." Should I not love them? Can gold, yes, fine gold, offer to me blessings such as these? Can it heal my broken heart? Can it give relief to my wounded spirit? Has it any peace or prospect of comfort for me on my death-bed? And what cannot—what has not—what will not—the precious word of God do at that awful season of trial? O my God, I would be deeply ashamed, that I love Your commandments so coldly—that they are so little influential upon my conduct—that they so often give place to objects of comparative nothingness in Your sight. O that my heart might be wholly and habitually exercised in them, that I may find the "work of righteousness to be peace, and the effect of righteousness, quietness, and assurance forever!"

128. Therefore I esteem all Your precepts concerning all things to be right: and I hate every false way.

The general contempt of religion acts upon the Christian's judgment no less than upon his affections. Is wickedness breaking loose to make void the law? Therefore he esteems it to be right. His judgment—instead of being shaken—is more determined. How beautiful is it to see the leaven of grace pervading the whole man! In the fervor of his heart he loves the commandments even above fine gold; but yet his "love will abound yet more and more in knowledge and in all judgment." His is an intelligent and universal regard to them—esteeming all the precepts concerning all things to be right. This constitutes his separate and exclusive character. He is readily known from the thoughtless worldling. But his difference from the professor, though really as marked in the sight of God, is far less perceptible to general observation. Consisting more in the state of heart, than in any external mark of distinction, it is often only within the ken of that eye, whose sovereign prerogative it is to "search the heart," and to "weigh the spirits."

Many profess to esteem the precepts to be right, so far as they inculcate the practice of those moral virtues, of which they may present some faint exhibition, and demand the abandonment of those sins, from the external influence of which they may have been delivered. But when they begin to observe the "exceeding breadth of the commandment"—how it takes cognizance of the heart, and enforces the renunciation of the world, the crucifixion of sin, and the entire surrender of the heart unto God; this searching touchstone separates them from the church, and exposes to open day the brand of hypocrisy upon their foreheads. "Herod did many things." And so the enemy still will allow a partial subjection to the precepts. But—as he well knows—one sin holds us his captive as well as a thousand. The willful contempt of one precept is the virtual rejection of all. All, therefore—not many—is the Christian's word. He fails in some—yes, in all—but all are the objects of his supreme regard—every duty, and every circumstance and obligation of duty—the evangelical as well as the moral precepts—teaching him to renounce himself in every part (his sins as a source of pleasure, and his duties as a ground of dependence): and to believe in the Son of God as the only ground of hope. He never complains of the strictness of the precepts!— but he is continually humbled in the recollection of his nonconformity to them. Every way, however pleasing to the flesh, that is opposed to the revealed will of God, is hated, as false in itself, and false to his God. This "godly sincerity" will apply to every part of the Christian Directory. So that any plea for the indulgence of sin (as if it admitted of palliation, or was compensated by some surplus duty, or allowed only for some temporary purpose) or any willful shrinking from the universality of obedience—blots out all pretensions to uprightness of heart. If holiness be really loved, it will be loved for its own sake; and equally loved and followed in every part. By this entire "approval of things that are excellent," we shall "be sincere and without offence unto the day of Christ."

O my soul, can you abide this close test? Have you as much regard to the precepts, as to the privileges, of the Gospel? Is no precept evaded, from repugnance to the cross that is entailed to it? Is no secret lust retained? Are you content to let all go? If my hatred of sin is sincere, I shall hate it more in my own house than abroad; I shall hate it most of all in my own heart. Here lies the grand seat of hypocrisy. And therefore may the great Searcher of hearts enable me to search into its depths! May I take the lamp of the Lord to penetrate into its dark interior hiding-places of evil! May I often put the question to my conscience, 'What does the Omniscient Judge know of my heart?' Perhaps at the time that the Church holds my name in esteem, the voice of conscience, as the voice of God, may whisper to me "That which is highly esteemed among men is an abomination in the sight of God." Some false way, yet undetected within, may keep me lifeless and unfruitful in the midst of the quickening means of grace. Let me look into my house—my calling— my family—my soul; and in the course of this search how much matter will be found for prayer, contrition, renewed determination of heart, and dependence upon my God! "O that my ways were directed to keep Your statutes! I will keep Your statutes; O forsake me not utterly." And oh! let my spirit be wounded by every fresh discovery of sin. Let my soul bleed under it. But specially and instantly let me apply to the "fountain opened for sin and for uncleanness." Here let me wash my soul from the guilt of sin, and regain my peace with God. And to Him, who opened this fountain, let me also repair for a large supply of spiritual strength. May His power and grace sharpen my weapons for the spiritual conflict, until every secret iniquity is overcome, and forever dispossessed from my heart!

And just as sin, besides its guilt, brings its own misery; so does this whole-hearted purity carry with it its own happiness. Can I forget the time, when, under Divine grace and teaching, I made a full presentment of myself, when I began to estimate myself as an hallowed, devoted thing—sacred—set apart for God? Was not this the first sunshine of my happiness? Nor was this offering made with momentary excitement, notional intelligence, forced acquiescence, or heartless assent. My judgment accorded with the choice of my heart. All was right in His precepts. All that was contrary to them was abominable. And will not this form the essence of the happiness of heaven, where every aspiration—every motion—every pulse of the glorified soul—in the eternity of life—will bear testimony to the holiness of the service of God?

129. Your testimonies are wonderful: therefore does my soul keep them.

Can the mere professor make this acknowledgment? He knows only the letter—the shell, which excites no interest. Yet hidden from his eye is an unsearchable depth, which will make the believer a learner to the end of his life. Even he, who "was caught up into paradise, and heard unspeakable words, which it is not lawful for a man to utter," was brought to this adoring contemplation, "O the depths of the riches both of the wisdom and knowledge of God!" Every way indeed is this revelation worthy of Him, the first letter of whose name is "Wonderful." It lays open to the heaven-taught soul what "eye has not seen, nor ear heard, neither has entered into the heart of man." Think of the Creator of the world becoming a creature—yes, "a curse for man." Think of man— guilty and condemned—made just with God by a righteousness not his own. Think of God bringing out of the ruinous fall more glory to Himself, and more happiness to man, than from his former innocence—in the display of His mercy—the glory of His justice, and the investment of sinners—not, as before; with a creature's righteousness, security, and reward, but with His own righteousness, guardianship, and glory. Think how "the way into the holiest of all" is thus "made manifest." Think how abounding grace is the death as well as the pardon of sin—the present as well as the everlasting life of the soul. These are among the stupendous discoveries of the sacred book, that bow the humble and reflecting mind to the confession—Your testimonies are wonderful! Let us therefore join with the Apostle, in "bowing our knees to the God and Father of our Lord Jesus Christ"—that we "might be able to comprehend with all saints" (for, blessed be God! the privilege is common to all His people) "what is the breadth, and length, and depth, and height: and to know the" unsearchable "love of Christ," "in whom are hid all the treasures of wisdom and knowledge."

And how delightful is the recollection of these testimonies being our "heritage forever!" For they are not less wonderful in their practical fullness, than in their deep unfathomable mysteries of love. Such is the infinite enlargement of this "heritage," that He who foreknew every thought that would find an entrance into the minds of His people, has here secretly laid up seasonable direction and encouragement for every, even the most minute occasion and circumstance of need. Here, again, is wrapped up, in words fitted by wisdom to receive the revelation, all that communion between God and man, throughout all ages of the Church, which is treasured up in the vast unsearchable depository of the Divine mind and purpose. Can we then forbear repeating the exclamation—Your testimonies are wonderful!

But it is not enough to 'adore the fullness of Scripture:' we must seek to imbibe and exhibit its practical influence. Holy admiration of the testimonies will kindle spiritual devotedness to them—Therefore does my soul keep them. The stamp of Divine authority upon them, while it deepens our reverence, commands our steady and cheerful obedience. To keep them is our privilege, no less than our obligation; and in this path we shall delight to persevere to the end.

But how affecting is the thought of the mass, who look at these wonders with a careless or unmeaning eye, unconscious of their interesting import! They pass by the door of the treasury, hardly condescending to look aside into it: or only taking a transient glance, which comprehends nothing of its inexhaustible stores. "I have written to them"—says the Lord, "the great things of My law: but they are counted as a strange thing." But far more wonderful is it, that we, enlightened, in answer to prayer (See verse 18), with "the Spirit of wisdom and revelation"—should often be so indifferent to the mysteries of redeeming love here unfolded before us, and should experience so little of their practical influence! Oh! let the recollection of our indolence, and want of conformity to them, never cease to humble us. Let us not enter into the testimonies, as a dry task, or an ordinary study; but let us concentrate our minds, our faith, humility, and prayer, in a more devoted contemplation of them. Every such exercise will extend our view of those parts, with which we had conceived ourselves to be competently acquainted: opening a new field of wonders on every side, far beyond our present contracted apprehensions.

And can any joy be imagined so sublime as the adoring contemplation of this revelation? It reflects even to angels a new and glorious manifestation of their God. It engages their every faculty with intense admiration and delight. And while they behold and worship with self-abasement, their obedience is lively. "With twain he" (the seraph before the throne) "covered his face, and with twain he covered his feet, and with twain he did fly." Thus may we study the same lessons, and with the same spirit. May our contemplation humble us in the dust, and animate us in the service of our God! Your testimonies are wonderful: therefore does my soul keep them.

130. The entrance of Your words gives light: it gives understanding to the simple.

'So "wonderful are Your testimonies," gracious God,' that even by touching as it were only their threshold, the entrance of Your words gives light and understanding unto my heart. The study commenced in simplicity and prayer, opens an entrance to the first dawning light of the word into the soul; often only sufficient to make darkness visible, but still "shining more and more unto the perfect day." Indeed all the spiritual light known in this dark world has flowed from the word, forcing its entrance, like the beams of the sun, upon the opening eyes of "a man that was born blind." It is a most striking instance of Divine condescension, that this word—so wonderful in its high and heavenly mysteries—should yet open a path so plain, that the most unlearned may find and walk in it. Indeed the entrance of the word into unintellectual and uncultivated minds, often gives an enlargement and elevation of thought, which is the earnest of the restoration of man to his original glory, when doubtless every mental as well as spiritual faculty was "filled with all the fullness of God." So astonishing is the power of this heavenly light, that from any one page of this holy book, a child, or even an idiot, under heavenly teaching, may draw more instruction than the most acute philosopher could ever attain from any other fountain of light! No—he may acquire a more intelligent perception of its contents, than the student, untaught by the Spirit of God, who may have devoted to its study the persevering industry of many successive years. For very possible is it to be possessed of all the treasures of literature, and yet to remain in total ignorance of everything that is most important for a sinner to know. The Apostle's paradox unfolds the secret, "If any man among you seems to be wise in this world, let him become a fool, that he may be wise." We do not mean to disparage human wisdom; but it is the pride of wisdom, so opposed to the simplicity of the gospel, which prevents us from "sitting at the feet of Jesus, and hearing His word." It makes the teacher instruct in "the words of man's wisdom," rather than in the knowledge of "Christ and Him crucified," and hinders the learner from receiving Christ in the light and love of the truth.

It is painful to remember how much light may be shining around us on every side, without finding an entrance into the heart. "The light shines in darkness; and the darkness comprehended it not." Not only the pride of human reason, but the love of sin, shuts out the light: "Men love darkness rather than light, because their deeds are evil." And thus because "the eye is evil, the whole body is full of darkness:" and "if the light that is in them is darkness, how great is that darkness!" Most awful is the view given us of the conflict between the contending powers of light and darkness, "The God of this world blinding the eyes of them that believe not, lest the light of the glorious gospel of Christ, who is the image of God, should shine unto them,"—the Almighty God resisting his hateful influence, and "shining into the hearts" of His people, "to give the light of the knowledge of the glory of God in the face of Jesus Christ." How necessary is it to watch vigilantly against the pride that "rebels against the light," and the indifference that neglects to cherish it! How much more entrance would have been given to the word, and consequently how much clearer would have been the diffusion of light in the soul, were we as earnest and diligent in secret prayer for heavenly teaching, as we are accustomed to be in the public hearing of the word!

But the enthusiast is not satisfied with the light of the word. The delusion of his own heart dreams of a light within—an immediate revelation of the Spirit, independent of the word. It cannot however be safe to separate the light of the Spirit from the light of the word. The word indeed moves in subserviency to the Spirit; but the light of the Spirit is nowhere promised separate from the word. If it does not always guide directly by the word; yet it is only manifested in the direction of the word. The word is in the matter, if not in the mode; and though the Spirit may by immediate light direct us to any path of duty, yet it is invariably to that path, which had been previously marked by the light of the word. Thus the Spirit and the word conjointly become our guide—the Spirit enlightening and quickening the word—and the word evidencing the light of the Spirit. Nor will their combined influence ever leave the church of God, until she has joyfully and completely entered into Immanuel's land, where she shall need no other light, than that of the glory of God, and of the Lamb, which shall shine in her forever.

But—Reader—rest not satisfied with whatever measure of light may have been hitherto given. Seek that the word may have "an entrance ministered unto you abundantly." The most advanced believer is most ready to acknowledge, how much of the word yet remains unexplored before him. Cultivate the disposition of simplicity—the spirit of a "little child"—willing to receive, embrace, submit to, whatever the revelation of God may produce before you. There will be many things that we do not understand: but there is nothing that we shall not believe. "Thus says the Lord"—is sufficient to satisfy reverential faith. To this spirit the promise of heavenly light is exclusively made. "The testimony of the Lord is sure, making wise the simple. The meek will He guide in judgment; the meek will He teach His way." It is beautiful to see a man like Solomon, endued with enlarged powers of mind—acknowledging himself to be a little child, afraid of trusting in his own light; and seeking instruction from above. But never will an unhumbled mind know the benefit of this Divine instruction. To such a student, the Bible must ever be a dark book; since its very design is to destroy that disposition which he brings to the inquiry. That knowledge, therefore, which is unable to direct our way to heaven—no, which by closing the avenues of spiritual light, obstructs our entrance there, is far more a curse than a blessing. Far more glorious is the simplicity of the word than the wisdom of the world.

"In that hour, Jesus rejoiced in spirit, and said, I thank You, O Father, Lord of heaven and earth, because You have hid these things from the wise and prudent, and have revealed them unto babes: even so, Father, for so it seemed good in Your sight."

131. I opened my mouth, and panted; for I longed for Your commandments.

When the "wonderful" character of God's "testimonies" is apprehended; and when their entrance has given light to the soul; something far beyond ordinary affection and desire is excited. A thirsty man—burning with inward heat on a sultry day, opening his mouth, and panting for some alleviation of his thirst—is a fine image of the child of God intensely longing for the attainment of his object. Or, if we suppose before us the man nearly exhausted by the heat of his race, and opening his mouth, and panting to take in fresh breath to renew his course; so would the believer "rejoice," like the sun, to "run his" heavenward "race." He cannot satisfy himself in his desires. The motions of his soul to his God are his life and his joy. It is a spring of perpetual motion beating within—perpetual, because natural—not a rapture, but a habit—a principle, having indeed its faintings, and its sickness, but still returning to its original spring of life and vigor. It seems as if the soul could never draw in enough of the influences of the spiritual life. Its longings are insatiable—as if the heart would "break with" the overpowering strength of its own desires; until at length, wearied with the conflict, the believer opens his mouth, and pants to fetch in a fresh supply of invigorating grace. He enjoys "a little reviving" in his Lord's commandments; enjoying the Lord Himself as his well-spring of refreshment.

Hear the man of God elsewhere giving, or rather attempting to give, expression to his pantings, "As the deer pants after the water-brooks, so pants my soul after You, O God. My soul thirsts for You; my flesh longs for You in a dry and thirsty land where no water is. I stretch forth my hands unto You; my soul thirsts after You as a thirsty land." Thus did Job open his mouth, and pant. "O that I knew where I might find Him! that I might come even to His seat!" And the church—pouring out her heart before the Lord, "With my soul have I desired You in the night; yes, with my spirit within me will I seek You early." St. Paul also describes the same intenseness of his own desire, "Not as though I had already attained, either were already perfect; but I follow after, if that I may apprehend that for which also I am apprehended of Christ Jesus. Brethren, I count not myself to have apprehended; but this one thing I do; forgetting those things which are behind, and reaching forth unto those things which are before, I press towards the mark for the prize of the high calling of God in Christ Jesus." But amid all these examples, and infinitely beyond them all—behold the ardor of our blessed Master in his work. Such was the panting of His heavenly desire, that, when "wearied with his journey," and "sitting at Jacob's well," He forgot even His natural want for His thirsty frame, in the joy of the conversion of a lost sinner to Himself.

And thus must our affections be fully engaged. The soul must be kept open to heavenly influence; so that, when the Lord touches us with conviction, inclines our hearts to Himself, and constrains us to His service, we may be ready to "exercise ourselves unto godliness," in receiving, cherishing, and improving the heavenly longing after His commandments; and may open our mouths, and pant for more advanced progress in them. We look not so much to the quantity, as to the activity of faith; always at work, stirring up a holy fire within, for the utmost stretch of human attainment: like men of large projects and high determinations, still aspiring to know more of God, both in the enjoyment of His love, and in conformity to His will. And shall we be ashamed of these feelings? Shall we not rather be deeply humbled, that we know so little of them—encouraged, if we have any springing of them—alarmed, if we be utterly destitute of their influence? Shall we not be opening our mouth, and panting, when any new path of service is opened before us? For if we are content to be strangers to this longing after God—this readiness for duty; what else can be expected, but "sliding back from the Lord by a perpetual backsliding?" Growing in sin, declining in love, and gradually relinquishing the habit of prayer, we shall shortly find little attaching to us but the empty name—Christianity without Christ. The world will despise these exercises as enthusiasm, the distemper of a misguided imagination. But is it—can it be—otherwise than a "reasonable service" as well as a bounden obligation, to give up our whole desires to Him, who is alone worthy of them? There can be no evidence of their sincerity, unless they are supreme.

But let union with Christ, and the life flowing from Him, be the constant spring of this holy ardor. Thus shall I enjoy a more habitual influence of His love—that all-constraining principle, which overcomes all my complaints of coldness and deadness of heart, and fills me with pantings and longing in His service. But am I ready to shrink from this elevated standard? If my heart is drawing back, let me force it on. Let me lay my command, or rather God's command, upon it. Let conscience do its office, until my heart is brought into actual and close contact with this touchstone of my spiritual prosperity. What then—let me ask myself—is the pulse of my desires after spiritual things? What exercises of grace do I find in them? What improvement of grace do I derive from them? Do I pant, thirst, long, after the enjoyment of heavenly pleasure? Do I mourn over, and conflict with, that indolence and indifference, which so often hinders my race? Oh! let me be found a frequent suppliant at the throne of grace; bewailing my dullness, yet "stirring up" my faith "to lay hold on" my God; seeking for larger views of the Gospel, a warmer experience of its promises, a more intense appetite for its enjoyments, and a more devoted attachment to its service. Surely such desires will issue in the confidence of faith. "My soul shall be satisfied as with marrow and fatness."

132. Look upon me, and be merciful unto me, as You do unto those that love Your name.

The highest ardency of holy desire is no ground of satisfaction before God. Nor does the believer in his most elevated moments forget his proper character—always a sinner—needing mercy every moment—in every duty. His prayer for mercy therefore suitably follows his exalted expression of love—Look upon me, and be merciful unto me. Mercy is indeed secured to him beyond the power of earth and hell to despoil him of it; but the comfortable sense of this mercy is given only according to the earnestness of his desires, and the simplicity of his faith. And this is indeed a blessing, with which no earthly source of satisfaction can compare. What are all the riches of the world without it, but splendid poverty, as little able to supply the place of Jesus in the soul, as the magnificent array of the starry skies is to compensate for the absence of the sun? It is night with the child of God—Egyptian night, "darkness which may be felt," until his Sun appear to chase away his gloom—until his Lord hear his cry—Look upon me, and be merciful unto me!

To have this portion of those that love the name of God, is, then, the grand object. To have our offering, as Abel's was, accepted with God—to walk as Enoch walked, with God—to commune with Him as Abraham and Moses were privileged to do—to be conformed with the holy Apostle to the death of Christ—in a word, to be interested in all the purchase of a Savior's blood, "this is the heritage of the Lord's servants"—this is the "one thing that we have desired of the Lord, and are seeking after," "this," with the dying Psalmist, "is all our salvation, and all our desire." "Remember me then, O Lord, with the favor that You bear to Your people; O visit me with Your salvation; that I may see the good of Your chosen: that I may rejoice in the gladness of Your nation; that I may glory with Your inheritance."

And yet, alas! how often has the power and deceitfulness of sin cast us into so lifeless a state, that we are not only living without the enjoyment of this portion, but at rest without it; scarcely knowing or caring whether the Lord look on us or not? Can we wonder, that our holy, jealous God, should "hide Himself," and "go and return to His place?" His next manifestations will probably be in the way of sharp conviction, making us to feel our distance, our coldness, our barrenness: awakening us to search into the cause; and, in the contrast of our sad condition with those who are walking in His favor, again bringing forth the cry—Look upon me, and be merciful unto me, as You do unto those that love Your name. The prayer of humility, earnestness, and perseverance, though it may be tried awhile, will surely never be forgotten. If therefore we cannot yet "sing in the ways of the Lord," yet let us not cease to mourn after Him, until He look upon us, and "satisfy us with His mercy." And oh! let us remember that there is but one way through which one gracious look, or one expression of tender mercy, can visit our souls. Let our eyes and heart then be ever fixed on Jesus. It is only in this His "beloved" Son that the Lord can look upon us, so as not to "behold iniquity in us." But we "are complete in Him." Here then let us wait; and when this our prayer has received its answer in the Lord's best time—whether it be in "the goings of our God in the sanctuary," or in the more secret manifestation of His love—Christians, "arise, and shine." Let it be known, that you have been on the mount with God, by the luster of your face, the adorning of your profession, before the world.

Lord! since our looks to You are often so slight, so cold, so distant, that no impression is made upon our hearts; do condescend continually to look upon us with mercy and with power. Give us such a look, as may touch us with tenderness and contrition, in the remembrance of that sin, unbelief, and disobedience, which pierced the hands, the feet, the heart of our dearest Lord and Savior. Oh! for that contrite spirit, in which we shall enjoy the look of Your special favor! Oh! for a glimpse of Your love, that will put our spiritual enemies to shame! Oh! for that sunshine of Your countenance, which brings present salvation to our souls!

133. Order my steps in Your word; and let not any iniquity have dominion over me.

To expect the favor of the Lord without an habitual desire of conformity to His image, is one among the many delusions of a self-deceiving heart. It is the peculiar character of the Christian, that his desires are as earnest for deliverance from the power as from the guilt of sin. Having therefore prayed for acceptance, he now cries for holiness. For even could we conceive the Lord to look upon him with a sense of His favor, he would still feel himself a miserable creature, until he has received an answer to his prayer—Let not any iniquity have dominion over me.

But it is often difficult to distinguish the power of temptation from the prevalence of sin, and thus precisely to ascertain, when iniquity may be said to have dominion over us. Is it not however the influence of temptation—not acting upon the mind, but admitted with consent into the heart? It is this actual consent of the will, obtained by the deceitfulness and solicitations of sin, that marks its real dominion. Light, knowledge, and conscience, may open the path of holiness; but while the will—the sovereign power in the soul—dissents, the reigning power of sin continues undisputed. Much care, however, much singleness, and a most jealous scrutiny of the springs of action, are required, accurately to determine the bias of the will, and consequently the dominion of iniquity. The perplexed, conflicting soul may mistake the rebellion for the dominion of iniquity—its continued impression upon the heart for its ruling sway. On the other hand, a constrained opposition of conviction may present some hopeful symptoms of deliverance, while the dominant principle is still unshaken. The present resolution to any particular act of sin may be weakened, while the love and habit of it remained unaffected. Sin is not always hated, when it is condemned, or even forsaken; nor are duties always loved in the act of their performance. The opposition to sin, which the awakened superficial professor considers as his evidence of uprightness of heart, is often only the unavailing resistance of a natural enlightened conscience to the ruling principle of the heart. The light and power of conscience may do much in condemning every known sin, and in restraining from many; in illustrating every known duty, and insisting upon the external performance of many; while yet the full dominion of iniquity is undisturbed. Were not Ahab and Judas as completely under his dominion after their repentance as they were before? Did not Balaam, with all his knowledge—and the young ruler, with all his natural loveliness and semblance of sincerity, "lack that one thing"—a heart delivered from the dominion of its own iniquity? Yet it is not occasional surprisals, resisted workings, abhorred lust, nor immediate injections of evil and blasphemous thoughts; but only the ascendancy of sin in the affections, that proves its reigning power. The throne can admit but of one ruler; and therefore, though grace and iniquity may and do co-exist within, they cannot be co-partners in one sovereignty. Yet do not forget that every sinful indulgence is for the moment putting the scepter into the hands of our worst enemies. The setting up of an usurper is the virtual dethronement of the rightful sovereign. The subjection to sin is therefore the rejection of Christ.

How inestimably precious is the thought, that deliverance from this cursed dominion is inseparably connected with a state of acceptance with God! The man who enjoys the unspeakable blessing of pardoned iniquity, is he "in whose spirit there is no deceit." He has a work done within him, as well as for him. His Savior is a whole Christ, "made of God unto him Sanctification" and complete "Redemption" as well as "Righteousness." He comes to the cleansing fountain, as the double cure of his iniquity—equally effectual to wash from its power, as from its guilt.

But let us duly estimate the value of David's preservation. He had been used to "hide the word in his heart," as his safeguard against sin, and from his own experience of its power he had recommended it to the especial attention of the young. Yet the recollection of his continual forgetfulness and conscious weakness, leads him to turn his rule into a matter of prayer—Order my steps in Your word;—implying, that if his steps were not ordered, from want of their keeping, iniquity would regain its dominion. And who of us have not daily need of this ruling discipline? Without it, all is disorder. Our scattered affections need to be "united" in one central principle, under the direction of the word. The universal influence of this rule also is so important. The word not only cheers our path, but orders our steps. Every act—every duty—are as steps in the heavenward path—guarding us from the devious paths on either side, beset with imperceptible danger, and spread with the fowler's snare. And what a blessed path would this be for us, if we had singleness and simplicity always to "look right on, and straight before us!" But alas! we are often only half-roused from our security. The word is forgotten; or there is an unreadiness to receive its Divine impressions. Our own wisdom is consulted: and, "or ever we are aware," iniquity regains a temporary dominion over us.

Now I would ask myself—What do I know of this godly, careful walk? Am I frequently during the day looking upward to my heavenly guide; and then looking into His word as my direction in the way; and lastly considering my heart and conduct, whether it is ordered in the word? The man, who has "the law of God in his heart," alone possesses the security, "that none of his steps shall slide." When I take therefore a step into the world, let me ask—Is it ordered in God's word, which exhibits Christ as my perfect example; so that, walking after Him, and following in His steps, I may be able to frame my temper and habits according to this unsullied pattern?

But let us mark, how fully is this prayer warranted by the special promise of the Gospel, "Sin shall not have dominion over you; for you are not under the law, but under grace." The law stirred up sin, and gave it increased power; while it left us to our unassisted exertions to subdue it. We watch, pray, and strive against it; yet, alas! it mocks our efforts—rages, yes, tyrannizes more than ever. But it is the cross of Calvary, that gave the child of God his first view of sin, that first made him loathe it, that first enabled him to contemplate a holy God without fear, and even with confidence. This—this alone—subdues his pride, rebellion, enmity, selfishness. In Him that hung there we trust as an Almighty conqueror; and we are made ourselves "more than conquerors through Him that loved us." His very name of Jesus marks His office, His crown, His glory. Here therefore—not in doubts and fears—not in indolent mourning for sin—here lies the appointed means of present relief—the only hope of final victory. Iniquity, even when subdued, will struggle to the last for dominion: but looking to and living on Jesus, we have the victory still. The more clear our view of Jesus, the more complete is our victory. Supplies of continual strength will ever be given to restrain the dominion of iniquity, and even to "keep under" its daily risings; except as they may be needful for the exercise of our graces, and be eventually overruled for the glory and praise of our faithful God.

134. Deliver me from the oppression of man: so will I keep Your precepts.

"Many are the afflictions of the righteous," from external as well as from internal enemies—not only from their own iniquity, but from the oppression of man. Yet "man is only the Lord's hand and sword," and he can only move under the overruling guidance of our Father's wisdom and love. Not indeed that the believer would (except in submission to the will of God) desire his deliverance from this trouble on account of personal pain and distress: but he sometimes finds peculiar circumstances of trial an unavoidable hindrance in the service of his God. And his conviction sends him to the throne of grace: and there he never makes interest in vain. "He cries unto the Lord because of the oppressors: and He sends a Savior, and a great one: and He delivers him."

The power of faith is indeed Omnipotent. Mountains are removed from their place, or they become "plains before" it; or the "worm" is enabled to "thresh them, and beat them small, and make them as chaff." Often is the Christian strengthened to overcome the most formidable opposition, and to "profess a good profession before many witnesses," who are "watching for his halting." The grace of Christ will make the hardest duty easy; and the love of Christ will make the sharpest trials sweet: yet, where in the continued exercise of faith the obstacles to conscientious service remain unmoved (as, for instance, a child of God restrained in the fetters of a worldly family from a free and avowed obedience), we may lawfully pray that the providence of God would deliver from the oppression of man, that we might keep His precepts.

A time of deliverance, as well as a time of persecution, has proved a season of extraordinary prosperity in the church of God. When "the Churches had rest throughout all Judea and Galilee and Samaria," they "were edified; and walking in the fear of the Lord, and in the comfort of the Holy Spirit, were multiplied." And thus in individual experience, whatever be the benefit of persecution, yet the weariness of a long-protracted conflict is often more than flesh and blood can bear; and which He who "knows our frame," will not refuse to look upon, and remove, in answer to the prayers of His afflicted people. At the same time, our proneness, self-indulgence, and our natural inclination to shrink from discipline—as needful as our food—require this prayer to be presented with exceeding caution and self-jealousy. There is a great danger, lest, in our eagerness to escape from the difficulties of our path, we should lose the most important benefit intended by them. We must therefore accompany the petition for deliverance with a sincere purpose to keep God's precepts. For how many have exposed the unsoundness of their own hearts, when the supplication has been heard, the deliverance granted, and the promise of obedience been forgotten!

Fellow-Christian! have your circumstances of trial ever dictated this prayer? How then have you improved your liberty, when the answer has been given? Has the "way of escape made" for you been kept in grateful remembrance? Has the effect of your deliverance been visible in an increasing love and devotedness to the Lord's service? Oh! let a special Ebenezer be set up to mark this special achievement of prayer. Let the mercy be connected with the sympathy of our "faithful and merciful High-Priest, who being Himself touched with the feeling of your infirmities," has pleaded for your support and release. And be encouraged henceforth to tread the ways of God with more firmness and sensible stay, "having your feet shod with the preparation of the Gospel of peace." But remember—the blessing of the cross is lost, if it does not issue in a song of praise—if we have not taken it up as a token of fatherly love. At all times the safest and shortest way to peace, is to let God use His own methods with us; to live the present moment to Him in the situation He has placed us; not dreaming of other circumstances more favorable to our spiritual prosperity; but leaving ourselves, our difficulties, our discouragements, in His hands, who makes no mistakes in any of His dispensations—but who orders them all, that they "may turn to our salvation, through our prayer, and the supply of the Spirit of Jesus Christ."

135. Make Your face to shine upon Your servant; and teach me Your statutes.

If the Lord deliver us from the oppression of man, and "make even our enemies to be at peace with us;" still, if we are in spiritual health, we shall be restless and uneasy, until He make His face to shine upon us. And in the Scripture revelation of God, "dwelling between the cherubim," and therefore on the mercy-seat—with the "rainbow," the emblem of "the covenant of peace" "round about the throne," as if to invite the access of sinners from every quarter—have we not full warrant to plead, "You who dwell between the cherubim, shine forth; stir up Your strength, and come and save us? Turn us again, O God; and cause

Your face to shine, and we shall be saved." Others we see eagerly asking, "Who will show us any good?" Alas! they will discover in the end, that they have "spent their money for that which is not bread, and their labor for that which satisfies not." The believer's incessant cry is—Let me see "the King's face." This is a blessing worth praying for. It is his heart's desire, his present privilege, and what is infinitely better—his sure and everlasting joy, "They shall see His face."

It is both important and interesting to mark the repetitions—always new—in this beautiful Psalm. David had just before prayed, "Look upon me, and be merciful unto me." Perhaps another passing cloud had darkened his sky. Again he darts up the same prayer, Make Your face to shine upon Your servant. Such cries in the mouth of this holy servant of God, must have been most hopeless petitions—no, the expression of the most daring presumption—had he not been acquainted with the only true way of access to God, joyfully led to renounce every other way, and enabled diligently to improve this acceptable approach to his God. Indeed whatever obscurity may hang over the question relating to the faith of the Old Testament believers, their confidence at the throne of grace shows them to have attained a far more distinct perception of Christian privilege, through the shadowy representations of their law, than is commonly imagined. Else how could they have been so wrestling and persevering in their petitions; overcoming the spirit of bondage, and breathing out the spirit of adoption in the expression of their wants and desires before the Lord? The prayers of the Old Testament church are not more distinguished for their simplicity, spirituality, and earnestness, than for their unfettered, evangelical confidence. When they approached the footstool of the Divine Majesty, with the supplications—Make Your face to shine upon Your servant—You who dwell between the cherubim, shine forth—it was as if they had pleaded—'Reconciled Father—You who sit upon a throne of grace, look upon us—Abba, Father, be gracious to us!'

Many, however, seem to despise this child-like confidence. They go on in heartless complaining and uncertain apprehensions of their state; as if doubting was their life, and as if they might rest upon the presumption, that the shining of God's face upon them is not indispensable to their salvation. But will they then be content to "be saved, yet so as by fire," instead of having an "entrance ministered unto them abundantly into the everlasting kingdom of our Lord and Savior?" Is it enough for them to be just alive, when "the things that remain," from want of being duly cherished, "are ready to die?" If they can be safe without a conscious interest in the favor of God, can they be so without the desire for it? Is not this assurance attainable? Is it not commanded? Is it not most desirable? This cold contentment clouds the integrity of their profession. For God's real people are living habitually either in spiritual enjoyment, or in restless dissatisfaction. Their dark seasons are times of wrestling supplication—seasons of deep humiliation, tenderness of spirit, and constant waiting upon God, until He makes His face to shine upon His servants. They can dispense with ordinary comforts. But it is death to be without Him. "All their springs are in Him." They estimate their happiness by the shining—and their misery by the clouding—of His face. This is the true principle of assurance, even if this most important blessing be not sensibly enjoyed.

How then stands the case between us and God? From ourselves originates the mist, which darkens the shining. His sovereign free grace blots the cloud away. We raise the mountains of separation. The Almighty power of our great Zerubbabel removes them. To ourselves then be all the shame. To Him be all the praise!

But how may we realize more constant sunshine?—Apart from the hindrances just alluded to, others are mainly to be found in mistaken or contracted views of the Gospel. Hence, therefore, the value of enlarged apprehensions of the Gospel of the grace of God—of its fullness, satisfying every claim, and supplying every want—of its freeness, unencumbered with conditions, and holding forth encouragement to the most unworthy—of its holiness, restraining the sinful hindrances to enjoyment—and of its security, affording permanent rest in the foundations of the covenant of grace. The life of faith will thus be maintained in more full contemplation of Jesus, and renewed reliance upon Him; and walking in closer communion with Him, our hope will be enlivened with the constant sense of reconciliation and love.

We need not wonder at the Psalmist's persevering determination to seek the shining of the Lord's face. This high privilege is connected no less with the Christian's public usefulness than with his personal enjoyment. For who is most likely to win others to the love of the Savior, and to the service of God—to enliven the drooping soul, or to recover the backslider? Is not he, who lives most in the sunshine of the Gospel, and who therefore has most to tell of its heavenly joy? But you say, 'My heart, alas! is so cold and barren, my affections so languid, my desires so faint, my sky so often clouded. I do not forget that I am a child; but a child in disgrace is too often my dishonorable character and wretched condition.' Then exercise your faith in going where David was accustomed to go. As a penitent child, "Arise and go to your Father" "only acknowledge your iniquity"—tell your complaint before Him— resort much and often to Him; be importunate; be patient; plead the name and merits of Jesus; and you will not, you cannot plead in vain; you will once more walk happily, holily, as well as confidently, in the light of your Father's countenance. And in marking more carefully His gracious dealings with your soul, you will be kept from formality, hardness, and despondency.

But we cannot expect this shining, save in the paths of God; and he who looks for comfort, while careless of duty, is only the victim of his own delusions. Well, therefore, does the child of God—longing for higher enjoyment, and learning more of his own ignorance, add this petition—Teach me Your statutes. And He who taught us this petition, will Himself, according to His promise, be our teacher in the way of holiness. And if, under His teaching, in the pathway to glory—our God makes His face to shine upon us, what more want we to beguile the toil and weariness of the way? And if one beam of His countenance, though but dimly seen through this sinful medium, exceeds the glories of ten thousand worlds—what will it be to live under the perpetual cloudless shining of His face!

Believer! does not this prospect invigorate every step of your journey? Your Lord is at hand. Soon will He appear to gladden with His inexpressible smile every soul that is in readiness for Him. Oh! seek to realize His approach, and with holy aspirations and joyful expectancy respond to His welcome voice. "He which testifies these things says, Surely I come quickly: Amen. Even so, come, Lord Jesus!"

136. Rivers of waters run down my eyes, because they keep not Your law. (Comp. Jer. 9:1; 14:17; Lam. 2:18)

If the Lord teaches us the privileges of His statutes, He will teach us compassion for those who keep them not. This was the mind of Jesus. His life exhibited one, whose "heart was made of tenderness." But there were some occasions, when the display of His compassion was peculiarly striking. Near the close of His life, it is recorded, that, "when He was come near, and beheld the city" "beautiful for situation, the joy of the whole earth"—but now given up to its own ways, and "wrath coming upon it to the uttermost," He "wept over it." It was then a moment of triumph. The air was rent with hosannahs. The road was strewed with branches from the trees, and all was joy and praise. Amid all this exultation, the Savior alone, seemed to have no voice for the triumph—no heart for joy. His omniscient mind embraced all the spiritual desolation of this sad case; and He could only weep in the midst of a solemn triumph. Rivers of waters run down my eyes, because they keep not Your law.

Now a Christian, in this as in every other feature, will be conformed to the image of his Lord. His heart will therefore be touched with a tender concern for the honor of his God, and pitying concern for those wretched sinners, that keep not His law, and are perishing in their own transgressions. Thus was "just Lot" in Sodom "vexed with the filthy conversation of the wicked." Thus did Moses "fall down before the Lord, as at the first, forty days and forty nights; he did neither eat bread nor drink water; because of all their sins which they had sinned, in doing wickedly in the sight of the Lord to provoke Him to anger." Thus also Samuel, in the anticipation of the Lord's judgments upon Saul, "grieved himself, and cried unto the Lord all night." Ezra, on a similar occasion, in the deepest prostration of sorrow, "rent his garment and his mantle, and plucked off the hair of his head and of his beard, and sat down astonished until the evening sacrifice." And if David was now suffering from the oppression of man, yet his own injuries never drew from him such expressions of overwhelming sorrow, as did the sight of the despised law of his God.

Need we advert to this tender spirit, as a special characteristic of "the ministers of the Lord?" Can they fail in this day of abounding wickedness—even within the bounds of their own sphere—to hear the call to "weep between the porch and the altar?" How instructive is the posture of the ancient prophet—first pleading openly with the rebellion of the people—then "his soul weeping in secret places for their pride!" Not less instructive is the great apostle—his "conscience bearing witness in the Holy Spirit to his great heaviness and continued sorrow in his heart for his brethren, his kinsmen according to the flesh." In reproving transgressors, he could only write to them, "Out of much affliction and anguish of heart with many tears," and in speaking of them to others, with the same tenderness of spirit, he adds, "Of whom I tell you even weeping." Tears were these of Christian eloquence no less than of Christian compassion.

Thus uniformly is the character of God's people represented—not merely as those that are free from, but as "those that sigh and that cry for all the abominations that be done in the midst of the land." They—they alone—are marked out for mercy in the midst of impending, universal ruin. The want of this spirit is ever a feature of hardness and pride—a painful blot upon the profession of the gospel. How wide the sphere presenting itself on every side for the unrestrained exercise of this yearning compassion! The appalling spectacle of a world apostatized from God, of multitudes sporting with everlasting destruction—as if the God of heaven were "a man that He should lie," is surely enough to force rivers of waters from the hearts of those who are concerned for His honor. What a mass of sin ascends as a cloud before the Lord, from a single heart! Add the aggregate of a village—a town—a country—a world! every day—every hour—every moment—well might the rivers of waters rise to an overflowing tide, ready to burst its barriers. We speak not of outward sensibility (in which some may be constitutionally deficient, and the exuberance of which may be no sign of real spiritual affection), but we ask—Do we lay to heart the perishing condition of our fellow-sinners? Could we witness a house on fire, without speedy and practical evidence of our compassion for the inhabitants? And yet, alas! how often do we witness souls on the brink of destruction—unconscious of danger, or bidding defiance to it—with comparative indifference! How are we Christians, if we believe not the Scripture warnings of their danger? or if, believing them, we do not bestir ourselves to their help? What hypocrisy is it to pray for their conversion, while we are making no effort to promote it! Oh! let it be our daily supplication, that this indifference concerning their everlasting state may give place to a spirit of weeping tenderness; that He may not be living as if this world were really, what it appears to be, a world without souls; that we may never see the sabbaths of God profaned, His laws trampled under foot, the ungodly "breaking their bands asunder, and casting away their cords from them," without a more determined resolution ourselves to keep these laws of our God, and to plead for their honor with these obstinate transgressors. Have we no near and dear relatives, yet "lying in wickedness—dead in trespasses and sins?" To what blessed family, reader, do you belong, where there are no such objects of pity? Be it so—it is well. Yet are you silent? Have you no ungodly, ignorant neighbors around you? And are they unwarned, as well as unconverted? Do we visit them in the way of courtesy or kindness, yet give them no word of affectionate entreaty on the concerns of eternity? Let our families indeed possess, as they ought to possess, the first claim to our compassionate regard. Then let our parishes, our neighborhood, our country, the world, find a place in our affectionate, prayerful, and earnest consideration.

Nor let it be supposed, that the doctrine of sovereign and effectual grace has any tendency to paralyze exertion. So far from it, the most powerful supports to perseverance are derived from this source. Left to himself—with only the invitations of the Gospel—not a sinner could ever have been saved. Added to these—there must be the Almighty energy of God—the seal of His secret purpose—working upon the sinner's will, and winning the heart to God. Not that this sovereign work prevents any from being saved. But it prevents the salvation from being in vain to all, by securing its application to some. The invitations manifest the pardoning love of God; but they change not the rebel heart of man. They show his enmity; yet they slay it not. They leave him without excuse; yet at the same time—they may be applied without salvation. The moment of life in the history of the saved sinner is, when he is "made willing in the day of the Lord's power"—when he comes— he looks—he lives. It is this dispensation alone that gives the Christian laborer the spring of energy and hope. The palpable and awful proofs on every side, of the "enmity of the carnal mind against God," rejecting alike both His law and His Gospel, threaten to sink him in despondency. And nothing sustains his tender and compassionate interest, but the assurance of the power of God to remove the resisting medium, and of His purpose to accomplish the subjugation of natural corruption in a countless multitude of His redeemed people.

The same yearning sympathy forms the life, the pulse, and the strength of Missionary exertion, and has ever distinguished those honored servants of God who have devoted their time, their health, their talent, their all, to the blessed work of "saving souls from death, and covering a multitude of sins." Can we conceive a Missionary living in the spirit of his work—surrounded with thousands of mad idolaters, hearing their shouts, and witnessing their abominations, without a weeping spirit? Indignant grief for the dishonor done to God—amazement at the affecting spectacle of human blindness—detestation of human impiety— compassionate yearnings over human wretchedness and ruin—all combine to force tears of the deepest sorrow from a heart enlightened and constrained by the influence of a Savior's love. This, as we have

243

seen, was our Master's spirit. And let none presume themselves to be Christians, if they are destitute of "this mind that was in Christ Jesus;" if they know nothing of His melting compassion for a lost world, or of His burning zeal for His heavenly Father's glory.

Oh, for that deep realizing sense of the preciousness of immortal souls, that would make us look at every sinner we meet as a soul to be "pulled out of the fire," and to be drawn to Christ;—which would render us willing to endure suffering, reproach, and the loss of all, so that we might win one soul to God, and raise one monument to His everlasting praise! Happy mourner in Zion! whose tears over the guilt and wretchedness of a perishing world are the outward indications of your secret pleadings with God, and the effusion of a heart solemnly dedicated to the salvation of your fellow-sinners!

'But feeble my compassion proves,
And can but weep, where most it loves;
Your own all-saving arm employ,
And turn these drops of grief to joy.'

137. Righteous are You, O Lord, and upright are Your judgments. 138. Your testimonies that You have commanded, are righteous, and very faithful.

The advancing Christian learns to adore the awful perfections of his God, and to acknowledge His righteous character and government, even when "his ways are in the sea, and His paths in the great waters." "Clouds and darkness are round about Him; righteousness and judgment are the habitation of His throne." We have already brought out the unvarying testimony of His people to the righteous character of His afflictive dispensations. Even from haughty Pharaoh was a similar acknowledgment extorted. Adonibezek also, under the blow of His hand, cried out, "As I have done, so God has requited me."

Yet in this path, "we walk by faith, not by sight." Often in Providence "his footsteps are not known." We cannot trace the reasons of the Divine mind. We must wait and see the "end of the Lord," when the disjointed pieces shall be compacted into one complete texture and frame-work. "At evening time there shall be light." Much more in the dispensation of grace do we hear the voice, "Be still, and know that I am God." Doubtless He could give His grace to all as well as to some. Yet none have a claim upon Him. "Is it not His to do what He will with His own?" "No, but, O man, who are you that replies against God?" "Shall not the Judge of all the earth do right?" Thus much is plain—enough to silence cavil, and justify God—grace is freely offered to all. Man's own will rejects it, and leaves him without excuse. Effectual grace is withheld from none, but those who deserve that it should be so. None are forced to sin. None are condemned without guilt. Therefore when we stand upon the ocean's brink, and cry, "Oh, the depth!" are we not constrained to the adoring acknowledgment—Righteous are You, O Lord, and upright are Your judgments? And if this be our praise, even while "we see but as through a glass darkly, and know but in part," how much more, in the world of uncloudy day, when we shall see "face to face, and know even as we are known"—shall we sing with reverential joy "the song of the Lamb—Great and marvelous are Your works, Lord God Almighty! just and true are Your ways, You King of saints!"

The young Christian, however, less able to grasp these deeper apprehensions, exercises himself chiefly in his more engaging perfections of long-suffering, goodness, and love. It is therefore a satisfactory evidence of growth in grace, when our habitual contemplation of God fixes upon our minds the more full and awful displays of His character; and we gather from thence an increase of light, peace, humility, and consolation. But the cross of Calvary harmonizes to our view at once the most appalling and the most encouraging attributes. Though His own declaration—that "he will by no means clear the guilty"—seemed to present an insurmountable barrier to the purpose of mercy; yet, rather than the glory of a God of love should be obscured, or His righteous law should be mitigated, "He spared not His own Son;" He "made Him, who knew no sin, to be sin for us."

And do not we naturally argue from His nature to His testimonies? If He be righteous, nothing unrighteous can come from Him. His testimonies, therefore, are His lively image—like Himself—righteous and very faithful—requiring nothing impossible—nothing unsuitable—perfect love to God and man, "our reasonable service," no less our privilege than our duty to render. None that are blessed with a spiritual apprehension of their nature, and are conformed and framed to them, will hesitate in setting their seal to the inscription, "The judgments of the Lord are true and righteous altogether." "The law is holy, and the commandment holy, and just, and good."

But let us take care to exhibit the practical influence of our contemplations of the character and government of God. The unconverted—far from understanding or subscribing to our acknowledgment—complain, "The ways of the Lord are not equal." "My punishment is greater than I can bear." And so opposed are the righteous judgments of God to the perverseness of corrupt nature, that even with the child of God there is much murmuring within, that needs to be stilled—much repining to be hushed—much impatience to be repressed—many hard thoughts to be lamented, resisted, and banished. Did we believe more simply, how much more joy would there be in our faith, and readiness in our submission! How clearly would our experience "show, that the Lord is upright; He is our rock, and there is no unrighteousness in Him!" "In returning" then "and rest shall we be saved; in quietness and confidence shall be our strength." In the submissive acknowledgment of the Lord's dispensations, "our peace" will "flow as a river;" more deep and extensive as it approaches the ocean, and fertilizing our souls with abundant spiritual peace and enjoyment.

139. My zeal has consumed me; because my enemies have forgotten Your words.

Such was David's high estimation of the testimonies of his God, that his spirits were consumed with vehement grief in witnessing their neglect. He could bear that his enemies should forget him; but his zeal could not endure, that they should forget the words of his God. Zeal is a passion, whose real character must be determined by the objects on which it is employed, and the principle by which it is directed. There is a true and a false zeal, differing as widely from each other, as an heavenly flame from the infernal fire. The one is fervent, unselfish affection, expanding the heart, and delighting to unite with the whole empire of God in the pursuit of a good, which all may enjoy without envious rivalry. The other is a selfish, interested principle, contracting the heart, and ready to sacrifice the good of mankind, and even the glory of God, to its own individual advantage. Were its power proportioned to its native tendency, or were it to operate extensively in an associated body, it would end in detaching its several members each from their proper center; in disuniting them from each other; and, as far as its influence could reach, crumbling the moral system into discordant atoms. Too often does this baneful principle exemplify itself in the Church—either in an obstinate opposition to the truth of the gospel, or in a self-willed contention for its own party."This wisdom descends not from above: but it is earthly, sensual, devilish." How much also of that misguided heat, that spends itself upon the externals of religion, or would "call fire down from heaven" in defense of fundamental truths, may be found among us, exposing its blind devotees to our Master's tender rebuke, "You know not what manner of spirit you are of!"

Often also do we see a distempered, counterfeit zeal, disproportioned in its exercise, wasting its strength upon the subordinate parts of the system, and comparatively feeble in its maintenance of the vital doctrines of Christ. Thus it disunites the Church by adherence to points of difference, instead of compacting the Church together by strengthening the more important points of agreement. Often again, by the same process in practical religion, are the "mint, anise, and cummin," vehemently contended for; "while the weightier matters of the law" are little regarded.

Widely different from this fervor of selfishness is that genuine zeal, which marks the true disciple of our Lord. Enlightened by the word of God, and quickened into operation by the love of Christ, it both shines and warms at the same moment. It is indeed the kindled fire of heavenly love, exciting the most heavenly desires and constant efforts for the best interests of every child of man, so far as its sphere can reach; and bounded only by a consistent regard to the general welfare of the whole. Thus earnest and compassionate in its influence, awakened to a sense of the preciousness of immortal souls, and the overwhelming importance of eternity, it is never at a loss to discover an extended sphere for its most vehement and constraining exercises. While it hates the sins that pass on every side before its view, it is all gentleness to the sinner; and would gladly weep tears of blood over those who are deaf to the voice of persuasion, could such tears avail to turn them from their iniquity. But, knowing all human unassisted efforts to be insufficient, it gives to the world its protest against the abominations, which it is too feeble to prevent; and then hastens to the secret chamber to pour out its wrestling desires in the tenderness of our Master's intercession, "Father, forgive them! for they know not what they do."

Such was the zeal of the ancient Lawgiver, whose spirit, though, as it regarded his own cause, "meek above all the men which were upon the face of the earth," "waxed hot" on witnessing the grievous dishonor done to his God during his absence on the mount. At the same time (as if most clearly to distinguish the holy burning from the heat of his own spirit) how fervently did he plead his people's cause in secret before his God, as he had manifested his concern for the honor of his God before the congregation! Surely he could have taken up this language—My zeal has consumed me; because my enemies have forgotten Your words. Burning with the same holy flame, the great Old-Testament Reformer bore his testimony against the universal prevalence of idolatry; making use of the arm of temporal power, and of the yet greater power of secret complaint, to stem the torrent of iniquity. The same impulse in later times marked the conduct of the Apostles: when, "rending their clothes, and running in among" a frantic multitude of idolaters, by all the power of their entreaties "they were scarcely able to restrain the people, that they had not done sacrifice unto them." On another occasion the great Apostle, forgetting "the goodly stones and buildings" that met his eye at Athens— found "his spirit stirred in him, when he saw the city wholly given to idolatry." In another city "was he pressed in spirit" by the intensity of his interest for the souls of his fellow-sinners and his Master's work.

Yet this is not a heat that wastes itself without a proportionate object. The truth of God is the grand object. Not one atom of its dust shall be lost. For its fundamentals all consequences must be hazarded—yes, life itself—if need be—sacrificed. Nor does this fervor expend itself in strong impulses that wear out without fruit. It is a constant affection in "a good thing." Nor is it an undisciplined burst of warm feeling, but a sober controlled exercise of Christian judgment. The Apostle—with his inexpressible abhorrence of idolatry—yet remained in the midst of it for two, perhaps three, years, faithfully employed in his Master's work; yet waiting for the fittest time of open protest against Diana's worship. So admirably was "the spirit of power and love" disciplined by "the spirit of a sound mind."

But, "compassed about, as we are, with so great a cloud of witnesses," let us yet turn aside to look unto One greater than them all— to One, whose example in every temper of Christian conduct affords equal direction and encouragement. Jesus could testify to His Father, "The zeal of Your house has eaten Me up." He was ever ready to put aside even lawful engagements and obligations, when they interfered with this paramount demand. Yet was His zeal tempered with a careful restraint from needless offence. Rather would He work a miracle, and retreat from publicity, than seem to give occasion to those that might desire it. And if we bear the stamp of His disciples, without rushing into offence in the waywardness of our own spirits, and while rejoicing to have our own "names cast out as evil," we shall at the same time be tender of any reflection on the name of our God, as on our dearest friend and benefactor. We shall feel any slight of His honor as sensitively as a wound to our own reputation; nor shall we hesitate to thrust ourselves between, to receive on ourselves any strokes that may be aimed at His cause. This combined spirit of self-denial and self-devotedness kindles the flame, which "many waters cannot quench, neither can the floods drown." 'I could bear'—said holy Brainerd—'any desertion or spiritual conflict, if I could but have my heart burning all the while within me with love to God, and desire for His glory.' It is indeed a delightful exercise to "spend and be spent" in the service of Him, who for our sakes was even consumed by the fire of His own zeal.

However, the surest evidence of Christian zeal is, when it begins at home, in a narrow scrutiny, and "vehement revenge" against the sins of our own hearts. Do we mourn over our own forgetfulness of God's words? Are we zealous to redeem the loss to our Savior's cause from this sinful neglect? And do we plainly show, that our opposition to sin in the ungodly is the opposition of love? And is this love manifested to the persons and souls of those, whose doctrines and practice we are constrained to resist, and in a careful restraint from the use of unhallowed "carnal weapons" in this spiritual "warfare?"

Perhaps the weak, timid child of God may be saying, 'I can do nothing for my God. I allow His words to be forgotten, with little or no success in my efforts to prevent it.' Are you then making an effort? Every work done in faith bears fruit to God and to His church. You may not see it. But let your secret chamber witness to your zeal: and the Lord "will not be unrighteous to forget your work and labor of love." He will even strengthen you for your dreaded conflict in the open confession of His cause, "For He has chosen the weak things of the world to confound the things that are mighty." Or, should peculiar trials restrain the boldness of your profession, you may be found in the end to have made as effectual a resistance to the progress of sin by your intercession before God, as those who have shown a more open front in the face of the world.

140. Your word is very pure: therefore Your servant loves it.

The Psalmist's love for the law of his God may account for the zeal he felt on account of its general neglect. All other systems of religion (or rather of "philosophy falsely so called") allure their disciples by the indulgence of carnal lust or self-complacent pride. The word of God outweighs them all in its chief excellence—peculiar to itself—its purity. "Every word is very pure—tried to the uttermost" in the furnace, and found to be absolutely without dross. Its promises are without a shadow of change or unfaithfulness. Its precepts reflect the holy image of their Divine Author. In a word, it contains 'truth without any mixture of error for its matter'—Therefore Your servant loves it.

'No one but a true servant of God can therefore love it, because it is pure; since he who loves it must desire to be like it, to feel its efficacy, to be reformed by it.' The unlettered believer cannot well discern its sublimity; but he loves it for its holiness. The mere scholar, on the other hand, admires its sublimity—but the secrets which it reveals (such as the pride of the natural heart struggles to conceal) forbid him to love it. Its purity, which is the matter of love to the one, excites enmity in the other. From "the glass" which shows him "his natural face"—his neglected obligations—his fearfully self-deluded state—and his appalling prospects—he turns away in disgust. The indulgence of sin effectually precludes the benefit of the most industrious search into the word of God. The heart must undergo an entire renewal—it must be sanctified and cleansed, yes, be "baptized with the Holy Spirit," before it can discern, or—when it has discerned—can love, the purity of the word of God.

Witness the breathings of Brainerd's soul in this holy atmosphere—'Oh, that my soul were holy, as He is holy! Oh, that it were pure, even as Christ is pure; and perfect, as my Father in heaven is perfect! These I feel are the sweetest commands in God's book, comprising all others.' 'Oh, how refreshing'—exclaims the beloved Martyn—'and supporting to my soul was the holiness of the word of God! Sweeter than the sweetest promise at this time, was the constant and manifest tendency of the word, to lead men to holiness and the deepest seriousness.'

The valuable end for which we "desire this word" is, "that we may grow thereby"—grow in purity of heart and conduct; learning to shrink from the touch of sin; "cleansing ourselves from all filthiness of flesh and spirit, and perfecting holiness in the fear of God." Our "esteem" for it, "more than our necessary food"—will be in proportion to our growth in grace, an evidence of this growth, and a constant spring of holy enjoyment.

An additional excitement to love its purity is the exhibition of that purity embodied in our perfect pattern, in Him, who was "holy, harmless, undefiled, and separate from sinners." For the habit of "beholding the Savior" with the eye of faith "in the glass of the word," conforms us to His image. But be it ever remembered, that its holiness can have no fellowship, and communicate no life, except in its own atmosphere. Oh, for a larger influence of the Spirit of God upon our souls, that we may enjoy the purifying delights of the word of God; that we may live in it, live by it to the glory of our dear Redeemer, and to the edification of His Church!

141. I am small and despised; yet do not I forget Your precepts.

Evidently David did not love the word for selfish gain. Small and despised was his condition, when the Lord first looked on him. It was also the reproach, which in the height of his glory he endured for the name of his God. Yet—stripped and destitute as he might be—did he not forget His precepts. The remembrance of his God was a cheering encouragement to his faith in his lowly condition; and no less his support in the far greater trials of his prosperity. Thus habitually did he realize the unspeakable privilege of an ever-present God!

The objects of the Lord's sovereign choice, whom He has stamped as a "peculiar treasure unto Him above all people," and whom at the day of His appearing He will bring forth as the "jewels" of His crown—are most frequently in their worldly condition—always in the eyes of the world, and in their own estimation—small and despised. And yet pride and hypocrisy in the natural heart will sometimes assume this character for selfish ends. This language of humility is not infrequently in the mouth of the professor, to enable him to maintain "a name to live" in the church of God. But are those who call themselves small and despised willing to be taken at their word? Are they content to be despised by those, whose esteem this "voluntary" spurious "humility" was meant to secure? Do they really believe themselves to be what they profess—false, vile, mean, deceitful creatures? Have they any experimental knowledge of the depth of inner wickedness, that God could open door after door in "the chamber of imagery" to confound them with the sight of greater, and yet "greater abominations!" When, therefore, they "take the lowest place," do they feel it to be their own place? Or does not the language of self-abasement mean in the eyes of God—'Come, see how humble I am?'

Christian! do not think these self-inquiries unnecessary for the cautious scrutiny of Your own heart. A self-annihilating spirit before men, as well as before God;—to feel small and despised, when we have a reputable name in the Church—is a rare attainment—a glorious triumph of victorious grace—usually the fruit of sharp affliction. This was the spirit of Brainerd—that meek and lowly disciple of his Master, who would express his astonishment that any one above the rank of "the beasts that perish" could condescend to notice him. But if we are small and despised, in the estimation of men, let us think of "Him, whom man despises—Him whom the nation abhors." Never was such an instance of magnanimity displayed, as when Pilate brought out the blessed Jesus, arrayed in the mockery of royalty, and with the blood streaming from His temples: and said, "Behold the man!" Then was there a human being, sustaining himself in the simple exclusive consciousness of the favor of God, against the universal scorn of every face. This was independence—this was greatness indeed. With such a pattern before our eyes, and such a motive touching our hearts, we may well account it "a very small thing, that we should be judged of man's judgment." What upheld "the man Christ Jesus," will uphold His servants also. "He committed himself to Him that judges righteously." Must we not desire to "know the fellowship of His sufferings"—yes, to rejoice in the participation of them?

Christian! do you love to be low, and still desire to be lower than ever? Small and despised as you are in your own eyes, and in the eyes of the world, "you are precious in the eyes of Him," who gave a price "for your ransom"—infinitely more precious than "Egypt, Ethiopia, and Seba," and who will suffer "none to pluck you out of His hands." Many may rebuke you; many may scorn you; even your brethren may treat you with contempt; yet your God, your Redeemer, will not depart from you, will not permit you to depart from Him; but will put His Spirit within you, and bring forth His precepts to your remembrance, that you may keep them, and many a sweet supporting promise for your consolation. Therefore "fear not, you worm Jacob; I will help you, says the Lord, and your Redeemer, the Holy One of Israel."

142. Your righteousness is an everlasting righteousness, and Your law is the truth.

The Psalmist in the midst of his trials could not forget the precepts, while he maintained so just a perception of their exalted character. His mind at this time seems to have been filled with the contemplation of the righteous government of God. He therefore repeats his adoration, not as applied to any particular instance, but as distinguishing the general character of His administration from everlasting.

But on whom is this government appointed to rest? Think of our Immanuel—the human brow encircled with Divine glory—the crucified hands wielding the scepter of the universe—Him, whom they mocked as the King of the Jews, seated on His own exalted throne, "King of Kings and Lord of lords!" "The government is upon His shoulder: and of the increase of His government and peace there shall be no end." How delightful to join Jehovah Himself in the ascription of praise, "Your throne, O God, is forever and ever; a scepter of righteousness is the scepter of Your kingdom!" How glorious also to praise that everlasting righteousness—the ground on which the administration of His church is framed—which Jesus "brought in," and "which is unto all them that believe;" which, when once clothed with it, is our infinite glory and reward!

"Every ordinance of man" is connected only with time. The Divine government has a constant reference to eternity, past and to come. "And I heard"—said the enraptured disciple, "the angel of the waters say; You are righteous, which are, and was, and shall be; because You have judged thus." Every instance, therefore, of His righteous administration, is that display of the Divine character which constrains the adoration of heaven. "One cried to another, and said, Holy, holy, holy, is the Lord of hosts: the whole earth is full of His glory." His law, "the manifestation of His righteousness"—is the truth. "Your word is true from the beginning! and everyone of Your righteous judgments endures forever."

This truth is the law of righteousness, which Jesus bound Himself to "fulfill"—to which He "came to bear witness," and for which He commended His people to His Father as the means of their sanctification; for what else is holiness, but the influence of truth, digested and practically embodied in the life and conduct? There may be fragments of truth elsewhere found—the scattered remnants of the fall. There may be systems imbued with large portions of truth deduced from this law. But here alone is it found perfect—unsullied. How carefully, therefore, should we test, by this standard, every doctrine—every revelation; receiving with implicit subjection all that is conformed to it; rejecting with uncompromising decision whatever will not abide the fiery trial. Most careful also should we be to preserve its unadulterated simplicity. Even the most seemingly trifling infusion of fundamental error is the grain of poison cast into the food, and making it "a savor of death unto death." Such was the error of the Galatian Church, "another gospel, yet not another"—not deserving the name—not putting ordinances in the stead of Christ (an error too gross to beguile a Christian profession), but what is far more subtle, and equally destructive, mixing them with Christ; thus impairing the integrity of the foundation, paralyzing the springs, poisoning the sources of life, yes, converting life itself into death. Let this church stand out as a beacon to our own—as a much-needed warning to each of her members.

But in a more general view, let us adore the Divine revelation, as bearing so full an impress of a "God that cannot lie"—of a "covenant ordered in all things" beyond human contrivance, "and sure" beyond the possibility of a change. How many dying testimonies have sealed the truth of the precious promises! Joshua, Simeon, and a "cloud of witnesses with which we are compassed about," have "set to their seals that God is true"—that "all the promises of God are in Christ Jesus yes and amen"—that "all are come to pass unto them, and not one thing has failed thereof." Equally manifest is the truth of His threatenings. Hell is truth seen too late. Those on the right hand and those on the left, at the great day of God, will combine their testimony to the declaration of the "Faithful and True Witness" "Heaven and earth shall pass away, but my words shall not pass away."

143. Trouble and anguish have taken hold on me: yet Your commandments are my delights.

Christian! expect not unmixed sorrow or uninterrupted joy as your present portion. Heaven will be joy without sorrow. Hell will be sorrow without joy. Earth presents to you every joy mingled with grief—every grief tempered with joy. To be accounted small and despised does not comprise the whole of your trials. Like the great apostle, you must expect not only trouble without, but anguish within. Others may not have it. But your Savior engages, "You shall." To all His people He has not meted out the same measure. Some have rebuke. Some have a scourge. But all have the cross, and this a daily cross—not a single or an occasional trial—but a life of trial—constant contradiction to the will—constant mortification of the flesh. And this takes hold of us. We cannot escape from it. Should we wish to escape it? This discipline, as Luther observes in his own way (and who was a better calculator in this school?), 'is more necessary for us, than all the riches and dignities of the whole world.' And the exercise of faith and patience in the endurance will bring more honor to God and profit to ourselves than a life of ease and indulgence. The instruction of the rod delivers us from its curse, and brings a substantial and enriching blessing.

But how precious is the sympathy of Jesus, "in all things made like unto His brethren"—enduring trouble and anguish inconceivable to human apprehension, "that He might be a merciful and faithful High Priest to support His tempted people!" How does it lift up our head amid the billows, when in communion with our Lord we can call to mind, that His sorrow was for the sake of His dear purchased people; that they might drink their lighter cup bereft of its bitter ingredients!

The Psalmist did not find that the Lord afflicted him to leave him in misery, but rather to increase his happiness. The precepts which he had not forgotten, were now his delights. The scriptural records of the trials of the Lord's people bear similar abundant testimony to the inexhaustible resources of support in the Book of God: and they are written for our learning, "that we through patience and comfort of the Scriptures might have hope." The child of God, whose thoughts are habitually occupied in the word, will always find it to be his food and light, his joy and strength; witnessing within, the presence and power of God, even where its sensible comfort may not be enjoyed.

But specially is affliction the time, that unfolds the delights of the word, such as more than counterbalances the painful trouble and anguish of the flesh. Such cheering prospects of hope and deliverance does it set forth! Such mighty supports in the endurance of trial does it realize! Truly the experimental power of the word in keeping the soul alive—much more than this—cheerful—sustained—established—is there any blessing like this—the fruit of the cross? Can we mourn over that cross, that brings so gainful a harvest? The bitterness of the cross then best realizes the delights of the commandments. But never does the believer more "rejoice in tribulation," than when the trouble and anguish which take hold of him, is for the love he bears to the name of his dear Lord.

Persecution for His sake, far from appalling him, only endears His service to his heart. It is in his eyes, "not a penalty endured, but a privilege conferred," "to suffer for His name's sake."

But contrast the condition of the child of God and the follower of the world, in the hour of affliction. The one in the midst of his troubles drinks of the fountain of all-sufficiency; and such is his peace and security, that, "in the floods of great waters they shall not come near unto him." The other, "in the fullness of his sufficiency, is in straits." David could look upward, and find the way of escape in the midst of his trouble: but for Saul, when trouble and anguish took hold of him, no source of comfort opened to his view. "God was departed from him, and was become his enemy." It was therefore trouble without support, anguish without relief—trouble and anguish; such as will at length take hold of them that forget God, when nothing will be left, but the unavailing "cry to the mountains and the hills to fall upon them, and cover them." Thanks be to God for deliverance from this fearful prospect! Thanks for the hope of unfading delights, when earthly pleasures shall have passed away! The first sheaf of the heavenly harvest will blot out the painful remembrance of the weeping seed-time which preceded it. The first moment of heaven will compensate for all the troubles and anguish of earth; and these moments will last throughout eternity. "Say to the righteous, it shall be well with him"—eternally well.

144. The righteousness of Your testimonies is everlasting: give me understanding, and I shall live. (Comp. verses 137, 138.)

What deep—weighty—impressive thoughts were exercising the Psalmist's mind! He had just marked the happy influence of the testimonies upon the believer's heart. Now he again recurs to their righteousness—as the Divine administration—not subject to the incessant variations of the human standard—but everlasting—of unalterable obligation—binding us unchangeably to God, and God to us. His creatures can virtually "make them void" by their rebellion; but they cannot change their character, or shake their foundation. No—themselves shall be the instruments of their fulfillment. Every word shall be established either by them as His obedient servants, or in and upon them as rebel transgressors. What solemn weight therefore is due to this Divine standard! It seems now to be trampled under foot; but its righteousness, inflexible in its demands, and unalterable in its obligations—will before long assert its sovereignty over the world, when every other standard shall have passed away. It will be the rule of the Divine procedure at the great day of decision. When the "great white throne" is set up—when "the dead, small and great, stand before God, and the books are opened, and another book is opened, which is the book of life;" and the dead are judged out of those things which were written in the books, "according to their works"—the acknowledgment will be made throughout the universe of God—The righteousness of Your testimonies is everlasting. How glorious is the confidence of being dealt with in that great day upon an everlasting foundation of righteousness!

But this view of the Divine righteousness and everlasting obligation of the testimonies, naturally suggests the prayer for a more spiritual, enlightened, and experimental acquaintance with them. Often before had the petition been sent up. But who can cry too often or too earnestly? One ray of this understanding is of far higher value than all the intellectual or speculative knowledge in the world. If its first dawn exhibits the infinite difference between light and darkness—if prayer for it implies a measure already received, still—Give me understanding—will be the cry—not of the "little child" whose spiritual perception is just opening—but of the "father who has known Him that is from the beginning." Let me know the holiness of Your testimonies—their extent—their perfection—their intimate connection with every part of my daily walk—with the restraint of my inclination, the regulation of my temper, the direction of every step of my path. And indeed the more devoutly we study them, the more shall we feel our need of supplication for Divine teaching, to give us more adoring and thankful views of the government of God, and to subjugate our caviling disposition to the humbling influence of faith.

The principle of spiritual and eternal life flows from the enlightened perception of the testimonies of God. Give me understanding, and I shall live. For "this is life eternal, that we might know You, the only true God, and Jesus Christ whom You have sent." His testimonies are the revelation of Himself. If then we "have an unction from the Holy One, and know all things," our knowledge of them will become more spiritual in its character, more experimental in its comforts, and more practical in its fruits. And thus, 'the life of God in the soul' will invigorate us for higher attainments in evangelical knowledge, and more steady advancement in Christian holiness. But how infinitely do we live below the full privilege of knowing God in His testimonies! Christians of a

Scriptural standard are "forgetting those things which are behind, and reaching forth unto those things which are before. Let us therefore, as many as be perfect, be thus minded."

And then—what will it be at the great consummation; when our God of love will have put His last hand to His glorious work; when the mark of all our aims—the term of all our hopes and desires—all that we have so long labored for—so earnestly panted after—so restlessly pursued—when all shall be attained? Then indeed we shall live a life worthy of the name—not as now under the shadowed glimmerings—but under the immediate full-eyed glory of His light and love; having escaped forever the deadliest of all dangers—sin—the very deadliness of death itself.

145. I cried with my whole heart; hear me, O Lord, I will keep Your statutes. 146. I cried unto You; save me and I shall keep Your testimonies.

This is indeed the "pouring out of the soul before the Lord," a beautiful and encouraging picture of a soul wrestling with God, in a few short sentences, with as much power and success as in the most continued length of supplication. Brief as are the petitions, the whole compass of language could not make them more comprehensive. Hear me. The whole heart is engaged in the cry. Save me—includes a sinner's whole need—pardon, acceptance, access, holiness, strength, comfort, heaven, all in one word—Christ. Save me—from myself, from Satan, from the world, from the curse of sin, from the wrath of God. This is the need of every moment to the end. I cried unto You.—What a mercy to know where to go! The way of access must have been implied, though not mentioned, in these short ejaculations. Hear me—must have been in the name of the all-prevailing Advocate. Save me—through Him, whose name is, Jesus the Savior. A moment's interruption of our view of Jesus casts for the time an impenetrable cloud over our way to God, and paralyzes the spirit of prayer. Prayer is not only the sense of guilt, and the cry of mercy, but the exercise of faith. When I come to God, I would always bring with me the blood of Christ—my price—my plea in my hand. He cannot cast it out. Thus am I "a prince, that has power with God, and prevail." Here is the warrant to believe, that my God does, and will hear me. Here is my encouragement to "look up"—to be "watching at His gate"—like the cripple at the "beautiful gate of the temple, expecting to receive somewhat of Him." Not a word of such prayer is lost. It is as seed—not cast into the earth, exposed to hazard and loss—but cast into the bosom of God—and here—as in the natural harvest, "he which sows bountifully, shall reap also bountifully." The most frequent comers are the largest receivers—always wanting—always asking—living upon what they have, but still hungering for more.

With many, however, the ceremony of prayer is everything, without any thought, desire, anxiety, or waiting for an answer. These slight dealings prove low thoughts of God, and deep and guilty insensibility;—that the sense of pressing need is not sharp enough to put an edge upon the affections. But are none of God's dear children, too, who in days past never missed the presence of God, but they "sought it carefully with tears"—now too easily satisfied with the act of prayer, without this "great object of it—the enjoyment of God?" Perhaps you lament your deficiencies, your weakness in the hour of temptation, your indulgence of ease, your unfaithfulness of heart. But is your cry continually ascending with your whole heart? Your soul would not be so empty of comfort, if your mouth were not so empty of prayer. The Lord never charges presumption upon the frequency or extent of your supplications; but He is often ready to "upbraid you with your unbelief," that you are so reluctant in your approach, and so straitened in your desires—that you are so unready to receive what He is so ready to give—that your vessels are too narrow to take in His full blessing—that you are content with drops, when He has promised "floods,"—yes "rivers of living water,"—and above all, that you are so negligent in praising Him for what you have already received.

We must not lightly give up our suit. We must not be content with keeping up the duty, without keeping up "continued instancy in prayer" in our duty. This alone preserves in temptation. Satan strikes at all of God in the soul. Unbelief readily yields to his suggestions. This is the element in which we live—the warfare of every moment. Will then the customary devotion of morning and evening (even supposing it to be sincere) suffice for such an emergency? No. The Christian must "put on the whole armor of God;" and buckle on His panoply with unceasing "prayer and watchfulness in the Spirit." If his heart be dead and cold, let him rather cry and wait as Luther was used to do, until it be warm and enlivened. The hypocrite, indeed, would be satisfied with the barren performance of the duty. But the child of God, while he mourns in the dust, "Behold I am vile!"—still holds on, though sometimes with a cry, that probably finds no utterance with his lips, that vents itself only with tears, or "groanings that cannot be uttered." And shall such a cry fail to enter into the ears of the Lord of Sabaoth? The Lord has heard the voice of my weeping. Lord, all my desire is before You; and my groaning is not hid from You.

But why is the believer so earnest for an audience?—why so restless in his cries for salvation? Is it not, that he loves the statutes of his God; that he is grieved on account of his inability to keep them; and that he longs for mercy, as the spring of his obedience? Hear me; I will keep Your statutes. Save me: and I shall keep Your testimonies—a most satisfactory evidence of an upright heart. Sin can have no fellowship with the statutes. As saved sinners, they are our delight.

Lord! You know how our hearts draw back from the spiritual work of prayer: and how we nourish our unbelief by our distance from You. Oh, "pour upon us this Spirit of grace and supplication." "Teach us to pray"—even our hearts—our whole hearts—to cry unto You. Give us the privilege of real communion with You—the only satisfying joy of earth or heaven. Then shall we "run the way of Your commandments, when You shall enlarge our hearts."

147. I prevented the dawning of the morning, and cried: I hoped in Your word. 148. My eyes prevent the night-watches, that I might meditate in Your word.

The Psalmist here brings before us not only the fervency, but the seasons, of his supplication. Like Daniel, he had set times of prayer, "three times a-day." Yet did not this frequent exercise satisfy him, without an habitual "waiting all the day upon his God." Prayer was indeed his meat, and drink, and breath. "I give myself unto prayer." His sketch of the "blessed man delighting in the law of his God, and"—as an evidence of this delight, "meditating therein day and night"— unconsciously furnished an accurate picture of himself. For early and late was he found in the work of God; preventing the dawning of the morning for prayer, and again the night-watches, that he might meditate in the word. But to look above the example of David to David's Lord—surely "it was written" most peculiarly "for our learning," that Jesus—after a laborious Sabbath—every moment of which appears to have been spent for the benefit of sinners; and when His body, subject to the same infirmities, and therefore needing the same refreshment with our own, seemed to require repose, "in the morning, rising up a great while before day, went out and departed into a solitary place, and there prayed." On another occasion, when intensely engaged in the service of His church, and about to lay her foundation in the choice of her first ministers, did His eyes prevent the night-watches. "He continued all night in prayer to God."

So long as the duty only of prayer is known, we shall be content with our set seasons. But when the privilege is felt, we shall be early at work, following it closely morning and night. While, however, family and social exercises are refreshing—while "the tabernacles of the Lord are amiable" in our view, and we delight to "wait at the posts of His doors;" yet it is the lonely, confidential communion with our God, "the door shut"—the Church as well as the world excluded—that makes our closest walk with God. Secret prayer is most likely to be true prayer. At least there is no true prayer without it. It was the "garden" prayer—separate even from His own disciples—that brought special support to the fainting humanity of Jesus. And if He needed this perfect retirement, whose affections were always fixed upon their center, what must be our own need, whose desires are so unstable and languishing! And how cheering is His succoring sympathy, knowing as He does experimentally the heart of a secret, earnest pleader! Such, doubtless, were David's cries—penetrating no ear, but His Father's—yet delightful incense there.

But to see the King of Israel, with all His urgent responsibilities, "sanctifying" such frequent daily seasons "with the word of God and prayer"—how does it expose the insincerity of the worldling's excuse, that the pressing avocations of the day afford no time for the service of God! It is not, that such men are busy, and have no time for prayer; but that they are worldly, and have no heart to pray. The consecrated heart will always find time for secret duties, and will rather, as David, redeem it from sleep, than lose it from prayer.

And does not the uniform experience of the Lord's people warrant the remark—how much our vital spirituality depends upon the daily consecration of the first-fruits of our time to the Lord? How often are opportunities for heavenly communion during the day unavoidably straitened! But the night watches and the dawning of the morning afford seasons free from interruption, when our God expects to hear from us, and when "the joy" of "fellowship with Him" will be "our strength" for active service, and our preservation from many a worldly snare. What a standard of enjoyment would it be, with our last thoughts in the night watches, to leave as it were our hearts with Him, and to find them with

Him in the morning, awaking as with our hearts in heaven! Surely the refreshments of our visits to Him, and His abidance with us, will often constrain us to acknowledge, "Truly our fellowship is with the Father, and with His Son Jesus Christ." The thoughts of God were clearly the first visitors to David's waking mind; and to this may be ascribed his habitual success in realizing His presence throughout the day. The lukewarmness and our want of spiritual enjoyment may often be traced to that morning indolence, which not only throws the business of the day into confusion, but also consumes the time in self-indulgence or trifling, which should have been given to sacred communion. For—not to speak of the seasonableness of the early hours for devotion—the very exertion made to overcome "this lust of the flesh," and to steal a march upon the demands of the world, is an exercise of self-denial, honorable to God, "that shall in no wise lose its reward." No remembrance of the past will be so refreshing at a dying hour, as the time redeemed for communion with God.

And, even should there be no actual enjoyment, at least let us honor God by expectancy. I hoped in Your word. There can be no exercise of faith in the neglect of prayer; but the ground of faith, and that which gives to it life, hope, and joy, is the view of God in His word as a promising God. Therefore when His Providence opens no present encouragement, let us seek it in His covenant. To hope in His word is to build up ourselves upon "our most holy faith" and to lay all our desires, all our cares, all our weights, and burdens, upon a solid, unsinking foundation.

Well, therefore, were David's night-watches employed in meditation in the word. For, in order to stay ourselves upon it in time of need, it must occupy our whole study, thought, and desire. Instability of faith arises from a want of fixed recollection of the promises of God. This superficial habit may suffice for times of quietness; but amid the billows of temptation we can only cast "anchor sure and steadfast" in an habitual and intelligent confidence upon the full, free, firm promise of the word. Let it therefore be the food of our meditation, and the ground of our support, when our suit seems to hang at the throne of grace without any tokens of present acceptance. Often will it lift up our fainting hands, and supply strength for fresh conflict, and the earnest of blessed victory. The ground is always sure for faith. May the Lord ever furnish us with faith enough for our daily work, conflict, consolation, and establishment!

149. Hear my voice according to Your loving-kindness: O Lord, quicken me according to Your judgment.

In the eyes of the world, David appeared "in all his glory," when seated on his throne, and surrounded with the magnificence of his kingdom. But never did he appear so glorious in the sight of God, as when presenting himself as a suppliant before the mercy-seat, seeking an audience of the King of Kings only to send up reiterated cries for quickening grace. And do I not need the same grace every moment, in every duty? Does not "the gift of God within me" need to be daily "stirred up?" Are not the "things that remain" often "ready to die?" Then hear my voice, O Lord; quicken me.

But to urge my suit successfully, I must "order my cause before God;" I must "fill my mouth with arguments." And if I can draw a favorable plea from the character of my Judge—if I can prove that promises have been made in my behalf, these will be most encouraging pledges of a successful issue. Now David had been so used to plead in cases of extremity, that arguments suited to his present distress were always ready at hand. He now pleads with God for quickening grace, on the ground of His own loving-kindness and judgment. Can He "deny Himself?"

And with what "full assurance of faith," may I ask to be heard on account of that transcendent proof of loving-kindness manifested in the gift of God's dear Son—not only as His chief mercy, but as the pledge of every other mercy—and manifested too at the fittest time—according to His judgment—after the inefficiency of the power of reason, and the sanctions of the law, to influence the heart, had been most clearly displayed! And what a plea is it to ask for quickening influences, that this is the very end for which this gift of loving-kindness was given, and that the gift itself is the channel, through which the quickening life of the Godhead is imparted! Could I ask for this grace on any other ground than loving-kindness? All ground of fitness or merit is swept away. On the footing of mercy alone, can I stand before Him. And how is my faith enlivened in retracing the records of my soul from the beginning—how He "betrothed"—how He "drew—me with loving-kindness!" May I not then cry, "Oh! continue Your loving-kindness?" And not less full is my conviction of His judgment, in dealing wisely and tenderly with me, according to His infallible perception of my need. Left to my own judgment—often should I have prayed myself into evil, and asked what it would have been my curse to have received. But I have learned, that the child must not be guided by his own will, but by his father's better mind—not the patient by his own humor, but by the physician's skill. Truly, even the Lord's corrections have been in judgment! And in the thankful remembrance of them my confidence for the time to come is established! Gladly will I "set to my seal," that "the Lord is a God of judgment;" and that "blessed are all those who wait for Him." He knows not only what grace is needed, but at what time. Not a moment sooner will it come; not a moment later will it be delayed. "As You will, what You will, when You will" (Thomas a Kempis)—is the expression of faith and resignation, with which all must be committed to the Lord, waiting for the end in humility, desire, expectation. And if in pleading my suit for a hearing according to His loving-kindness, my poor, polluted, lifeless petitions should find no liberty of approach; may I be but enabled to direct one believing look to "the Lamb that is in the midst of the throne!" and I will not doubt that my feeblest offering shall come up as a memorial before God.

Verses 150-176

150. They draw near that follow after mischief: they are far from Your law. 151. You are near, O Lord: and all Your commandments are truth.

The imminent danger in which David was living quickened his cries to his God. Often does the Lord permit this pressing trial!, Seldom, but in extremity, are our graces brought to their full exercise. Confidence is then shaken from man, and established in God. For now it is that we enjoy our God as "a very present help in trouble," and that our dependence on His commandment is a true and solid foundation of comfort to our soul. A dreadful character is indeed drawn of the ungodly—They are far from God's law—and that not from ignorance, but from willful enmity. This is God's witness against them; and they are not ashamed to consent, that this "witness is true." No wonder, therefore, that those, that are far from God's law, should draw near to follow after mischief. But if they draw near, the Lord is nearer still. "I am your shield"—says He to His distressed child—who echoes back the promise in the cheerfulness of faith, "You are my hiding place, and my shield: I hope in Your word." Elisha knew the power of this shield, when he quelled the alarm of his terrified servant. He beheld them draw near that follow after mischief. But the eye of faith assured his heart; and when "the Lord opened the eyes of the young man," he too was enabled to testify—You are near, O Lord!

But near as the Lord is to His people as their outward shield, is He not yet nearer still, as dwelling in their hearts? Here is "His temple," His desired habitation—like Zion of old, of which He said, "This is my rest forever; here will I dwell, for I have desired it." This is the dwelling, which, once possessed of its Divine Inhabitant, will never be left desolate.

Our spiritual enemies, like David's persecutors, are ever present and active. The devouring "lion," or the insinuating "serpent," is near to follow after mischief; and so much the more dangerous, as his approaches are invisible. Near also is a tempting, ensnaring world: and nearer still a lurking world within, separating us from communion with our God. But in turning habitually and immediately to our stronghold, we can enjoy the confidence—You are near, O Lord. Though "the High and Lofty One, whose name is Holy;" though the just and terrible God, yet are You made near to Your people, and they to You, "by the blood of the cross." And You manifest Your presence to them in "the Son of Your love."

Indeed to the Son Himself, the nearness of His Father's presence was a source of consolation and support, when they drew near, that followed after mischief. "He is near"—said he, "which justifies Me: who will contend with Me? let us stand together. Who is my adversary? Let him come near to Me. Behold! the Lord God will help Me: who is he who shall condemn Me? Lo they all shall wax old as does a garment: the moth shall eat them up." "Behold," said He to His affrighted disciples, as His hour drew near, "the hour comes, yes is now come, that you shall be scattered everyone to his own, and shall leave Me alone: and yet I am not alone, because the Father is with Me." And thus His people in earthly desolation flee to the promises of their God; and in the recollection of His faithful, ever-present help, "set to their seal," that all His commandments are truth. The mischief intended for them only proves, that "You, Lord, will bless the righteous; with favor will You compass him as with a shield."

But may the Lord not only be brought near in our interest in Him, but may we be kept near in communion with Him! Let our hearts be sacred to Him. Let us be most careful to watch against any strangeness with this beloved Friend, and to cultivate a growing cordiality and closeness in our walk with Him. If our character is formed by the society in which we live, what "treasures of wisdom and knowledge" should we find, what a spirit of unbounded love should we imbibe—by a nearer and more constant communion with Him; willing as He is to impart Himself freely, inexhaustibly unto us! In a backsliding state, we must expect to lose this heavenly nearness. In a state of darkness, it is the exercise of faith, to believe that unseen He is near; and the practical influence of faith will lead us to speak, and pray, and think, and praise, "as seeing Him who is invisible." In a state of enjoyment, let us anticipate the time when He will be ever near to us.

"And I heard a great voice out of heaven, saying, Behold! the tabernacle of God is with men, and He will dwell with them, and they shall be His people, and God Himself shall be with them, and be their God."

152. Concerning Your testimonies, I have known of old, that You have
   founded them forever.

The "truth of the commandments," which the Psalmist had just
asserted, was an everlasting foundation. He stated it not upon slight
conviction. But he knew it—and that not recently—but as the result of
early consideration—he had known it of old. It is most important to have
a full certainty of the ground of our faith. How else can we have that
"good thing—a heart established with grace?"—how "continue in the
faith grounded and settled?"—how be kept from being "moved away
from the hope of the gospel?" Praised be God! We feel our ground to be
firm. As God is the same, so must His testimonies be. We cannot
conceive of His promising without performance, or threatening without
effect. They are therefore expressly revealed as a firm foundation, in
express contrast with this world's fairest promise.

But let us mark this eternal basis of the testimonies. The whole plan
of redemption was emphatically founded forever. The Savior "was
foreordained before the foundation of the world." The people of God are
"chosen in Christ before the world began!" The great Author "declares
the end from the beginning," and thus clears His dispensations from any
charge of mutability or contingency. Every event in the church is fixed,
permitted, and provided for—not in the passing moment of time, but in
the counsels of eternity. All God's faithful engagements with His people
of old are founded forever upon the oath and promise of God—the two
"immutable things, in which it is impossible for God to lie." May we not
then "have strong consolation" in venturing every hope for eternity upon
this rock? nor need we be dismayed to see all our earthly stays, "the
world, and the lust, and the fashion of it—passing away" before us. Yet
we are most of us strangely attached to this fleeting scene, even when
experience and Divine teaching have instructed us in its vanity and it is
not until repeated proofs of this truth have touched us very closely in the
destruction of our dearest consolations, that we take the full comfort of
the enduring foundation of God's testimonies, and of the imperishable
character of their treasure.

Now let me realize the special support of this view in a dying hour: 'I
am on the borders of an unknown world; but "my hope makes not
ashamed" at the moment of peril it is as "an anchor of the soul, sure and

steadfast;" and in the strength of it I do not fear to plunge into eternity. "I know whom I have believed, and am persuaded that He is able to keep that which I have committed to Him against that day." I know—not His sufficiency merely, but His All-sufficiency. I know His conquering power over the great enemies of my soul. I know that He has "spoiled the principalities and powers" of hell, of the strength to triumph over His ransomed people. I know also, that He is "the Lord; He changes not;" His word changes not; His testimonies abide the same: I have known of old, that He has founded them forever.' Thus we look for the removing of those "things which are shaken, as of things that are made, that those things which cannot be shaken may remain." The scoffer may say, "If the foundations be destroyed, what can the righteous do?"—Let God Himself give the answer, "Lift up your eyes to the heavens, and look upon the earth beneath: for the heavens shall vanish away like smoke, and the earth shall wax old like a garment, and those who dwell therein shall die in like manner; but my salvation shall be forever, and my righteousness shall not be abolished."

153. Consider my affliction, and deliver me: for I do not forget Your law.

Another note of the child of sorrow! Hated by the world—vexed by his restless enemy—chastened by his God—burdened with his "body of death"—what else can he do but cry—Consider my affliction! How manifestly is this world, not our rest, but our exercise for rest! Well is it that our "days are few," when they are so "evil." But how could we hold on as we do, had we not our Savior's pitying heart and Almighty help? The want of this sympathy was the overwhelming sorrow, that well-near "broke His" sorrowing "heart" "I looked for some to take pity, but there was none; and for comforters, but I found none." This depth of trial combined with every other part of His unknown sufferings to make Him "such an High Priest as became us," "touched with the feeling of our infirmities"; considering our afflictions: and, "in that He Himself has suffered being tempted, able to support them that are tempted." With what sympathy did He consider the affliction of His people in Egypt!, "I have surely seen the affliction of My people which are; in Egypt, and I know their sorrows." At a subsequent period, "his soul was grieved for the misery of Israel"—a cheering example of that compassionate interest, with which "in all His people's afflictions He is afflicted." Well may His people take encouragement to pray, Consider my affliction. "Now, therefore, let not all the trouble seem little before You, that has come upon us."

Yet is He not only sympathizing to consider, but mighty to deliver. "Who is this glorious" conqueror with His "dyed garments" of victory, "traveling in the greatness of His strength? I that speak in righteousness—mighty to save." Such did the noble confessors in Babylon—such did Daniel in the den of lions—find Him, fully justifying their unwavering confidence in His love and power. And what age of the Church has been wanting in testimony, that "the Lord knows how to deliver the godly out of temptations," and that "He who has delivered, does deliver, and will even to the end deliver?" The consciousness that we do not forget His law, is our plea, that He would consider our affliction, and deliver us; and is of itself an evidence, that the affliction has performed its appointed work. Let me then expect in my affliction the fulfillment of His gracious promise, "Because he has set his love upon Me, therefore will I deliver him; I will set him on high, because he has known My name. He shall call upon Me, and "I will deliver him: I will be with him in trouble; I will deliver him, and honor him." In the midst of my trials I would prepare my hymn of praise for His kind consideration and faithful deliverance, "I will be glad and rejoice in Your mercy: for You have considered my trouble; You have known my soul in adversities, and have not shut me up into the hand of the enemy; You have set my feet in a large room!" Let me then remember my affliction, only as it may be the means of increasing my acquaintance with my tender and Almighty friend. Poor and afflicted as I may be, let me be more poor and afflicted still, if I may but have fresh evidence that He "thinks upon me"—that He considers my affliction, and in His own gracious time and way will deliver me.

154. Plead my cause, and deliver me; quicken me according to Your word.

Oppressed as the Psalmist appeared to be by the weight of his affliction, he is at no loss where to apply for help. He carries his righteous cause to Him, who "stills the enemy and the avenger" "Plead my cause, O Lord, with them that strive with me: fight against them that fight against me. Take hold of shield and shield, and stand up for my help. Draw out also the spear, and stop the way against them that persecute me; say unto my soul, I am Your salvation." Thus must we throughout our warfare maintain "the patience of hope," waiting for the Lord, "until He plead our cause, and execute judgment for us." If there is an accuser to resist, "we have an advocate" to plead, who could testify of His prevailing acceptance in the court of heaven, "Father, I thank You, that You have heard Me. And I knew that You hear Me always." Our Redeemer does indeed plead our cause successfully for our deliverance; when but for His powerful advocacy we must have stood speechless in the judgment—helpless, without any prospect of acceptance. Awful indeed was the cause which He had to manage. Our adversary had the law on his side. We could not deny the charge, or offer satisfaction. We could neither "stand in the judgment," nor flee from the impending wrath. But at that moment of infinite peril, our cause was pleaded by a "Counselor," who never was nonsuited in court, who brought irresistible pleas, and produced satisfaction that could not be denied. The voice of deliverance was heard in heaven, "Deliver them from going down to the pit: I have found a ransom." This ransom is no less than the price of His own "precious blood," "shed for many for the remission of sins," a ransom, which has merited and obtained eternal deliverance for His people, and which still pleads for the expiation of the guilt, which attaches to their holiest services, and defiles their happiest approaches to their God. When therefore Satan accuses me: yes, when my own heart condemns me, I may look upward to my heavenly Advocate—Plead my cause, and deliver me. "O Lord, I am oppressed; undertake for me. You will answer, O Lord, my God."

Poor trembling sinner! take courage. "Your Redeemer is strong—He will thoroughly plead your cause," and leave no charge unanswered. But you say 'How know I that He speaks for me?' Yet if not for you, for whom does He speak? Who needs an advocate more than you? He pleads indeed nothing favorable of you; but much, very much for you. For He pleads the merit of His own blood, "that takes away the sin of the world"—even that great sin of "unbelief," of which His Spirit is now "convincing" you; and which you are now made to feel, lament, and resist, as the bitterest foe to your peace. And does He not "ever live to make intercession for you?" Why then hesitate to apply the certain and consoling inference, that "he is able to save to the uttermost?" Why discouraged by the sight of sin, temptation; backsliding, difficulty, and fear, arising before you on every side; when after you have taken the most extended view of the prospect o f sorrow, this one word "uttermost" goes beyond it? If you feel it hard to believe, send up your cry, "Help my unbelief." Only do not dishonor Him by willful despondency; and do not add the sin of disobedience, in delaying this moment to come to Him.

After all, however, even while exercising faith in our heavenly Advocate, we must mourn over our sluggishness in His service. Well, therefore, do we accompany our pleading for deliverance with the supplication—Quicken me! Every moment's perseverance depends upon this Divine supply. Blessed be God for the sure warrant of expectation— According to Your word! Here we shall receive not only the living principle, but its lively operation; not only the fire to kindle the lamp, but the oil to feed the flame. For He who is our Advocate to plead for us, and our Savior to deliver us, is also our quickening Head, filled with "the residue of the Spirit" to "revive His work." "You have ascended on high, and have received gifts for men: yes, for the rebellious also, that the Lord God might dwell among them." Do we therefore want a heart to pray, to praise, to believe, to love? Let us only look to an ascended Savior, sending down the life-giving influence from above, as the purchase of His blood, and the fruit of His intercession. Thus will our hope be enlivened, our faith established, and the graces of the Spirit will abound to the glory of our God.

155. Salvation is far from the wicked; for they seek not Your statutes.

How striking the contrast!—how awfully destitute the condition! They have no one to consider their affliction—no one to deliver them— no one to plead their cause. Indeed, all the misery that an immortal soul is capable of enduring throughout eternity is included in this sentence— Salvation is far from the wicked. The full picture of it is drawn by our Lord Himself, "The rich man died, and was buried; and in hell he lifted up his eyes, being in torments, and sees Abraham afar off, and Lazarus in his bosom." The present enjoyment of salvation is far from the wicked. "There is no peace, says my God, to the wicked." Their common employments are "sin." Their "sacrifice is an abomination." Their life is "without Christ, having no hope, and without God in the world." But who can tell the curse of eternity, with this salvation far from them? To be eternally shut out from God—from heaven! To be eternally shut in with the enemies of God, and the heirs of hell! Fellow-Christians—look from what you have escaped—what you were, when "you were sometimes afar off,"—what you would have been now and forever, had you not "in

Christ Jesus been made near by the blood of Christ:" and then "if you hold your peace, the stones will immediately cry out" against you.

But whence this inexpressibly awful condition of the wicked? Is not salvation offered to them? Are they shut out from hope, and sternly refused an interest in the covenant? Oh! no! it is their own doing, or rather their own undoing. Would they but seek the ways of God, they might plead for deliverance; yes, they might have a prevailing Advocate to plead their cause, and deliver them. But now salvation is far from them, because "they are far from God's law." It does not fly from them; but they fly from it. Every act is a stride of mind, more or less vigorous in departure from God. No—such is their pride, that "they will not even seek His statutes." They "desire not the knowledge of His ways." They say to God, "Depart from us;" God, therefore, will say to them, "Depart from me." They say to Christ, "We will not have this man to reign over us;" He will say of them, "Those My enemies, that would not I should reign over them, bring here, and slay them before me." It is not then so much God that punishes them, as those who punish themselves. Their own sin—the necessity of the case—punishes them. They "will not come to Christ, that they might have life:" "so that they are without excuse"— die they must.

But who are the wicked? Alas! this is a melancholy question, as involving within its sphere so much that passes for amiable, virtuous, and lovely, in the estimation of the world. Not to speak of those, whose name is broadly written upon their foreheads; it includes "all that forget God," however blameless their moral character, or their external Christian profession. It is determined upon immutable authority—it is the decree of our eternal Judge, "If any man have not the Spirit of Christ, he is none of His;" and if none of His, then it follows in unavoidable consequence, that salvation is far from him.

Oh! could we but persuade such of their awful state. Oh! could we awake them from their death-like, deadly sleep—slumbering on the brink of ruin! on the borders of hell! But they are closed up in their own self-esteem, or in the favorable comparison drawn between themselves and many around them; forgetting that the rule, by which they will be judged, is not the world's standard of moral rectitude, but the statutes of a holy, heart-searching God; forgetting too, that all may be decency without, while all is corruption within. Let them test their hearts by an honest and prayerful scrutiny of the statutes; and while they must confess themselves guilty before God, a sense of danger would awaken the hearty cry for salvation which would not then be far from them. For "the Lord is near unto all them that call upon Him, to all that call upon Him in truth. He will fulfill the desire of them that fear Him; He also will hear their cry, and—will save them."

O You Almighty Spirit, whose power is alone able to "turn the hearts of the disobedient to the wisdom of the just," "raise up Your power, and come among us;" "rend the heavens, and come down;" rend the hearts of sinners, of the ungodly, the moral, the naturally amiable, the self-righteous. "Fill their faces with shame, that they may seek Your name, O Lord."

156. Great are Your tender mercies, O Lord; quicken me according to Your judgments.

It is most cheering to pass from judgment to mercy—from the awful state of the wicked, to adore the mercies of God to His own people. We were naturally no better than they. The most eminent saved sinner looks on himself with wonder, "Is not this a brand plucked out of the fire?" Never will he lose the remembrance, "Who makes you to differ?" To mercy—rich mercy alone—we trace the distinction between those that are "quickened," and those that remain "dead in trespasses and sins."

But let us mark the features of this mercy. How great in extent! Estimate its greatness by the infinite debt which it blots out—the eternal ruin from which it saves—the heavenly crown to which it raises. Trace it to the mind of God—that first eternal purpose of mercy, which set us apart for His glory. Mark it in that "time of love," when His mercy rescued us from Satan, sin, death, and hell, and drew us to Himself. As soon might we span the arch of heaven, as fully grasp the greatness of His mercy. And then how tender is it in its exercise! Such was the first beam of mercy that "visited us." Such has been the continued display. So natural, as from a Father. So yearning, "as one whom his mother comforts!" Such a multitude of those tender mercies! The overflowing stream follows us through every step of our wilderness journey. The blessing "compasses us about," abounds towards us, keeps us steadfast, or restores us when wandering, and will preserve us to the end. Happy are we—not in the general perception—not in the hearsay report—but in the experimental enjoyment of it. "Bless the Lord, O my soul, and all that is within me, bless His holy name." But what poor returns have we made for this infinite love! Surely the petition for quickening grace suits us

273

well. This was the constant burden of David's prayer. For he was not like many professors, who can maintain their assurance in a lower and careless walk. No, he was a believer of a very high standard; desirous not only of proving his title to the blessing, but of living in its habitual and active enjoyment.

Often as this petition has been brought before us, in the course of this Psalm, it is too important ever to be passed over. Let us at this time use it for the purpose of individual self-inquiry. In what respects do I need quickening grace? Are my views of sin, and especially of the sin of my own heart, slight and superficial? Do they fail in producing humility, abasement, tenderness of conscience, circumspection of conduct? If it be so—Quicken me, O my God! Does my apprehension of a Savior's love serve to embitter sin to me? to crucify sin in me, to warm and enliven my heart with love to Him, and zeal in His service? If I am convicted of coldness to such a Savior, and sluggishness in such a service, I need to pray—O Lord, quicken me! And how do I find it with regard to prayer itself? Are not my prayers general—unfrequent—wandering? Is not my service too often constrained, a forced duty, rather than a privilege and delight? O Lord, quicken me!

Yet many Christians, through a mistaken perception, know not when they have received the blessing. They have looked for it in strong and sensible excitement; and in defect of this they sink into despondency. Whereas the solid influence is independent of sensations, and consists in a tender sensibility of sin, a spiritual appetite for the gospel, active energy in Christian duties, and continual progress in heavenly exercises. But under no circumstances must the evil of a dead and drooping state be lightly thought of; obscuring as it does the difference between the believer and the worldling, or rather between the believer and the formalist. O believer, you have great need to carry your complaint again and again unto the Lord! 'Quicken me—quicken me—according to Your judgments—according to those gracious promises, which are the method of Your proceedings, and the rule of Your dispensations of grace.' You cannot be too earnest to welcome the breathings of the Spirit, or too cautious, that your indolence resists not His Divine impression. When He quickens you with His influence, do you quicken Him with your supplications, "Awake, O north wind; and come, you south: blow upon my garden, that the spices thereof may flow out." Persuade—entreat—constrain His stay. Enlivened by His energy, how happy, and in your own sphere how useful, a member of the Church of Christ you may be found! Your soul will be invigorated—your graces strengthened—and your affections elevated—in humble, cheerful, steady dependence upon the Savior, and in daily renewed devotedness to His service. The more the spiritual life is thus "exercised unto godliness, the more delightfully will you realize the active service and everlasting praise, which will constitute the perfection of heavenly enjoyment."

157. Many are my persecutors and my enemies; yet do I not decline from Your testimonies.

David's experience is common to us all. Many, indeed, are our persecutors and enemies. This is a solemn cost. Let those who are setting out in the Christian course count it well. From neglect of our Lord's rule of Scriptural calculation, many seem to begin well; but they have been "hindered"—they turn back; they are zealous but inconsiderate; warmhearted, but ignorant of themselves, their work, and their resources. They were allured at first, perhaps, by an interest in the Gospel—some delusive excitement of love to the Savior—the picture of the paths of "pleasantness and peace," or the joys of heaven. The cross was out of sight, and out of mind. But this promise of ease and happiness was no less foolish and unwarrantable, than that of a soldier, utterly forgetful of his profession, and who should promise himself peace at the very time that he was called out to the wars. Surely, if like God's ancient people, we begin our road in sunshine, it is well to be provided against the storms, which will soon overtake us. We would say therefore to all—specially to sanguine beginners—Let your course be commenced with serious consideration, and zealous self-scrutiny. Beware of hasty determinations. See to it, that your resources are drawn, not from your own resolutions, or from the sincerity and ardor of your love; but from the fullness that is treasured up in Jesus for your present distress. Feel every step of your way by the light of the sacred word. If you expect Christian consistency to command the esteem of an ungodly world, you have forgotten both your Master's word and example; and you will soon be ready to exclaim—Many are my persecutors, and my enemies. For if their hostility is not always active, the enmity "is not dead, but sleeps." If, however, their unexpected surprisals and inveteracy should daunt you in the conflict, you are again forgetting the word of cheering support in the most awful crisis, "My grace is sufficient for you; for My strength is made perfect in weakness." Thus the word of God will be "the armor of righteousness on the right hand and on the left." Presumption is cast down, self-confidence is humbled, and the trembling simplicity of dependence upon an Almighty arm is upheld and honored.

Count then upon the difficulties that beset the heavenly path. You will never pluck the Rose of Sharon, if you are afraid of being pierced by the thorns which surround it. You will never reach the crown, if you flinch from the cross in the way to it. Oh! think of the honor of bearing this cross. It is conformity to the Son of God. Let the mind be deeply imbued with the remembrance of his daily cross of suffering and reproach; and we shall gladly "go forth without the camp, bearing His reproach," yes—even "rejoicing, if we are counted worthy to suffer shame" with Him and for Him. Indeed, what is our love, if we will not take up a cross for Him? How can we be His followers, without His cross? How can we be Christians, if we are not confessors of Christ before a world that despises His Gospel?

But a steady, consistent profession is no matter of course. The crown is not easily won. Many are our persecutors, and our enemies. Persecution, to the false professor, is an occasion of apostasy; to the faithful servant of Christ, it is the trial of his faith, the source of his richest consolations, the guard of his profession, and the strength of his perseverance. It drives him to his God. He casts himself upon his Savior for immediate refuge and support; and the quickening influence, which he had just been seeking, enables him to say—Yet do I not decline from Your testimonies. Thus did the great Apostle, at the time, when his persecutors were many, and human help even from his friends had failed him, maintain an unshaken confidence in the service of his God, "At my first answer"—he tells us, "no man stood with me, but all men forsook me. Notwithstanding, the Lord stood with me, and strengthened me." David himself often acknowledged the same principle of perseverance under similar trials, "Lord, how are they increased that trouble me! Many are those who rise up against me. Many there be, which say of my soul, There is no help for him in God. But You, O Lord, are a shield for me; my glory, and the lifter-up of my head. O God the Lord, the strength of my salvation, You have covered my head in the day of battle."

But have we never taken a devious path in declining from the Lord's testimonies, to escape the appointed cross? Do we never shrink from "the voice of him that reproaches" and blasphemes, by reason of the enemy and the avenger? Can we always in the integrity of our heart appeal to an Omniscient God, "All this is come upon us; yet have we not forgotten

You, neither have we dealt falsely in Your covenant; our heart is not turned back, neither have our steps declined from Your way: though You have sore broken us in the place of dragons, and covered us with the shadow of death?" This profession is not the foolish confidence of boasting; but the fulfillment of the covenant promise, "I will put My fear in their hearts, that they shall not depart from Me." So beautifully does the promise of perseverance connect itself with the duty of persevering! And so clearly in this, as in every other way, does the "wrath of man" ("howbeit he means not so, neither does his heart think so") "praise God." How glorious is the display of the power of His grace in the constancy of His people! like the rocks in the ocean, immoveable amid the fury of the waves; like the trees of the forest, "rooted and established" by every shaking of the tempest! Must not the world, in witnessing the total defeat of their enmity against the Lord's people (or rather its eventual results in their increased prosperity), be constrained to confess to the honor of God, "Surely there is no enchantment against Jacob, neither is there any divination against Israel: according to this time it shall be said of Jacob and of Israel—What has God wrought!"

158. I beheld the transgressors, and was grieved; because they kept not Your word.

We shall not tire in listening to this repeated expression of the Psalmist's tenderness for the honor of God. No trouble from his many persecutors and enemies came so near to his heart, as the sight of the dishonor and contempt of God's word. The glory of God was dearer to him than life. O that every recollection of this tried servant of God might deepen the special mark of acceptance upon our too cold and indifferent hearts! Our joys and sorrows are the pulse of the soul. A fellowship with the joys of angels over repenting sinners will be accompanied with bitterness of godly sorrow over the hardness and impenitency of those, who keep not the word of God.

But even here we need much and earnest prayer, in order to obtain a clear perception of our real principles. Sin is so subtle in its nature and workings that it insinuates itself into our holiest desires, and often so far interweaves itself into the graces of the Spirit, as greatly to mar their beauty, and obstruct their operations. How often is zeal for the honor of God mingled with the unhallowed fire of our own spirit! True zeal is indeed a precious fruit of the Spirit. Its other name is love—active, self-denying, compassionate love for sinners. 'Let me never fancy I have zeal'—said a Christian of a very high order—'until my heart overflows with love to every man living.' If then we are really under its holy influence, we shall lose no opportunity of active exertions on behalf of wretched transgressors: and the limits of our zeal will be only the limits of a fallen world. Especially within our own sphere shall we employ all our labors and pains to stem the tide of unrighteousness, "saying unto the fools—deal not foolishly—How long, you simple ones, will you love simplicity? Turn, turn, why will you die?"

But the fervency of zeal will express itself in something more difficult than personal service. We can often warn and plead with transgressors, when we are sinfully backward in sending up sighs and cries on their behalf; and in presenting these poor lepers by faith to that great and good Physician, whose "power present to heal" has been so abundantly manifested. This is indeed zeal of rare attainment through our own unbelief. But it brings its own rich blessing to the soul; because it is the zeal of the compassionate Jesus; who, though He looked round on sinners with anger, "being grieved for the hardness of their hearts," did not forget to plead on their behalf, "Father, forgive them; for they know not what they do." It was the zeal and love of Him, who so identified His Father's interest with His own, that He endured the reproaches cast upon Him in His bosom. And should not the members feel, when the Head is wounded? Should not we consider every dishonor done to Jesus as a shaft piercing our own bosom? Can we bear to behold all around us united in a conspiracy against the honor, and—if it were possible— against the life, of our dearest friend and benefactor, and not be painfully grieved? Yet genuine grief must begin with our own heart, "all of us mourning, everyone for his iniquity." The wickedness of others will stir up the conviction within our own conscience, "I do remember my faults this day." And when once we begin the enumeration, where shall we end? Who can understand his errors? Cleanse me from secret faults. Enter not into judgment with Your servant."

159. Consider how I love Your precepts; quicken me, O Lord, according to Your loving-kindness.

Love for the precepts, such as this Psalm describes, is a distinguishing characteristic of a child of God. The transgressors neither love the precepts, nor desire quickening grace to keep them. For though "not grievous" in themselves, they are too strict, too humbling for the unrenewed, proud, worldly heart. Love therefore to them—not being the growth of the natural man—must be "a plant which our heavenly Father has planted," a witness of the Spirit of adoption, and the principle of Christian devotedness. And how encouraging is the recollection of the Lord's readiness to consider how we love His precepts! "I know Abraham, that he will command his children and his household after him, and they shall keep the way of the Lord, that the Lord may bring upon Abraham that which He has spoken of him." Thus also did He challenge "the accuser of the brethren," to "consider His servant Job that there is none like him in the earth, a perfect and an upright man, one that fears God, and eschews evil."

But while love of the precepts realizes the full confidence of the Lord's consideration, the consciousness of its imperfection and scanty measure will always prevent us from urging it as the ground of acceptance. Christian! you know not—or at least you allow not—the proud boast, "God, I thank You, that I am not as other men are." No, rather—your constant cry to the end is—Quicken me. Your plea is not merit, but mercy. Not that you deserve to be helped—because you love the precepts: but you desire and trust to be helped—according to Your loving-kindness. And what must be the loving-kindness of a God of infinite love! Only do not sit still, and wait for the breezes of His love. Rather call to the "north wind to awake, and to the south wind to blow," to fill your sails, and urge you on. God—His word, His works, His perfections, His holiness; Jesus—His pity, His love, His grace—is your delight, your chief delight; yet how infinitely is it below the scriptural standard of privilege, attainment, and expectation!

Under the painful influence of straitened desires and heartless affections, how refreshing is it to mark the springs of life flowing from the loving-kindness of the Lord! Yes, indeed—He is the overflowing spring of His church. Every mercy is His grace. Every holy suggestion is His influence. Even the passing thought that our Christian progress proceeds from our own resources, opens the door of fearful departure from God. And yet such is the self-deceitfulness of the heart, that, in the very act of professing to "rejoice in Christ Jesus," the Omniscient eye traces a "confidence in the flesh." The real dependence is on the "mountain that stands strong," not on "the favor that makes" it so. Even our first father, in his original unimpaired strength, could "not quicken his own soul." Can we wonder that the fallen nature, even though

279

partially upheld by Divine power, is changeable and unstable? The most advanced Christian needs the supply to the end, as much as he did in his first stage of infantile weakness. And will he not continue to need it throughout eternity, in every exercise of adoring service, as well as for his active existence?

But when we ask for this quickening, are we expecting, as we ought to be, a large answer to our prayer? Or are we "limiting" our God, by the scanty apprehensions of our poor faith? Remember He is glorified—not in possessing, but in dispensing His gifts. If we really expect His blessing, can we be satisfied without it? It is not our unworthiness, but our unbelief, that stops the current. Would that we gave Him full credit for His exuberant flow of free, rich, ceaseless mercy!

Blessed Jesus! we plead Your promise to be filled. We have life from You; but give it us "more abundantly"—as much as these houses of clay—as much as these earthen vessels—can contain. Our taste of Your love, and our knowledge of its unbounded fullness, encourage our plea to ask You still for more—Quicken us according to Your loving-kindness. Often as the Psalmist had repeated this prayer for quickening grace, it was not a "vain repetition." Each time was it enlivened with faith, feeling of necessity, and ardent affection: and should we, in the consciousness of our weakness and coldness, offer it a hundred times a-day, it would never fail of acceptance.

160. Your word is true from the beginning: and everyone of Your righteous judgments endures forever.

The "loving-kindness and the truth of God" were two heavenly notes, on which "the sweet Psalmist of Israel" loved to dwell—His "loving-kindness" in giving, and His "truth" in fulfilling—His gracious promises. Indeed the displays of His truth—whether to His Church collectively, or to His people individually—have always been every way worthy of Himself. Often has His word seemed on the eve of being falsified, clearly with the design of a brighter and more striking display of its faithfulness. The very night previous to the close of the four hundred and thirty years, Israel was, to all human appearances, as far from deliverance as at any former period. But "the vision was for an appointed time:" nothing could hasten, nothing could delay it; for "it came to pass at the end of the four hundred and thirty years, even the self-same day it came to pass, that all the hosts of the Lord went out from the land of Egypt." At a subsequent period, the family of David appeared upon the point of extinction; and it seemed as if the promise of God would fall to the ground. But to exhibit the word of God, as true from the beginning, a providential, and almost a miraculous, interference was manifested. When Athaliah destroyed all the seed-royal of the house of Judah, Joash was stolen away, put under a nurse, hid in the house of the Lord six years, and in God's appointed time brought forth to the people as the fulfillment of the express promise of God, "Behold! the king's son shall reign, as the Lord had said of the sons of David." "Whoever is wise, and will observe these things, even they shall understand the loving-kindness of the Lord."

And thus have many of His own people been tempted in seasons of despondency to "charge God foolishly." But who of them has not afterwards, in some unexpected deliverance, "set to his seal"—Your word is true from the beginning? "The Lord shall judge His people, and repent Himself for His servants, when He sees that their power is gone, and there is none shut up or left." And how do these recollections put to shame the suggestions of unbelief, and strengthen our confidence in the prospect, or even in the present endurance, of "manifold temptations!"

The full acknowledgment of the truths of God's word is the ground of all our peace and comfort. The believing reception of the testimony opens to us a free access to God. We stand before Him self-condemned, and yet we believe that "there is no condemnation." "The Spirit bears witness" to and "with our spirits," that "this God is our God forever and ever" "unto death," in death, and through eternity. In this simplicity of rest upon the testimony, we go to our God, like Abraham, in sensible helplessness, but in assured confidence, "strong in faith, giving glory to God."

Many, however, have been so used to indulge the pride of their own reasonings, that they scarcely know how to read the Book of God without caviling. If they believe while it is in their hands, they are not prepared to give a reason of their faith. They have ventured into conflict with the enemy with unproved armor, and so have been shaken and troubled. Or perhaps their faith does not reach the whole testimony: and therefore, being partial only it is not genuine. For if we do not give full credence to all, we do not give true credence to any. We do not receive it on the authority of God, but only so far as our reasoning can explain it, or our will may approve it. What need then have we to pray for a teachable simplicity of faith—not asking—'What think you?' but, "How read you?" In this spirit we shall hold our anchor on solid ground; and should we again be "tossed with the tempest," we shall look to Him, who stills the storm, and there shall be "a great calm." Confidence simply built upon the word of God, will endure the storms of earth and hell.

Yet we may loosely believe all, while we practically believe none. The generalities of truth have no influence without an individual application. The summary look of acquiescence will miss all the solid blessings of a reverential and experimental faith. But to find—as the woman of Samaria found—that 'it is all true,'—because it answers to our convictions, our wants, and our feelings to know that the promises are true, because they have been fulfilled in us—this is tasting, feeling, handling—this is indeed blessedness—this makes the word unspeakably precious to us, "a treasure to be desired." To have the witness in ourselves that "we have not followed cunningly devised fables," but that it is "a faithful saying, and worthy of all acceptance, that Christ Jesus came into the world to save sinners"—this is indeed "life from the dead." Oh! how should we seek thus to receive the word "with much assurance!" The Israelites were not satisfied with inquiring respecting the manna, "What is this?" or with discovering that it had descended from heaven; but they gathered it each for himself, and fed upon it as their daily bread. Nor will it be of any avail to us to prove beyond contradiction, and to acknowledge with the fullest assurance, the truth of God's word, unless we thus embrace it, and live upon it as our heavenly portion. Faith alone can give this spiritual apprehension, "He who believes, has the witness in himself." But if the word be the truth of God from the beginning, it must be eternal truth in its character and its results; like its Great Author in every particular—enduring forever. "Forever, O Lord, Your word is settled in heaven; Your faithfulness is unto all generations." Here is the rock of my confidence. How could I rest my hope on any salvation, that did not proceed from the primary, unchangeable, eternal mind? What assurance could I have elsewhere, that the grand plan might not be defeated by some unexpected combination? Whereas every act of reliance in His faithfulness establishes more firmly His title to my confidence, and strengthens the soul into a habit of intelligent, vigorous faith.

Lord! give unto us that "precious faith," which makes the acknowledgment of the truth of Your word from the beginning, and its endurance forever, the spring of continual life and consolation to our souls.

161. Princes have persecuted me without a cause: but my heart stands in awe of Your word.

So contrary are the principles of God and the world! God chastens His people for their sin; the world persecutes them for their godliness. So it has been from the beginning, and will continue to the end. David had before mentioned his persecutors as many. Now he tells us, that they were, like those of David's Lord, the princes of the earth. In both cases, however, was it confessedly without cause. Had it been with cause, it would have been his shame. Now it was his glory. In the former case it would have been his own—here it was his Master's—cross.

His awe of God's word was the gracious restraint to his own spirit. And this godly fear has always marked the people of God. Witness Joseph, Moses, Nehemiah, and the Jews, and the three Babylonish captives. Josiah also obtained a special mark of acceptance. For the man "that trembles at God's word," whether he be found on the throne or on the ash-heap, is the man, "to whom the Lord will look." And certainly where, as with David, the wrath of princes and the wrath of God are weighed against each other; who can doubt, but that it is better to incur the persecution of men by a decided adherence to the word of God, than the wrath of God by declining from it?

Our Savior, "knowing what was in man," had clearly fore-warned and fore-armed His disciples against these difficulties. The trial at the first onset proved too hard for them; Peter's heart stood in awe of the persecuting princes, and in a moment of temptation he disowned his Master: but when "the Spirit of power" was poured from on high, such was the holy awe, in which himself and his brethren stood of God's word, that they declared, in the face of the whole council, "Whether it be right in the sight of God to hearken unto you more than unto God, judge you. We ought to obey God rather than men." 'I fear God,'—Colonel Gardiner used to say—'and I have nothing else to fear.'

Indeed the spirit of adoption—the Christian's distinguishing character and privilege—produces an awe of God; a dread of sinning against the tenderest Father, of grieving the dearest Friend. And this awe of God will naturally extend to His word; so that we shall be more tenderly afraid of disregarding its dictates, than the most faithful subject of breaking the law of his beloved Sovereign. There is nothing slavish or legal in this fear. It is the freedom and the holiness of the Gospel, the very soul of religion; the best preservative of our joys and privileges; and the best evidence of their scriptural character. We shall find, with David, this principle a valuable safeguard against the richest allurements, or the more powerful reproach of men, to go "beyond the word of the Lord to do less or more."

But what must be the state of that heart, where the word of the great God—the Creator and Judge of the earth—commands no reverence! Could the sinner hear a voice from heaven, addressed distinctly to himself, would he dare to reject it? Yet "we have a more sure word, whereunto we do well that we take heed;" that we receive it with silent awe, bow before it with the most unlimited subjection, and yield ourselves entirely to its holy influence. But if it does not stand infinitely higher in our estimation than all—even the best—books of man, we have no just perception of its value, nor can we expect any communication of its treasures to our hearts. The holiness of God is stamped upon its every sentence. Let us then cherish an awe of His word, "receiving it"—not as a common book, "not as the word of men, but as it is in truth, the word of God", in the true spirit of Cornelius and his company, "Now therefore are we all here present before God, to hear all things that are commanded you of God."

162. I rejoice at Your word, as one that finds great spoil.

The awe in which we should stand of God's word, so far from hindering our delight in it, is, as we have just hinted, the most suitable preparation for its most happy enjoyment. In receiving every word of it as the condescending message from Him, before whom angels veil their faces, we shall rejoice at it, as one that finds great spoil. Often had David found great spoil in his many wars; but never had his greatest victories brought him such rich spoil, as he had now discovered in the word of God. The joy in this treasure (like that of the church at the advent of Christ [Isaiah 9:3], described by this figure) evidently implied no common delight. If then the saints of old could so largely enrich their souls from their scanty portion of the word; must not we, who are favored with the entire revelation of God, acknowledge, "The lines are fallen unto us in pleasant places; yes, we have a goodly heritage?"

This expressive image may remind us, that the spoils of this precious word are not to be gained without conflict: Here "the kingdom of heaven suffers violence." Our natural taste and temper revolt from the word. Our indolence indisposes for the necessary habitual effort of prayer, self-denial, and faith. But still "the violent do take the kingdom by force." No pains are lost—no struggle is ineffectual. What great spoil is divided as the fruit of the conflict! What abundant recompense is in reserve for the "good soldier of Jesus Christ," who is determined, in Divine strength, to "endure hardness," until he overcomes the reluctance of his heart for the spiritual duty? It is not a sudden flash, or impression upon the imagination; but the conqueror's joy in spoiling the field of conflict—solid and enriching. Sometimes indeed (as in the Syrian camp, 2 Kings 7:8), we find the spoil unexpectedly. Sometimes we see the treasure long before we can make it our own. And when we gird ourselves to the conflict, paralyzed by the weakness of our spiritual perceptions and the power of unbelief; many a prayer, and many a sigh, is sent up for Divine aid, before we are crowned with victory, and as the fruit of our conquest, joyfully appropriate the word to our present distress.

But from a cursory, superficial reading of the word of God, no such fruit can be anticipated. When therefore the flesh or the world have deadened our delight, and taken from us this great spoil, should we not arm ourselves for repossession of it? Should we be unaffected by our loss? Oh, then, since there are such treasures found and enjoyed in this field of conflict, let us not lose our interest in them by the indulgence of presumption, heartlessness, or despondency. Before we attempt to read, let us cry to the Lord, under the sense of utter helplessness to perform one spiritual act, for His powerful help and Almighty teaching. Then we shall persevere with unconquerable and unwearied vigor, and not fail to share in the blessed spoil of victory, views of a Savior's dying love—an interest in the precious blessings of the cross—great spoil, "unsearchable riches."

163. I hate and abhor lying: but Your law do I love.

We can neither stand in awe of God's word, nor rejoice at it, unless we abhor all contrary ways. And here lies the spiritual conflict. For so opposed are our natural affections to the character and will of God, that we love what God hates, and we hate what God loves. Our new principle and bias, however, as directly falls in with the dictates of God's law, as before we have revolted from it. Lying is now hated and abhorred as contrary to "a God of truth;" and the law is now loved, as the reflection of His image, and the manifestation of His will. David had before prayed to have "lying ways removed from him," and a love for the law of God

285

imparted. His utter detestation shows, that these ways had been removed, and a renewed inclination to the law granted to him.

To have avoided lying, and to have practiced the law, might have been sufficient for the regulation of his outward conduct. But his was the religion of the heart—not meant only to control his actions; but to renew his habits, motions, tempers, and taste. He would not therefore only refrain from lying, or manifest a disinclination to it—he must hate and abhor it as hell itself. Nor was external conformity, or approval of the law, his standard: he must love it. If sin was counted common, fashionable, venial, profitable, or pleasant; if contempt was cast upon the law of God—this stopped him not. Every sin, though only a hair's breadth deviation from the rule, was in his eyes hateful, defiling, damning. He would "resist unto blood, striving against it." Every act, desire, and habit of conformity, with whatever shame it might be attended, was his delight. Such, Christian, should be our standard. Lord! humble us in the daily sense of deviation and defect. Give to us larger desires, growing conformity to Your perfect rule.

Well had it been for Eve and for her children, had she turned from the tempter's lie with this strong determination. But, "You shall not surely die"—has from that fatal moment been a most effectual instrument in captivating unwary souls. So plausible is it in itself, so agreeable to our natural inclinations, that it is readily cherished, even where the first contact with temptation assures the wretched victims, that its "deceit is falsehood." But they do not hate and abhor it: they do not flee from it, as a concern for the honor of God and their own safety would lead them; and therefore justly are they "given up to believe it" as the fruit of their delusion, and the punishment of their unfaithfulness. Oh! if we are ever tempted by the flattery and allurements of the world, let us only mark the opposition of their standard, taste, maxims, and pursuits to the truth of God, and we shall turn away with hatred and abhorrence.

The "overseers of the purchased flock" of Christ—yes, all "who earnestly contend for the faith which was once delivered unto the saints" will anxiously watch any deterioration of doctrine or principle—any deviation from the simplicity of the Gospel, and brand it as a lie. "I have not written unto you"—said the venerable Apostle, "because you know not the truth; but because you know it, and that no lie is of the truth. Who is a liar, but he who denies that Jesus is the Christ?" How does the great Apostle teach us to look at the adulteration of the doctrine of grace before referred to—a system not of faith, but of fear—not of joy, but of slavish awe—not of confidence, but of doubt—palsying the springs of life: withering, blighting, chilling the glow of love; "entangling again the free-born children of God in a yoke of bondage!" The champion of the faith would not tolerate it for a moment. And he bids his people hate and abhor it, even though from an angel's mouth, as the beguiling lie of the great "corrupter" of the church. Equally would he have us abhor the licentious abuse of the gospel flowing from the same source, "Shall we continue in sin, that grace may abound? God forbid!"

After all, however, this verse must include an abhorrence of the literal sin of lying in all its forms. A lie is so gross a sin, that we might be disposed to spiritualize this expression, rather than to analyze some of the plausible shapes, in which the sin may be detected in our own profession. Exaggeration, a false gloss, a slight deviation (hardly perceptible) from the straight line, excuses made to one another, which we dare not make to God, want of accuracy in relating what we hear—all these are forms of lying to be shunned, hated and abhorred by the man, who is really "walking in the light, and having fellowship with God," as much as the more palpable falsehoods, with which the world abounds, which it excuses, and even boasts of.

Believer! would you have your hatred and abhorrence of every kind of lying yet further deepened? Would you summon every passion of the soul, "indignation, vehement desire, zeal, revenge"—against it? Then learn to abhor it, not only as your enemy, but as God's. Pray that the arrow of conviction may be dipped in the blood of Christ; and then, however deep and painful be the wound, it cannot be mortal. Mortal indeed it will be to the sin, but healing to the soul. Pray that your hatred of sin may flow from a sense of reconciliation; for never will it be so perfect, as when you feel yourself sheltered from its everlasting curse. To lie before your Savior as His redeemed sinner, and to wash His feet with your tears of contrition, will be your highest and happiest privilege on this side heaven. In this spirit and daily posture you will most clearly manifest the inseparable connection of hatred of lying ways with a love for the law of God.

164. Seven times a day do I praise You, because of Your righteous judgments.

David had just spoken of his fear, joy, hatred, and love. He now expresses his love in praise. And indeed it is the mixture of praise with prayer, that makes this Psalm so complete an exhibition of Christian experience. Early and late, and habitually throughout the day, have we seen this man of God "give himself to prayer." But his "spirit of supplication," in strict conformity with the Apostolic rule, was ever mingled "with thanksgiving." Indeed, self-love—the sense of want—may prompt us to pray. But love to God is the spirit of praise. The neglect, therefore, of this service is robbing God, no less than ourselves. Not that He needs it, but that He deserves and desires it. Not that it brings any merit to us, but that it strengthens our dependence, and elevates our love. If then we feel it to be "good, lovely, and pleasant," it will be as needless to define its frequency, as to prescribe the limit of our service to a beloved friend, to whom our obligations were daily increasing. The casuistry of love would answer all the entangling scruples of a bondage system. We should aim at living in praise, as the element of our souls, the atmosphere of our enjoyment, our reward more than our duty—that which identifies our interest with heaven, and forms our fitness for it.

Young Christians indeed sometimes unwarily bring themselves into "bondage," in forcing their consciences to a frequency of set times for duty, interfering with present obligations, or pressing unduly upon the weakness of the flesh. Our rule of service, though not measured by our indolence, yet should be accommodated to those legitimate daily engagements, which, when "done as to the Lord," form as real and necessary a part of our religion, as the more spiritual sacrifices of prayer and praise. To observe any particular time (beyond the Sabbath, and the "morning and evening sacrifice") because it is the time—however wearied our spirits may be, or however immediate obligations may interfere—is to forget the weighty instruction of one well qualified to speak, "Bodily exercise profits little." Rather let us "go, and learn what that means—I will have mercy, and not sacrifice." Growth in grace will, however, gradually mold our profession into habitual communion with God. As our views become more solid and settled, each duty of the day will find its proper place, our services will become more free, and our obedience more evangelical.

But the formalist considers seven times a-day—to be an infringement of the sacred canon, "Be not righteous overmuch." He pays his customary service twice a-day; he says his prayers and his praises too; and his conscience slumbers again. And alas! there are times of slumber, when we little differ from him. Oh! let us be alarmed at every symptom of such a state, and "find no rest to our spirit," until we have regained, some measure of this frame of hearty and overflowing praise. If there be a heavenly nature, there must be a heavenly work. Tongue and heart should be set on fire by love. Thus we will go to our work, whatever it may be, and sing at it.

But the Christian sometimes feels, that he has no heart, and—he almost fears—no right to praise. Having no sensible token of love to call him forth, his harp "hangs upon the willows;" nor does he care to take it down, even to "sing one of the Lord's songs in this strange land." But how many have found with Bunyan—'When I believe and sing, my doubting ceases!' "Meat comes out of the eater,"—cheering rays out of the darkest cloud. Endeavor therefore to bring to mind some spiritual, or even temporal, mercies. Or, if recollection fails you, open your Bible; turn to some subject of praise, such as the song of the Angels at the birth of our Savior, or the song of the Redeemed to the honor of the Lamb. Have you no part or interest in it? Do you not need the Savior? Can you be happy without Him? Then inquire, and feel, and try, whether you cannot give "thanks unto God for His unspeakable gift." Perhaps, your notes may rise into praise, and in the excitement of praise, prayer will again mingle itself with its customary enjoyment. It is your sinful folly to yield to that continual depression, which unfits you for the exercise of your duties and your privileges. How fully do our Liturgical services elevate and sustain the ascent of the soul heavenward! Language better adapted for strengthening its feeble aspiration will not readily be found; consecrated as it is in the remembrance of its acceptable use by a throng of the Lord's favored people during successive generations, now united to the general assembly above, and worshiping with everlasting acceptance "before the throne of God and the Lamb."

The Lord's righteous judgments in His word are a constant matter for praise. Such light, food, and comfort! Such a stronghold of God! Such a firm hope to anchor on! Such a clear rule to walk by! Truly the distinguishing favor of this gracious gift stirs up the song, "Praise the Lord." Add to which—the righteous judgments—His decrees and declarations respecting His Church—occupied the Psalmist's "midnight," as well as his daily, song. "O Lord, You are my God"—said the enraptured prophet in the name of the Church, "I will exalt You, I will praise Your name; for You have done wonderful things; Your counsels of old are faithfulness and truth." Inscrutable indeed they may sometimes appear; and opposed to our best prospects of happiness; yet the language of faith in the darkest hour will be, "We know that all things work together for good to them that love God, to them who are the called according to His purpose." But neither seven times a-day, nor "seventy times seven," will satisfy us in heaven. Then our song—even "the song of Moses and the Lamb"—will still be "the Lord's righteous judgments;" and for this ever "new song" the harps of God will never be unstrung, and never out of tune, throughout an eternity of praise. But a moment, and we shall be engaged in this heavenly employ—no reluctancy of the spirit—no weariness of the flesh. Every moment is hastening on this near, this cheering, this overwhelming glorious—prospect. Blessed be God!

165. Great peace have they which love Your law, and nothing shall offend them.

Here is the happiness of a child of God summed up in one word— peace. Looked at with an eye of sense, slighted by the world, and often chastened with "the rod of affliction," he is an object of pity. But look at him with the eye of faith—he loves the law of his God, and his heritage is peace. Every feature of the covenant bears some resemblance to its nature; full of grace, peace, and love. Two of the agents are fitly represented by the lamb and the dove—emblems of peace. The tendency of its principles "is first pure," "then peaceable." Its present enjoyment and privilege is peace—great peace. Its end will be universal, eternal peace.

Christian! have you not discovered the connection of peace with love for the law—the whole revealed will of God? Looking at it as the law of truth—was not its disturbance of your peace of self-satisfaction and self-delusion the first step to the attainment of solid peace? You learned to see yourself as God sees you. Every fresh view humbled you more deeply. Your dissatisfaction exercised you in an anxious and diligent search for true peace. And then, looking at it again as the "law of faith"—here is your ground of peace laid open. Your way to God is clear—your acceptance free—your confidence assured—your communion heavenly. "Being justified by faith, you have peace with God through our Lord Jesus Christ;" yes—you are "filled with peace, all peace in believing." And have you not equal reason to love this law, as a law of obedience? Here is your question answered, "Lord! what will You have me to do?" Let "this word dwell in you richly in all wisdom;" and it will be your daily directory of life and conduct. You will "delight in it after the inner man." Walking in the light of it, you will go on to the full enjoyment of peace. "Taking" cheerfully your Savior's "yoke upon you, and learning of Him, you will" ever "find rest unto your soul." "All His paths are peace."

Professor! what do you lose by your indulged indifference to the law of God? Conscience tells you, that you are a stranger to this peace—this great peace. A secret root of idolatry cankers the principles of peace. Notions will not bring it. Nothing but vital godliness—the love for God's law, "the truth received in the love of it"—will realize the blessing.

Young Christian! be not disheartened, though your love to the law be so weak, interrupted, clouded, that sometimes you fear that you have no love at all. Do you not mourn over its coldness? Do you not desire to love? Seek to know more of the constraining influence of the love of Christ. If your chariot-wheels now, like those of the Egyptians, drive heavily, you will then move, like the chariots in the prophet's vision, "upon wheels and upon wings." At least you are on the way to peace. Stir up the habit of diligent faith; be active—be more earnest in dependence on the Lord. Soon will He visit you with His cheering sunshine, and bless you with His heavenly peace. "The Lord is your shepherd:" and dwelling near the shepherd's tent, "you shall not want." Nothing comes to you without His appointment; and whatever He takes away was only what He had first given, and leaves you nothing but to say, "Blessed be the name of the Lord!" Whatever He lays upon you is infinitely less than you deserve, and with the fatherly design "to do you good at the latter end." Whatever He gives you is peace, great peace, "perfect peace:" and though at best, as to its actual enjoyment, it is only a chequered gift, linked with "this world's tribulation;" yet, as the earnest of that "peace into which the righteous shall enter, when taken away from the evil to come," it is an incalculable blessing.

The steadfastness of our profession is a most important fruit of this blessing—Nothing shall offend them. The daily cross, the humbling doctrine, the fiery trial—which, by offending the professor, detect the unsoundness of his heart—these are the principles of strength and

291

consolation to the faithful lover of God's law. Those "had no root in themselves," who were stumbled by "tribulation or persecution." Hence there was no love in their hearts; consequently no peace in their experience, and no stability in their course. The frequency of such cases in a day of profession is a most painful subject of observation. A course of religion, commenced under the impulse of momentary excitement, is like a "reed shaken by the wind." The first breath of the storm beats down all resolutions, that were not formed upon the conviction of utter helplessness, and in entire dependence upon Divine grace. Light without love ends in fearful ruin. Genuine love to the law alone keeps the soul—a love of no common character—a devoted, persevering attachment. The claim of the law is above every other. Everything—even life itself—if need be—must be sacrificed for it. And when it has been thus embraced on a fair calculation of its cost, from a deep sense of its value, and with a spiritual perception of its character and application to our necessities—there will be no stumbling-block.

Indeed genuine love will prove our safeguard against all grounds of offence. The doctrine of the total depravity of man is objected to: but love to the law of God, molding our minds into its heavenly impression—will remove all ground of offence. The pride of man's wisdom revolts from the doctrine of the cross, and the freeness of the grace of God. But we love it as a part of the law of faith. It suits our case. It answers our need, and therefore here also nothing offends us. Thus, whatever be the hindrance—whether from Satan or himself—whether from the enmity of the world, or the inconsistencies of the church—the believer, while he mourns over these things, is not offended at them, or at the Gospel through them. He has learned a more Scriptural standard, and to exercise a more discriminating judgment. Love to the law of God enables him, instead of being "tossed to and fro" in doubtful perplexity, to "make straight paths for his feet." If his cross be grievous, he seeks from the Lord a quiet spirit; and thus, "in patience possessing his soul," he finds "the yoke easy, and the burden light." His difficulties exercise and strengthen his faith, and add fresh testimony to the faithfulness of the promise. Whether therefore his way be dark or light, his soul is at peace. In the enjoyment of his Savior's love, he has the witness in his own heart, that "the work of righteousness"—of love to the law of his God, "shall be peace; and the effect of righteousness quietness and assurance forever."

166. Lord, I have hoped for Your salvation, and done Your commandments.

The great peace connected with the love of God's law, is at once the fruit of faith, and the motive of obedience. And the enjoyment of it leads the man of God to give renewed expression to his faith and devotedness. "Faith, which works by love," is no less the characteristic of the Old, than of the New Testament, Church. For mark here the principle and the object of faith—I have hoped for Your salvation—and the practical influence of faith—I have done Your commandments. "Walked not believers always in the same spirit? Walked they not in the same steps?"

Faith is the exercise of the soul in a sense of need, in desire, and in trust. Faith goes to God on the ground of the promise; hope in the expectation of the thing promised. Thus hope implies the operation of faith. It appropriates to itself the object of faith. The power to take hold of the promises of faith, and to stay our souls upon their "everlasting consolation," is the energy of "a good hope through grace"—such as "makes not ashamed." Conscious unworthiness may give a trembling feebleness to the hand of faith; but the feeblest apprehension of one of the least of the promises of the gospel assures us of our interest in them all. Why may we not set all the fullness of the covenant before the weakest as well as before the strongest believer, and proclaim to both with equal freedom the triumphant challenge, "Who shall lay anything to the charge of God's elect? Who is he who condemns?" Every believer is alike interested in the gospel of grace. "There is no difference" in the righteousness of the gospel, which is "the righteousness of God"—nor in the imputation of it, which is "unto all and upon all," nor in the subjects—which is them that believe—nor in the means of its application, which in all cases is "by faith of Jesus Christ,"—nor in the need of the blessing, "All have sinned" without difference. All therefore are justified without difference. The only difference regards the strength or weakness of the faith, by which the righteousness is more or less distinctly appropriated, and its consequent blessings enjoyed. No soul, however, can sink into perdition, that grasps the promise of Christ with the hand of faith, be that hand ever so weak and trembling; though if the promise did not hold us more firmly by its unchangeableness, than we hold it by our faith, who could ever attain the blessing?

Not that our interest in the Gospel is transient or uncertain. For though the perception of it may be often interrupted, yet is it not still in the Bible, in the covenant of God, in the heart of God? And is it not constantly renewed in the exercise of faith? The repetition of the same act of faith is therefore equally necessary every successive moment, as at the first moment of our spiritual life. What ever be our standing in the Gospel, faith will always realize to the end the same hope for God's salvation. Indeed the neglect of the cultivation of its habitual exercise materially weakens its operation in great emergencies. Let it then be regarded as the breathing of the soul. Let it be constantly exercised in the daily occasions of need; and we shall enjoy its clear light and active influence upon occasions, where its special energy is required.

Now is not this sometimes your experience? You are distressed by an unsuccessful struggle with wandering, defiling imaginations. You know the promise, and the remedy. But "the shield of faith" has been laid by. You have therefore to seek it, when you want it at hand for the present moment; and thus you lie powerless, at a distance from the cure, instead of being able to bring your sin at once to Jesus—'Lord, this is my trouble; this is the "plague of my heart;" "but speak the word only, and Your servant shall be healed.'" Thus the indolent neglect of the quickening principle greatly impairs its powerful energy, and the "confidence and rejoicing of hope" flowing from it. If "the life in the flesh is" not "a life of faith on the Son of God," no solid rest or acceptance can be known.

But on what ground is this hope for the Lord's salvation built? On His faithfulness, not on our sincerity; on His promises, not on our frames; on His unchangeableness, not on our constancy. It is built, not on the work of grace in us, but on the work of Christ for us; a work which has satisfied every claim, provided every security, and pledged all the Divine perfections on our behalf; a work so finished and complete, that all the difficulties of salvation on the part of God are removed; and the sinner, finding no hindrance in the way but himself, is warranted, though covered with guilt and defilement, to apply for full, immediate, and unconditional forgiveness. What then hinders the instant reception of the privilege, but disbelief of the record? It is this which dares to "make God a liar;" which therefore must not, as is too often the case, be lamented as an infirmity (except indeed in cases of constitutional weakness); but watched, prayed against, and resisted, as a deep and aggravated sin. The present enjoyment of the blessing is indeed often marred by looking at the fruits of faith (contrition, love, diligence, &c.) as prerequisites for believing, instead of looking to the object of faith, to put away our sin, and to produce these fruits in us. This not only binds our sin upon us, but robs God of His honor;—and, while it restrains His blessing on our souls, reflects upon His wisdom and grace, who has laid the foundation of a sinner's hope on His own dear Son, irrespective of any warrant of faith in himself. We want to be enlivened with sensible comfort, as a ground for our believing in Christ; or, if we look for it from faith, it is from faith as an act (in which respect it is no more a proper ground for comfort than any other grace,) instead of looking for it from the object of faith. Thus we not only lose the peace and joy we are seeking, but we lose it by our mistaken way of seeking it.

The fullness of Christ, and the promises of God in Him, are the only basis of a full assurance of salvation: and this basis is equally firm at all times, and under all circumstances. "You are complete in Him." Your title at this moment is as perfect, your interest as secure, as ever it will be at the day of "the redemption of the purchased possession." Awakened sinner! let not then a sense of unworthiness paralyze your faith. As a guilty sinner, you are invited. As a willing sinner, you are welcome. As a believing sinner, you are assured. Why hesitate then to "lay hold on eternal life?" Is it presumption in the drowning man to attempt to swim to the rock of safety? Why then should not the sinking soul cast itself upon the "Rock of Ages?" Lord, I have hoped for Your salvation.

Believer! "Behold!" says your Lord, "I come quickly; hold that fast which You have, that no man take your crown." "Hold fast your confidence and the rejoicing of your hope." This is of no trifling importance. An established confidence ought to result from, and to witness to, your interest in the Lord's salvation. For without it, you have no relief from the spirit of bondage; no enlargement in duties; no enjoyment of privileges; no "growth in grace, and in the knowledge of the Savior;" no honored usefulness in the Church of God. "The things which remain will be ready to die." Rest not, then, satisfied with an occasional gleam of light and joy, while your horizon is overcast with doubts and fears. Waste not time in heartless complaints, that would be far better employed in a vigorous habit of faith. Live above frames and feelings, upon this glorious truth—'Christ has undertaken for me.' He lives, and reigns, and pleads for every sinner that trusts in Him. Exercise your dependence upon Him in importunate and persevering supplication. "Give all diligence"—at all times—in all ways, private and public, "instant in season and out of season." Thus "an entrance into" the joy, peace, and glory of "the everlasting kingdom of our Lord and Savior, will be richly ministered unto you." You shall be released from the prison-house of despondency, and shall breathe the free atmosphere of adoption and heavenly love.

But remember, that this "assurance of hope," even in its weakest and lowest influence, is a practical principle—I have done Your commandments. "Every man that has this hope in Him purifies himself, even as He is pure." All obedience that springs not from this source is of a low and legal character; the fruit of self-will, self-righteousness, self-sufficiency. Evangelical obedience can only flow from Evangelical faith and hope. Love to Christ catches fire from the perception of His love to us. Without this perception, all is weariness, toil, and travail of soul in His service; duty, not privilege; constraint, not delight; conscience, not love. Hence the most assured believers will be the most devoted servants of their Master. "The joy of the Lord" "the joy of faith," of acceptance, of communion, "is their strength." They live by faith; and as they believe, they love; they deny themselves; they lay themselves out for their Master's work; they conquer all that opposes their progress.

We cannot, therefore, do His commandments without a hope for His salvation. For only in proportion as we have assured our title to the promises of the Gospel, can we take hold of them, plead them, or experience their support. When therefore our hope is indistinct, we are almost left to our own unassisted resources; and our course will probably end in "perpetual backsliding." Active devotedness flows from assured acceptance. Where there is no certainty, there can be little love, little delight, little diligence. Let us walk in sunshine, and we shall work cheerfully and honorably for God.

Keep then the eye fixed on Christ as the ground, and on obedience as the evidence, of our hope. Thus will our own confidence be more established; and others, beholding in us the power of our Christian hope, will be led to say, "We will go with you, for we have heard that God is with you."

167. My soul has kept Your testimonies; and I love them exceedingly.
168. I have kept Your precepts and Your testimonies: for all my
ways are before You.

Those only who have hoped in the Lord's salvation can express this
joyful delight in His precepts. The Christian does not acknowledge the
popular separation of duty and privilege, according as it may be
constraint or indulgence to his inclination. Every part of his walk
identifies these terms of distinction. If it is his duty, it is no less his
privilege, to love the precepts. Nothing holds him to them—nothing
enables him thoroughly to keep them, but love. All resolutions, vows,
covenants, would be as ineffectual to bind him, as the green withs to
fasten the giant. David had not done the commandments from constraint;
but his soul kept them; yes, he loved them exceedingly. Indeed, the bias
of the new nature to keep the precepts is as prevalent, as that of the old
nature to break them. Once the believer would have wished the law of
God blotted out of the universe, or at least exchanged for a more
indulgent dispensation. But now that it is written in his heart, even its
restraint is delightful to him; and as he gains a closer intimacy with it,
and a clearer discernment of its spirituality, he loves it exceedingly. Not
one, indeed, of the precepts or testimonies does he keep as he ought, and
as he desires; but there is not one of them that he does not delight in, and
most anxiously desire to fulfill. Thus every feature of the Divine image is
inwrought in the soul, beautiful in its place and proportion; and all other
graces grow in connection with love to the testimonies.

Nor let our consciousness of daily failures restrain this strong
expression of confidence. The most humble believer need not hesitate to
adopt it 'as an evidence of grace, not as a claim of merit.' This frequent
repetition marks the godly jealousy of the man of God, mindful of his
own self-deceitfulness and manifold infirmities, and "giving" careful
"diligence to make his calling and election sure." David knew himself to
be a poor sinner; but he was conscious of spirituality of obedience,
exceeding love to the word, and an habitual walk under the eye of his
God—the evidences of a heart (often mentioned in the Old Testament)
"perfect with Him." 'Christ alone kept the old law, and He enables us to
observe the new.'

The active love to the word should be cultivated on the principle of
our public walk before God. We must not study the Scripture merely for
our present gratification, or to furnish materials for our Christian

communion. We ought rather, from every step in the history of Christ, as well as from the more finished course of instruction in the Epistles, to be gathering some help to "set the Lord always before us"—realizing the interest that He takes in us, and His presence with us as our Father, Governor, Teacher, Comforter, Friend.

Now, let us ask—Do our souls thus keep the Lord's testimonies habitually, perseveringly? Does conscience testify that, with all our defects and sinful mixture, they are uppermost in our minds; that our love rises above the worldly rules of expediency, prudence, or the example of those around us (the too common measurement of scanty obedience)—as if it could never burn with sufficient fervor in His service, "who loved us, and gave Himself for us?" Why, then, should we shrink from this acknowledgment of "simplicity and godly sincerity?" If we are ready to own, that "without Christ we can do nothing;" that His Spirit "has wrought all our works in us;" that "by the grace of God we are what we are;" that our hope of acceptance is grounded only upon the finished work on the cross—why should we refuse to confess the grace of God in us? Yet we must not forget, that allowed unfaithfulness, neglect of secret prayer, impurity of motive, or any "iniquity regarded in the heart"—though they will not loosen the ground of our hope—will obscure the comfort of our Christian confidence. How beautiful is that princely spirit, which will not serve the Lord "of that which costs us nothing;" that not only longs for holiness as the way to heaven, but loves heaven the better for the holy way that leads to it, and for the perfect holiness that reigns there eternally!

But never let us lose sight of the recollection, that all our ways are before God! that every act, every thought, every desire, every word, is registered by conscience as His viceregent, and laid up in His book of remembrance! Well would it be for us, if we walked less before men, and more before God; if in secret, in business, at home and abroad, we heard the solemn voice, "I am the Almighty God: walk before Me, and be perfect." We may be unreprovable in the sight of men, while it is a mere artificial walk, grounded upon base external principles—a "walking after the flesh"—not before God. Even the engagements of active duty may be the subtle snare of the great enemy to divert us from intense personal religion, and to spoil the hidden walk of communion with God, by concentrating the mind upon a more public, and, apparently, a more useful walk. Thus too often the vital principle of religion sinks into a stated formal habit. "Walking with God" is the secret spring of the

Christian. "Walking before God" is the manifestation and the exercise of the hidden principle. For in all things, private as well as public, the most trivial as well as the most weighty, to have our eye fixed in dutiful reverence upon the Omniscient, Omnipresent eye of Jehovah—what solemnity would it give to our whole behavior! what influence would it have upon our public professions, our general conversation, our secret duties! We should be energetic in "serving our own generation by the will of God;" and yet, while walking before men, should be truly "walking before God"—all our ways before Him, "done" in His sight, "as to Him," and accepted in His favor.

When, therefore, I am about to venture upon any line of conduct, let me consider the watchful eye, that pierces into the deepest recesses of my thoughts, and brings, as it were, to daylight, my principles, my motives, and my ends. Above all, let me ever recollect, that he, before whom are all my ways, is He who hung upon the cross for my sins. Let me then walk, as if He were standing before me in all the endearing obligations of His love. Oh, do not I owe Him sacrifice for sacrifice, heart for heart, life for life? Then surely I cannot be dead, insensible, sluggish in keeping His precepts. I cannot forbear to show this practical proof of my love to Him. Let not, then, the fear of legality make me neglect this privilege of "keeping the commandments" of my beloved Master and Lord. Let me live under the solemn recollection, "You, God, see me;" and in the joyful assurance, "You, God, love me;" and His ways will be to me holiness, happiness, heaven.

169. Let my cry come near before You, O Lord; give me understanding, according to Your word. 170. Let my supplication come before You: deliver me according to Your word.

We mark David here, where he always loved to be, a supplicant at the throne of grace. Many had been his cries and supplications. His petition now is—that they may come near before his Lord. Oh, that our wants of every moment were felt with the same pressure, and carried to the Lord with the same faith, earnestness, humility, and perseverance! Richness of expression, and fluency of utterance, are the mere shell and shadow of prayer. The life of prayer is the cry of the heart to God. The eloquence of prayer is its earnestness. The power of prayer is that, which comes not from education, or from the natural desire of the man; but that "which is from above" "the spirit of supplication" "the spirit of adoption." The

299

urgency of present need calls for instant prayer. The soul is at stake; the enemy is within the walls, perhaps within the citadel. Oh, what a privilege to know, that we have a "strong habitation, whereunto we may continually resort;" to be able to remind the Lord, "You have given commandment to save me: for You are my rock and my fortress!"

But then we must see that our cry comes before—comes near before—the Lord; that nothing blocks up the way, or interrupts the communication. If we are believers, the way is open: "the middle wall of partition is broken down." Oh, let us be excited to greater nearness of communion, "Having boldness to enter into the holiest by the blood of Jesus, by a new and living way, which He has consecrated for us, through the veil, that is to say, His flesh," why should we be backward to come? Had we not seen the way marked by this blood of sprinkling, we should (if we have had any sight into our own hearts) no more have dared to take one step into the awful presence of God, than to rush into the devouring flame. If in a moment of extremity, we had felt that we must pray or perish, we should have had no boldness to open our mouth before God, much less to expect that our supplication would come near before Him, had we not been "made near by the blood of Christ." But what an amount of privilege is it, that this way to God is always open; that, as members of Christ, we stand in the sight of God as pure as Christ is pure; that we have not only "access," but "access with confidence;"— yes, with the same confidence as the Son of God Himself! For the Father is never weary of delighting in His dear Son, or in those who are one with Him. If He, therefore, takes our names into the holy place; if He offer sacrifice and incense for us, and sprinkle us with His blood, we "are complete in him" "in Him," therefore, let us "glory." "Having an High-priest over the house of God; let us draw near with a true heart, in full assurance of faith."

But where we feel as if we did not, could not, reach the throne of grace, "is there not a cause?" Our distance from God must be traced to a deeper origin than the dullness and insensibility of our hearts. The real difficulty of prayer, and indeed the actual inability to pray, arises in many, and probably in most, cases, from an indistinct perception of the way of access. We must admit this, not only in those who are totally ignorant of Christ, but also in the cases of weak, unestablished, or negligent Christians. Through ignorance of the fullness and freeness of the gospel in the one, and indulgence of sin or secret unwatchfulness in the other, the way of access (only perceptible by the eye of faith) becomes obscured, the desire faint, the spiritual strength weakened. And instead of the acknowledgment, "The Lord has heard the voice of my supplications," we have the mournful complaints, "My soul cleaves to the dust—oh, that I were as in months past!" It must be so; for prayer without faith is a heartless ceremony in the spirit of bondage. That which gives to it life and acceptance is the believing apprehension of Christ. The ignorant and self-righteous may find it a matter of course (as easy as it is fruitless) to bow their knee in the form of prayer. But the light that darts in upon the awakened conscience reveals something hitherto unknown of God and of themselves, and shows the ground of confidence, for a self-condemned sinner, to be a matter of the deepest mystery, and most amazing difficulty. Such a confidence, however, God has laid open to us. We cannot honor Him more than by making use of it. All that come in the name of Jesus are welcome. Why, then, penitent sinner, should not you be welcome? The throne of grace was raised for sinners such as you. You cannot want larger promises or a better plea. You come, not because you are worthy, but because you are bid, to come. Take the command and lay it upon your conscience. Christ is your only way to God. Faith is the act and exercise of coming to Christ. Faith, therefore, will bring you to God, if you have not hitherto come; or restore you to God, if you have wandered from Him.

But there may be a secret departure from God even in the engagement of active service, or in the exercises of social religion. For if these duties are substituted for secret communion with God, "the things that remain in us will be ready to die;" ordinances will fail to enrich; Christian fellowship will bring no refreshment; and the soul, while blessed with the abundance of means of grace, "in the fullness of its sufficiency will be in straits." Indeed, if our affections and feelings are moved in social exercises, and are cold and insensible when we are alone with God, it is a bad symptom of our state. What, then, do we know of the comforts of the closet? Do we pray, because we love to pray, or only because our consciences constrain us to the duty? Does the Lord mark those secret transactions with Himself, that manifest our hearts to be really drawn to Him? Is it any pressing business of our soul's salvation that brings us to God? Are our services enlivened with spiritual manifestations of Christ? It is possible long to continue in the outward course of duty: and yet not one of our prayers to come near before the Lord. We have not come in the appointed way; and, therefore, we have not really come at all. Or if the name of Christ has been affixed to our prayers, it has been as a component part of a formal system, not as an exercise of dependence in seeking acceptance with God.

But it may be, that we have backslidden from God, in a habit of indulged coldness or willful iniquity. Now if we would expect "the candle of the Lord again to shine upon our heads, and His secret to be upon our tabernacle," we must rest satisfied with nothing short of the full restoration of our privileges. We must return to the Lord with deepened contrition in His appointed way, and wait for Him to look upon us, and once more to let our supplication come near before Him. He had "gone, and returned to His place, until we acknowledged our offence, and sought His face;" and He is now sitting on a "throne of grace, waiting that He may be gracious." Again and again, therefore, let us fall down at His feet, and never cease to pray, until we feel that our cry and supplication come near before Him, and spiritual understanding of our case, and deliverance from our danger, are given. As a God of wisdom and yearning mercy, we may trust Him to "perform all things for us." Let Him then judge for the time and means of our deliverance. Only let it be according to His own word of faithfulness, and we "shall yet praise Him."

It is beautiful to observe the oil of the Psalmist's faith feeding the flame of his supplication. Every petition is urged upon the warrant of a promise—according to Your word. The promises were the very breath of his supplication; exciting his expectation for a favorable answer, and exercising his patience, until the answer should come. Though in possession of so comparatively small a portion of the blessed book, he seemed always to find a word for the present occasion; always able to show to his God His own hand and seal. Alas! sometimes, with the whole word of God before us, we are at a loss to appropriate one of its innumerable promises to the present emergency. Yet with all our contracted views of the covenant, still our interest in it is not denied. Such is the condescension of our tender Father, that He accepts even the stammering language of faith in His children! The cry "Abba, Father"— 'though' (as Luther sweetly expresses it) 'it is but a cry; yet it does so pierce the clouds, that there is nothing else heard in heaven of God and His angels.' And how delightful is the thought that God's elect—as they will shortly be gathered a countless multitude around the heavenly throne—so do they now hold spiritual communion with each other, while "they cry day and night" before their Father's throne of grace! True it is—we understand not one another's tongues. Yet does our loving Father understand us all. Nor do our different dialects cause any confusion in heaven—rather do they unite, and form one cloud of incense, ascending with continual acceptance and delight in His presence. Ineffable is the delight, with which our Beloved enjoys that communion with His people, "which He purchased with His own blood" "O my dove, that are in the clefts of the rocks, in the secret places of the stairs, let me see your countenance, let me hear your voice; for sweet is your voice, and your countenance is lovely."

171. My lips shall utter praise, when You have taught me Your statutes.

How happy is it to bring to God a heart as large in praise as in prayer! The answer of the supplication for spiritual understanding and deliverance naturally issues in the sacrifice of praise. Guilt had sealed David's lips; while living in sin, and restrained alike the utterance of praise and prayer. But when awakened to a sense of his sin, how earnest were his cries!, "Restore to me the joy of Your salvation. O Lord, open my lips; and my mouth shall show forth Your praise." And if guilt or unbelief has made us dumb, his petitions will tune our hearts to the "songs of Zion." When the Lord has taught us in His statutes the revelation of Himself, as having given His dear Son for us and to us, "the tongue of the dumb is made to sing." "Thanks be to God for His unspeakable gift!"

And do I not remember "the time of love," when I first knew myself to be "a brand plucked out of the fire"—a redeemed sinner—a pardoned rebel—destined for a seat on the throne of God—indulged with a taste, and assured of the completion, of heavenly bliss? This was a work worthy of God—a work, which none but God could have wrought. What mercy is this! Everlasting! Unchangeable! Let me cast myself daily upon it; yes, let me bury myself in it! What gratitude is demanded! My lips shall utter praise, now that He has taught me His statutes. "O Lord, I will praise You; though You were angry with me, Your anger is turned away, and You comfort me."

Again—I seemed to have sunk beyond all help. No means, no ministers, no providences, could reach my extremity. All were "physicians of no value," tried and tried again: but tried in vain. But "in weakness" thoroughly felt, "strength was made perfect." The threatening clouds were dispersed; the breaches were healed; the veil of unbelief was rent. "The right hand of the Lord has brought mighty things to pass." "He has both spoken unto me, and Himself has done it," and it is "marvelous in our eyes." Let my stammering lips utter praise. What a display of power! It is the spark preserved in the ocean unquenched, the drop in the flames unconsumed; the feather in the storm unshaken. "Who is a God like unto You? Not unto us, O Lord, not unto us; but unto Your name give glory."

And again—I was perplexed in a dark and bewildered path. Every dispensation appeared to frown upon me. One dark hour had blotted out all the recollections of my former comforts; and it was as if I never could, never should, rejoice again. But little did I think how the Lord was "abounding towards me in all wisdom and prudence"—how His arrows were sharpened with love—how He was "humbling me, and proving me, to know what was in my heart" and in the moment of chastening was speaking to me, "I know the thoughts that I think towards you, thoughts of peace, and not of evil, to give you an expected end." What a display of "wisdom!" My lips shall utter praise; for if I "should hold my peace, the stones would immediately cry out."

The thought of what I was before my conversion—what I have been since—what I am now, overwhelms me with shame and with praise. "Lord, how is it that You should have manifested Yourself to me, as You have not unto the world?" "Who am I, O Lord God, that You have brought me hitherto?" And how much more "that You have spoken of Your servant for a great while to come!" For You have prepared for me a happy eternity in Your unclouded presence. Should not then my praise be bubbling up, as from a fountain—pouring forth, as from a rich treasure-house? Should not my instrument, if not always employed, be always kept in tune? Forward we may be in prayer. But how backward we are in praise! Self-love may constrain the one. Only the love of God will quicken the other. And yet ought we not to be more touched in receiving mercies, than we were in asking for them? In the one case we only knew them by testimony or report. In the other we know them by our own experience. We hear of one, who had much forgiven, and who "loved much." And surely the more sin pardoned—the more mercies received—does not God justly expect of us more love in the heart—more utterance of praise from the lips?

And yet who of us are fit to praise, except those whom God has taught? The "new song" ill accords with the old heart. God vouchsafes His grace for the praise of His grace. Ought not we then to glory in our Savior—a privilege as high as to enjoy Him—no—the very means of increasing our enjoyment of Him, in the active excitement of our love, and every grace for His sake? Let not the enemy rob me, as too often he has done, of my high privilege. Let me prize secret prayer. Let me be separated from an ensnaring world. Let me dread separation from my God; and if ever estranged from Him, let me never rest, until, by "receiving the atonement," always presented and accepted on my behalf, I once more walk in the light of His countenance. Let me then fix the eye of my faith, weak and dim as it may be, constantly upon Jesus. He must do all for me, in me, by me; He must teach me more and more of the statutes of my God, that my heart may be delightfully engaged with my lips in uttering His praise.

172. My tongue shall speak of Your word; for all Your commandments are righteousness.

To speak of God and for Him, will be the desire and delight of him, whose heart and lips have been taught to utter praise. Yet alas! how seldom is "our conversation seasoned with grace!" So much of this poor world's nothing! So little of Jesus! 'If only five minutes can be redeemed for prayer, for Scripture, or for thought; let it be seized as an inestimable jewel. If we can pass five minutes less in foolish or ensnaring company, secure the advantage.' If vain words are flowing up from the bottom, look on the restraint that represses them from our lips as a triumphant mercy. This active energy of Christian discipline will communicate a fragrance to our conversation, most acceptable to our beloved Lord; and will make our "lips" enriching, feeding, and instructive to His church. And truly when we see how hardly men judge of Him, how they count His "commandments grievous," and His ways "unequal," it will be delightful to bear our testimony, that all His commandments are righteousness; restraining the power of sin, and conforming the soul to His image.

"Lord, open my lips, that my tongue may speak of Your word." Honor me, O my God, by helping me to show, that all Your commandments are righteousness. In our own atmosphere, and our own spirit, how often do we pour out our words without waiting on the Lord for unction and power; speaking of the things of God without His presence and blessing! Were we living fully in the atmosphere and breathing of prayer, enriched with habitual meditation in the word; how much more fluent would our tongue be to speak of His word "to the use of edifying!" It would be made really our own, known experimentally;

and then how cheering, how enlivening the conversation of the man of God! His "light so shines before men, that" they are constrained to "glorify His Father which is in heaven."

Perhaps, Believer, supposed inability, natural bashfulness, or want of seasonable opportunity, may restrain your lips. But under the most unfavorable circumstances something may generally be said or done in the service of God. And while it is well carefully to watch against the "talk of the lips, which tends only to poverty;" beware, lest, through the scrupulous tenderness of conscience, "Satan get advantage" to shut the mouth of the faithful witnesses of God, and thus to weaken that cause, which it is your first desire to support. Guard then against the influence of unbelief. Bring your weakness and inability daily to the Lord. Let any dreaded inconsistency of profession be searched out, examined, and lamented before Him, and opposed in dependence on His grace; but never let it be made a covering for indolence, or supply fuel for despondency. Consider how your interest in a Divine Savior makes your way open to bring all your wants to Him. Be encouraged therefore to ask for the Spirit of God to guide your lips: that a poor weak sinner may be permitted to "show forth the praises of Him," who is surrounded with all the Hosts of Heaven.

When however our silence has arisen from the too feeble resistance of our natural carelessness and indolence, the recollection of many important opportunities of glorifying our Savior, lost beyond recall, may well excite the prayer, "Deliver me from blood-guiltiness, O God; and my tongue shall sing aloud of Your righteousness." Oh! to have the preciousness of souls deeply impressed upon our hearts! Oh! for that compassionate love, that would never suffer us to meet a fellow-sinner without lifting up our hearts to God on his behalf: without making an effort to win his soul to Christ, and manifesting an earnest desire for his salvation! What loss is there to our own souls in these neglected opportunities of blessing the souls of others! For never do we receive richer fruit to ourselves, than in the act or endeavor to communicate to others. The heart becomes enlarged by every practical exercise of Christian love. Yet much simplicity, much unction from above, much tenderness of heart, much wisdom combined with boldness—is needed in our daily conversation, that we may "make manifest the savor of the knowledge of Christ in every place;" and especially, that our very desires to bring sinners to the Gospel may proceed, not from a goading conscience, much less from pride and vainglory; but from the pure source of love to Christ and to our fellow-sinners. For even if we are as "full of matter" as Elihu was, nothing will be said for God—nothing, that will "minister grace to the hearers," unless the influence of the Divine Spirit fills our hearts, as "a well of water, springing up into everlasting life"—a blessing to all around us.

173. Let Your hand help me: for I have chosen Your precepts.

David, having engaged himself to a bold profession of his God, now comes to seek His needful supply of help. Let Your hand help me. And if we may "come to the throne of grace," that we may find "grace to help in time of need," when should we not come? For is not every moment a "time of need," such as may quicken us to flee to the "strong tower," where "the righteous runs, and is safe?" Besieged without; betrayed within; "wrestling against flesh and blood," and yet "not against flesh and blood" only: disputing every inch of ground, yet often discouraged by the little ground we seem to gain; surely we need all the help of Omnipotence to sustain us in the tremendous conflict. We may plead our choice of His precepts, in looking for His help. David had before "taken the testimonies of God as his heritage"—including all the precious promises of the Gospel, extending to every necessity of time, and to every prospect of eternity. He now confesses his obligation, in choosing the precepts—a happy choice, the influence of the Spirit upon his heart.

This choice is the distinctive mark of the Lord's people—the exercise of a well-instructed and deliberate judgment; prompt obedience in the simplicity of faith. It is the choice of all the precepts—no other than the voluntary acknowledgment of our Baptismal obligations. Many carnal suggestions offer themselves the moment that the purpose is forming into the choice. "The things that were gain to us," and which now must be "counted loss for Christ," (should we allow their weight in the balance at this crisis) will bring much hesitation and perplexity. Conferences "with flesh and blood" are most subtle hindrances to Christian determination. 'What will the world say? If I go too far, I shall give offence; I shall lose all my influence, and blast all my prospects of eventual benefit to those around me.' The apprehension also of losing the affection and of incurring the displeasure of those whom my heart holds dear, is most fearful. And then this sacrifice is too costly to make; that pleasure too hard to resign. Such thoughts—the injections of the tempter—are ever at the door; and even when effectual resistance is offered, the struggle is most severe. But it is such a mighty help in this conflict, when one desire has taken sole possession of the heart, "Lord, what will You have me to do?"—when we are so crucified to worldly influence, whether of pleasure, profit, fear, or esteem, as to be ready to act upon the resolution, "Therefore henceforth know we no man after the flesh." Now the heavenly beauty of the religion of the gospel breaks in upon us.

Experience of our own weakness, and of the great power of the world, is gradually preparing us for victory over it. We shall then most specially find our happiness in losing our own will; and our Master's cross will be a delightful burden; like wings to a bird, or sails to a ship; assisting, instead of retarding, our course. The more we trust to His help and guidance in everything, the more we shall be able to do, and the more delightful will His service be to us.

The lack of a determined choice is the secret of the halting profession that prevails among us. A compromise is attempted with the world. "The offence of the cross" begins to "cease." A middle path of serious religion is marked out, divested of what is called needless offensiveness. But the religion that pleases the world will never be acceptable with God; nor can the religion that pleases God, be ever accommodated to the inclination of the world. Oh! we shall do well to consider, whether the way of the Lord's precepts may not be found too hard, too strait, too unfrequented; whether we are prepared to brave the pointed finger and whispered scoff of the ungodly, and perhaps the mistaken opposition of beloved friends. Often has the profession of Christ been hastily taken up and relinquished. He who wishes to abide by it, must daily learn this lesson, "Without Me you can do nothing:" and in conscious helplessness, he will often breathe the cry—Let Your hand help me.

Nor is this petition needful only in the first determination of this choice. In the growing and more decided conviction of its superior happiness, and in the daily endeavor to live in it, we shall find increasing need for the same acknowledgment of helplessness, and the same cry for support. Dependence is a principle of deep humility and mighty energy. The thought that we are entering upon the work in the Lord's strength is a great stay. Blessed indeed is that helplessness, that makes us lie in the bosom of our Savior, supported and cherished! Blessed be God for the "help laid" for us "upon one that is mighty;" so that our insufficiency and all-sufficiency are visible at one glance: and "when we are" most "weak, then are we" most "strong!" "Those who war against you shall be as nothing, and as a thing of nothing. For I the Lord your God will hold your right hand, saying unto you, Fear not, I will help you."

174. I have longed for Your salvation, O Lord; and Your law is my delight.

Before we close this Psalm, let us dwell once more upon this word—salvation. Common as is its use, to the believer it has a constant freshness and an infinite meaning. Do we wonder at his longing for it? Look at its fullness—including all the mercy of the everlasting covenant. Look at its ground—that work of Calvary's cross once "finished," and leaving nothing to be filled up or improved; standing out in all its glorious completeness; constraining the admiration—and encouraging the confidence, of the chief of sinners; but wholly disclaiming all assistance from the most eminent saint. Look at its simplicity—not keeping the sinner aloof from the Savior, not hedging up or bewildering the open freeness of his path, but bringing to him immediate peace and joy in resting upon the great atonement of the gospel. Mark its unchangeableness—independent of and above all frames and feelings, so that, while "walking in darkness" we can "stay upon our God," expecting salvation even from the hand that seems ready for our destruction; leaving it to our heavenly Father to frown or to smile, to change as He pleases from the one to the other; and looking at every aspect of His countenance, as only a different arrangement of the same features of ineffable paternity; and the different, suitable, and seasonable expression of unchangeable covenant love.

Is not this an object for the longing of the soul, that feels its own pressing wants, and sees in this salvation an instant and full supply? This longing marks the character of evangelical religion—not merely duty, but delight. The mind wearies in the continued exertion for duty; but it readily falls in with delight. Duties become privileges, when Christ is their source and life. Thus every step of progress is progress in happiness. The world's all to the believer is really nothing. It presents nothing to feed the appetite, or quench the thirst, of an immortal soul. Indeed the creatures were commissioned to withhold consolation, until every desire was concentrated in the single object. "You, O God, are the thing that I long for;" until the sinner has found rest in the answer to his prayer, "Say unto my soul, I am Your salvation." And now he enjoys his earthly comforts, "as not abusing them," because he loves them as God would have them loved, and longs for His salvation above them all. This is true religion; when the Lord of all occupies that place in the heart, which He fills in the universe—There He is "All in all." Here the believer cries, "Whom have I in heaven but You? and there is none upon earth that I desire beside You." Oh, what a privilege is it to have Him in heart, in thought, and in view; to be rejoicing in His presence; and to be longing for a more full conformity to His image, and for a more lively enjoyment of His love! If this be but earth, what must heaven be! This longing is a satisfactory evidence of the work of God. It exercises the soul in habitual contemplation of the Savior, in nearer communion with Him, and supreme delight in His law. Such desires will be unutterably increased, and infinitely satisfied in the 'fruition of His glorious Godhead.'

But the Lord often brings this charge against His professing people, "You have left your first love." The principle is not dead, but the energy is decayed. Human nature is prone to apostasy. Slumber unconsciously steals upon the soul. Faith is not in habitual exercise. The attraction of the Savior is not felt. His love is not meditated upon. The soul is satisfied with former affections to Him. There is little heart to labor for Him. The means of communion with Him are slighted. The heart naturally becomes cold in spiritual desires, and warm in worldly pursuits and too often without any smitings of conscience for divided love.

Some professors indeed consider this declension of affections to be a matter of course. The young convert is supposed to abound most in love, and, as he advances, his fervor gradually subsides into matured judgment. Those indeed, who "have no root in themselves," lose their lively affections, and their religion with them. But surely the real principle of love cannot decay; that is, our esteem of God cannot be lowered: our longing for His salvation cannot languish; our delight in its enjoyment cannot diminish, without guilt and loss to our souls, He claims our love, and it is most unreasonable to deny Him His own. He is the same, as when we first loved Him. Then we thought Him worthy of our highest love. Do we now repent of having loved Him so much? Have we found Him less than our expectations? Can we bestow our heart elsewhere with stricter justice, or to better advantage? Do not all the grounds of our love to Him continue in full force? Have they not rather increased every day and hour? What would an indulgent husband think of incessant and increasing attentions repaid with diminished affection? Oh! let us be ashamed of our indolence, and "remember" the times when our longings for His salvation were more intense; when our communion with Him was more heavenly; when we were ready to labor and suffer for Him, and even to die to go home to His presence. Let us "repent" with deeper contrition, and "do our first works:" never resting until we can take up afresh the language of delight—I have longed for Your salvation, O Lord.

Some, however, of the Lord's dear children are distressed in the conscious coldness of their spiritual affections. But if it be a mark of the decay of grace to "lose our first love," it is at least a mark of the truth of grace to mourn over this loss. There is always a blessing for those "that hunger and thirst after righteousness." These restless desires are the beating pulse of the hidden life; and if there be not always a sensible growth of desire and enjoyment, there may be (as with the trees in winter) growth at the root, in a more fixed habit of grace and love, in a deeper spirit of humility, and in a more established self-knowledge and simplicity. Yet the shortest way of peace will be to look off from our longing for this salvation, to the salvation itself. For nothing is more desecrating to this great work—nothing is more paralyzing to its saving power, than the incorporating with it the admixture of our own experience as the ground of hope. The most Christian feelings must find no place at the foundation. Indeed their continual variation renders them, especially in the hour of temptation, very uncertain. Yet amid all these fluctuations, Christ may always be safely trusted. While therefore our coldness humbles us before Him, let not brooding despondency cover His precious cross from view. Let not our eyes be so filled with tears of contrition, as to obscure the sight of His free and full salvation. "Looking" singly "unto Jesus" as our peace and our life, is at once our duty, our safety, and the secret principle of our daily progress heavenward. We shall but realize the perception of our own emptiness in the contemplation of His unbounded fullness.

But the connection between longing for salvation, and delight in the law, is at least an incidental evidence, that right apprehensions of salvation must be grounded upon the word or law of God; and that a religion of feeling is self-delusion. Our delight is not only in His love, but in His law. And so practical is Christian privilege, that longing for salvation will always expand itself in habitual delight in the law: which in its turn will enlarge the desire for the full enjoyment of salvation. All spiritual desire therefore, that is not practical in its exercise, is impulse, excitement; not, as in this man of God, the religion of the heart; holiness, delight.

Would that this beautiful Psalm might quicken us to be followers of Him, who evidently knew so much of the heavenly joys of religion! Why should we not, why do we not determine to know as much of God as we can? Why are our longings for His salvation so transient and so few? The religion of thousands who bear the name is of a very different stamp; empty instead of solid; withering instead of profitable; insipid instead of delightful. If there be any exercise, it is only "the door turning upon hinges," movement without progress. The head is stored with knowledge, but there is no unction in the heart, "ever learning, and never able to come to the knowledge of the truth."

But the soul that really longs shall "not be ashamed of its hope." Even to taste the present fruits (though it be but a taste) in a sense of reconciliation, liberty of access, a beam of the love of Jesus in the heart, is unutterable enjoyment. It strengthens the soul for endurance of trials, and for a devoted, self-denying, obedient service. But there are heights and depths of Divine love yet unexplored. He who has given large apprehensions of them to others, "is rich in mercy to all that call upon Him." The fountain of everlasting love is ever flowing, ever full; and He who commands us to "open our mouths wide," has promised, "I will fill them." After all, however, the grand consummation is the object, to which these longings for salvation stretch with full expansion. The fullness and likeness of God; the complete and everlasting deliverance from sin; the glorious "manifestation of the sons of God;" the coming of the Lord. Then—not until then—will they be fully and eternally satisfied. Praised be God! "Now is our salvation nearer than when we believed."

Lord of all power and might! create in our souls a more intense longing for Your salvation, and a more fervent delight in Your law. And as our longings for Your salvation increase, oh! nail us to the door-posts of Your house, that we may be Your happy servants forever!

175. Let my soul live, and it shall praise You; and let Your judgments help me.

There must be life, in order to praise. For how can the dead speak? Yet is it as natural for the living soul to praise, as for the living man to speak. And is not the life that the Psalmist is now praying for, the salvation for which he was longing? The taste that he has received makes him hunger for a higher and continued enjoyment; not for any selfish gratification, but that he might employ himself in the praise of His God. Indeed, the close of this Psalm exhibits that pervading character of praise which has been generally remarked in the concluding Psalms of this sacred book. Yet he alone is fitted for this heavenly exercise, of whom it has been said, "This my son was dead, and is alive again." And how will he, who has "looked to the hole of the pit whence he was dug," who has been awakened to a sight of that tremendous gulf, from which he is but "scarcely saved," long to give utterance to the effusions of a praising heart! How will he cry for the quickening influence of "the Lord and Giver of life," to stir him up to this delightful privilege! Praise springs from prayer—Let my soul live, and it shall praise You. When the breathing of life into our souls enlivens our services, we become, in the noblest sense, "living souls."

Too often, however, the consciousness of inconsistency, carelessness, and unspirituality, damps our song. But let every recollection of our sin be accompanied with an humble yet assured confidence in the Lord's pardoning grace. The abominations of a desperately wicked and unsearchably deceitful heart may well lead us to "abhor ourselves in dust and ashes." Yet in the lowest depths of abasement, the Savior's blood, applied to the conscience, "cleanses from all sin." He who once "passed by us, and saw us polluted in our blood, and said unto us, when we were in our blood, Live"—still "holds our souls in life;" covering our daily infirmities, and maintaining our everlasting acceptance before God.

But while the song of praise dwells on our lips for life thus freely given, let us guard against all hindrance to its growth and influence. For if the life within waxes low, praise will be dull and heartless. But when the assured believer cries with acceptance—Let my soul live, and it shall praise You—see how his spirit kindles with holy fire, "Blessed be the God and Father of our Lord Jesus Christ, which according to His abundant mercy has begotten us again unto a lively hope by the resurrection of Jesus Christ from the dead!" The work of praise is now his nature, his element, his delight. No wonder, then, that he continues his cry for the daily renewal of his spiritual life, that he may return to this sweet foretaste of heaven—Let my soul live. And, indeed, this life—the more it is known, the more will it form the constant matter for prayer. For what besides makes existence tolerable to a child of God? The mere actings of a sickly pulsation can never satisfy him. Considering how much nearer he might live to God than he has yet known, he longs for more vigorous influence of the Divine principle. In his most active enjoyments, his insufficiency for this sacred work presses upon him, and stirs up petition for help—Let Your judgments help me. Give me such an enlightened apprehension of Your word, of Your character, and of Your perfections as the God of my salvation, as may furnish abundant matter of unceasing praise; so that my daily exercise may be, "Giving thanks always for all things unto God and the Father, in the name of our Lord Jesus Christ."

176. I have gone astray like a lost sheep: seek Your servant; for I do not forget Your commandments.

The natural disposition to wander from the fold is constant ground for prayer for the help of the Lord's judgments, to give us clearer light and preserving principles. Yet our need of this safeguard opens to us a most humbling truth. Who can gainsay the testimony from the mouth of God—that "all we like sheep have gone astray?" But how afflicting is the thought, that this should not only be the description of a world living without God, but the confession even of God's own people! And yet where is the child of God that does not set his own seal with shame to the confession—I have gone astray like a lost sheep? "Who can understand his errors?" If he be not found, like Peter, in the open path of wandering; yet has he not need to cry, "Cleanse me from secret faults?" Is he never led away by sense, fancy, appetite? If the will be sincere, how far is it from being perfect! And only a little yielding, a little bending to the flesh, giving way to evil—who knows what may be the end of this crooked path? Who knows what pride, waywardness, earthliness, may be working within, even while the gracious Lord is strengthening, guiding, comforting His poor straying sheep? That they should ever wander from privileges so great, from a God so good, from a Shepherd so kind! What can induce them to turn their backs upon their best Friend, and sin against the most precious love that was ever known, but something that must, upon reflection, fill them with shame! The blame is readily cast upon the temptations of Satan, the seductive witcheries of the world, or some untoward circumstances. But whoever deals with himself must trace the backsliding to his own heart, "This is my infirmity." And have we replaced what we have wilfully yielded up, with anything of equal or superior value? May it not be asked of us, "What fruit had you in those things, whereof you are now ashamed; for the end of those things is death."

But there is no enjoyment while distant from the beloved fold. It is as impossible for the child of God to be happy, when separated from his God, as if he were in the regions of eternal despair. He has not lost—he cannot wholly lose—his recollection of the forsaken blessing. In struggling, weeping faith, he cries—Seek Your servant. 'I cannot find my way back: the good Shepherd must seek me. Once I knew the path: but now that I have wandered into bye-paths, I am no more able to return, than I was to come at first. I have no guide but the Shepherd whom I have left.' How cheering, then, is His office character!, "Behold I, even I, will both search My sheep, and seek them out: as a shepherd seeks out his flock in the day that he is among his sheep that are scattered; so will I seek out My sheep, and will deliver them out of all places where they have been scattered in the cloudy and dark day" Cannot I set my seal to His faithful discharge of His office, "He restores my soul?"

If I want further encouragement to guide my steps homeward, let me think of His own description of tender faithfulness, and compassionate yearnings over His lost sheep; not showing it the way back to the fold, and leaving it to come after Him: but "laying it upon His own shoulders, and bringing it home:" all upbraidings forgotten; all recollection of His own pains swallowed up in the joy, that He has "found the sheep which was lost." Let me remember the express commission, that brought the Shepherd from heaven to earth, from the throne of God to the manger, and thence to the garden and cross, "to seek and to save that which was lost." Let me see upon Him the especial mark of "the Good Shepherd, giving His life for the sheep." Let me observe this sacrifice, as covering the guilt of my wanderings, and opening my way to return—yes, drawing me into the way. Surely then, I may add to my contrite confession the prayer of confidence—seek Your servant. I cannot forbear to plead, that though a rebellious prodigal, I am still Your servant, Your child: I still bear the child's mark of an interest in Your covenant. Though a wanderer from the fold, I do not forget Your commandments. Nothing can erase Your law, which was "written in my mind and inward parts" by the finger and Spirit of God, as an earnest of my adoption, as the pledge of my restoration. What man writes is easily blotted out; what God writes is indelible. Let me then lie humbled and self-abased. But let me not forget my claim—what has been done for me. Thus, again, I hope to be received as a "dear" and "pleasant child;" again to be clothed with "the

315

best robe," to be welcomed with fresh tokens of my Father's everlasting love, and to be assured with the precious promise, "My sheep shall never perish, and none shall pluck them out of My hand."

Such, Christian reader, would be the application we should make of this verse to ourselves; and such a penitent confession of our backslidings, united with a believing dependence on the long-tried grace and faithfulness of our God, would form a suitable conclusion to our meditations on this most interesting Psalm. We would unite the tax-collector's prayer with the great Apostle's confidence; and, while in holy brokenness of heart we would wish to live and die, smiting upon our bosom, and saying, "God be merciful to me a sinner:" the remembrance of our adoption warrants the expression of assurance, "I know whom I have believed, and am persuaded that He is able to keep that which I have committed to Him against that day." Yet, as it regards the experience of David, is there not something striking, and we had almost said, unexpected, in the conclusion of this Psalm? To hear one, who has throughout been expressing such holy and joyful aspirations for the salvation of his God, such fervent praises of His love, that we seem to shrink back from the comparison with him, as if considering him almost on the verge of heaven—to hear this "man after God's own heart," sinking himself to the lowest dust, under the sense of the evil of his heart, and his perpetual tendency to wander from his God, is indeed a most instructive lesson. It marks the believer's conflict sustained to the end:— the humility, and yet the strength, of his confidence; the highest notes of praise combining with the deepest expressions of abasement—forming that harmony of acceptable service, which ascends "like pillars of smoke" before God. And thus will our Christian progress be chequered, until we reach the regions of unmixed praise, where we shall no longer mourn over our wanderings, no longer feel any inclination to err from Him, or the difficulty of returning to Him—where we shall be eternally safe in the heavenly fold, to "go no more out."

"That is why they are standing in front of the throne of God, serving him day and night in his Temple. And he who sits on the throne will live among them and shelter them. They will never again be hungry or thirsty, and they will be fully protected from the scorching noontime heat. For the Lamb who stands in front of the throne will be their Shepherd. He will lead them to the springs of life-giving water. And God will wipe away all their tears." Revelation 7:15-17

Made in United States
Troutdale, OR
01/10/2025

27720310R00176